PARALLEL EXCHANGE RATES IN DEVELOPING COUNTRIES

Parallel Exchange Rates in Developing Countries

Edited by

Miguel A. Kiguel
Central Bank of Argentina and the World Bank

J. Saul Lizondo
International Monetary Fund

and

Stephen A. O'Connell
Associate Professor of Economics
Swarthmore College
Pennsylvania

First published in Great Britain 1997 by
MACMILLAN PRESS LTD
Houndmills, Basingstoke, Hampshire RG21 6XS
and London
Companies and representatives
throughout the world

A catalogue record for this book is available from the British Library.

ISBN 0–333–64294–5

First published in the United States of America 1997 by
ST. MARTIN'S PRESS, INC.,
Scholarly and Reference Division,
175 Fifth Avenue,
New York, N.Y. 10010

ISBN 0–312–16558–7

Library of Congress Cataloging-in-Publication Data
Parallel exchange rates in developing countries / edited by Miguel A.
Kiguel, J. Saul Lizondo, and Stephen A. O'Connell.
    p. cm.
Includes bibliographical references and index.
ISBN 0–312–16558–7 (cloth)
1. Foreign exchange rates—Developing countries—Econometric
models—Case studies. 2. Economic stabilization—Developing
countries—Econometric models—Case studies. 3. Developing
countries—Economic policy—Econometric models—Case studies.
I. Kiguel, Miguel Alberto, 1954– . II. Lizondo, José Saúl.
III. O'Connell, Stephen A.
HG3881.P2924   1997
332.4'56'091724—dc20   96–34337
                                                              CIP

10   9   8   7   6   5   4   3   2   1
06 05 04 03 02 01 00 99 98 97

Printed in Great Britain by
The Ipswich Book Company Ltd
Ipswich, Suffolk

To Claudia, Lucrecia, and Ginny

Contents

Notes on Contributors

Yaw Ansu received his Ph.D. in the Department of Engineering-Economic Systems at Stanford University. He is an Economic Advisor in the Office of the Senior Vice President for Development Economics and Chief Economist of the World Bank. He has worked in both the research and operations sections of the World Bank, most recently in the Bank's Resident Mission in Kenya.

Janine Aron holds an Economic and Social Research Council Fellowship at the Centre for Study of African Economies, Institute of Economics and Statistics, Oxford University. She received her D. Phil in Economics from Oxford University, where she held lectureships at Merton and Jesus Colleges. She has been a visiting lecturer at the Universities of the Witwatersrand and Cape Town in South Africa and has held research consultancies with the World Bank, the European Commission, and other organizations. Her current research focuses on foreign exchange and treasury bill auctions in sub-Saharan Africa and real exchange rate models for South Africa.

Ibrahim A. Elbadawi is the Research Director of the African Economic Research Consortium in Nairobi, Kenya, where he is on leave from the World Bank. He received his Ph.D. from Northwestern University and has held visiting positions at Yale University and the University of Gezira, Sudan. His empirical research on economic growth and structural adjustment in sub-Saharan Africa has appeared in numerous professional journals and books.

Nita Ghei is currently the correspondent in Washington, DC for *The Economic Times*, of India. She has served as a consultant to the National Institute for Public Finance and Policy, New Delhi and to the Research Department of the World Bank. Her research focuses on exchange rate policy in developing countries.

Ricardo Hausmann is the Chief Economist of the Inter-American Development Bank. Dr Hausmann has served as the Minister of Coordination and Planning of Venezuela, as a member of the Board of Directors of the Central Bank of Venezuela, and as Chairman of the Joint Development Committee of the International Monetary

Fund and World Bank. Dr Hausmann is Professor of Economics at IESA, Venezuela's leading Graduate School of Business, where he founded the Center of Public Policy. He holds a Ph.D. in Economics from Cornell University and has been a Visiting Fellow at Oxford University and at CEPREMAP in Paris. He has held research consultancies at the World Bank, the Inter-American Development Bank, and the International Monetary Fund, and has published widely on issues relating to macroeconomic adjustment, international finance, and fiscal policy.

Steven B. Kamin is a Senior Economist in the International Finance Division of the Federal Reserve Board, where he follows financial and economic developments in Mexico. He has also served as Senior Economist for international financial affairs at the Council of Economic Advisers, and as a consultant for the World Bank. Mr Kamin received a Ph.D. in Economics from MIT in 1987, and has published research on various topics in international and development economics.

Graciela L. Kaminsky is currently an Economist in the Division of Monetary Affairs at the Board of Governors of the Federal Reserve System, and a Visiting Associate Professor at the Department of Economics, Johns Hopkins University. She received her Ph.D. from MIT and was an Assistant Professor of Economics at the University of California at San Diego before joining the Board of Governors. She has been a Consultant and Visiting Scholar at the IMF and World Bank and has published extensively on empirical issues in open economy macroeconomics.

Daniel Kaufmann studied Economics and Statistics at the Hebrew University of Jerusalem and received his Ph.D. in Economics at Harvard University. He has held a number of posts at the World Bank and was one of the authors of the World Development Report 1991, *The Challenge of Development*. He was appointed Principal Economist in the World Bank's newly-formed Department for the Former Soviet Union in late-1991, and in 1992 became the Bank's first Chief of Mission in Ukraine. He is currently a Visiting Scholar at the Harvard Institute for International Development. His work has taken him to Latin America, Africa, East Asia and Eastern Europe. He has published on various macroeconomic and sectoral issues of policy relevance.

Miguel A. Kiguel is currently the Deputy General Manager for Economics and Finance and the Chief Economist at the Central Bank of Argentina, where he is on leave from the Research Department of the World Bank. He did his undergraduate work at the University of Buenos Aires and holds a Ph.D. in Economics from Columbia University. Dr Kiguel has taught at the University of Maryland (College Park) and at Georgetown University. His research on stabilization policy, exchange rate policy, and other macroeconomic issues has appeared in a number of professional journals.

J. Saul Lizondo received his Ph.D. in Economics from the University of Chicago. He has been a professor of economics at the Autonomous Technological Institute of Mexico and the University of Tucuman in Argentina, and is currently a Deputy Division Chief at the International Monetary Fund. Dr Lizondo publishes regularly in the area of open economy macroeconomics. His research on foreign exchange regimes and balance of payments management includes numerous contributions to the theory of dual exchange rates.

Nancy P. Marion is a Professor of Economics at Dartmouth College. She received her Ph.D. in Economics from Princeton University. She has served as a consultant to the IMF and has held research positions at the National Bureau of Economic Research, the Institute for International Economics, and the Board of Governors of the Federal Reserve System. She has published extensively in the area of open economy macroeconomics and exchange-rate policy.

Stephen A. O'Connell is an Associate Professor of Economics at Swarthmore College. He received his Ph.D. in Economics from MIT and has taught at the Universities of Pennsylvania and Dar es Salaam and served as a Research Associate at the University of Nairobi. Dr O'Connell has been a Ford Foundation/International Affairs Fellow of the Council on Foreign Relations and a visiting scholar at the Centre for Study of African Economies, Oxford University. He serves as a Resource Person for the African Economic Research Consortium and has been a consultant to the Governments of Tanzania and Sweden and to the research department at the World Bank. His research on macroeconomic policy in sub-Saharan Africa has appeared in a number of professional journals.

Sule Özler is Associate Professor of Economics at the University of California at Los Angeles. She received her Ph.D. from Stanford University and has been a Ford Foundation Fellow at the National Bureau of Economic Research and a National Fellow at the Hoover Institution. She has published on a variety of issues in empirical macroeconomics including the debt crisis and the impact of political instability on growth. Her current research focuses on the differential impact of macroeconomic and trade policies on employment patterns of men and women in developing countries.

Acknowledgments

The authors would like to acknowledge the guidance and encouragement of Vittorio Corbo at an early stage in the research. Stephen Kamin and Ibrahim Elbadawi contributed substantially to developing the overall methodology, and J. Saul Lizondo contributed a survey of the theoretical literature. We are grateful to the large number of colleagues who commented constructively at various stages of the project, including but not limited to David Bevan, Timothy Besley, Jagdeep Bhandari, Vittorio Corbo, Paul Collier, Valpy FitzGerald, Robert Flood, Michael Gavin, Mark Gersovitz, David Greenaway, Stephen Golub, Pablo Guidotti, Charles Harvey, Benno Ndulu, Donald O'Connell, Frances Stewart, Moshe Syrquin, and Aaron Tornell. Special thanks go to Janine Aron for arranging a conference at the Centre for Study of African Economies, Oxford University. Nita Ghei provided invaluable research assistance as well as collaborating in the writing of Chapter 1. We thank Racquel Luz for excellent secretarial assistance and Satya Kapur for expert administrative support. Sampriti Ganguli, Heather Maloney, Mary Anne Stewart, and Jude Uzonwanne all assisted in the editorial process, and we thank them for their efforts. We are grateful to our commissioning editors, Giovanna Davitti and Tim Farmiloe of Macmillan, for their encouragement and support. Finally, we note that the views expressed in this book are not necessarily those of the World Bank, the International Monetary Fund, or affiliated institutions.

Buenos Aires, Argentina
Washington, DC
Swarthmore, PA
December 1995

Overview

This book brings together a set of case studies of parallel foreign exchange systems, defined as systems in which a market-determined exchange rate, typically applying to financial transactions but often to a portion of trade transactions as well, coexists with one or more official, typically managed exchange rates. Such arrangements are extremely common among developing countries. At the end of 1993, 25 percent of the 158 developing country members of the International Monetary Fund (IMF) had separate official exchange rates for some portion (or all) of their capital account and/or invisible transactions. Fully 82 percent maintained restrictions on payments for capital account transactions and, of this group, 60 percent maintained restrictions on current transactions as well. Of the 100 developing countries listed in the *World Currency Alert*, nearly 20 percent had black markets with premia above 25 percent.

The book originated as a World Bank research project whose aim was to enhance the empirical basis for policy advising by generating a body of evidence on the macroeconomic behavior of parallel foreign exchange systems. To exploit the strong similarities between legal dual exchange rate systems and illegal, black market systems, our sample included a set of Latin American countries – Argentina, Mexico, and Venezuela – that had implemented dual exchange rate regimes in the 1980s and a set of African countries – Ghana, Sudan, Tanzania, and Zambia – whose illegal parallel markets had acquired macroeconomic significance by the 1970s and appeared to play a central role in macroeconomic dynamics in the 1980s. Turkey rounded out the sample of developing countries with substantial black markets and a set of European episodes with legal dual exchange rates – from Belgium, France, and Italy – were added to the sample in order to generate a comparison across widely divergent levels of development.

By the late 1980s, the theoretical literature on dual exchange rate systems was well developed and a smaller but important literature applied similar macroeconomic models to the study of illegal black markets. The case study authors therefore had access to a common fund of 'stock-flow' models of the type described in Chapter 1 of this book. The main objective of the project was to learn how these systems operated in practice. The analysis was to focus on the period

1

from roughly 1965 to 1990 and, in some cases, on a single multiyear episode within this longer period. The resulting sample of parallel exchange rate episodes is of course far from random. The period is dominated by the oil price shocks of 1973–4 and 1979–80 and the debt crisis of the 1980s, and ends before the renewal of private capital flows to developing countries in the early 1990s. This was a period of extraordinary balance of payments pressures and within it we are studying a set of countries (excluding the European cases) in which parallel exchange rates were asked, whether intentionally or not, to bear a major share of this pressure.

We asked the authors to develop a detailed analysis of the forces leading to the adoption or emergence of a parallel foreign exchange market, the macroeconomic properties of the system when in place, and the experience with exchange rate unification, whether successful or unsuccessful. They were to describe the structure of trade and exchange controls and to identify the major sources and uses of foreign exchange in the parallel market. We encouraged econometric modeling, particularly with regard to the factors determining the parallel premium and the mechanisms through which the premium fed back into the macroeconomy. Beyond this, we strongly encouraged the authors to pursue issues of particular interest or importance in the country they were studying. The aim was to produce a richly diverse set of case studies with a common analytical core. In this preface, we provide a brief road map of the book, indicating the key concerns and findings of each chapter.

OVERVIEW OF THE CHAPTERS

Chapter 1 by Nita Ghei, Miguel Kiguel, and Stephen O'Connell provides an overview of the macroeconomics of parallel foreign exchange markets, drawing mainly on the case studies but also on the broader literature. It introduces the stock-flow model that forms the analytical framework for the case studies and shows how this model is used to derive an econometric specification for the premium and to motivate empirical work on balance of payments leakages. In a postscript, it updates the authors' narratives, briefly summarizing developments in each country's foreign exchange markets up to the time of writing (December 1995). Finally and most importantly, it distills the main findings and policy lessons of the book:

- The *coverage* of the parallel rate – and particularly the degree to which current account transactions take place at the parallel rate – varies substantially across countries and over time and is a more fundamental determinant of the macroeconomic properties of a parallel exchange rate system than its legality or illegality.

- The premium is determined in the short run by portfolio equilibrium and in the longer run by variables such as trade policy and the fiscal deficit. It is a forward-looking variable, reacting sensitively to news affecting the expected rate of depreciation of the official exchange rate. Devaluations of the official rate, taken alone, have only a transitory effect on the premium.

- Parallel rates provide only limited insulation of domestic prices from external shocks and virtually none from persistently expansionary domestic macroeconomic policies.

- Leakages become important when the premium is large and persistent (for example, above 20 percent on average). Increases in the premium stimulate export smuggling and import over-invoicing and legal channels, if any, are used for speculation against the official exchange rate.

- There is an inverse relationship between the insulation of reserves and the insulation of domestic prices. Systems of extreme foreign exchange rationing achieve a high degree of insulation of reserves but at the cost of the parallel rate becoming a dominant force in domestic price formation.

- Successful exchange rate unification requires above all that the initial *level* of the unified rate be consistent with portfolio equilibrium and that the post-unification exchange rate regime be consistent with the fiscal deficit. Whether unification is to a fixed or flexible exchange rate – or even whether it precedes or follows the establishment of fiscal control – is less important. In many cases, exchange rate unification implies a positive fiscal shock and therefore a reduction in inflation relative to the counterfactual of continued parallel rates.

Perhaps the most fundamental lesson identified in Chapter 1 is a negative one:

- Parallel exchange rates cannot substitute for fiscal and monetary policy in reconciling inflation targets with a sustainable balance of payments.

In Chapter 2, Steven Kamin studies Argentina's use of exchange controls in the period from 1983 to 1989. Argentina's history of exchange controls dates back to the 1930s, involving brief periods of capital account convertibility interspersed with longer periods in which capital account transactions were subject either to a floating dual rate or to a fixed (sometimes dual) rate with rationing and a black market. Kamin presents econometric evidence suggesting first that the parallel exchange rate in the 1980s was determined in an efficient financial market characterized by a high degree of substitutability between domestic and foreign assets, second, that the spread between the free rate and the commercial rate responded to macroeconomic fundamentals as predicted by stock-flow models, with portfolio determinants playing a key role in the short run, and third, that export pre-financing provided an important channel for net capital movements during the exchange control period, undermining the separation of current and capital accounts and the insulation of reserves (an effect that was also produced by intervention in the financial market).

Kamin's overall assessment of Argentina's use of exchange controls is mixed. He argues that controls helped initially to absorb speculative pressures on the commercial rate following the collapse of the Austral Plan and the outbreak of the Malvinas War in 1981 and 1982. In particular, a unified devaluation sufficient to contain these pressures would have imposed an excessive inflationary and contractionary shock and unduly threatened the solvency of firms with large external debts. These macroeconomic benefits were soon exhausted, however and his view is that, for the bulk of the period under study, exchange controls were a costly and ineffective attempt to avoid the fiscal and exchange rate adjustments needed to restore macroeconomic sustainability.

Chapter 3 by Graciela Kaminsky examines Mexico's dual exchange rate regime of 1982–7. For most of its history, Mexico had exchange rate stability and few exchange controls. This began to change first with a loss of fiscal control during the early 1970s and then more definitively with the introduction of a dual exchange rate system following the debt crisis of August 1982. The Mexican authorities managed the financial rate, allowing it to depreciate dramatically on the introduction of the system and then during the crises of July 1985 and November 1987, but intervening heavily at other times to prevent excessive increases in the premium.

Kaminsky focuses on the degree to which the dual system insulated domestic prices from speculative capital movements and enhanced the Bank of Mexico's control over its international reserves. She addresses the first issue using a monthly structural vector autoregression (VAR) for the parallel premium and five key macroeconomic variables (output, the money supply, interest rates, prices, and the commercial exchange rate). Estimating separate VARs for the dual exchange rate period and the earlier unified exchange rate period (the latter VAR excluding the parallel premium), she finds little evidence that the dual system either altered the domestic inflation process or insulated domestic prices from shocks to the capital account.

To address the issue of reserve insulation, Kaminsky applies Hamilton's (1988) filter to a quarterly measure of capital flight, allowing the data to assign each observation to a 'high-capital flight' or 'low-capital flight' regime. She finds that substantial portions of the dual period are identified as high-capital flight observations and concludes that there is little evidence that the dual regime substantially enhanced the control of reserves.

On the basis of these results, Kaminsky rejects the benchmark of complete insulation of reserves and prices. This rejection is based in part on the dynamic behavior of variables *within* the dual regime – something the VAR methodology is well suited to capture – and in part on a comparison of these relationships across regimes. The latter comparison is more ambitious; in effect, the unified exchange rate period of 1976–82 is used to construct an econometric counterfactual to the use of dual rates in 1982–9. When data on a unified episode are available, this approach has clear advantages over the use of a 'judgmental' counterfactual for the period of parallel rates. However, modeling choices impose their own limitations; in Kaminsky's VAR analysis, the counterfactual is undercut by the omission of a variable capturing capital account shocks during the unified regime. Incorporating such a variable seems a useful direction for further work.

In Chapter 4, Ricardo Hausmann examines the Venezuelan experience with dual exchange rates between 1983 and 1989. The Venezuelan Government had used a temporary dual system with great success following the collapse of the oil markets in the early 1960s, allowing the parallel rate to absorb capital account pressures while phasing in a 30 percent devaluation of the commercial rate over a period of 3 years.

The 1983 arrangement was modeled after the earlier one, aiming for a devaluation of 39.5 percent over 3 years. The actual experience was dramatically different, however; the dual regime was abandoned in 1989 after a cumulative devaluation of over 700 percent.

Hausmann provides a detailed chronology of macroeconomic developments leading up to and during the dual regime period. A hallmark of the Venezuelan dual regime was a high degree of insulation of reserves from current account movements. Exports in Venezuela are dominated by the public sector (mainly oil), leaving very little scope for capital movements through smuggling or 'leads and lags' in the settlement of export-financing claims, while on the import side the government used the exchange control regime to impose a broad import quota on the private sector. To incorporate these features, Hausmann extends the dual exchange rate model of Kiguel and Lizondo (1990) to the case in which the government receives export revenues and manages the current account through an import quota.

In Hausmann's model, import quotas protect the current account, but in doing so over-constrain the system, rendering the equilibrium potentially unstable in the absence of a fiscal adjustment. Hausmann shows that the response to a devaluation of the commercial rate depends on whether the fiscal fundamentals are in place and then applies the model ingeniously to differentiate Venezuela's experience with the devaluations of 1984 and 1986. His descriptive analysis highlights the importance of inventory behavior by importers in determining the dynamics of output and the current account during adoption or abandonment of dual exchange rates, a theme not stressed in the theoretical literature.

Hausmann ultimately traces the failure of the Venezuelan dual exchange rate system to an inconsistency between the fiscal deficit and exchange rate policy. He argues that while import controls can be employed to prevent such an inconsistency from depleting reserves in the short run, this occurs – in the absence of sufficient fiscal adjustment – at the cost of an exploding parallel premium. In this view, the key failure of Venezuelan policy during the 1980s was the failure to make a sufficient fiscal adjustment in the face of lower oil prices. Hausmann argues that the substitution of exchange restrictions for fiscal adjustment was a poor intertemporal bargain for the country, producing substantial real exchange rate volatility and strong incentives for illegal activity during the 1980s and finally requiring an excessively contractionary adjustment when the system was abandoned in 1989.

With its focus on the extension of exchange controls to the current account, Hausmann's paper provides a natural bridge between the Argentinian and Mexican experiences and those of the African countries of the sample. Hausmann argues – based largely on the burst of inflation that accompanied exchange rate unification in 1989 – that Venezuela's system provided substantial insulation of domestic prices relative to what would have prevailed under unified exchange rates. However, domestic price controls were also lifted at the time of unification, suggesting that some portion of the observed insulation may have been due to price controls rather than to the dual regime. In the African cases, where price controls were absent or ineffectual, the parallel rate played a key role in domestic price formation.

Chapter 5 by Yaw Ansu focuses on the Ghanaian parallel market, one that was extraordinary by the early 1980s for the size of its premium and the degree to which the official exchange rate had become redundant even for current account transactions. At the time of adoption of the Economic Recovery Program in 1983, the black market exchange rate was 20 times the official rate. Smuggling was the only source of import supply on the margin, so that domestic prices fully reflected the parallel exchange rate, rather than the official rate. May (1985) estimated that more than half of the cocoa crop was being smuggled to Cote d'Ivoire in the early 1980s.

Ansu's chapter focuses first on the role of trade and exchange controls in the macroeconomic deterioration of 1973–83 and then on the gradual and ultimately successful move to a unified, market-determined exchange rate between 1983 and 1989. Ghana in the 1970s is a classic study in the use of trade and exchange controls to support macroeconomic policies that are inconsistent with low inflation and therefore with external balance under a fixed exchange rate. Exports declined as the exchange rate became increasingly overvalued and official exports fell even more rapidly given the smuggling incentive generated by a growing parallel premium. Imports fell as well as the authorities tightened exchange controls in preference to devaluing the official exchange rate. The decline in trade volumes drove down export and import tax revenues, producing a vicious circle of higher fiscal deficits, increased monetary growth and inflation, tighter controls, and a higher parallel premium. Ansu's econometric evidence confirms the role of exchange rate overvaluation and low domestic interest rates in driving the parallel premium and the negative influence of the premium on cocoa exports.

The Ghanaian decline was successfully reversed starting in 1983 and Ansu argues that trade and exchange rate reforms, supported by contractionary fiscal and monetary policy, played a key role in the reversal. In contrast to the Latin American cases, the process of exchange rate unification was gradual and focused on restoring convertibility on the current account. An initial maxi-devaluation and crawling peg were followed by the gradual transfer of trade transactions to market-determined exchange rates. The government introduced an auction for the allocation of official foreign exchange and in 1988 licensed private foreign exchange bureaus to deal in trade-related transactions. Capital controls were retained throughout the process, but by the late 1980s the average premium between the bureau rate and the black market rate was small.

Ghana's experience of the 1980s illustrates the close link between trade policy and exchange rate policy when exchange controls are applied to the current account. Ghana's exchange rate unification was essentially a gradual liberalization of import controls combined with the elimination of an indefensible and largely irrelevant official exchange rate. Economic activity had already shifted to the parallel exchange rate; this is evident in the fact that the maxi-devaluation of 1983 had virtually no cost-push effect on domestic prices (Chhibber and Shafik, 1991; Younger, 1993). Ansu rightly emphasizes the importance of fiscal correction in making this move to market-determined exchange rates consistent with a tolerable inflation rate; this is one of the central lessons of the entire set of case studies. More controversially perhaps, he argues that the Bank of Ghana's willingness to absorb the revaluation of the government's external debt arrears generated by devaluation helped to ensure the success of the fiscal adjustment in the 1980s. This expedient had no effect on a comprehensive measure of the public sector deficit, so the claim that it made an important difference suggests either an information asymmetry between the government and its creditors (domestic or external) or an accounting illusion on the part of these creditors.

In Chapter 6, Ibrahim Elbadawi takes up the case of the Sudan, where tight exchange controls on both capital and current accounts predated political independence in 1956. An ambitious and mainly domestically financed development program generated an increase in inflation in the 1970s and created a strongly overvalued official exchange rate. At the same time, the successive OPEC oil shocks transformed the economy into one heavily dependent on the remittances of Sudanese nationals working in the Gulf States. The authorities handled the deteriorating external situation by introducing a dual exchange rate and creating a series of concessional schemes to attract worker remittances.

Elbadawi argues that the Sudanese experience illustrates an important non-equivalence between economies in which the bulk of trade takes place at the black market rate and those in which a single, market-determined, officially recognized exchange rate applies to all transactions. Even when domestic prices have adjusted to the parallel rate, he argues, an increase in the premium interacts with expectations of official devaluation to increase uncertainty about relative prices and paralyze supply responses to changes in the effective real exchange rate. A central role of exchange rate unification, in such cases, is to reduce uncertainty.

Elbadawi uses the standard stock-flow model to derive a reduced-form equation for the parallel premium, emphasizing that fiscal deficits affect the premium not only through the stock of domestic money but also through the effect of money growth on expectations of official devaluation. He uses the regression results to characterize the long-term relationship between inflation and the premium, finding evidence of the type of trade-off emphasized by Pinto (1989, 1991) (see the Tanzania discussion below). He also finds a negative effect of the premium on official exports and trade tax revenues and a positive effect on capital flight, confirming the central role of the parallel foreign exchange rate in Sudan's macroeconomic dynamics. In the end, the central lesson of the Sudanese case is the dysfunctional nature of exchange controls when used as a palliative for a loss of fiscal control. Unlike the other case studies, the Sudanese case ends in the early 1990s with macroeconomic upheaval and an exploding premium associated with political instability and renewed loss of fiscal control.

Chapter 7 by Daniel Kaufmann and Stephen O'Connell studies Tanzania, a country whose reorientation of macroeconomic policy, beginning in the mid-1980s – reversing a decline dating from the early 1970s – brings out strong parallels to Ghana. The authors summarize their earlier work on the Tanzanian parallel market (Kaufmann and O'Connell, 1991; O'Connell 1992), presenting empirical results that confirm the importance of portfolio determinants of the premium, in the short run and 'flow determinants' like trade policy and the terms of trade, in the long run. They then use the Tanzanian case to explore the linkage between the parallel premium and the inflation rate. Pinto (1989, 1991) argued that when the public sector is a net buyer of foreign exchange from the private sector, an overvalued official

exchange rate levies an implicit tax on the private sector. The result is
that inflation is lower than it would be under a unified exchange rate –
or, equivalently, that exchange rate unification must be accompanied
by fiscal contraction if it is to take place without a long-term rise in
inflation. Kaufmann and O'Connell extend Pinto's (1989, 1991) analysis to incorporate effects operating through the government's
domestic currency receipts and expenditures – such as export taxes
and customs revenues – and through the changes in trade volume that
accompany successful unification. They argue, in line with Morris
(1995) and recent work by Agénor and Ucer (1995), that the 'shadow'
fiscal impact of parallel exchange rates can vary widely from case to
case – even from year to year – and can as easily be negative as
positive. For Tanzania, they find that by the time of unification in
the mid-1980s, the premium was exerting a net negative effect on the
public finances.

Chapter 8 by Janine Aron and Ibrahim Elbadawi focuses on Zambia, a country whose macroeconomic fortunes in the 1970s and 1980s
were dominated by a secular decline in copper prices and a series of
reforms and reversals in macroeconomic policy. The authors provide a
rich set of econometric results linking the parallel premium with the
rest of the macroeconomy. They begin by examining the statistical
properties of parallel rates and the premium, attributing the secular
increase in the short-term volatility of the monthly parallel premium
to increased policy uncertainties and transitory bubbles and crashes
associated with market thinness. They specify and estimate an annual
model for the parallel premium, finding it to be cointegrated with the
market fundamentals suggested by theory. Both aid and the terms of
trade are among the fundamentals but have theoretically ambiguous
effects; here (as in Chapter 7) the net effect of an increase in either
variable is to lower the premium.

They next investigate the effects of the premium on recorded and
unrecorded trade. A careful and detailed model of copper export
supply allows for a regime shift in the mid-1970s, when shortages of
foreign exchange and skilled manpower became binding. The data
indicate a strongly negative supply effect of import rationing, as
proxied by the parallel premium, during the supply-constrained post-
1975 period. With respect to unrecorded trade, the authors use partner
trade data to estimate import overinvoicing and report some evidence
of a positive linkage between overinvoicing and the parallel premium.

The Zambian experience underscores the centrality of credible fiscal
adjustment in supporting a durable decline in the parallel premium. It

also illustrates the important role of external shocks, however, consistent with the finding – both for Zambia and other countries in the sample – that variables like the terms of trade can have long-term effects on the premium for given domestic policy settings.

In Chapter 9, Sule Özler studies the Turkish black market, whose macroeconomic importance inspired some of the early empirical literature on black markets (for example, Olgun, 1984). Like Sudan, Turkey's foreign exchange black market had traditionally been generously supplied by remittances from Turkish nationals working abroad. Economic shocks and poor fiscal management culminated in a balance of payments crisis in the late 1970s, in which the premium rose to nearly 60 percent.

The Turkish experience of the 1980s was one of gradual and complete exchange rate unification, first on the current account – a process largely completed in the first half of the 1980s and formalized in the acceptance of Article VIII status in the IMF in 1989 – and then on the capital account. Özler's chapter focuses on the capital account liberalization and particularly on the role of domestic foreign currency accounts in facilitating currency substitution and altering the behavior of the premium. The analysis points to one of the often-neglected effects of capital account liberalization, which is to increase inflation by lowering the base for the inflation tax.

In Chapter 10, Nancy Marion complements her own earlier comparison of dual exchange rate experiences in Europe and Latin America (Marion, 1994), also undertaken as part of the World Bank project. Marion (1994) found that spreads were markedly higher and more persistent in Latin America than in Europe; that a greater share of current account transactions took place at the financial rate in the Latin American cases, and that while portfolio variables were important determinants of the spread in both groups, foreign interest rates were relatively less important and the commercial exchange rate and the fiscal deficit relatively more important in determining the spread in Latin America than in Europe. She argues on the basis of these findings that while European dual systems were typically designed primarily to insulate domestic interest rates, Latin American dual markets were designed to allow the authorities to delay an across the board devaluation.

In Chapter 10, Marion extends her earlier work to include a direct examination of the insulation properties of the European dual exchange rate regimes. The analysis focuses, as before, on Belgium's extended dual exchange rate regime (1957–90) and the shorter episodes in Italy and France following the move to floating among the industrial countries in the early 1970s. She begins by deriving the wedge between domestic and foreign asset returns when financial transactions are channeled through one exchange rate and commercial transactions through another. The overall distortion can be decomposed into a 'static' part, that prevails whenever the premium is non-zero and interest payments are channeled through the commercial market and a 'dynamic' part, that arises whenever the premium is expected to change over the holding period of the assets. Marion then uses a standard stock-flow model to derive a reduced-form equation for the premium – the 'observable part of the distortion' – and finds that portfolio variables are important determinants of the premium in the short term, as predicted by theory.

Why do countries impose dual rates, given the welfare losses associated with the distortion of intertemporal trade? The issue is discussed at length in Chapter 1; however, Marion's decomposition suggests the fundamental attraction of dual rates to a country facing speculative capital flows. A positive but declining spread (as might prevail if the regime were a temporary measure or if there were temporary pressures for capital outflows) has the effect of making foreign assets unambiguously less attractive relative to domestic assets than under unified rates. When the capital account would otherwise be in temporary deficit – or a unified exchange rate temporarily depreciated, with potentially adverse effects on the inflationary process – a dual exchange rate system levies the equivalent of a temporary tax on all financial transactions. Moreover, dual rates are administratively efficient – relative to taxes or discretionary direct capital controls – and the implied tax rate adjusts automatically to the degree of pressure on the capital account. The more fundamental issues are therefore (1) whether dual rates indeed provide meaningful insulation from shocks to capital flows, relative to unified rates and (2) whether dual rates generate important administrative or other costs relative to unified rates – costs in terms of corruption, for example or loss of macroeconomic discipline or credibility – that are larger than the 'welfare triangles' associated with small and relatively stable wedges between asset returns.

Marion focuses on the first of these issues and particularly on the insulation of domestic interest rates from shocks to foreign interest rates and of international reserves from speculative capital movements. She finds some – though weak – evidence of interest rate insulation. With regard to international reserves, she uses data for France and Italy to argue that trade financing undercuts the insulation of reserves, to a greater degree if the authorities do not impose regulations on leads and lags in the settlement of commercial claims.

Marion's chapter, together with her *World Bank Economic Review* article (Marion, 1994), gives the first systematic empirical look at the European dual exchange rate experience. The picture is one of very small distortions, perhaps some insulation with respect to foreign interest rate shocks, and potentially significant slippage through trade credit transactions at the commercial rate. With capital mobility now significantly higher than in the early 1970s, further work may want to focus on what these episodes can tell us about insulation with respect to domestic fiscal or political shocks or other events generating shifts in the perceived credibility of exchange rate targets. Countries may be prepared to tolerate significant slippage during normal times if dual rates can prevent severe crises, but, on the other hand, they may feel that maintaining a dual system is a constant invitation to uncertainty regarding the authorities' willingness to subordinate macroeconomic policy to exchange rate targets. These considerations apply equally to developing countries with substantial capital mobility.

NEW DIRECTIONS

The case studies in this book bring to bear a wealth of information on the macroeconomics of parallel exchange rate regimes. There are clear lessons for countries with substantial parallel foreign exchange markets, including many in Eastern Europe and the former Soviet Union and also Venezuela, Nigeria, and others that have maintained or recently reimposed tight exchange controls. Exchange controls and parallel markets do best when asked to do least. They do not enhance macroeconomic stability when fiscal and monetary policy are incompatible with stability.

What paths did our case study countries follow in the 1990s? The majority maintained or deepened the movement away from exchange controls that they had initiated by the late 1980s (see the postscript to Chapter 1). Argentina and Mexico went to full convertibility of their currencies. The removal of all restrictions on payments on the current and capital accounts in these countries eliminated the parallel market for foreign exchange. In Turkey, Ghana, Tanzania, and Zambia, the gradual elimination of restrictions on payments on the current account and an easing of capital controls drastically reduced the size of the parallel market and drove the premium to insignificant levels. This experience was not unanimous, however: Venezuela, in an extraordinarily sharp reversal, reimposed exchange controls in June 1994, almost 5 years after the unification of 1989; the parallel premium there reached 80 percent in late 1995. Sudan slid further into a civil war and the Sudanese parallel market is at least as large now as in the late 1980s, with an extremely high premium.

These developments reflect broader trends among developing countries. As a result of reforms undertaken during the 1980s and early 1990s, an increasing number of countries now face the task of managing highly open economies while maintaining market-oriented trade and exchange rate policies. For these countries, attention has shifted from the problem of establishing convertibility for current account transactions to that of choosing the appropriate degrees of exchange rate flexibility and of convertibility for capital account purposes. We are therefore back to the issue of managing the capital account, but in a context of basic macroeconomic stability – a role in which dual exchange rates, ironically, have perhaps their greatest theoretical appeal. What evidence is there here for the view (for example, Dornbusch and Kuenzler, 1993) that dual exchange rates represent the right choice for most developing countries in the mid-1990s?

For the countries in our sample and others in similar macroeconomic environments, dual rates probably carry more dangers than benefits for the immediate future. The reason is that dual rates and fiscal responsibility are substitutes in the short run. Choices regarding exchange-rate regime can therefore interact strongly – at the policy level or in the perceptions of investors or both – with choices regarding fiscal adjustment. These interactions raise dangers both in the operation of a parallel exchange rate regime, as choices are continually made between tightening exchange controls and adjusting monetary and fiscal policy and at the time of adoption (or abandonment) of parallel exchange rates, when market participants may view the choice of regime as a signal about the authorities' overall macroeconomic policy stance.

Our case studies dramatically illustrate the dangers that arise during the operation of parallel regimes. Nearly all of the countries of our sample made a transition *within* the parallel exchange rate period from a system that generated moderate distortions and moderate macroeconomic benefits to one that generated negligible benefits and major distortions. With regard to adoption, consider the case in which the balance of payments is under pressure from capital outflows. The adoption of exchange controls in such a situation almost by definition signals an unwillingness to raise real interest rates high enough to defend a unified fixed rate, to spend a large amount of international reserves, or to tolerate the cost-push effect of a unified devaluation or depreciation of a floating rate. While such an unwillingness may well be an optimum response to capital flows that are at odds with the fundamentals, it may also be interpreted as a signal that the authorities do not have the resolve or the ability to exercise control over the fiscal fundamentals. Governments committed to fiscal reform may therefore feel that hard-fought increases in credibility are too valuable to be endangered by the adoption of a policy tool that would be equally appealing to a government whose commitment was weaker than their own.

What of countries with established records of macroeconomic stability and with institutional structures to maintain this independently of the exchange rate regime? Such countries are unlikely to use exchange controls as a substitute for macroeconomic adjustment, so that black market or legal dual rates, if adopted, are unlikely to diverge persistently from official rates. Incentives for illegal transactions are likely to remain small, controls are unlikely to be extended to the current account, and the maintenance of current account convertibility will itself limit the distortion from capital controls by providing a substantial conduit for short-term capital movements. Parallel exchange rates may well provide meaningful insulation in such situations, allowing a managed commercial or official exchange rate to retain a leading role in price formation for traded goods, while protecting international reserves from temporary external shocks and speculative capital movements. Are these benefits likely to outweigh the potential costs? The answer will vary according to the circumstances of the particular country. But our results suggest caution. The experiences analyzed here suggest that governments often overestimate the net benefits of parallel rates, with ultimately damaging effects on policy credibility and economic performance.

REFERENCES

Agénor, Pierre-Richard and E. Murat Ucer (1995) 'Exchange Market Reform, Inflation, and Fiscal Deficits', *Working Paper WP/95/78* (Washington, DC: IMF, African and Research Departments).

Chhibber, Ajay and Nemat Shafik (1991) 'Exchange Reform, Parallel Markets and Inflation in Africa: the Case of Ghana', in Ajay Chhibber and Stanley Fischer (eds), *Economic Reform in Sub-Saharan Africa* (Washington DC: World Bank), pp. 39–49.

Dornbusch, Rudiger and Luis Tellez Kuenzler (1993) 'Exchange Rate Policies: Options and Issues', in Rudiger Dornbusch (ed.), *Policymaking in the Open Economy* (New York: Oxford University Press), pp. 91–126.

Hamilton, John (1988) 'Rational Expectations Econometric Analysis of Changes in Regime: an Investigation of the Term Structure of Interest Rates', *Journal of Economic Dynamics and Control*, vol. 12, pp. 385–423.

Kaufmann, Daniel and Stephen A. O'Connell (1991) 'The Macroeconomics of the Unofficial Foreign Exchange Market in Tanzania', in Ajay Chhibber and Stanley Fischer (eds), *Economic Reform in Sub-Saharan Africa* (Washington, DC: World Bank), pp. 50–65.

Kiguel, Miguel and J. Saul Lizondo (1990) 'Adoption and Abandonment of Dual Exchange Rate Systems', *Revista de Análisis Económico*, vol. 5, no. 1, pp. 2–23. Previously *Development Research Department Discussion Paper* No. 201 (Washington, DC: World Bank).

Marion, Nancy P. (1994) 'Dual Exchange Rates in Europe and Latin America', *World Bank Economic Review*, vol. 8, no. 2, pp. 213–45.

May, Ernesto (1985) 'Exchange Controls and Parallel Market Economies in Sub-Saharan Africa: Focus on Ghana', *PPR Working Paper* No. 771 (Washington, DC: World Bank).

Morris, Stephen (1995) 'Inflation Dynamics and the Parallel Market for Foreign Exchange', *Journal of Development Economics*, vol. 46, pp. 295–316.

O'Connell, Stephen A. (1992) 'Short and Long Run Effects of an Own-funds Scheme', *Journal of African Economies*, vol. 1, no. 1, pp. 131–50.

Olgun, Hasan (1984) 'An Analysis of the Black Market Exchange Rate in a Developing Economy: the Case of Turkey', *Weltwirtschaftliches Archiv*, vol. 120, pp. 324–47.

Pinto, Brian (1989) 'Black Market Premia, Exchange Rate Unification, and Inflation in Sub-Saharan Africa', *World Bank Economic Review*, vol. 3, no. 3, pp. 321–38.

Pinto, Brian (1991) 'Black Markets for Foreign Exchange, Real Exchange Rates and Inflation', *Journal of International Economics*, vol. 30, pp. 121–36.

Younger, Stephen (1993) 'Testing the Link Between Devaluation and Inflation: Time Series Evidence from Ghana', *Journal of African Economies*, vol. 1, no. 3, pp. 369–94.

1 Parallel Exchange Rates in Developing Countries: Lessons from Eight Case Studies

Nita Ghei, Miguel A. Kiguel, and Stephen A. O'Connell[1]

INTRODUCTION

Parallel foreign exchange systems are those in which a market-determined exchange rate, typically applying to financial transactions but often to a portion of trade transactions as well, coexists with one or more pegged exchange rates. Such arrangements are common in developing countries. In some cases governments respond to a balance of payments crisis by creating a legal parallel (or dual) foreign exchange market for financial transactions. The objective is to avoid the short-term effects of a depreciation of the exchange rate on domestic prices while maintaining some degree of control over capital outflows and international reserves. In other cases, extensive controls on foreign exchange restrict access to official markets and lead to the emergence of an illegal parallel market. The illegal market then grows in importance as the authorities respond to a deteriorating balance of payments by tightening and extending exchange controls.

The importance of parallel markets and their effect on overall economic performance generally depends on the size of the parallel premium, defined as the percentage gap between the parallel and official exchange rates. Table 1.1 shows the diversity of cross-country experience. Median values of the end of year black market premium range from below 10 percent in most Asian countries and the few industrialized countries that adopted official dual exchange rate systems to above 50 percent in many African and Latin American countries. Premiums generally increased in the 1980s relative to the 1970s, as countries responded to severe balance of payments problems

Parallel Exchange Rates

TABLE 1.1   *The parallel premium, selected countries*
(based on end-of-year figures)

Country	Median premium			Maximum premium	
	1970–9	*1980–9*	*1990–4*	*1970–89*	*1990–4*
Low premium					
Thailand	−0.2	−1.5	0.5	5.1	3.8
Malaysia	0.3	0.6	−0.1	8.2	0.6
Venezuela	0.4	75.2	5.2	213.0	7.1
Belgium	1.0	1.3	0.5	9.9	2.7
France	0.7	2.8	0.4	12.6	1.4
Italy	2.8	1.4	0.8	13.4	5.0
Indonesia	2.2	3.4	2.1	15.5	16.4
Mexico	0.0	17.7	1.8	66.0	6.8
Uruguay	4.4	7.1	20.7	73.0	30.6
South Africa	5.8	4.4	2.3	33.7	2.7
Morocco	4.6	5.8	2.1	17.0	13.1
Philippines	7.7	4.9	2.4	50.0	7.1
South Korea	11.0	6.1	1.2	23.5	4.0
Turkey	9.1	8.4	2.4	52.8	3.8
Colombia	4.4	12.7	8.4	28.3	16.9
Israel	26.5	5.8	0.7	70.0	3.5
Group median	2.4	3.7	1.7		
Moderate premium					
Bolivia	5.5	17.6	0.6	293.0	5.5
Ecuador	8.0	34.2	5.8	96.1	26.4
India	17.4	13.1	8.4	93.7	23.3
Kenya	16.8	15.2	9.3	44.9	107.1
Chile	8.3	18.5	8.1	1 260.0	18.7
Pakistan	26.9	14.8	2.6	211.9	14.2
Brazil	11.1	43.1	198.6	173.0	202.8
Syria	5.7	213.4	300.9	1 046.5	318.7
Dominican Republic	26.5	36.0	6.4	213.0	51.1
Sri Lanka	73.8	15.2	7.4	237.4	24.3
Argentina	55.8	43.3	11.1	363.0	42.4
Malawi	51.7	41.4	31.7	108.0	44.4
Group median	18.2	24.6	9.4		
Large premium					
Peru	51.2	27.0	10.4	278.9	16.1
Nigeria	37.8	85.5	42.5	456.6	354.6
Zaire	106.0	13.6	196.9	295.0	260.0
Ethiopia	41.1	103.9	180.0	226.0	233.3
Zambia	102.5	40.8	33.3	361.9	212.0
Sudan	85.4	78.8	99.8	344.4	1 011.0

Egypt	80.0	106.1	1.6	248.4	56.3
Ghana	66.3	142.0	−0.4	4 263.7	11.4
Tanzania	95.5	214.3	19.4	301.4	78.0
Algeria	59.5	332.5	207.7	418.6	339.0
Group median	73.5	100.0	49.4		

The premium is defined as $100 \times [(B - E)/E]$, where B and E are the parallel and official exchange rates. 'Low', 'moderate', and 'high' premium countries are those with median premiums for the 1970–89 period of below 10 percent, between 10 and 50 percent, and above 50 percent, respectively.
SOURCES   Parallel exchange rates are from International Currency Analysis, Inc., *World Currency Yearbook* (various years) and Kaufman and O'Connell (1991) for Tanzania. Official exchange rates are from IMF, *International Financial Statistics*.

by tightening controls on foreign exchange transactions. Even countries with low or moderate premiums tend to experience episodes of relatively high premiums, consistent with the use of parallel rates as a safety valve; however, among the high-premium countries, it is not unusual for the premium to remain extremely high for periods of 5 years or more (for example, Ghana 1980–6 and Tanzania 1973–86).

Although the macroeconomic behavior of parallel foreign exchange markets has been extensively studied in the theoretical literature, evidence on how these systems work in practice has been, until recently, relatively limited.[2] This chapter draws on the case studies in this volume and on the broader literature to provide an overview of experience with parallel foreign exchange markets in developing countries. We focus on issues of short- to medium-term macroeconomic policy, leaving discussions of efficiency and growth aside but providing pointers to the relevant literature where appropriate.[3]

The case studies in this volume cover the period from roughly 1965 to 1990. For many developing countries, the macroeconomic reforms of the 1980s included the adoption of more market-oriented exchange rate regimes, culminating in the late 1980s and early 1990s with a move to full convertibility at least for current account purposes. Coupled with the strong reversal of capital flows to reforming countries in the early 1990s, this development has driven parallel premiums lower on average in the 1990s than they have been in decades. However, one does not have to look far to find countries in which they are flourishing (for example, in portions of the former Soviet Union) or being re-established (for example, Venezuela and Nigeria). In

Appendix 2, (pp. 73–6) we provide a brief update on developments in the case-study countries up to the time of writing.

Economists advocated dual exchange rates for industrial countries early in the post-war period (Triffin, 1947) and again in the transition to floating rates in the early 1970s as a way to protect international reserves and insulate the prices of traded goods from external shocks. More recently, Dornbusch (1986b) and Dornbusch and Kuenzler (1993) advocated the use of dual exchange rates in developing countries as a way to prevent transitory shocks to the capital account from affecting prices and wages. The theoretical advantages of dual rates are straightforward. A dual system is more effective than a single pegged or managed rate at insulating international reserves from capital outflows, because these lead to a depreciation of the parallel rate rather than to a loss in reserves. It is more effective than a single floating rate in limiting the impact of capital outflows on domestic prices, because current account transactions are conducted at the (pegged or managed) commercial exchange rate. In principle, similar properties apply to black market systems; exchange controls protect international reserves, while some current account transactions continue to take place at the more appreciated official rate.

How effective have parallel foreign exchange markets been in maintaining external balance and controlling inflation? In practice, parallel markets provide temporary relief at best from the trade-off between price adjustment and reserve adjustment under unified exchange rates. Severe exchange controls are required if parallel markets are to insulate international reserves from capital flows meaningfully and such controls become virtually impossible to enforce when the incentives for capital outflows are strong and persistent. Insulation of domestic prices is also partial and temporary and attempts to enhance the insulation of prices – for example, by maintaining convertibility for a wide range of current account transactions – end up undermining the insulation of reserves. Parallel foreign exchange markets are emphatically not an effective way to maintain low inflation in the longer term.

What determines the size of the premium and what are the mechanisms through which the premium feeds back into macroeconomic performance? The case studies provide evidence on four fundamental links between parallel exchange rates and the domestic economy. First, the parallel exchange rate is the price of foreign assets. Portfolio balance considerations dominate in its short-term determination and help to explain the volatility of the premium and its rapid reaction to 'news'. Second, parallel foreign exchange markets are heavily used in the financing of illegal trade. Changes in the premium alter the 'parallel' trade balance in the short term and, in the medium to long term, other factors affecting illegal trade – such as export taxes and penalties for illegal transactions – help to tie down the value of the premium. Third, the parallel rate affects domestic price formation. In cases of extreme import rationing, for example, import prices tend to be determined solely by world prices and the parallel rate, with no role for the official rate. Finally, the spread between the parallel and official exchange rates acts as a shadow tax/subsidy scheme, penalizing individuals who surrender foreign exchange at the official rate and rewarding those who purchase at the official rate. Because governments are often substantial net buyers or sellers of foreign exchange *vis-à-vis* the private sector, the adoption and the unification of parallel rates have important fiscal implications not captured in standard calculations of the fiscal or quasi-fiscal deficit.

The relative importance of these linkages varies from country to country and there are numerous interactions between the channels. Certain common features emerge, however, in the determination of the parallel premium and its effect on other macroeconomic variables. The premium increases as a result of a real appreciation or an excess of money growth over the rate of official depreciation; it also increases with news of an impending devaluation of the official rate, the latter effect accounting for some of the most spectacular spikes in the premium. Official devaluations are typically associated with reductions in the premium, but the duration of this effect depends a great deal on the accompanying macroeconomic policies. Devaluations taken in isolation have virtually no long-term effect on the premium. 'Shadow' fiscal effects of the premium can be quite large – 10 percent of gross domestic product (GDP) in some cases – and, in many cases, the net effect is a fiscal loss, implying that a reduction in the premium will provide a fiscal bonus.

Our final topic is exchange rate unification. There is considerable diversity in the speed with which markets are unified and the type of exchange rate regime ultimately adopted. Experience shows that unification often takes place rapidly at times of macroeconomic crisis, as parallel exchange rates cease to be useful in protecting international reserves. There are also cases of successful gradual unification, however, particularly in highly distorted economies where unification moves in tandem with price deregulation and trade liberalization. The key to successful unification is choosing an exchange rate regime that is consistent with underlying fiscal and monetary policies. Countries that maintain money-financed budget deficits cannot succeed in unifying into a fixed exchange rate, as inflation would quickly lead to an overvalued real exchange rate. Whether countries unify to a flexible exchange rate system or a crawling peg is of secondary importance.

The chapter is organized as follows. Following the introduction of a simple classification of parallel foreign exchange systems, we discuss the adoption or emergence of parallel exchange rate systems and the reasons these arrangements were preferred to unified ones. We then introduce the standard 'stock-flow' model of the parallel premium, which we use in the section following to motivate our own cross-country regression results on the premium and to summarize the more detailed findings of the chapters. We then summarize the findings regarding insulation and the effect of the premium on illegal trade and then look at unification experiences and the fiscal effects of exchange rate unification. The final section concludes the paper with a summary of the major policy lessons.

A SIMPLE CLASSIFICATION

At the heart of any parallel foreign exchange market is a set of exchange restrictions assigning certain transactions to the pegged or managed exchange rate and others (perhaps implicitly) to the parallel rate. The details vary widely from country to country.[4] For most macroeconomic purposes, however, the array of parallel systems observed in developing countries can be reduced to a simple classification according to the coverage and legality of the parallel rate (Table 1.2).

The most fundamental distinction is with respect to coverage. Virtually all systems assign capital outflows and usually inflows as well to the parallel rate. The key distinction is between systems in which the free rate applies mainly to the capital account and those in which it also applies to a broad range of current transactions. The case in which exchange controls apply solely to the current account is not observed in practice, because such controls are virtually unenforceable in the absence of convertibility restrictions on the capital account. Although taxes and quantitative restrictions on trade help determine the level of the premium in a parallel system, both theory and the available evidence – from Indonesia, Uruguay, and (until recently) the members of the Communauté Financière d'Afrique (the CFA zone), all with open capital accounts – suggest that in the absence of capital controls, the parallel market remains thin and the premium small even in the presence of substantial tariffs, quantitative restrictions, and illegal trade.

Given the high costs of enforcement, governments typically tolerate a substantial amount of parallel market activity even when such activity is illegal. A distinction can be made between systems in which transactions at the parallel rate are largely tolerated (whether legal or not) and those in which a substantial threat of enforcement is present most of the time. However, the case study evidence suggests that the degree of effective legality is much less important for macroeconomic behaviour than the coverage of the parallel rate.

Bearing in mind that coverage and legality are matters of degree rather than discrete categories and that parallel systems evolve over time, Table 1.2 gives an approximate classification of parallel market episodes in the case study countries over the period from 1970 to 1990. Beginning with the upper left quadrant, the European experiences with dual exchange rates involved legal parallel rates applying mainly

TABLE 1.2   *Classification of case study episodes, 1970–90*

	Coverage of the parallel rate			
	Mainly capital account		*Capital and current accounts*	
Transactions	*Country*	*Years*	*Country*	*Years*
Legal or tolerated				
	Argentina	1981–9	Ghana	1983–7
	Europe	Various*	Tanzania	1984–90
	Ghana	1987–90	Venezuela	1983–9
	Mexico	1982–8	Zambia	1987–8
	Turkey	1980–4		
Illegal				
			Ghana	Before 1983
			Sudan	Entire period
			Tanzania	Before 1984
			Turkey	1970–9
			Zambia	Except 1987–8

* Includes Belgium 1957–90, France 1971–4, and Italy 1973–4.
SOURCE   Country case studies.

to the capital account. Argentina (1981–9) and Mexico (1982–8) represent extended episodes of narrow coverage and effective legality; in the case of Argentina, the parallel rate was initially a legal dual rate (1981 and 1982) but became an illegal (but tolerated) black market rate on reimposition of exchange controls. Venezuela (1983–9) represents a legal dual system buttressed by severe foreign exchange rationing for imports. Auction-based parallel markets in Ghana (1986–7) and Zambia (1987–8) also involved a legal free rate that applied to a broad range of current transactions. The black market systems that operated in the 1970s in Ghana, Sudan, Tanzania, Turkey and Zambia were accompanied by extensive foreign exchange rationing on the current account; the table shows the transitions experienced by some of these countries as they implemented macroeconomic reforms and moved towards convertibility on the current account (and for Turkey on the capital account as well).

ADOPTION OR EMERGENCE OF PARALLEL FOREIGN EXCHANGE MARKETS

Our sample illustrates the two main ways in which parallel foreign exchange markets emerge and become macroeconomically important in developing countries. In the first, the authorities split the foreign exchange market in order to phase in a devaluation when capital outflows prompt a balance of payments crisis. In the second, the parallel market developed gradually in response to efforts to maintain an overvalued exchange rate.

Dual Markets to Stem Capital Outflows

Official dual exchange rate systems, with a floating rate for capital account transactions and one or more pegged rates for current account transactions, were generally adopted on a transitional basis at times of balance of payments crisis. The main objective in these episodes was to phase in the required devaluation when problems of macroeconomic management were compounded by capital outflows. Mexico's dual system, for example, was adopted in August 1982 as part of a policy response to the debt crisis. The system was viewed as a temporary measure to smooth out the possibly adverse effects of the much needed devaluation on domestic prices. Venezuela's system of February 1983 was also adopted on a temporary basis to deal with collapsing oil revenues and massive capital flight during the debt crisis. The use of dual rates in Venezuela was modeled in part on a successful previous experience: in 1960, the government had instituted a dual system as a way of phasing in an official devaluation of 35 percent over a period of 3 years. The aim in 1983 was similar, as the government envisioned a 3-year transition to a unified fixed-rate system, with a cumulative devaluation of 39.5 percent.

In Argentina, legal dual exchange rate systems were adopted in response to balance of payments crises several times in the 1980s. A dual system was adopted in June 1981 when Argentina faced a large fiscal deficit, accelerating inflation, an overvalued exchange rate, large capital outflows, and extensive private sector indebtedness. A similar situation led to the readoption of a dual system in July 1982, after a brief attempt at unification. In addition to these episodes, Argentina had a semi-legal parallel exchange rate system through most of the 1980s, since periods of full convertibility (and a truly unified exchange rate) were few.

In most cases the adoption of the system was prompted mainly by fears that the nominal depreciation required to restore external balance in the short term would result in an unacceptable and potentially permanent burst of inflation.[5] A unified exchange rate would likely have to overshoot its equilibrium level, producing a dramatic fall in real wages and facing the authorities with a difficult choice between accommodating increased wage demands and forcing a severe recession.[6] In Mexico and Argentina, such concerns led the authorities to use the commercial rate as a nominal anchor whose fluctuations were to be minimized or at least smoothed out over time. In Venezuela, the dual regime was instituted in an election year and was designed in part to protect the prices of wage goods. Figure 1.1 illustrates these points using the Mexican financial dual system. The financial rate overshot its medium run level upon adoption of the dual regime in August of 1982; when the authorities devalued the commercial rate 3 months later, the magnitude of the devaluation was significantly below the initial movement in the financial rate.

Official dual systems have also been used for brief periods by three of the four African countries in our set of case studies. Ghana and Zambia both had short-lived foreign exchange auctions applying to a substantial share of external transactions in the 1980s. In Sudan, where a pegged dual rate had been used to attract worker remittances and

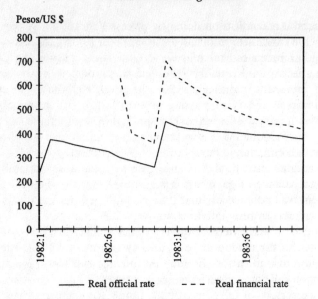

FIGURE 1.1   *Real exchange rates, Mexico, 1982–83*

NOTE   Monthly real exchange rates are calculated as nominal exchange rates deflated by Mexico's consumer price index. An increase is a real depreciation.

other transactions since the early 1970s, the illegal parallel market was legalized for a brief period starting in mid-1983. In contrast to Mexico and Venezuela, the dual exchange rate systems in Ghana and Sudan were instituted as part of broader attempts to move towards a unified, market-determined, official exchange rate and reduce the importance of the illegal parallel market. In both cases, the dual regime allowed for efficiency gains in the allocation of foreign exchange while continuing to protect, temporarily, the real incomes of groups subsidized by the overvalued official rate. The importance of the latter objective is illustrated dramatically by Zambia's 1987 short-lived dual system, which was quickly abandoned when the resulting increases in the prices of wage goods led to riots in the Lusaka Copper belt.

Unofficial Parallel Markets to Maintain Overvalued Exchange Rates

Unofficial (black) parallel foreign exchange markets exist as a matter of course in most developing countries, in response to ongoing restrictions on capital account transactions in the official foreign exchange market. While capital controls may be in place for the same reasons as official dual exchange rates – to insulate the economy from temporary shocks to the capital account – they are typically also (and often primarily) intended to influence the allocation of private wealth between domestic and foreign assets over the longer run. The underlying motivation may be fiscal (see p. 47) or controls may represent an attempt to increase domestic investment and growth.[7]

As with official dual systems, foreign exchange black markets become important at times of balance of payments crisis. However, in contrast to the official case, where adoption is often temporary and part of an overall policy adjustment, a growing black market typically reflects a systematic bias against devaluation. Exchange controls are extended to cover not only the capital account but also a broad set of current account transactions. These controls are then gradually tightened in an attempt to resolve fundamental inconsistencies between the exchange rate and the pressure of expansionary macroeconomic policies.

The typical pattern is one where the economy faces a gradual worsening in the balance of payments as a result of expansive monetary and fiscal policies that raise inflation and lead to overvaluation of the official exchange rate. The government fails to correct this imbalance by tightening macroeconomic policy or devaluing the official rate, choosing instead to increase restrictions on the private sector's access to foreign exchange at the official exchange rate. Expectations of a possible maxi-devaluation of the official rate or of a further tightening of foreign exchange controls add to the excess demand for foreign exchange in the short term by encouraging inventory accumulation by importers and portfolio substitution away from domestic assets. These forces support the demand for foreign exchange in an illegal market. The supply is provided by exporters of goods, tourists, and domestic workers abroad, all of whom find it profitable to divert foreign exchange from the official to the illegal market.

Each of our case studies of illegal parallel markets presents a period in which the above sequence of events is to some extent applicable. Turkey's black market, which had emerged in the early 1940s, expanded significantly in the 1970s, in a period characterized by mounting macroeconomic imbalances and an overvalued official exchange rate. In Sudan, the 1970s were characterized by expansive macroeconomic policies aimed at supporting ambitious economic development programs. These policies, together with exogenous shocks like the oil price increase of the mid-1970s, resulted in inflation and an appreciating real exchange rate. The authorities responded primarily by broadening and tightening exchange controls, with the result that the black market expanded to serve a growing volume of illegal transactions on both the current and capital accounts. Ghana's black market also grew substantially in the 1970s, the result of a reluctance to devalue in spite of rising inflation, balance of payments problems, and an overvalued exchange rate. Excess demand for official foreign exchange drove the premium from 50 percent in 1974 to more than 2000 percent in 1982. The emergence of a large premium in the parallel market followed a similar pattern in Tanzania and Zambia.

Why was a tightening of foreign exchange controls preferred over across-the-board devaluations of the official rate or contractionary macroeconomic policy as the way to deal with balance of payments problems? In Tanzania reluctance to devalue was established in the 1960s, rooted in arguments that a devaluation would generate only a weak supply response in exports of agricultural goods and would impose a contractionary and inflationary supply shock on the import-dependent industrial sector. By the early 1980s these arguments gave way to a lingering ideological opposition to market- determined prices and to concerns that devaluation would trigger political instability (Loxley, 1989; Hyden and Karlstrom, 1993). In Ghana the maxi-devaluation of 1971 was followed immediately by a military coup. It is safe to say that the association of these two events, whether causal or not, exercised a strong influence against subsequent devaluations in Ghana. In Zambia, exchange rate policy evolved beginning in the early 1970s as a shifting bargain between the government, external creditors, and an urban constituency subsidized by overvalued exchange rates. Political pressures made overvaluation increasingly hard to avoid as urbanization proceeded and copper prices – and, with them, real incomes – declined starting in the mid-1970s.

STOCK-FLOW MODELS OF THE PREMIUM

At the core of many theoretical models of parallel exchange rates (the literature is surveyed in Agénor (1992) and Lizondo (1990)) is a 'stock-flow' structure borrowed from an earlier monetarist literature on flexible exchange rates. The 'stock' element states that the parallel exchange rate is determined in the short term by the requirement that existing stocks of domestic and foreign assets be willingly held. The 'flow' element is a description of how asset stocks evolve over time. Most of the case study authors used a stock-flow model to derive an empirical model of the premium. In this section we lay out the basic elements of such models.

Assuming that domestic and foreign assets are imperfect substitutes, a simple version of portfolio equilibrium states that the (desired = actual) share of domestic assets in total financial wealth is a decreasing function of the expected yield differential in favor of foreign assets. Denoting home country private holdings of domestic and foreign assets by M and f, respectively, we have

(1)
$$\frac{M}{Bf} = \lambda(i^* + {}_t\Delta \log B_{t+1} - i; \, x_P)$$
$$(-)$$

where i^* and i are the interest rates on foreign and domestic assets, B is the parallel exchange rate, and x_P is a vector of other variables affecting portfolio equilibrium (for example, measures of relative liquidity or risk or indicators of the tightness of capital controls). The expected yield on foreign assets, in domestic currency terms, is $i^* + {}_t\Delta \log B_{t+1}$, where ${}_t\Delta \log B_{t+1} \equiv {}_t \log B_{t+1} - \log B_t$ is the anticipated rate of depreciation of the parallel exchange rate (the notation ${}_t \log B_{t+1}$ denotes the market's forecast of B_{t+1} in period t). We assume in equation (1) that interest income is repatriated at the parallel rate, as in a black market system; a similar formula holds when interest payments are assigned to the commercial rate, as in many legal dual systems (see Chapter 10). Note also that if substitution is mainly between domestic and foreign currencies rather than interest-bearing assets, the right-hand side of equation (1) takes the simpler form $\lambda({}_t\Delta \log B_{t+1}; \, x_P)$.

Analysis usually focuses on (one plus) the parallel premium $z \equiv B/E$ (where E is the official or commercial exchange rate) rather than the parallel rate, because it is the premium that encourages leakages between the official and parallel markets. Solving for B/E in equation (1) and taking logs, we can write

$$\log z_t = g(m_t, f_t, i^* + {}_t\Delta \log B_{t+1} - i; \, x_P).$$
$$(+) \, (-) \qquad (+)$$

The premium is therefore an increasing function of the stock of domestic financial assets, m (measured in foreign exchange at the official exchange rate) and a decreasing function of the stock of foreign assets, f and the expected yield differential in favour of these assets. Alternatively, since $_t\Delta \log B_{t+1} = {}_t\Delta \log z_{t+1} + {}_t\Delta \log E_{t+1}$, we can write equation (1) as a dynamic equation for the premium (Dornbusch et al., 1983):

$$\log z_t = h(m_t, f_t, {}_t\Delta \log z_{t+1}, v_{ot}; x_P)$$

(2) $\quad\quad\quad\quad (+)(-)\quad (+)\quad\quad (+)$

where $v_o \equiv i^* + {}_t\Delta \log E_{t+1} - i$ is the deviation from uncovered interest parity at the official exchange rate.

Equation (2) underscores the forward-looking nature of the premium. Today's premium depends not only on the expected future premium but also on the expected rate of depreciation of the official (or commercial) exchange rate. Under rational expectations, we can solve equation (2) forward, eliminating $_t z_{t+1}$ and expressing the current premium as a function of current and all expected future values of asset stocks, interest rates, and official depreciation. The premium will react not only to the current values of m, f, and v_o, but also to news about any of the macroeconomic variables – or political variables – that determine these variables over time.

The 'flow' element of theoretical models of parallel exchange rates comes from the behavioral equations and identities governing the evolution of asset stocks over time. Consider first the private stock of net foreign assets. Since capital account transactions are assigned to the parallel exchange rate, f changes over time only (1) if the central bank intervenes at the financial rate or (2) if the private sector is able, legally or illegally, to acquire (or dispose of) foreign assets at the official exchange rate. In the latter case, the system is said to be subject to 'leakages' (Lanyi, 1975). While the details vary widely from model to model, both intervention and leakages have the feature that net capital outflows are an increasing function of the premium:

$$\Delta f = f(z; x_f).$$

(3) $\quad\quad\quad\quad (+)$

A rise in the premium therefore tends, other things being equal, to produce an inflow of foreign exchange into the parallel market. This increase in net foreign assets then influences the evolution of the premium through the portfolio equilibrium condition. The vector x_f in equation (3) captures other determinants of net capital outflows under the parallel regime, including variables affecting the incentives for illegal trade.[8] Below we estimate a version of the Dornbusch *et al.* (1983) model that combines equation (3) with the portfolio equilibrium condition (p. 38); the empirical evidence on the premium and illegal trade is taken up on p. 49.

Note that equation (3) is the basis of the original 'flow' models of the black market premium that treated the private capital account (Δf) as predetermined and viewed the parallel exchange rate as clearing the flow market for foreign exchange arising from illegal transactions (Pitt, 1974; Sheikh, 1976; May, 1985). In these models, one would invert equation (3) to obtain

$$z = f^{-1}(x_t, \Delta f),$$
(4)
$$(+)$$

which express the premium as a function of predetermined net capital flows and variables determining illegal transactions.

Stock-flow models, in contrast, endogenize capital flows and emphasize the dominant role of portfolio factors in the short-term behavior of the premium. 'Flow' equations like equation (4) remain important in the long run, however, when capital flows are tied down by the steady-state condition $\Delta f = 0$. Variables included in x_f can therefore play a dominant role in determining the long-term value of the premium.[9] A rise in export taxes, for example, lowers the premium in the long run, by diverting a larger share of aggregate exports into the parallel market (de Macedo, 1987). A real appreciation increases the premium by lowering aggregate exports, which reduces the flow supply of foreign exchange in the parallel market for a given share of the exports smuggled (Dornbusch *et al.*, 1983; Kamin, 1993). A rise in import tariffs or in the implicit tariff associated with quantitative restrictions (for example, foreign exchange rationing) raises the premium by increasing the smuggling and underinvoicing of imports (de Macedo, 1987; O'Connell, 1992). We summarize evidence on these determinants on p. 40.

Stock-flow models often have the property that the steady state is homogeneous of degree one in all nominal variables, so that a nominal devaluation of the official exchange rate has only a short-term effect on the premium. Equation (2) is consistent with this property, since the exchange rate E affects the portfolio equilibrium only indirectly through the real variables M/E and B/E. Equation (4) is also consistent with homogeneity provided that the official exchange rate is not among the variables in x_f. This in turn requires homogeneity of degree one of the underlying supplies and demands for illegal foreign exchange, a property that may or may not hold depending on the details of smuggling and detection and penalty technologies (Kamin, 1993). On p. 41 we summarize evidence from the case studies and elsewhere in support of the proposition that devaluations have only a short-lived effect on the premium.

The second 'flow' element in stock-flow models is the determination of the overall current account, which equals the total change in net foreign assets $\Delta f + \Delta r$, where r is the net foreign assets of the public sector. The formal models used in this book treat the capital stock as exogenous, focusing on issues of medium-term macroeconomic adjustment rather than long-term growth.[10] The most common specification for the current account takes government spending as given and links private spending (and thus saving) to financial wealth and real income. The current account then becomes a decreasing function of total financial wealth, $m + zf$:

$$\Delta f + \Delta r = c(m + zf; x_C),$$
(5)
$$(-)$$

where x_C is a vector of other determinants of the current account, including output, the terms of trade, external assistance, and government spending. 'Descriptive' and 'optimizing' traditions in the parallel exchange rate literature differ according to whether the private saving behavior in equation (5) is explicitly derived from an intertemporal optimization problem (Lizondo, 1991). The descriptive tradition is more common in empirical work and is used in the models in this book.

Although r includes all public sector net foreign assets, it is typical in this literature to treat the change in long-term external government debt as predetermined and to focus on the net international reserves of the monetary authority. The change in reserves – and therefore the change in r in equation (5) – reflects the intervention rule followed by the central bank. In the case of extreme foreign exchange rationing, for example, an additional flow equation $\Delta r = -k$, where k is the change in other net foreign assets of the public sector, would limit private sector imports to current foreign exchange inflows to the central bank, net of government imports (for example, see Chapter 4 by Hausmann in this volume). The domestic price of imports would be endogenously determined, as in any quota-constrained regime. At the other extreme, if the authorities maintain convertibility for current account transactions at the official exchange rate, the change in reserves would be determined as a residual by equation (5).

The third flow element is the supply of real money balances, m. Assuming that the fiscal deficit is financed solely through money creation, the government's flow budget constraint can be written as the following accounting identity:

$$(6) \qquad \Delta m = d - (\Delta \log E)m + \Delta r,$$

where d is the fiscal deficit, measured in foreign exchange at the official exchange rate.[11] Equation (6) brings out the potentially central role of fiscal policy in the adoption of a parallel regime and the determination of the premium. Consider first a unified exchange rate that is depreciated at a predetermined rate (which may be zero). Since the growth in real domestic money balances (Δm) is tied down by the growth in real money demand, a sustained increase in the deficit leads to a deterioration of the balance of payments ($\Delta r < 0$). If the policy authorities regard fiscal adjustment as excessively costly, a tightening of capital controls and/or the imposition of a dual exchange rate may appear an attractive way of protecting reserves from capital outflows (and possibly even creating a captive demand for domestic assets, raising the base for the inflation tax). If reserve losses continue even under capital controls, foreign exchange rationing can be used to target the portion of the current account deficit that is financed through official reserve movements. Floating the exchange rate is always an option – this sets Δr to zero in equation (5) and endogenizes both the level and the rate of change of the exchange rate. However, fears of inflation or of excessive volatility of the real exchange rate may make this an equally unattractive option.

Once a parallel system is in place, changes in the deficit affect asset stocks and feed through to the premium through the portfolio equilibrium condition and the current account. In the long term, equation (6) ties the premium and the fiscal deficit together via the requirement that the rate of crawl – which is linked to the premium through the portfolio equilibrium condition – be sufficient to finance the fiscal deficit ($d = (\Delta \log E)m$). As in the standard literature on the inflation tax 'Laffer curve', both the comparative statics and the dynamics depend on whether the elasticity of money demand with respect to expected depreciation is above or below unity (see Fischer and Easterly, 1990; Morris, 1995). On p. 46 we use equation (6) together with the portfolio equilibrium condition to derive and estimate a long-run specification for the premium as a function of the fiscal deficit and the real money stock.

A final element of stock-flow models is a specification of domestic price formation. Denoting the domestic prices of traded and non-traded goods by P_T and P_N, we can write the domestic price level as

$$(7) \qquad\qquad P = P_T^{\alpha} P_N^{(1-\alpha)} = P_T q^{(1-\alpha)},$$

where α is the share of traded goods in consumption and $q \equiv P_N/P_T$ is the real exchange rate. The parallel exchange rate affects the domestic price level both directly through the portion of traded goods that is assigned to the parallel rate (Lizondo, 1991) and indirectly through wealth effects that alter total spending and the real exchange rate (Guidotti and Végh, 1988). The direct effects depend on the trade and exchange rate system. In a legal dual system, the authorities often assign some portion of imports to the parallel rate, in order to limit the claim on international reserves arising from imports assigned to the official rate. In this case, the domestic prices of imports simply reflect the exchange rate to which they are assigned. However, imports can also be assigned to the parallel rate implicitly, as when the authorities ration foreign exchange at the official rate for certain categories of import. In this case, the exchange control system acts like a set of import quotas and smuggling becomes the marginal source of the protected imports. The share of imports that are effectively priced at the parallel rate can then be much larger than the share actually smuggled, since domestic prices of the quota-protected imports will reflect the marginal cost of supplying these to the domestic market through smuggling.

Equations (6) and (7) in combination form the basis of a long-term relationship between inflation and the parallel premium that has received considerable attention in the literature on exchange rate unification (for example, Lizondo, 1987, 1991; Pinto, 1989, 1991). To illustrate, suppose that imports are the only goods consumed ($\alpha = 1$) and that foreign exchange is tightly rationed for all private sector imports. In this case, import prices reflect only the parallel exchange rate, not the official rate, so that $P = B$. Suppose furthermore that domestic tax revenues are fixed at t in real terms and that the government spends an amount g (also entirely on imports), purchasing the required foreign exchange from the central bank at the official exchange rate E. Then in a steady state ($\Delta m = \Delta r = 0$), the consolidated budget constraint given by equation (6) can be written (Lizondo, 1994):

$$(8) \quad \Delta \log Pm' + \left(\frac{B-E}{B}\right) g = \Delta \log Pm' + \left(\frac{z-1}{z}\right) g = g - t$$

where $m' \equiv M/P$ is the real money stock measured at domestic prices, rather than at the official exchange rate. Equation (8) says that the deficit, when measured at shadow prices, is financed not only by the inflation tax but also by the spread between the official exchange rate and the parallel rate. Exchange rate unification (which sets $z = 1$) removes this implicit source of financing. If the deficit remains unchanged at shadow prices, inflation tax revenues must rise to offset the loss in implicit financing. This means a rise in the inflation rate provided the economy is on the 'good' side of the inflation tax Laffer curve.

The analysis underlying equation (8) has been generalized in a number of directions. Lizondo (1991, 1994) allows a variable portion of private sector trade (imports and exports) to be conducted at the official exchange rate and traces out the implied long-term trade-offs between the inflation rate and the shares of trade assigned to the official rate. Kaufmann and O'Connell (Chapter 7 in this volume), Morris (1995) and Agénor and Ucer (1995) extend the analysis to allow the possibility that unification lowers inflation – for example, by allowing the public sector to be a net seller rather than a net buyer of foreign exchange *vis-à-vis* the private sector. On p. 59 we provide evidence on the 'shadow' fiscal effect of the premium for five of the case study countries.

MACROECONOMIC DETERMINATION OF THE PREMIUM

Equations (2)–(8) provide the bare bones of a parallel exchange rate model. They leave open a host of issues discussed in the country studies, from the determination of output, interest rates, and the official exchange rate to the detailed structure of exchange controls and the factors governing transitions between dual and unified exchange rate regimes. In this section we use the basic structure to motivate econometric work on the macroeconomic determination of the parallel premium. A number of the case studies also included econometric work on leakages, which we discuss on p. 48 in connection with the insulating properties of parallel exchange rates.

The Premium Equation

The authors generally proceeded by imposing a set of simplifying
assumptions on the basic structure, deriving the implied expression
for the steady-state premium, and then estimating this along with a
flexible specification of short-term dynamics. To illustrate this
approach, we apply a variant of the Dornbusch *et al.* (1983) model
of black markets to quarterly data for 21 developing countries.

Figure 1.2 shows the stock-flow structure of the model, with the
premium on the vertical axis and the stock of foreign assets on the

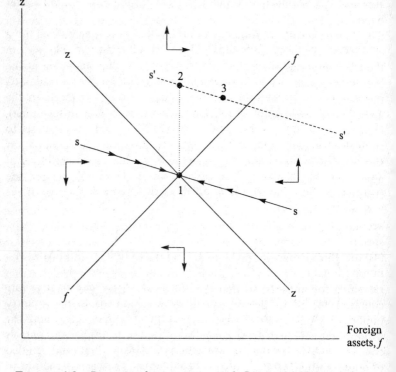

FIGURE 1.2   *Dynamic adjustment in a stock-flow model of the premium.*

NOTE   The arrows show dynamics corresponding to the steady state at point
1. An unanticipated rise in real money balances shifts the steady state to point
3: the premium jumps from 1 to 2 and then adjusts to 3 along the new saddle
path *s's'*.

horizontal. The exchange rate is assumed to follow a predetermined crawl, with the possibility of occasional maxi-devaluations. For given real money balances m, the downward-sloping schedule zz shows the portfolio equilibrium condition equation, (3), as a demand function for foreign assets, under the steady-state assumption $_t\Delta Z_{t+1} = 0$. The dynamics lead away from this schedule: above it portfolios are shifted towards foreign assets, requiring an expected increase in the premium, while below it the premium must be expected to decline. The schedule is downward sloping because a rise in private holdings of foreign assets requires a decline in the premium to rebalance private portfolios.

The supply of foreign assets is predetermined at any point in time but evolves according to equation (4) for Δf. We assume that illegal trade is the only source of leakages, so that Δf is the illegal trade surplus. The ff schedule is the schedule along which illegal trade is balanced. The ff schedule is drawn under the assumption that the illegal trade surplus is an increasing function of the premium and that an increase in private wealth increases illegal outflows. The first of these assumptions is central to models of parallel exchange rates, as indicated above, while the second would prevail if, for example, the increase in desired spending associated with higher wealth led to a rise in the domestic prices of quota-protected and non-traded goods, increasing the incentive for import smuggling and reducing the flow of smuggled exports. Above the ff line the illegal trade balance is in surplus and foreign assets increase over time, while below it foreign assets fall.[12] Under rational expectations, dynamic adjustment to the steady state at point 1 takes place along the saddle path ss.

Conspicuously absent here are equation (5) for the overall current account (or equivalently for international reserves, since we have specified the change in private net foreign assets Δf) and equation (4) for the change in real money balances. We can think of the international reserves as being held constant through foreign exchange rationing for imports, so that $\Delta r = 0$; in this case, the main role of equation (5) is to determine the endogenous domestic price of imported goods. With respect to the fiscal accounts, the implicit assumption here is that the deficit is continuously adjusted to enforce consistency between the real money stock and the predetermined rate of crawl, so that M/E is constant. The model is simple, but its fundamental stock-flow mechanism survives a variety of complications. Agénor (1994), for example, derived an identical diagram in a model that incorporates a commercial banking sector, informal domestic loan markets, and endogenous output.

Starting at point 1, the diagram shows the short- and long-term
effects of an unanticipated burst of monetary financing that permanently increases real money balances. The *zz* schedule shifts upwards,
since a rise in the premium is required to re-establish the portfolio
equilibrium at a fixed level of foreign assets. The *ff* schedule also shifts
upwards, but by less because a rise in the premium sufficient to restore
the portfolio equilibrium produces a strong incentive for illegal outflows. The new steady-state equilibrium is at a point like 3. Dynamic
adjustment begins with a jump in the parallel premium. This restores
portfolio equilibrium at point 2, but generates a surplus in the illegal
current account that produces a gradual rise in private net foreign
assets. The economy then converges to point 3 along the new saddle
path $s's'$.

Stationary equilibria at points like 1 and 3 take the form

(9)
$$\log z_t = z(\log m_t, \ _t\Delta \log E_{t+1}; x_P, x_f),$$
$$(+) \qquad (+)$$

where x_P and x_f contain other variables entering the portfolio equilibrium and illegal trade equations. Drawing on Ghei and Kiguel (1992),
we apply a dynamic version of equation (6) to data for 21 developing
countries, a sample including but not limited to the case study
countries. The data are quarterly for the period from 1970 to 1990,
omitting episodes of unified exchange rates. We model the unobserved
expected rate of depreciation as a decreasing function of the stock of
international reserves and an increasing function of the degree of
exchange rate overvaluation. Overvaluation is also unobservable, but
we proxy it by the difference, $\hat{e}$, between the real exchange rate and its
own centered 12-quarter moving average.

Dickey–Fuller tests suggest that all series are first-difference stationary for the sample. To capture both the long-term relationship (in
equation (9)) and the short-term dynamics, we estimate the equation
in error-correction form (Banerjee *et al.*, 1993):

(10)
$$\Delta \log(z) = \alpha_0 + \alpha_1 \Delta \log(m) - \alpha_2 \Delta \log(r) + \alpha_3 \Delta \hat{e} - \alpha_4 \log(z_{-1})$$
$$+ \beta_1 \log(m_{-1}) - \beta_2 \log(r_{-1}) + \beta_3 \hat{e}_{-1}.$$

In this representation, the long-term relationship in equation (9) is
captured by the ratios β_i/α_4. The parameter α_4 is positive and
below unity in absolute value, implying that deviations from the
long-term relationship are erased over time. The βs are non-negative,
as indicated by our discussion. The parameters $\alpha_1 - \alpha_3$ capture the

short-term effects of changes in real money balances, reserves, and overvaluation on the premium; the theory implies that these are all non-negative.

The results appear in Appendix 1. They broadly support the model and corroborate the more detailed findings provided in the chapters below. The long-term effects are generally of the right sign and in the case of the real money stock are often statistically significant. The error-correction restriction on α_4 is satisfied in all cases and the adjustment speed is significantly greater than zero in all cases but one. The other αs suggest an important role for portfolio and wealth effects in the short term. These short-term impacts are also generally of the right sign and are rarely significant when of the wrong sign. While little weight should be placed on any individual country's results here – this is a stripped-down model in which x_P and x_f are excluded and no country-specific features are incorporated – the results are indicative of the robust empirical appeal of stock-flow models. They also indicate, not surprisingly, that the role of the macroeconomic 'fundamentals' is more readily detected econometrically in the high-premium countries than in the countries with moderate premia.[13]

The Premium Equation: Results from the Case Studies

Table 1.3 gives a summary of the main econometric results from the more detailed premium equations estimated in the case studies. The premium equation was in most cases derived from a stock-flow model. The case studies differ with respect to the frequency of the data, the details of the estimation procedure, the degree to which variables like real money balances, expected depreciation, and the real exchange rate were endogenized, and the inclusion of country-specific details.[14] The table identifies short- and long-term effects where possible, indicating with + or − the direction of the estimated impact over each horizon. Asterisks identify results that are statistically significant at the 10 percent level or better.

An expansion of money balances (measured in dollars at the official exchange rate) raises the premium in the short term in all cases. In Sudan, Turkey, and Mexico, it raises the premium in the long term as well. Given the link between fiscal deficits and money growth in these countries, this suggests that a major reason for persistently high premia is inconsistency between the deficit and the rate of crawl of the exchange rate. An increase in the interest parity differential increases

TABLE 1.3 *Determinants of the parallel premium*

		Argentina	Ghana	Mexico	Sudan	Tanzania	Turkey	Zambia
Portfolio determinants								
Real money	SR	(+)		+‡	(+)	(+)	(+)	(+)§
balances, M/E	LR			+§	(+)	(+)	(+)	
Official interest	SR				(+)	(+)	(+)	
parity deviation, $i^* +_t \Delta \log E_{t+1} - i$	LR		(+)	+‡	+		−	(+)
'Flow' determinants								
Official real	SR			+‡	(+)	(+)	(+)	
exchange rate (increase = appreciation)	LR	(+)	(+)	+‡	(+)§	(+)	(+)	
External aid	SR							
	LR					−		
Terms of trade	SR							
	LR	(−)/+*				−		(−)§
Export tax rate	SR	(−)	+		(−)			
	LR							
Import tariff rate	SR	+/−†			(+)§			
	LR							
Real output	SR	(−)		+‡				
	LR	(−)	−	+†				

Parentheses refer to estimated effects that are statistically significant at the 10 percent level or better.
* Effects operating through dollar import prices (−) and dollar export prices (+) were estimated separately and imply conflicting conclusions regarding the terms of trade effect.
† Results for import tariffs (+) and quantitative restrictions (−) were both insignificantly different from zero.
‡ Results reported here are impulse responses from a structural vector autoregression (see Chapter 3). Short-run effects refer to a 1 year horizon and long-run to 3 years. Significance levels not reported.
§ Very close to significance at the 10 percent level.
SOURCE: Country chapters (including earlier versions).

the premium in the short term, as predicted by the theory; in some cases, this effect persists in the long term. Since variation in this variable is dominated by changes in expected depreciation, this implies a powerful role for exchange rate expectations in determining the premium.

A real appreciation of the official exchange rate increases the premium both in the short term and over time. Since exchange rate expectations are already captured in the interest parity variable, this result points to the effect of overvaluation on trade flows: a real appreciation reduces aggregate exports and (holding trade policy constant) increases imports; for a given premium, this means a decreased flow supply of dollars and an increased flow demand. The premium rises both in the long term to restore balance in the parallel current account (equation 3) and in the short term through expectations of higher future premia.

Table 1.3 shows results for foreign aid inflows and the terms of trade for a number of countries. These variables have potentially complex effects on the premium. They affect both the flow supply of foreign exchange at the parallel rate (for example, through direct leakages of reserves) and the flow demand (for example, through spending effects that increase the demand for smuggled imports or – in the opposite direction – through an induced liberalization of foreign exchange rationing). They also may affect expectations of future policy. Their net effect on the premium is therefore theoretically ambiguous. The estimated effects are generally statistically insignificant. They tend uniformly to be negative, however, suggesting that these variables affect the parallel trade balance mainly through favorable policy and flow supply effects rather than through income effects that raise total spending.

The evidence on trade policy is limited to Argentina, Ghana, and Sudan, but in these cases the variables generally enter with the right sign, indicating that tightening of restrictions on imports or a cut in the export tax rate increases the premium. In the Tanzanian case, adoption of an own-funds scheme, which amounts to a liberalization of imports at the parallel rate, appears to increase the premium, as predicted by the theory.[15]

Do Devaluations Affect the Premium?

We mentioned above that theoretical models of parallel exchange rates often – but not always – have the feature that one-off devaluations of the official exchange rate have no long-term effect on the premium. In the case of Argentina, the author tested this homogeneity restriction econometrically and was unable to reject it. In the other case studies, where this restriction was not formally tested, the descriptive evidence suggests that in the absence of supporting macroeconomic policies, the effect of a devaluation of the official rate on the premium is negative but very transitory.

Figure 1.3 shows the devaluation/premium cycle that can emerge if policy makers devalue the official exchange rate while failing to address the underlying sources of high monetary growth or to accommodate these through continual exchange rate adjustments. In the Sudan, each of four maxi-devaluations of the 1980s brought down the premium significantly. After each devaluation, however, the premium began to rise again, reaching very high levels (exceeding 100 percent) before being brought down again through a new devaluation. A similar picture prevailed in Venezuela, where a premium emerged on the implementation of the dual exchange rate system in 1983 and reached 200 percent by late in that year. The devaluation of early 1984 cut the premium nearly in half, but in the absence of a change in underlying policies, the premium resumed its increase until a second maxi-devaluation was implemented in late 1986. The devaluation–premium cycle was finally eliminated when the foreign exchange market was unified in 1989.

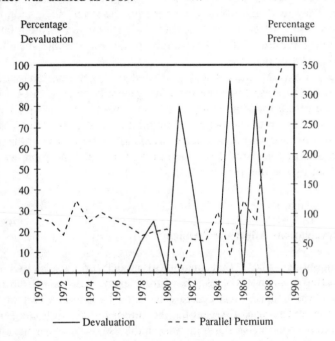

FIGURE 1.3   *Devaluation and parallel premium, Sudan, 1970–89*
SOURCES: Official exchange rate from IMF, *International Financial Statistics*; parallel rate from International Currency Analysis, Inc., *World Currency Yearbook*

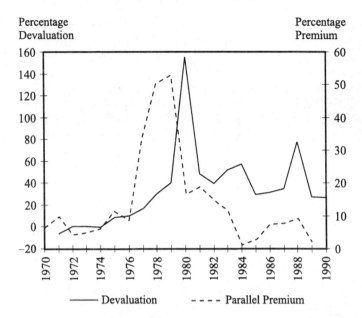

FIGURE 1.4   *Devaluation and parallel premium, Turkey, 1970–89*
SOURCES: Official exchanges rate from IMF, *International Financial Statistics*; parallel rate from International Currency Analysis, Inc., *World Currency Yearbook*

Figure 1.4 gives an example of the role of macroeconomic adjustments in achieving more sustained reductions in the premium. In Turkey, the premium rose dramatically during the late 1970s and early 1980s as a result of problems in the external sector and acute macroeconomic instability. It was brought down definitively by the devaluation in 1981, which was part of a broader package that included a reduction in the budget deficit and adoption of a crawling peg. In similar fashion, Ghana's premium was reduced permanently with the devaluation of 1983, thanks to a broad-based macroeconomic reform program that combined fiscal austerity with the adoption of a more flexible exchange rate and substantial new aid inflows.

While the evidence suggests that devaluations have negligible long-term effects on the premium, the short-term effects can be substantial. Since the parallel rate is forward looking, these effects may well occur in advance of the devaluation, as market participants come to anticipate a parity change. Developments that increase the probability or expected size of a devaluation increase the expected rate of depreciation of the parallel rate (since the premium does not change in the long-term), causing portfolio substitution away from domestic assets and raising the premium immediately, often in spectacular fashion. The premium then falls when the devaluation takes place and may indeed fall by nearly the full amount of the official depreciation, since much of the adjustment of the parallel rate has already taken place.

Figure 1.5 shows this effect at work in the run-up in the Tanzanian parallel premium preceding the maxi-devaluation of April 1986. The 1986 devaluation marked the end of a protracted struggle over exchange rate policy that had produced two failed International Monetary Fund (IMF) programs in the early 1980s and culminated in the resignation of President Nyerere in 1985. The Government of Tanzania had implemented its own macroeconomic reforms in 1984, including a minor devaluation and the introduction of an own-funds

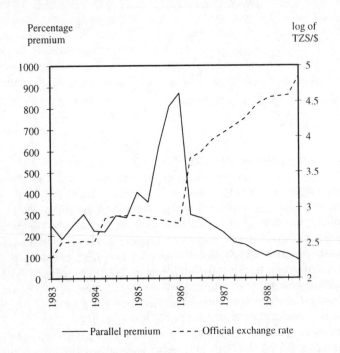

FIGURE 1.5 *Parallel premium and official exchange rate, Tanzania, 1983–88*
NOTE: Data are end of quarter
SOURCES: Official exchange rate from IMF, *International Financial Statistics*; parallel rate from International Currency Analysis, Inc., *World Currency Yearbook and Kaufmann and O'Connell, 1991*

scheme for imports, but it was clear that a major agreement with the IMF was on the cards and that it would be accompanied by a maxi-devaluation. At its pre-devaluation peak, the premium reached nearly 800 percent.

Episodes such as the Tanzanian one – or the very similar Zambian one of 1983 (Chapter 8) – are complicated by the fact that causality is likely to run from the premium to the official exchange rate as well as from expectations of the exchange rate to the premium. In Tanzania, the rise in the premium in 1985 and 1986 produced strong incentives for the diversion of official foreign exchange into the parallel market and may have pressured the authorities into altering the size and/or timing of the 1986 devaluation. Kamin (1993) and Edwards (1989) found strong evidence of this two-way causality in cross-sectional studies of devaluation episodes in developing countries and Kaminsky's vector autoregressions for Mexico in this volume (Chapter 3) suggest the same conclusion. As mentioned earlier, the case study authors handled the joint endogeneity of the official exchange rate and exchange rate expectations in the premium equation by modeling endogenous variables directly (for example, Sudan, Tanzania, and Zambia) and/or estimating with instrumental variables (for example, Tanzania and Turkey).

Fiscal Deficits and the Premium

There is a positive and statistically significant correlation across developing countries between long-term averages of the fiscal deficit and parallel premium.[16] The deficit can affect the premium not only through increases in real money balances, but also through a variety of other mechanisms. By equation (6), for example, a rise in the fiscal deficit requires a rise in inflation tax revenues in the long term. Given real balances m, this requires an increased rate of crawl of the exchange rate (which equals the inflation rate in steady state), which in turn means a shift in private portfolios away from domestic assets. If leakages are tightly controlled so that foreign assets are fixed, the required portfolio shift can only occur through a rise in the premium. Other mechanisms include the effect of higher deficits on expectations of future money growth or official devaluation or on the demand for capital flight via anticipations of higher taxation of domestic assets. Higher fiscal deficits may also lead to a tightening of foreign exchange rationing as a way of compressing private sector imports, with the premium reflecting the binding import quota (Greenwood and Kimbrough, 1987).

The scope for detailed country by country econometric work on the relationship between the fiscal deficit and the premium is limited by the lack of adequate or sufficiently high-frequency fiscal data. One way to address this is through the use of pooled data, which we do in a preliminary fashion in equation (12) below. The equation is taken from Ghei and Kiguel (1992) and uses annual data from 1970 to 1989. The panel comprises the 19 developing countries for which fiscal data were available and in which the average premium exceeded 10 percent. The sample includes all of the case study countries except for Turkey.[17] The estimation uses the random effects procedure (see Hausman and Taylor, 1981) to account for unobservable, country-specific effects. Since this procedure requires the same number of observations for each country, the dummy variable DU is used to account for periods of unified exchange rates.[18]

$$\log(\text{premium}_{it}) = 0.62 + 0.24 \log(m_{i,\,t-1}) + 0.36 \log(d_{i,\,t}) + -3.24 DU_{i,\,t}$$

(11)   (5.87) (2.61)   (2.28)   (−7.77)

$$R^2 = 0.26, \quad DW = 1.40.$$

While these estimates should clearly be treated gingerly, they provide some further corroboration of the importance of the fiscal deficit in determining the premium.

Equation (11) has causality running from the fiscal deficit to the premium, as do the various channels described at the outset of this subsection. While this assumption is often plausible, there are cases in which causality may run in the opposite direction, leading to simultaneous equation bias in equation (11). An important example is when exchange controls extend to the current account and illegal trade is substantial. Increases in the premium may then reduce the revenue from trade taxes by increasing the share of trade that takes place through illegal channels. Ghana's revenue collapse in the early 1980s, for example, was directly related to the smuggling of the majority of the cocoa crop to next-door Cote d'Ivoire (May, 1985). In Tanzania, the introduction of the own-funds window in 1984 was associated with an increase in customs revenues (between 1983 and 1987) of 4.5 percent of GDP, even though underinvoicing was widely thought to be a serious problem in that window.

Deficit Finance, Capital Controls, and Inflation

With inflation determined by seigniorage requirements in the long term, capital controls have the potential to lower inflation by (1) increasing the demand for the real monetary base (recall equation (6)), (2) allowing the government to pay below-market interest rates on its domestic borrowing, and (3) slowing the outflow of other taxable domestic assets (Agénor and Montiel, 1996).[19] Parallel foreign exchange markets frustrate this objective to some degree by reopening the domestic financial market to world markets; Haque *et al.* (1993), for example, found that intertemporal saving and investment behavior is governed by foreign interest rates (adjusted for expected depreciation) rather than by controlled domestic rates, even in the presence of capital controls. However, asset substitution is almost certainly costlier – and the share of domestic assets in private portfolios higher – in the presence of capital controls than without. Consistent with this view, the evidence suggests that liberalization of capital controls can impose a substantial inflationary shock (Giovannini and de Melo, 1993; Adam *et al.*, 1996). Thus Özler (Chapter 9), for example, attributes the high Turkish inflation of the late 1980s in part to the effect of capital account liberalization, while Adam (1995) made a similar argument for Zambia in the early 1990s.

Holding aside the residual effectiveness of capital controls in creating a 'captive' demand for domestic assets – a gain that may come at considerable cost in terms of efficiency and growth, according to the literature on financial repression (McKinnon, 1973; Shaw, 1973; King and Levine, 1993) – a more important lesson of the case studies is that parallel exchange rate regimes do not free governments from the requirement of consistency between fiscal policy and exchange rate policy. In countries that fail to control monetary growth, the parallel rate depreciates and domestic inflation continues even if the government keeps a fixed official exchange rate. The resulting overvaluation places increasing pressure on the balance of payments and the leakages and distortions associated with increasingly tight controls eventually force an accommodating devaluation of the official rate. In Venezuela, for example, while inflation did not increase significantly during the early phase of the dual system, it eventually increased from 10 percent in 1982 to approximately 30 percent in 1988, mainly because the authorities failed to adopt restrictive policies to deal with external imbalances. In Argentina, inflation rose from 150 percent in 1982 to over 600 percent in 1985 as a result of large budget deficits and protracted problems in the balance of payments. In the longer term, inflation is determined by domestic policies and little is gained by having a parallel foreign exchange market.

INSULATION OF RESERVES AND PRICES

In theory, parallel systems insulate both international reserves (and thus the money stock) and domestic prices from transitory shocks to the capital account, relative to what would prevail under unified exchange rates. Shocks are absorbed by movements in the parallel rate rather than in reserves, while the prices of traded goods remain tied down by the official rate. In practice, the picture is more complicated. This is mainly because countries follow macroeconomic policies that are inconsistent with a low average premium. Insulation in such cases is far from complete and it is a declining function of the average size of the premium and the length of time it has been in place. Not surprisingly, there is a trade-off between insulation and reserves and insulation of prices. In this section we summarize evidence from the case studies on the mechanisms underlying these conclusions.

Incomplete Separation

First, the authorities often choose not to separate the markets fully. Trade finance, for example, is typically allowed at the commercial rate, as a way of stabilizing the environment for private traders and supporting the insulation of traded goods' prices; but this provides a channel for speculative capital movements, as in the use of export pre-financing facilities in Argentina (Chapter 2) or trade credit in France and Italy (Chapter 10).

Legal separation is also undercut by high current account deficits, which induce the authorities to sacrifice convertibility for current transactions. As we emphasized above, parallel systems are typically adopted or become prominent in developing countries at times of balance of payments crisis. In these situations, ongoing inconsistencies between domestic macroeconomic policy and the exchange rate regime, present in many of our case studies, are often supplemented by mechanisms that further worsen the current account, such as inventory accumulation by importers expecting an official devaluation or a tightening of import rations (for example, see Chapter 4 on Venezuela).[20]

In our sample, Ghana, Tanzania, Sudan, Zambia, Turkey, and Venezuela all had periods in which capital controls or a dual exchange rate were accompanied by severe foreign exchange rationing for imports. In Ghana and Tanzania in the early 1980s, for example, reserves dropped nearly to zero, so that although the exchange rate was nominally pegged, the central bank was unable to intervene in support of the domestic currency. The exchange control regime in these cases implied no commitment on the part of the central bank to finance a payments imbalance on even a subset of current account transactions. Reserves were therefore effectively insulated; however, the resulting compression of imports meant an increase in the share of trade being financed at the parallel rate, undercutting the insulation of prices (Chhibber and Shafik, 1991; Younger, 1993; see Kaufmann and O'Connell, Chapter 7 in this volume). The failure of domestic price insulation is sometimes underscored by the imposition of direct price controls – Tanzania and Venezuela are leading examples – but these bring problems of their own when the pressures in question are not transitory.[21]

Leakages Through Illegal Trade

Illegal transactions undercut the insulation of reserves by diverting official foreign exchange to the financing of private capital flows and they undercut price insulation by involving the parallel rate directly in the pricing of traded goods. Evidence in the case studies suggests that illegal trade is both substantial and sensitive to the premium, particularly in the African cases.

Empirical attempts to assess the effects of the premium on reserve leakages generally take one of two approaches. The first focuses on the relationship between the premium and measures of illegal transactions. For Argentina (Chapter 2) and Zambia (Chapter 9), the authors use partner trade data to measure the amount of trade misinvoicing. The results are tenuous – not surprisingly, given the low quality of the data – but they support the theoretically predicted positive link between the premium and the supply of foreign exchange from misinvoicing (see also McDonald, 1985).

The second approach is to look at the relationship between the premium and official trade flows while holding constant the determinants of aggregate (legal plus illegal) trade. In this approach, the premium is viewed as altering the *share* of aggregate trade that takes place through illegal channels. In all four cases for which evidence is available (Argentina, Ghana, Sudan, and Zambia), a rise in the parallel premium reduces a major category of official exports (cocoa and copper, respectively, in Ghana and Zambia, aggregate exports in Argentina, and worker remittances and aggregate exports in Sudan). The combined effect of overvaluation and a high parallel premium can be stunning: in Ghana, for example, exports fell (in real terms) from 37 to 22 percent of GDP between 1971 and 1990.

Interactions between illegal exports and the parallel premium are particularly dramatic around official devaluations, when changes in the premium are large. In a sample of 40 devaluation episodes, Kamin (1993) found that anticipatory increases in the parallel premium play an important role in explaining the decline in official exports preceding devaluations and that the immediate post-devaluation decline in the premium helps account for their surprisingly rapid recovery thereafter. Changes in the premium in these episodes dominate changes in the real official exchange rate, suggesting that what appear to be movements in aggregate exports are instead largely shifts of exports between official and unofficial markets.

Import Rationing and Domestic Prices

We have seen how the use of import rationing to avoid exchange rate devaluation or macroeconomic adjustment can initiate a cycle of falling official exports, tighter controls, and higher premia. In such a situation, the amount of foreign exchange available for distribution at the official exchange rate shrinks and the official exchange rate becomes increasingly irrelevant in the determination of domestic prices. These developments have striking implications for policy towards the official exchange rate. First, they are likely to undercut the political resistance to devaluation, both from the formal wage sector and from the recipients of official foreign exchange.[22] Second and relatedly, they reduce the likely cost-push effect of a maxi-devaluation, since such a policy simply amounts to an undercutting of rents to the residual recipients of official foreign exchange. The

Ghanaian case provides a striking case in point: the official exchange rate played virtually no role in domestic price formation in the waning years of the exchange control regime and the maxi-devaluations of the mid-1980s had virtually no perceptible impact on inflation (Chapter 5; see also Chhibber and Shafik, 1991; Younger, 1993).

Intervention at the Financial Rate

A final reason for incomplete insulation is that the authorities may be tempted to intervene at the financial rate in order to prevent an excessive rise in the premium. In Mexico, such a policy was motivated by the desire to limit the incentives for illegal transactions and to avoid a vicious circle driven by private sector expectations as to the necessity and size of the prospective devaluation of the commercial rate (Dornbusch, 1986b). Due in part to this official intervention, capital flight was actually larger after introduction of the dual system than before (Chapter 3).

UNIFICATION

Full unification refers to the adoption of a single exchange rate for all external transactions, with full convertibility if the exchange rate is managed. *Partial unification* refers to the adoption of a single exchange rate for all current account transactions, while maintaining convertibility restrictions and therefore a parallel market for portfolio and capital account operations. In this section we summarize the evidence from numerous unification attempts, both failed and successful, in the sample (see also Pinto, 1989; Agénor, 1992; Agénor and Ucer, 1995). Appendix 2 (pp. 73–6) updates these accounts through to 1995.

Full Unification in a Crisis

Most of the countries that originally created an official parallel market to deal with a balance of payments crisis eventually decided to unify the market. Paradoxically, the decision was not part of a well-planned strategy but instead occurred during a second crisis when inflation was high and the premium was on the rise. Thus, Venezuela, after 6 years of operating a multiple system, unified its foreign exchange market in February 1989 by floating the exchange rate. In Mexico, unification was part of a package aimed at stabilizing prices and restoring the external balance. The decision was made following the stock market crash of October 1987, in the face of accelerating inflation and a rapidly depreciating parallel exchange rate. Argentina unified under a floating exchange rate to control an explosive hyper-inflation in 1989. These experiences suggest that parallel systems are typically abandoned not because they are no longer 'needed' but because they are no longer useful in protecting reserves and maintaining low inflation. Moreover, crises may offer policy makers an opportunity to institute reforms that would have been politically costly at other times. A dual regime may long since have exhausted its macro-economic benefits, but unification was postponed because of political opposition.

A number of the former socialist economies have recently eliminated dual exchange markets as part of broader efforts to bolster market forces. As in earlier cases, unification occurred during a period of crisis, although in these countries the process was part of major systemic reforms. In Poland, for example, unification was essential to secure the credibility of the fixed exchange rate (Lipton and Sachs, 1990). Moreover, the measure was a natural instrument for rationalizing prices after years of price controls and poorly functioning markets. Similar arguments motivated the rapid unification of the foreign exchange market in Russia.

Gradual Unification in Highly Distorted Economies

In countries with widespread exchange controls, unification tends to be a long process. In Turkey it took nearly a decade, beginning in 1980 with a maxi-devaluation and a schedule for phasing out multiple exchange rates. In subsequent stages the government adjusted exchange rates, liberalized imports, and relaxed controls on the capital account. The process was completed in 1989, when residents were permitted to purchase foreign securities; since then the black market has essentially disappeared.

In Africa most economies that regulated foreign exchange have opted for partial – and gradual – unification. In Ghana, the reform process began in 1983 and included monetary and fiscal restraint, increases in producer prices, relaxation of import controls, and a more flexible management of the official exchange rate. As a result, the system – which initially consisted of an official, fixed-rate market and a thriving black market – has been transformed into two legal markets with floating rates and a negligible spread between them and a small illegal market. The black market premium declined from above 2000 percent at the beginning of 1983 to 24 percent in April 1988, when the second legal market became operational and practically absorbed the black market. The spread between the two legal markets declined gradually and has remained around 5 percent since April 1990.

Tanzania was well on the way to partial unification by the early 1990s. The premium declined from over 700 percent in 1986 to approximately 50 percent in 1990. Comprehensive reforms have gradually succeeded in liberalizing markets and restoring macroeconomic stability. In 1984, the authorities devalued and introduced an own-funds scheme that allowed holders of (illegal) foreign exchange to obtain import licenses freely. By 1986 this window was financing one-third of the total imports. The government devalued again in 1986 and adopted a crawling peg as part of a macroeconomic reform package heavily supported by external assistance. More recently, private foreign exchange bureaus have been authorized to deal in trade-related transactions at market-determined exchange rates.

Ingredients for Successful Unification

A common element in the above episodes is that unification was sustained. Argentina (in 1989), Mexico, and Turkey were successful in this respect, while Ghana and Tanzania have moved gradually but steadily and remain on a course that may well lead to full unification. Successful unification requires two ingredients. First, the exchange rate must be reasonably close to the rate that would clear the market for portfolio transactions in the short term. These transactions are the main short-term determinants of reserve or exchange rate movements under a unified regime. Second, the exchange rate system must be consistent with underlying credit and fiscal policies. In practice, this means that if monetized deficits create inflationary pressures the authorities need to adopt some form of crawling peg to keep the parallel market from re-emerging.

The theoretical literature offers only limited guidance on choosing a unified exchange rate. Lizondo (1987) and Kiguel and Lizondo (1990) noted that much depends on whether unification is anticipated and on the exchange rate regime adopted, such as a floating rate or a crawling peg. If the change is anticipated, the unified rate will coincide with the parallel rate; otherwise there would be opportunities for capital gains. In other cases the theory is more ambiguous. An unanticipated unification to a crawling peg occurs at the parallel exchange rate if the central bank maintains a stock of international reserves but is likely to occur at some rate between the official and parallel rates if the central bank is willing to lose reserves. The results of unifying to a floating exchange rate are also unclear.

In practice, however, the unified exchange rate generally coincides with or is close to the parallel rate. This was the case in Argentina and Venezuela in 1989 and in Mexico in 1987. When unification is anticipated, this choice probably reflects the need to maintain asset market equilibrium in the short term (which in a parallel regime takes place at the parallel rate). Experiences vary in countries that choose partial unification and maintain controls on the capital account because in those cases it is only necessary for the exchange rate to balance current account transactions.

The exchange rate system adopted after unification varies according to circumstances. Ghana and Turkey chose a crawling peg, Venezuela (in the 1960s) and Mexico opted for fixed exchange rates, and Venezuela (in the 1980s) and Argentina used floating rates. A fixed exchange rate is possible only if fiscal and monetary policies support stable prices. If the economy faces inflationary pressures, unification can be maintained only if the authorities adopt a flexible exchange rate system or crawling peg.

Failure to unify successfully can often be traced to an inconsistency between the new exchange rate regime and the stance of fiscal and monetary policy. In Argentina, for example, two attempts at unification failed in the early 1980s because the government funded large budget deficits by printing money while trying to use the exchange rate as an anchor for inflation. Macroeconomic imbalances were still large when unification was finally accomplished, but this time the government devalued the exchange rate rapidly enough to avoid a real appreciation.

Countries that attempt to bring down inflation and improve the external balance at the time of unification must adopt fiscal and monetary policies that support these objectives. Ghana, Mexico, Turkey, and Venezuela all cut their budget deficits and tightened domestic credit to support the removal of foreign exchange controls. Although inflation did not always fall, the exchange rate was allowed to depreciate sufficiently to avoid severe overvaluation and the macroeconomic situation usually improved.

Attempts at partial unification in Sudan and Zambia were unsuccessful. In 1979 Sudan tried to unify its foreign exchange market as part of a liberalization and stabilization program. The government shifted a growing number of transactions from the official market to a legal parallel market, in an attempt to reduce the importance of the illegal parallel market. Lax domestic policies, however, led to the reappearance of a large black market premium and an expansion in the number of black market transactions. In Zambia two attempts at unification failed. The first effort (1983–5), based on a crawling peg, was abandoned after large adverse changes in the terms of trade led to increases in the premium. The second episode (1985–7) was an attempt to reduce the volume of transactions in the black market by using an auction system in the official market. However, without the support of compatible monetary and fiscal policies, the premium rose and the black market continued to thrive.

Experience in Latin America suggests that rapid unification is desirable, particularly when inflation is rising. The Latin American economies were less distorted than others in the sample, however, and their capital markets were better integrated into world financial markets. Thus, parallel foreign exchange markets (and relatively large premiums) were difficult to sustain because agents could easily find ways to beat the system. In economies with extensive price controls, barriers to trade, and thin financial markets, a gradual approach to unification could well be appropriate. In Turkey, Ghana, and, to some extent, Tanzania, unification has moved in tandem with structural reforms to expand the role of the market in determining resource allocation – an approach that has been largely successful.

Last, but not least, success depends on the government's commitment, which must be strong enough to outlast the short-term adverse consequences, such as an increase in inflation or a drop in real wages, that unification may bring. When inflation increased after unification in Venezuela, the authorities were determined to rely on monetary and fiscal policies to control it rather than resorting to a parallel market. In contrast, the government of Zambia was unwilling to accept the sharp depreciation required and abandoned efforts to unify the market.

Unification and some Pleasant (Shadow) Fiscal Arithmetic

We have seen that the parallel exchange rate often plays a role in determining the domestic prices of traded goods, either through the legal assignment of certain trade transactions to the free rate or through the use of illegal foreign exchange in import smuggling. In such cases, central bank purchases of export proceeds at the (over-valued) official exchange rate represent an implicit tax on exporters and the sale of foreign exchange to private sector importers at the official rate represents an implicit subsidy. While these effects do not show up as central bank cash flows – assuming the central bank intervenes only at the official rate, if at all – they create a potentially powerful linkage between exchange rate unification and inflation (Lizondo, 1987, 1991; Kharas and Pinto, 1989; Pinto, 1989, 1991). In this section we provide rough estimates of the fiscal effect of unification for five of the case study countries.

To motivate the calculation, we return to the consolidated budget constraint of the public sector (equation (7)) and disaggregate the government's nominal expenditure and revenue flows into those denominated in domestic currency (D) and foreign exchange (D^*). We impose the steady-state assumption that reserves are not changing, so that the government's net purchases of foreign exchange from the central bank, D^*, are exactly equal to the private sector's export remittances, x^*, minus its purchases of official foreign exchange for imports, m^*. Deflating by the domestic price level P, we then have

$$(12) \qquad \text{Inflation tax} + (e^s - e)(x^* - m^*) = e^s D^* + \left(\frac{D}{P}\right),$$

where e is the ratio of the official exchange rate to the domestic price level and similarly for the shadow real exchange rate e^s.

Holding the shadow public sector deficit (the right-hand side) con-stant, equation (12) points to two fundamental determinants of the nature of the link between inflation and unification. The first is whether the government is receiving implicit revenues or making net payments to the private sector due to overvaluation (that is, whether the second term in equation (12) is positive or negative). Since the shadow exchange rate is above the official rate in the presence of exchange controls, this depends on whether the government is a net buyer or seller of foreign exchange *vis-à-vis* the private sector. If the government is a net buyer, unification (which sets $e = e^s$) will reduce the government's implicit financing and require an increase in revenues from the inflation tax.

The second determinant is whether increases in inflation increase or decrease the inflation tax. If the inflation elasticity of demand for the monetary base is below unity, increases in inflation imply increases in seigniorage in the steady state, whereas if it is above unity, increases in inflation reduce real money demand sufficiently to reduce the revenues from the inflation tax (cf. Fischer and Easterly, 1990). Thus, if the typical case is that the government is a net buyer of foreign exchange from the private sector and the inflation elasticity of money demand is below unity, exchange rate unification constitutes a fiscal shock that will raise inflation unless conventional taxes are increased or expenditures reduced (Pinto, 1989).

The full effect of unification is more complicated than suggested here, because unification may have substantial effects on the components of the shadow real deficit or be associated with changes in real income or real wealth that alter money demand directly. First, substantial portions of the domestic currency budget may in fact be indexed to the official exchange rate, so that the government receives implicit revenues (or generates implicit subsidies) from overvaluation on these flows as well as on its foreign exchange flows. A second budgetary effect of unification is a revenue boom associated with the shift of trade flows from legal to illegal channels. We have already emphasized the importance of this effect in countries such as Ghana and Tanzania, where chronic overvaluation had moved a large portion of external trade onto parallel channels. Third, when foreign exchange rationing is extensive, exchange rate unification – unless it is associated with a major increase in tariffs or quantitative restrictions – implies a liberalization of trade. The price of importables must therefore fall domestically relative to the price of non-traded goods and the price of exportables must rise. If the government's spending patterns are fixed in terms of goods, these relative price movements will alter the real deficit as long as the government's spending pattern differs from that of the private sector.[23]

The relationship between inflation and unification has received considerable attention in the theoretical literature. Less is known, however, about the magnitude of the shadow fiscal effect in practice.

Table 1.4 shows our estimates for five of the case study countries. These estimates are rough and partial; problems in measuring public sector deficits are well known and we require heroic assumptions regarding the shadow equilibrium exchange rate. Our results suggest, however, that the outcome in practice is often more pleasant (and the implications of parallel exchange rates correspondingly more unpleasant) than emphasized in the literature. Recent findings by Morris (1995) and Agénor and Ucer (1995) corroborate these results.

The first set of columns in Table 1.4 summarize the shadow gain or loss associated with the pricing of foreign exchange transactions at the overvalued official exchange rate. We call this the 'central bank profits effect' to emphasize the analogy with the familiar quasi-fiscal gain or loss from central bank intervention in a multiple exchange rate system (see Sherwood, 1956; Dornbusch, 1986a,b; Lizondo, 1991).[24] We use the parallel rate as the hypothetical unified rate; as discussed above, this is broadly consistent with actual experience in successful unifications, particularly when the system has been in place for some time.

As discussed above, the qualitative effect on central bank profits depends primarily on whether the central bank is a net buyer or a net seller of foreign exchange to the private sector. In Zambia, for example, the central bank was a net seller to the private sector and thus it suffered losses.[25] The same applies to Tanzania, where the central bank was a net seller to the private sector in all the years but one. In Venezuela, the buying and selling rates were different, but the central bank was a net seller by such large amounts that this factor dominated and the central bank suffered losses. In Argentina, the central bank was a net buyer of foreign exchange from the private sector and thus benefited from the dual exchange rate system.

The magnitude of the effect on central bank accounts may be quite significant. Estimations range from a positive 3.5 percent of GDP for Argentina to a negative of 25.4 percent of GDP for Venezuela.[26] The absolute size of these estimates is biased upwards if the parallel exchange rate overestimates the true value of foreign exchange; however, the estimated effects remain significant even after correcting for a possible bias. For example, using a shadow exchange rate equal to 60 percent of the parallel exchange rate in the case of Venezuela reduces the estimated average effect on central bank profits from 20.5 percent to 4.7 percent of GDP (see also Chapter 7 for Tanzania).

The second set of columns in Table 1.4 give the change in the domestic currency component of the budget associated with unifica-

TABLE 1.4 Fiscal effects of parallel exchange rates

| Country | Effects on shadow central bank profits (percentage of GDP)* | | | | Effects on shadow domestic currency budget[†] | |
	Number of years[‡]	Maximum	Minimum	Average	Channel	Direction of effect
Argentina	7	3.5	1.3	2.1	Reduction in export tax revenue from underinvoicing	–
Sudan	–	–	–	–	Reduction in revenues from trade taxes	–
Tanzania	14	0.4	−9.8	−4.5	Reduction in import (customs and sales) tax revenues; increased marketing board revenues as a result of lower producer prices for exports	+/−
Venezuela	4	−14.7	−25.4	−20.5	Not calculated	
Zambia	2	−12.2	−16.2	−14.2	Increased revenues from imports (customs and sales taxes)	+

* The shadow gain or loss associated with pricing foreign exchange transactions at the overvalued exchange rate.
[†] The change in the domestic currency component of the budget associated with unification.
[‡] The number of years of data used in the calculation.
SOURCE: Country chapters and authors' calculations.

tion. With the exception of Tanzania, the effect on the domestic currency budget could be assessed only in qualitative terms. For Tanzania (Chapter 7), the authors assume that some components of the domestic currency budget (custom duties, sales taxes on imports, and producer prices for exports paid to farmers by parastatals) are fully indexed to the exchange rate, while other components (other tax revenue and public sector wages) are indexed to domestic prices. Under these assumptions, multiple rates have both positive and negative effects on the domestic currency budget. On the one hand, a large spread allows the government to keep producer prices low, thereby reducing expenditures. On the other hand, it reduces declared imports, thereby reducing revenues from import taxes. From 1976 to 1989, the parallel system in Tanzania generated an estimated net positive effect equivalent to 2.1 percent of GDP per year on average. For other countries, the limited available evidence suggests a mixed picture. For example, an increase in the premium seemed to reduce revenues from trade taxes in Argentina and Sudan, but the opposite appears to have occurred in Zambia.

It is clear from Table 1.4 that the fiscal effect of parallel rates is not uniform across countries. There are countries with shadow central banks profits and others with shadow losses; in some, the domestic currency budget improves and in others it worsens. Furthermore, these two components do not necessarily work in the same direction.

Casual evidence suggests that Ghana and Mexico (not included in Table 1.4) incurred fiscal losses from having parallel exchange rate systems. In Ghana, most tax revenues in the early 1970s were related to trade. As official imports and exports (particularly cocoa) collapsed as a result of the large premium in the parallel market, trade taxes fell from around 8 percent of GDP in the early 1970s to just 1 percent in 1982. In Mexico, the public sector is a net 'producer' of foreign exchange, as revenues from oil exports far exceed the cost of servicing the public external debt. For example, oil exports generated around US$16 billion in 1983 and 1984, while net official external transfers were, respectively, US$4.2 billion and US$6.2 billion. On average, the public sector generated US$10 billion in those years and in all likelihood was a net seller of foreign exchange to the private sector.

More often than not, parallel foreign exchange markets tended to generate fiscal losses in the countries studied. Most of these losses did not appear directly in the budgetary accounts, but were instead generated by net sales of foreign exchange to the private sector at over-valued exchange rates. In most of the countries in the sample the public sector was a net producer of foreign exchange, either because public sector enterprises were the main exporters in the economy (as in Mexico, Venezuela, and Zambia) or because the public sector received large external transfers, some portion of which was channeled to the private sector (as in Ghana and Tanzania). In these cases, an earlier or faster unification would have reduced the public sector's real domestic financing requirement, which, other things being equal, would have reduced inflationary pressures.

FINAL THOUGHTS

Experience with parallel exchange rates in developing countries has, on the whole, been disappointing. Most of the countries in our sample tolerated high premia for long periods, undercutting the insulating effects of these arrangements and damaging the allocation of resources and growth. The studies do not indicate any clear gains from keeping the system in place.

Legal dual systems were misused more often than not, both because they were maintained too long and because the premium was excessive. Venezuela, for example, maintained the dual system for 6 years, Mexico for 5 years, and Argentina for 8 years, (counting official and quasi-official parallel exchange rates). The average premiums during these periods were 30 percent in Mexico, 44 percent in Argentina, and 120 percent in Venezuela. In Argentina and Venezuela, the governments made no clear efforts during this 'temporary' period to restore external balance by altering monetary and fiscal policies. It is unlikely that the macroeconomic gains from protecting reserves and avoiding inflation in these countries were larger than the costs resulting from the misallocation of resources. These experiences weaken the case for recommending the adoption of dual exchange rates, even in circumstances where, theoretically, such a recommendation would be appealing.

In other cases, the parallel market was a quasi-permanent arrangement, the result of prolonged periods of overvalued exchange rates and expansionary macroeconomic policies. In Ghana and Tanzania, for instance, the authorities had to rely on extensive foreign exchange controls to avoid a full depletion of reserves. The large premiums in these economies (exceeding 700 percent at times) were clear evidence of a dramatic inconsistency between exchange rate policy and monetary and fiscal policies.

Although examples of macroeconomic mismanagement associated with the coexistence of official and parallel foreign exchange markets are numerous, in some cases parallel systems were used judiciously. Belgium had a dual exchange rate system for more than three decades and the system did not lead to major distortions (Chapter 10). Colombia has maintained an unofficial parallel market for years, while preserving the macroeconomic balance. In these cases, however, the premium was kept low on average (approximately 2 percent in Belgium and 6 percent in Colombia); larger premiums were tolerated only as a short-term safety valve during crises. Serious distortions were avoided in these countries because the governments followed sound macroeconomic policies. What is more difficult to determine is whether the parallel regime delivered greater macroeconomic benefits than a unified rate would have.

How important is unification? Large and persistent parallel premiums create numerous microeconomic distortions and induce rent seeking and corruption. Recent empirical studies find that increases in the premium are associated with reductions in long-term economic growth (Easterly, 1992, 1994; Fischer, 1993; Barro and Lee, 1994). The evidence strongly suggests that a determined transition to unified exchange rates for current account purposes should be a high priority for countries with large and persistent premiums. Convertibility for capital account purposes is less urgent, as long as the premium remains low on average; moreover, maintaining convertibility on the current account allows substantial leeway for capital flows, tending to reduce the distortionary effect of capital controls.

With respect to the speed of unification, we find two distinct successful patterns. In countries such as Argentina, Mexico, and Venezuela, where the parallel foreign exchange market was introduced to deal with capital flight, unification proceeded rapidly, generally as part of a comprehensive stabilization–liberalization package. Unification meant convertibility for both current and capital account transactions.

In contrast, unification in Ghana, Tanzania, and Turkey occurred in phases, with reductions in the premium accompanying a gradual shift of transactions to a more market-determined official exchange rate. These economies were more heavily controlled in most respects at the outset and to some degree the liberalization of exchange controls was constrained by the feasible pace of reform in other areas (for instance, trade and price controls). Experience indicates that legalization of the existing parallel foreign exchange market is a good first step towards full unification.

Last, but not least, a puzzling question arose from the study. In most cases, the exchange control system generated large parallel premiums and important fiscal losses. The large premiums had detrimental effects on exports and growth while providing only limited insulation from external shocks. Surely a 'rational' government would have pushed for unification. Why, in the face of this evidence, was unification typically delayed, relative to initial intentions and half-hearted (and therefore unsuccessful)? The answer may lie in the realm of political economy. Even when parallel exchange rates are adopted on an explicitly transitional basis, interest groups with enough political clout to deter devaluation or macroeconomic contraction at the outset are likely to resist the policy adjustments necessary for early unification. Moreover, the parallel system itself creates rents and, potentially, new vested interests. In a dismaying proportion of cases, unification had to await a renewed crisis (Argentina and Venezuela) or the steady hollowing-out of the official economy, rents and all (Ghana and Tanzania).

NOTES

1. We are extremely grateful to Saúl Lizondo who played a pivotal role in the preparation and management of the research project, prepared background material for this chapter, and spent long sessions discussing the findings. We also thank David Bevan, Vittorio Corbo, Robert Flood, Steven Kamin, and seminar participants at Swarthmore College, Oxford University, and the World Bank for helpful comments and William Shaw and S. Akkaya of the World Bank for information used in Appendix 2. Portions of this chapter are taken from our recent survey of parallel exchange rates (Kiguel and O'Connell, 1995). The fourth section of this chapter is entirely new, as are the Appendices and much of the fifth section; other sections have been revised to focus more specifically on the case study countries.

2. Lizondo (1990) provided a non-technical survey of the theoretical literature on parallel foreign exchange markets. Agénor (1992) focused on black markets and Edwards (1989) on the related issue of exchange rate misalignment. Montiel *et al.*, (1993) provided an integrated model of foreign exchange black markets and informal financial markets in developing countries.

3. Bhagwati (1978) provided extensive evidence on the microeconomic efficiency implications of departures from unified exchange rates. Adams and Greenwood (1985) studied the efficiency properties of capital controls; see also Mathieson and Rojas-Suarez (1993) and the references therein. The growth literature has recently used the parallel premium as a measure of overall distortions; Barro and Lee (1994), Easterly (1994), and Fischer (1993) all found a negative and statistically significant effect of the premium on growth in cross-sectional data. Easterly (1994) developed a theoretical model in which a higher premium imposes an implicit tax on exports and reduces the steady-state growth rate.

4. These are summarized in the annual publication *Exchange Arrangements and Exchange Restrictions* by the International Monetary Fund (IMF). See Einzig (1934) for an early and thorough taxonomy of exchange controls.

5. In Brazil, for example, the devaluations of the mid- and late 1970s were associated with a permanent increase in inflation (Kiguel and Liviatan, 1988).

6. Overshooting is a common feature of floating exchange rates. It is associated with the maxi-devaluation option as well, since the real depreciation required to stem private capital outflows in the presence of generalized uncertainty regarding macroeconomic events may well be larger than the real depreciation consistent with restoration of macroeconomic balance in the medium term.

7. See Mathieson and Rojas-Suarez (1993) for a discussion of alternative motivations for and forms of capital controls.

8. Short-term net capital movements can also take place through manipulation of 'leads and lags' in remitting export proceeds or purchasing foreign exchange for imports or through the use of trade financing, which is a capital account transaction that is typically allowed at the official rate in a parallel exchange rate system (see Chapters 3 (Argentina) and 10 (Europe) in this volume). This means that even when the authorities are not attempting to influence the parallel rate through intervention, the private sector has some scope for accumulating foreign assets by swapping domestic money for international reserves. Portfolio equilibrium therefore may involve both movements in the parallel rate and discrete adjustments of private foreign assets. Variables such as the interest parity deviation may therefore also enter equation (3).

9. Theoretical models in the dual exchange rates literature sometimes have the property that the premium is zero in the long run (for example, Guidotti and Végh, 1988; Bhandari and Végh, 1990; Agénor and Flood, 1992). This reflects an assumption that only one side of the flow market for foreign exchange operates at any non-zero level of the premium. With import tariffs or quotas (for example, foreign exchange rationing) in place, a flow demand – for import smuggling and underinvoicing – exists whenever the premium is below the implicit tariff rate (de Macedo, 1987) and the premium will generally be positive in the long run.

10. Exogenous growth in real GDP is easy to incorporate in these models. Steady-state conditions such as $\Delta f = 0$, for example, would take the

form $\Delta(Bf/Py) = 0$, where P and y are the domestic price level and real GDP, respectively. This condition would require the parallel trade surplus, as a share of GDP, to equal $(g - r)f$, where r is the foreign real interest rate and g is the growth of real GDP.

11. Net interest payments are included in the deficit. Equation (4) is a simplified version of the consolidated public sector budget constraint; see Anand and van Wijnbergen (1989) and Agénor and Montiel (1996) for a detailed analysis incorporating growth and alternative means of government finance.

12. We draw ff upward sloping, which requires that the direct effect of the premium on illegal trade flows dominates the indirect effect operating through the impact of changes in the premium on financial wealth and therefore on spending, plus the effect of interest income on the parallel current account.

13. Ghei and Kiguel (1992) used this finding to reinterpret Marion's (1994) result that domestic macroeconomic variables like the fiscal deficit were more important in determining the premium in Latin American dual exchange rate systems than in European dual systems. They argue that this does not necessarily indicate that the set of relevant fundamentals differs between the two groups of countries; rather, the underlying relationship may simply be harder to detect in Europe given the low and stable premia.

14. For additional variations on this theme, see the premium equations estimated by Agénor (1990), Azam and Besley (1989), Chhibber and Shafik (1991), Kamin (1993), Kharas and Pinto (1989), and Phylatkis (1992).

15. In an own-funds scheme, individuals are granted import licenses without being asked where they obtained their foreign exchange. Unless exports are simultaneously liberalized, this tends to raise the premium because the flow demand for foreign exchange increases while the flow supply, in the absence of strong output effects from the import liberalization, is unaffected. O'Connell (1992) provided a theoretical treatment.

16. Using annual data for the period 1976–89, the cross-country correlation between the average fiscal deficit and the average parallel premium for the 33 developing countries in Table 1.1 (excluding South Africa) is 0.39 and is statistically significant.

17. The countries are Algeria, Argentina, Bolivia, Brazil, Chile, Dominican Republic, Ecuador, Egypt, Ethiopia, Ghana, Malawi, Mexico, Nigeria, Peru, Sudan, Tanzania, Venezuela, Zaire, and Zambia. All had average premia above 25 percent except Mexico (10 percent).

18. Source: IMF, *International Financial Statistics* and World Bank data. The money stock variable is $m = a[M2/EP^*y]$, where P^* and y are the US Consumer Price Index and home country real GDP and the constant $a > 0$ is set so that m equals the ratio of $M2$ to nominal GDP in the initial year. This adjusts for growth in nominal money demand associated with real income growth and 'imported' inflation. The deficit variable is the nominal fiscal deficit deflated by nominal GDP.

19.   Fischer and Easterly (1990) provided a useful summary of seigniorage and the fiscal accounts.

20.   Kiguel and Lizondo (1990) pointed out that by increasing private financial wealth, the initial depreciation of the parallel rate on adoption of a dual system can itself raise private spending and deteriorate the current account.

21.   Bevan *et al.* (1990) and O'Connell (1995) analyzed the macroeconomic effects of Tanzanian price controls, arguing that in concert with across-the-board import quotas and a rigid government spending requirement they overconstrained the system, producing a money overhang and a severe contraction of output. Hausmann's argument in Chapter 4 is similar in style: he omits price controls but models the parallel foreign exchange market explicitly, arguing that full government control of both current and capital accounts produced an exploding premium and a need for fiscal adjustment to regain a viable equilibrium.

22.   In a related argument, Ndulu (1986) argued that in sub-Saharan Africa more generally, the rapid development of parallel markets for goods and foreign exchange starting in the mid-1970s undercut the ability of governments to deliver patronage and therefore made governments more open to market-based reforms by the mid-1980s.

23.   Finally, an exchange rate unification that restores convertibility for current account purposes will typically raise real income through a trade-liberalization effect; this increases money demand, directly lowering the inflation rate required to generate any amount of real seigniorage (Collier, 1989).

24.   The analogy is not perfect because the shadow effects we calculate do not manifest themselves as actual cash flows when the parallel regime is in operation. Nonetheless, the gains or losses under a multiple exchange rate system must be calculated relative to a 'reference' exchange rate – typically the commercial rate or some other official rate – and thus implicitly involve a counterfactual. Our shadow central bank profits effect embeds the calculation in a full specification of the counterfactual. What emerges looks exactly like the quasi-fiscal effect, but using the unified rate as the reference rate. Thus, our calculation for Venezuela, for example, allows for official foreign exchange transactions occurring at more than one exchange rate.

25.   The estimations shown here for Venezuela and Zambia differ from those presented by the respective authors in their individual case studies. Although the Venezuelan oil company (PDVSA) is publicly owned and the Zambian copper company (ZCCMC) is largely publicly owned, the estimations of the fiscal effect on central bank accounts in the individual case studies treat these companies as part of the private sector. The estimations presented here include those companies as part of the public sector.

26.   Due to lack of detailed information, in the estimation for Argentina central bank foreign exchange sales to and purchases from the private sector include only those arising from merchandise trade transactions and the central bank buying exchange rate includes export taxes and subsidies.

REFERENCES

Adam, Christopher S. (1995) 'Fiscal Adjustment, Financial Liberalization, and the Dynamics of Inflation: Some Evidence from Zambia', *World Development*, vol. 23, no. 5, pp. 735–50.

Adam, Christopher S., Benno Ndulu and Nii Kwaku Sowa (1996) 'Liberalization and Seigniorage Revenue in Kenya, Ghana and Tanzania'. *Journal of Development Studies*, vol. 32, no. 4, pp. 531–53.

Adams, Charles and Jeremy Greenwood (1985) 'Dual Exchange Rate Systems and Capital Controls: an Investigation', *Journal of International Economics*, vol. 18, 43–63.

Agénor, Pierre-Richard (1990) 'Stabilization Policies in Developing Countries with a Parallel Market for Foreign Exchange', *IMF Staff Papers*, vol. 37, no. 3, pp. 560–92.

Agénor, Pierre-Richard (1992) 'Parallel Currency Markets in Developing Countries: Theory, Evidence, and Policy Implications', *Princeton Essays in International Finance* No. 188 (Princeton, NJ: International Finance Section, Department of Economics, Princeton University).

Agénor, Pierre-Richard (1994) 'The Macroeconomics of Informal Financial Markets', mimeo (Washington, DC: IMF).

Agénor, Pierre-Richard and Robert P. Flood (1992) 'Unification of Foreign Exchange Markets', *IMF Staff Papers*, vol. 39, no. 4, pp. 923–47.

Agénor, Pierre-Richard and Peter J. Montiel (1996) *Development Macroeconomics* (Princeton, NJ: Princeton University Press).

Agénor, Pierre-Richard and E. Murat Ucer (1995) 'Exchange Market Reform, Inflation, and Fiscal Deficits', *Working Paper WP/95/78* (Washington, DC: IMF, African and Research Departments).

Anand, Ritu and Sweder van Wijnbergen (1989) 'Inflation and the Financing of Government Expenditure: an Introductory Analysis with an Application to Turkey', *World Bank Economic Review*, vol. 3, no. 1, pp. 17–38.

Azam, Jean-Paul and Timothy Besley (1989) 'General Equilibrium with Parallel Markets for Goods and Foreign Exchange: Theory and Application to Ghana', *World Development*, vol. 17, no. 12, pp. 1921–30.

Banerjee, Anindya, Juan Dolado, John W. Galbraith, and David F. Hendry (1993) *Co-integration, Error Correction and Econometric Analysis of Non-Stationary Data* (Oxford: Oxford University Press).

Barro, Robert J. and Jong-Wha Lee (1994) 'Losers and Winners in Economic Growth', in Michael Bruno and Boris Pleskovic (eds), *Proceedings of the World Bank Annual Conference on Development Economics, 1993* (Washington, DC: World Bank), pp. 267–314.

Bevan, David, Paul Collier and Jan W. Gunning, with Arne Bigsten and Paul Horsnell (1990) *Controlled Open Economies: a Neoclassical Approach to Structuralism* (Oxford: Oxford University Press).

Bhagwati, Jagdish, N. (1978) *Foreign Trade Regimes and Economic Development* (Cambridge, Mass.: Ballinger).

Bhandari, Jagdeep S. and Carlos A. Végh (1990) 'Dual Exchange Markets Under Incomplete Separation', *IMF Staff Papers*, vol. 37, no. 1, pp. 146–67.

Chhibber, Ajay and Nemat Shafik (1991) 'Exchange Reform, Parallel Markets and Inflation in Africa: the Case of Ghana', in Ajay Chhibber and Stanley Fischer (eds), *Economic Reform in Sub-Saharan Africa* (Washington, DC: World Bank), pp. 39–49.

Collier, Paul (1989) 'Exchange Rates and Exchange Controls in Developing Countries', *Greek Economic Review*, vol. 12, pp. 132–47.

de Macedo, Jorge Braga (1987) 'Currency Inconvertibility, Trade Taxes, and Smuggling', *Journal of Development Economics*, vol. 27, pp. 109–25.

Dornbusch, Rudiger (1986a) 'Multiple Exchange Rates for Commercial Transactions', in Sebastian Edwards and Liaquat Ahamed (eds) *Economic Adjustment and Exchange Rates in Developing Countries* (Chicago, Ill: University of Chicago Press), pp. 143–76.

Dornbusch, Rudiger (1986b) 'Special Exchange Rates for Capital Account Transactions', *World Bank Economic Review*, vol. 1, no. 1, pp. 1–33.

Dornbusch, Rudiger and Luis Tellez Kuenzler (1993) 'Exchange Rate Policies: Options and Issues', in Rudiger Dornbusch (ed.), *Policymaking in the Open Economy* (New York: Oxford University Press), pp. 91–126.

Dornbusch, Rudiger, Daniel V. Dantas, Clarice Pechman, Roberto Rocha, and Demetri Simoes (1983) 'The Black Market for Dollars in Brazil', *Quarterly Journal of Economics*, vol. 98, pp. 25–40.

Easterly, William, R. (1992) 'Endogenous Growth in Developing Countries with Government-induced Distortions', in Vittorio Corbo, Stanley Fischer, and Steven B. Webb (eds), *Adjustment Lending Revisited: Policies to Restore Growth* (Washington, DC: World Bank), pp. 160–76.

Easterly, William, R. (1994) 'Economic Stagnation, Fixed Factors, and Policy Threshholds', *Journal of Monetary Economics*, vol. 33, pp. 525–57.

Edwards, Sebastian (1989) *Real Exchange Rates, Devaluation and Adjustment: Exchange Rate Policies in Developing Countries* (Cambridge, Mass: MIT Press).

Einzig, Paul (1934) *Exchange Controls* (London: Macmillan and Co., Ltd).

Fischer, Stanley (1993) 'The Role of Macroeconomic Factors in Growth', *Journal of Monetary Economics*, vol. 32, no. 3, pp. 485–512.

Fischer, Stanley and William R. Easterly (1990) 'The Economics of the Government Budget Constraint', *World Bank Research Observer*, vol. 5, no. 2, pp. 127–42.

Ghei, Nita and Miguel A. Kiguel (1992) 'Dual and Multiple Exchange Rate Systems in Developing Countries: Some Empirical Evidence', *Policy Research Working Paper Series* No. 881 (Washington, DC: World Bank).

Giovannini, Alberto and Martha de Melo (1993) 'Government Revenue from Financial Repression', *American Economic Review*, vol. 83, no. 4, pp. 953–63.

Greenwood, Jeremy and Kent P. Kimbrough (1987) 'Foreign Exchange Controls in a Black Market Economy', *Journal of Development Economics*, vol. 26, 129–43.

Guidotti, Pablo and Carlos Végh (1988) 'Dual Exchange Markets and Incomplete Separation', *IMF Staff Papers*, vol. 37, no. 1, pp. 146–67.

Haque, Nadeem U., Kajal Lahiri, and Peter J. Montiel (1993) 'Estimation of a Macroeconomic Model with Rational Expectations and Capital Controls for Developing Countries', *Journal of Development Economics*, vol. 42, no. 2, pp. 337–56.

Hausman, J.A. and W.E. Taylor (1981), 'Panel Data and Unobservable Individual Effects', *Econometrica*, vol. 49, no. 6, pp. 1377–98.

Hyden, Goran and Bo Karlstrom (1993) 'Structural Adjustment as a Policy Process', *World Development*, vol. 21, no. 9, pp. 1395–404.

International Currency Analysis, Inc. (various years) *World Currency Yearbook* (formerly *Pick's Currency Yearbook*; continued as monthly *Currency Alert*) (Brooklyn, New York: International Currency Analysis, Inc).

International Monetary Fund (various years), *International Financial Statistics* (Washington, DC: International Monetary Fund).

Kamin, Steven B. (1993) 'Devaluation, Exchange Controls, and Black Markets for Foreign Exchange in Developing Countries', *Journal of Development Economics*, vol. 40, no. 1, pp. 151–69.

Kaufmann, Daniel and Stephen A. O'Connell (1993) 'Exchange Controls and the Parallel Premium in Tanzania: 1965–1990', mimeo, Swarthmore, PA: Swarthmore College.

Kharas, Homi and Brian Pinto (1989) 'Exchange Rate Rules, Black Market Premia and Fiscal Deficits: the Bolivian Hyperinflation', *Review of Economic Studies*, vol. 56, pp. 435–47.

Kiguel, Miguel and Nissan Liviatan (1988) 'Inflationary Rigidities and Orthodox Stabilization Programs: Lessons from Latin America', *The World Bank Economic Review*, vol. 2, no. 3, pp. 273–98.

Kiguel, Miguel and J. Saul Lizondo (1990) 'Adoption and Abandonment of Dual Exchange Rate Systems', *Revista de Análisis Económico*, vol. 5, no. 1, pp. 2–23 (previously *Development Research Department Discussion Paper No. 201* (Washington, DC: World Bank).

Kiguel, Miguel and Stephen A. O'Connell (1995) 'Parallel Exchange Rates in Developing Countries', *World Bank Research Observer*, vol. 10, no. 1, pp. 21–52.

King, Robert G. and Ross Levine (1993) 'Finance and Growth: Schumpeter Might Be Right', *Quarterly Journal of Economics*, vol. 108, pp. 717–37.

Lanyi, Anthony (1975) 'Separate Exchange Rates for Capital and Current Transactions', *IMF Staff Papers*, vol. 22, pp. 714–49.

Lipton, David and Jeffrey D. Sachs (1990) 'Creating a Market Economy in Eastern Europe: the Case of Poland', *Brookings Papers on Economic Activity*, vol. 1, 75–147.

Lizondo, J. Saul (1987) 'Exchange Rate Differential and Balance of Payments Under Dual Exchange Markets', *Journal of Development Economics*, vol. 26, no. 1, pp. 37–53.

Lizondo, J. Saul (1990) 'Multiple Exchange Rates and Black Market Exchange Rates: a Non-technical Survey', mimeo (Washington, DC: IMF).

Lizondo, J. Saul (1991) 'Alternative Dual Exchange Rate Regimes: Some Steady-state Comparisons', *IMF Staff Papers*, vol. 38, no. 3, pp. 560–81.

Lizondo, J. Saul (1994) 'A Note on Dual Foreign Exchange Markets with Official Rationing: Predetermined vs. Floating Exchange Official Exchange Rate', *Journal of Development Economics*, vol. 44, pp. 429–39.

Loxley, John (1989) 'The Devaluation Debate in Tanzania', in Bonnie Campbell and John Loxley (eds), *Structural Adjustment in Africa* (New York: St Martins), pp. 13–36.

McDonald, Donough (1985) 'Trade Data Discrepancies and the Incentive to Smuggle', *IMF Staff Papers*, vol. 32, no. 3, pp. 668–92.

McKinnon, Ronald (1973) *Money and Capital in Economic Development* (Washington, DC: Brookings Institution).

Marion, Nancy, P. (1994) 'Dual Exchange Rates in Europe and Latin America', *World Bank Economic Review*, vol. 8, no. 2, pp. 213–45.

Mathieson, Donald J. and Liliana Rojas-Suarez (1993) 'Liberalization of the Capital Account: Experience and Issues', *Occasional Paper* No. 103 (Washington, DC: IMF).

May, Ernesto (1985) 'Exchange Controls and Parallel Market Economies in Sub-Saharan Africa: Focus on Ghana', *PPR Working Paper* No. 771 (Washington, DC: World Bank).

Montiel, Peter J., Pierre-Richard Agénor, and Nadeem U. Haque (1993) *Informal Financial Markets in Developing Countries* (Oxford: Basil Blackwell).

Morris, Stephen (1995) 'Inflation Dynamics and the Parallel Market for Foreign Exchange', *Journal of Development Economics*, vol. 46, pp. 295–316.

Ndulu, Benno (1986) 'Governance and Economic Management', in Robert J. Berg and Jennifer Seymour Whitaker (eds), *Strategies for African Development* (Berkeley: University of California Press), pp. 81–110.

O'Connell, Stephen A. (1992) 'Short and Long Run Effects of an Own-funds Scheme', *Journal of African Economies*, vol. 1, no. 1, pp. 131–50.

O'Connell, Stephen A. (1995) 'Monetary Adjustment and Policy Compatibility in a Controlled Open Economy', *Journal of African Economies*, vol. 4, no. 1, pp. 52–82.

Phylatkis, Kate (1992) 'The Black Market for Dollars in Chile', *Journal of Development Economics*, vol. 37, pp. 155–72.

Pinto, Brian (1989) 'Black Market Premia, Exchange Rate Unification, and Inflation in Sub-Saharan Africa', *World Bank Economic Review*, vol. 3, no. 3, pp. 321–38.

Pinto, Brian (1991) 'Black Markets for Foreign Exchange, Real Exchange Rates and Inflation', *Journal of International Economics*, vol. 30, pp. 121–36.

Pitt, Mark (1974) 'Smuggling and the Black Market for Foreign Exchange', *Journal of International Economics*, vol. 16, pp. 243–57.

Sheikh, Munir A. (1976) 'Black Market for Foreign Exchange, Capital Flows and Smuggling', *Journal of Development Economics*, vol. 3, pp. 9–26.

Shaw, Edward (1973) *Financial Deepening in Economic Development* (New York: Oxford University Press).

Sherwood, Joyce (1956) 'Revenue Features of Multiple Exchange Systems: Some Case Studies', *IMF Staff Papers*, vol. 5, pp. 74–107.

Triffin, Robert (1947) 'National Central Banking and the International Economy', *Postwar Economic Studies* No. 7 (Washington, DC: Board of Governors of the Federal Reserve System).

Younger, Stephen (1993) 'Testing the Link Between Devaluation and Inflation: Time Series Evidence from Ghana', *Journal of African Economies*, vol 1, no. 3, pp. 369–94.

TABLE A.1 *Error-correction regressions for the parallel premium in 21 developing countries: dependent variable:* $\Delta \log z_t$

	Constant	$\Delta \log m_t$	$\Delta \log r_t$	$\Delta overal_t$	$\log z_{t-1}$	$\log m_{t-1}$	$\log r_{t-1}$	$overal_{t-1}$	Adjusted R^2	DW
High-premium countries										
Egypt	−0.71 (−2.60)	1.95 (2.47)	−0.04 (−0.5)	2.15 (2.46)	−0.10 (−2.11)	0.06 (2.33)		0.29 (0.63)	0.62	2.20
Ethiopia	−1.69 (−1.86)	−3.00 (−2.04)	0.01 (0.07)	−1.09 (−1.78)	−0.19 (−2.26)	0.25 (1.95)		−0.76 (−1.69)	0.14	2.11
Ghana	−6.34 (−4.45)	−0.58 (−1.54)	−0.21 (−0.56)	0.14 (11.08)	−0.57 (6.22)	0.93 (4.56)		0.03 (1.49)	0.86	1.92
Nigeria	−1.72 (−1.91)	0.84 (1.62)	−0.12 (−0.68)	0.54 (2.12)	−0.37 (−3.83)	0.32 (2.87)	−0.18 (−2.56)	0.49 (2.67)	0.35	2.22
Tanzania	0.54 (0.67)	0.44 (0.84)	0.05 (0.45)	0.03 (1.17)	−0.32 (−3.49)	0.02 (0.18)	−0.14 (−2.15)	0.20 (1.36)	0.26	2.15
Zambia	1.13 (0.98)	0.91 (1.68)	−0.07 (−0.54)	0.05 (0.38)	−0.14 (−1.91)	−0.17 (−0.99)		0.27 (2.03)	0.07	1.97
Argentina	−11.44 (−2.17)	1.22 (1.52)	−1.01 (−2.42)	0.07 (0.07)	−0.94 (−6.55)	1.85 (2.83)	−0.90 (−3.86)	−2.17 (−1.12)	0.46	2.02
Bolivia	−2.06 (−1.97)	1.78 (2.38)	−0.14 (−0.46)	−0.88 (−0.47)	−0.23 (−2.23)	0.26 (1.59)		1.09 (0.68)	0.23	2.61
Brazil	0.86 (0.21)	1.95 (1.92)	−1.15 (−1.59)	−14.81 (−0.30)	−0.40 (−3.43)	−0.16 (−0.38)		415.63 (1.36)	0.21	1.94
Chile	1.72 (0.95)	1.20 (0.68)	−2.83 (−5.35)	0.04 (1.73)	−0.35 (−3.67)	−0.25 (−1.19)		−0.01 (−0.81)	0.69	2.29
Dominican Republic	−2.09 (−2.22)	−0.88 (−0.89)	−0.18 (−1.21)	1.12 (3.65)	−0.24 (−3.20)	0.57 (2.85)	−0.43 (−3.11)	−0.20 (−1.06)	0.39	2.46
Peru	−5.51 (−1.46)	2.07 (0.98)	−0.53 (−0.78)	−0.03 (−0.11)	−0.24 (−2.51)	0.66 (1.39)		0.01 (−0.05)	0.07	1.91
Venezuela	−9.79 (−2.36)	2.81 (2.62)	−1.11 (−1.36)	−0.07 (0.61)	−0.63 (−5.90)	1.00 (2.40)		0.04 (0.53)	0.80	1.02

TABLE A.1 (Continued)

	Constant	$\Delta\log m_t$	$\Delta\log r_t$	$\Delta overal_t$	$\log z_{t-1}$	$\log m_{t-1}$	$\log r_{t-1}$	$overal_{t-1}$	Adjusted R^2	DW
Moderate-premium countries										
Colombia	-3.33	-1.15	-0.46	0.08	-0.41	0.81	-0.65	0.03	0.19	2.37
	(-1.22)	(-0.52)	(-0.56)	(1.84)	(-3.55)	(1.48)	(-1.95)	(0.84)		
Ecuador	-1.97	-1.28	0.04	0.03	-0.17	0.24		0.01	0.20	1.39
	(-2.12)	(-1.76)	(0.14)	(3.47)	(-2.60)	(1.99)		(1.43)		
India	-1.60	6.82	-2.17	-0.43	-0.80	0.01		-0.10	0.42	1.98
	(-0.75)	(1.74)	(-1.88)	(-1.10)	(-6.53)	(0.04)		(-0.36)		
Kenya	0.63	-2.67	-0.16	0.18	-0.35	-0.17		0.07	0.16	2.02
	(0.66)	(-2.13)	(-0.51)	(1.60)	(-3.75)	(-1.20)		(0.70)		
Mexico	-4.65	0.39	-0.92	0.00	-0.15	0.42		0.00	0.07	2.72
	(-1.31)	(0.39)	(-1.83)	(0.26)	(-1.75)	(1.22)		(-0.88)		
Pakistan	0.95	1.52	0.12	0.11	-0.40	-0.19		0.11	0.25	2.23
	(0.64)	(0.90)	(0.39)	(0.70)	(-3.93)	(-1.10)		(1.34)		
Turkey	-12.23	3.79	-2.66	0.01	-0.67	5.96	-6.47	-0.02	0.08	2.39
	(-0.51)	(0.49)	(-0.77)	(0.15)	(-0.56)	(2.28)	(-2.65)	(-0.56)		
Uruguay	-0.75	-0.65	0.12	0.05	-0.48	0.39	-0.57	0.05	0.48	1.75
	(-0.74)	(-0.36)	(0.34)	(2.39)	(-4.84)	(1.33)	(-2.20)	(2.82)		

The numbers in parentheses are t-statistics. Data are quarterly, end of period. The period of estimation is 1970:1–1990:4, excluding the following episodes of unified exchange rates: Argentina, 1976:4–1980:4; Chile, 1977:4–1981:2; Colombia, 1977:3–1981:2; Ecuador, 1973:3–1974:4. For Venezuela (1983–9) and Mexico (1976–87), estimation was only for the dual exchange rate period. 'High-premium' and 'moderate-premium' countries are those with average parallel premiums above 35 percent and between 10 and 35 percent, respectively. For definitions of the variables see the text. *DW* is the Durbin–Watson statistic. The regression for Bolivia includes the following two dummy variables: DUMMY1: 1.97 (3.73) for the period of the hyperinflation and DUMMY2: −0.99 (−1.67) for the period following the hyperinflation.

SOURCES: IMF, *International Financial Statistics* and International Currency Analysis, Inc., *World Currency Yearbook* (various years)

APPENDIX 2: RECENT DEVELOPMENTS IN THE CASE STUDY COUNTRIES

Although the balance of payments crises of the 1970s and 1980s had important internal origins in most cases, external shocks – such as the increase in world interest rates in the early 1980s and the subsequent reversal of voluntary capital flows to developing countries – were a contributing factor. The external situation reversed rather dramatically in the early 1990s, as many countries that had implemented market-based reforms and restored macroeconomic stability became the recipients of major capital inflows. While large inflows of capital raise important issues of macroeconomic management, none of the countries in our sample responded to these inflows using dual exchange rates or exchange controls. Those that maintained or reimposed controls during the 1990s did so, as before, to deal with capital outflows whose origins were at least partly traceable to a lack of fiscal control. In this appendix we briefly outline developments in the case study countries in the 1990s.

Argentina (Chapter 2) and Mexico (Chapter 3) successfully achieved and maintained a fully unified exchange rate through the 1990s. Even in the peso crisis of December 1994, the Mexican authorities did not seriously contemplate either a return to dual or multiple exchange rates or the imposition of controls that would give rise to a parallel foreign exchange market. Any such action would have been perceived as anti-market and would have weakened the credibility of the Mexican government's commitment to the liberalization program. In any case, the speed at which the IMF and the US government assembled a rescue package made it unnecessary to consider anything as drastic as a reversal of free-market policies.

Similar considerations underlay the decision of the authorities to maintain full convertibility of the Argentine peso in the wake of the Mexican crisis. The peso had been made fully convertible in 1991, as part of the convertibility program that was announced following a fresh surge of inflation in 1991. The program committed the government to fix the exchange rate and to back the monetary base fully with international reserves while removing all exchange controls. A fully convertible currency was the cornerstone of the program and is seen as the key factor in maintaining its credibility. Convertibility was maintained through 1995, even as foreign capital inflows fell dramatically in response to the Mexican crisis and to problems in Argentina's own banking system. Austerity measures announced in March

1995 achieved modest further decreases in inflation – the CPI actually declined 0.5 per cent that month – but at a substantial cost in terms of increased unemployment. However, the exchange rate has remained unified and, as the government works on solving the problems of the domestic banking sector, it is likely to remain so. The clear subordination of monetary and fiscal policy to exchange rate policy presents a dramatic contrast to the use of exchange controls to postpone adjustment during the 1980s.

Venezuela (Chapter 4) and Sudan (Chapter 6) offer sharp contrasts to both Mexico and Argentina. Following the exchange rate unification of March 1989, Venezuela maintained a unified floating exchange rate for approximately 5 years. However, a fiscally induced balance of payments crisis in the spring of 1994 caused a sharp depreciation of the bolivar. Exchange controls were reimposed along with controls on domestic prices and an illegal parallel market emerged. The authorities experimented briefly with foreign exchange auctions in May 1994, as a way of increasing the supply of foreign exchange to the domestic banking system. This succeeded in narrowing but not eliminating the parallel premium and, in June 1994, the authorities depreciated the exchange rate substantially and fixed it at the new rate of 170 bolivars per US dollar. Domestic prices have nearly doubled in the 15 months since then, suggesting that the bolivar is now significantly overvalued. The parallel premium reached 80 percent late in 1995.

Sudan (Chapter 6) regressed severely through the 1990s. A military takeover of the government in June 1989 ended a short-lived democratic experiment. After initial attempts at restoring controls as part of a populist agenda, the new government embarked on a large-scale liberalization and privatization program. However, the ongoing civil war meant that these structural reforms were undertaken in a very unstable macroeconomic environment. War-related expenditures and low revenues produced fiscal deficits averaging 16 per cent of GDP in the early 1990s and inflation reached almost 100 per cent. The government replaced a system of multiple rates with a single official rate in 1995, but exchange controls remain and the illegal parallel market has continued to flourish with a very high premium. This situation is unlikely to change without a peaceful settlement of the civil war.

The macroeconomic situation remains precarious in Ghana (Chapter 5), but there is room for optimism. Reforms undertaken during the 1980s brought slow but substantial gains, reaching a high point in 1991 with real GDP growth of 5.3 per cent, a fiscal surplus of 1.5 per cent of GDP, and inflation down to 16 per cent. The situation then deteriorated in 1992, as a huge – election-related – increase in public sector wages and a fall in government revenues increased the fiscal deficit by over six percentage points of GDP. This fiscal crisis was rapidly addressed, however, without a reversal of trade or exchange rate policy. By 1993, the parallel premium was down to 3 percent. Market-oriented reforms have now been sustained for over a decade and real GDP growth has averaged 4 percent through the 1990s. Ghana formally accepted the obligations of Article VIII status in the IMF in 1994.

Tanzania (Chapter 7) sustained the reform program that was launched in 1986 through the 1990s. Almost all trade restrictions were lifted over the years, culminating with the elimination of the import licensing system and surrender requirements for exports in 1993. The exchange rate was officially unified in the same year. Although some restrictions on the capital account were retained, the parallel market has been virtually eliminated and is now thought to serve mainly illegal activities, including tax evasion. The macroeconomic environment, which improved significantly between 1990 and 1992, showed signs of slippage in 1993 as a tax reform designed to rationalize the customs tax structure and decrease incentives for tariff evasion produced a major decline in revenues. However, beginning January 1994, the government increased its efforts to restore macroeconomic stability. While difficulties remain, the government's broad commitment to pro-market policies is unlikely to change. Substantial backtracking on trade and exchange rate policy is particularly unlikely given the modest but evident success of these policies in promoting exports and the close attention of external donors to these policies.

In Zambia (Chapter 8), both the inflation rate and the parallel premium rose dramatically following the 1988 imposition of a fixed exchange rate regime. The authorities then adopted a dual exchange rate arrangement in 1990, as part of an IMF program. Unification to a managed official rate took place in April 1991 and through 1992 the Bank of Zambia operated an Open General License (OGL) window, allocating foreign exchange on a non-market basis at the official exchange rate. The exchange rate underwent substantial nominal depreciation during the OGL period. A major departure occurred in October of 1992 when the government licensed private foreign exchange bureaus. By the end of that year, the government adopted the bureau rate for sales through the OGL window, thus unifying the official exchange rate structure around a market-based exchange rate.

The parallel premium fell sharply throughout 1992, reaching extremely low levels upon unification of the bureau and OGL rates.

Turkey (Chapter 9) avoided any reversal in the 1990s of the policy gains of the previous decade, although high inflation has remained a serious problem. Large capital inflows – responding to events in world capital markets and to the perceived durability of Turkey's move to a market-oriented trade and exchange rate regime – put pressure on domestic prices and appreciated the real exchange rate early in the 1990s. Some portion of the high inflation of the early 1990s may be the result of a fall in the base for the inflation tax due to capital account liberalization, as argued by Özler in Chapter 9. Inflation peaked at 110 percent in 1994, as the authorities implemented a large nominal devaluation in an attempt to unwind the real appreciation. Notwithstanding massive capital outflows following the devaluation, no restrictions were imposed and the black market did not re-emerge. The macroeconomic situation improved in 1995, but inflation appears to be continuing at approximately 80 percent. While the public sector deficit remains within IMF limits, the current account has shown some deterioration through 1995, consistent with a revival of short-term capital inflows and renewed pressure on the exchange rate. The authorities have been attempting to sterilize the inflationary impact of these inflows and ease pressure on the real exchange rate. The imposition of exchange controls is not under consideration and the exchange rate is likely to remain unified.

The 1990s did not see a re-emergence of dual exchange rates in Western Europe (Chapter 10). Belgium was the last country in the West to unify its exchange rate, on 5 March 1990, abandoning the dual exchange rate arrangement that had been in place since 1955. Belgium's unification can be traced primarily to her obligation as a member of the European Community (EC). Given the EC target of a full liberalization of intracommunity capital movements by 1992, Belgium would have had to unify in 1992 if it had not done so earlier. The 1990 unification followed several years of a minimal spread and occurred at a time when there was little danger of a speculative attack on the currency.

2 Parallel Markets and the Effectiveness of Exchange Controls in Argentina: 1981–9

Steven B. Kamin[1]

INTRODUCTION

Argentina's history of exchange controls and parallel exchange markets dates from the beginning of the 1930s and has persisted, with occasional episodes of liberalization, nearly to the present. The most recent unbroken period of exchange controls in Argentina lasted from early 1982 to the end of 1989 and coincided with one of the most turbulent periods of macroeconomic crisis in Argentina's history. Faced with balance of payments problems, accelerating inflation, and severe private sector indebtedness, the authorities imposed exchange controls as an alternative to a mix of real devaluation and fiscal adjustment that would have secured long-term stability, but at the cost of short-term contraction. In the absence of fundamental reforms, the macroeconomic crisis deepened, leading to the hyperinflations of mid-1989 and the first quarter of 1990. This hyperinflation, in turn, generated balance of payments pressures so strong as to force the abandonment of exchange controls and the floating of the currency in December 1989.

This chapter reviews Argentina's experience with exchange controls and parallel exchange markets during the 1980s and evaluates the impact of these institutions upon macroeconomic performance and policy. The second section provides a historical overview of this period, highlighting the factors which motivated the government's exchange market policies. The third section describes the role and structure of the parallel market during the 1980s. In the fourth section, the influence of the parallel market premium over the official balance of payments and official exchange rate policy is examined. The fifth section presents an evaluation of Argentina's exchange-control policy as an instrument to achieve various macroeconomic objectives, while the final section concludes.

To summarize our findings, we conclude that exchange controls were never sufficiently effective in Argentina to allow the authorities to set the official exchange rate independently of the 'market-clearing' rate for more than short periods of time. Depreciations of the parallel market rate, by causing diversions of export receipts to the parallel market and reductions in short-term capital inflows, consistently undermined the official balance of payments and prompted devaluations of the official exchange rate. Efforts to contain the parallel market premium through contractionary monetary policy proved to be costly and ultimately counterproductive. Hence, exchange controls served only to delay necessary adjustments of the official exchange rate, not to postpone them permanently.

In consequence, exchange controls usually were not supportive of the government's aim to stabilize the economy. As a partial exception to this view, we find that during the balance of payments crisis of the early 1980s exchange controls may have played a positive role in insulating the economy from wide, speculative swings in the free-market exchange rate. By 1983, however, this crisis had largely subsided. During the remainder of the 1980s, exchange controls were used repeatedly to support short-term stabilization programs built around fixed exchange rates to the neglect of fundamental adjustment policies. Given continued inflationary financing of the fiscal deficit, these programs would have failed, even if exchange controls had been fully effective in segmenting the commercial and parallel exchange markets. As described above, however, leakages to the parallel market repeatedly caused the process of balance of payments deterioration to accelerate significantly, thereby hastening the abandonment of these programs.

HISTORICAL OVERVIEW

Prior to the 1980s, exchange restrictions had been in effect in Argentina from 1931 to 1959, 1964 to 1967, and 1971 to 1976 (see Fundacion de Investigaciones Latinoamericanas, 1989; Guissari, 1989). In each case, the application of exchange controls initially was motivated by balance of payments problems. However, the controls generally were not removed immediately after the crisis subsided, but only after an extended experience with these controls, which generally were accompanied by other interventionist policies, provoked a backlash by a new administration with a stronger taste for liberalization. As will be shown below, Argentina's most recent experience with exchange controls has followed this pattern closely.

The Evolution of Balance of Payments Problems: 1976–81

Following the overthrow of the civilian government in March 1976, the new military government unified the exchange markets, largely decontrolling current account transactions by November 1976 and capital account transactions by December 1978. The highest priority for the authorities was to reduce inflation, which had declined from its peak of 348 percent in 1976 but still registered at 170 percent in 1978, notwithstanding partial fiscal adjustment (see Table 2.1). To accelerate the disinflation, in December 1978 the authorities began to depreciate the exchange rate at a preannounced pace that was to gradually decline over time. It was hoped that under the *tablita* ('little

TABLE 2.1   *Selected macroeconomic and external indicators*

	Real GDP growth (%)[*]	CPI Inflation (%)[†]	Fiscal deficit GDP (%)[‡]	Merchandise exports ($M)[§]	Merchandise imports ($M)	Current account ($M)[§]
1976	0.0	348	11.7	3 918	2 765	651
1977	6.4	160	4.7	5 651	3 799	1 126
1978	−3.2	170	6.5	6 401	3 488	1 856
1979	7.0	140	6.5	7 810	6 028	−513
1980	1.5	88	7.5	8 021	9 394	−4 774
1981	−6.6	131	13.3	9 143	8 431	4 712
1982	−4.9	210	15.1	7 623	4 859	2 353
1983	3.0	434	15.2	7 835	4 119	2 436
1984	2.6	688	11.9	8 100	4 118	−2 495
1985	−4.3	385	6.0	8 396	3 518	−952
1986	5.7	82	4.7	6 852	4 406	−2 859
1987	2.2	175	5.5	6 360	5 343	4 235
1988	−2.6	388	7.4	9 134	4 892	1 572
1989	−4.5	4 924		9 573	3 864	−1 305

[*] *Carta Economica.*
[†] Fundacion de Investigaciones Latinoamericanas database.
[‡] Rodriguez (1994).
[§] IMF, *International Financial Statistics Yearbook* (1991).

Index, 1981:5=100

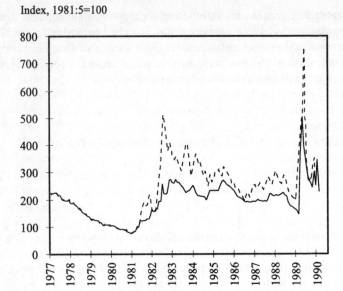

——— Commercial   - - - - Parallel

FIGURE 2.1   *Real parallel and commercial exchange rate indices*
NOTE: Real exchange rates are defined here as $E(P^*/P)$ and $E_p(P^*/P)$,
respectively, where E and E_p are the commercial and parallel rates (pesos/$),
P^* is the US wholesale price index, and P is the consumer price index for
Argentina.
SOURCE: Country case study.

table,' in reference to the table of preannounced exchange rates)
program, the rate of price growth would eventually converge to the
declining rate of exchange rate depreciation. In fact, inflation declined
more slowly than anticipated, exceeding the rate of exchange rate
depreciation under the *tablita* and appreciating the real exchange rate,
shown in Figure 2.1.[2]

This appreciation contributed to a turnaround in the current
account balance from a $1.8 billion surplus in 1978 to deficits exceed-
ing $4.5 billion in 1980 and 1981. These deficits initially were financed
by a surge in capital inflows motivated by a combination of high
domestic interest rates and the low rate of expected exchange rate
depreciation guaranteed by the *tablita*. By 1980, however, the growing
overvaluation of the real exchange rate led to expectations of a corrective devaluation, causing the private sector to reverse its prior stance
by reducing external borrowing and sending capital abroad, leading to

substantial declines in international reserves. Continued heavy borrowing during 1980–1 reflected government borrowing to maintain the overvalued exchange rate, as well as distress borrowing by firms in the tradeables sector that were adversely affected by the real appreciation of the exchange rate. Between the end of 1978 and the end of 1981, the total external debt rose from $12.5 billion to $35.7 billion.

In the face of this deterioration in the balance of payments, the government was forced to devalue the currency by 10 percent in February 1981 and by 23 percent in April, subsequently abandoning the *tablita* and replacing it with a series of more frequent exchange rate adjustments.

The Transition to a Dual Exchange Market: 1981–2

By mid-1981, the authorities faced at least six key economic problems remaining as the legacy of the preceding period.

(1) A highly overvalued exchange rate, still 37 percent more appreciated in real terms than its December 1977 value.
(2) Severe capital outflows reflecting amortizations on recently acquired external debt and private capital flight motivated by expectations of continuing devaluation.
(3) An expansion of the fiscal deficit from a recent low of 4.7 percent of gross domestic product (GDP) in 1977 to 13.3 percent of GDP in 1981.
(4) An acceleration of consumer price inflation from a low of 3.4 percent (monthly basis) in August 1980 to 9.4 percent in June 1981.
(5) A reduction in economic activity leading to declines in real GDP of 6.6 percent in 1981 and 4.9 percent in 1982.
(6) A dangerous degree of indebtedness, both domestic and external, in both the financial system and the private non-financial sector.

No single policy package could have corrected all of the problems listed above. Implicitly, the strategy chosen by the authorities was to address the most pressing problem, the balance of payments crisis, while attempting to limit the adverse consequences of measures taken in this area for the other areas of concern. Correcting the balance of payments problem through devaluation alone would have substantially increased inflation and by increasing the domestic currency value of external debt, it also would have brought about widespread bankruptcy and financial instability. A complementary program of severe fiscal adjustment and tight monetary policy might have reversed capital flight and strengthened the balance of payments, but it was believed that such policies would further jeopardize the solvency of the highly indebted private sector. Faced with these constraints, the authorities opted for a dual exchange market combining a slower real depreciation of the exchange rate used for trade transactions with a floating exchange rate to absorb the pressures on the capital account. In late June 1981, a fixed commercial rate was applied to all imports, most exports, and repayments of previously contracted external debt. All remaining transactions were to take place at the floating financial exchange rate. In addition, the authorities initiated an exchange rate guarantee program for private entities willing to reschedule their external debt. Its purpose was to relieve balance of payments pressures on the Central Bank, as well as to protect firms with high external debt against subsequent depreciation (Banco Central de la Republica Argentina, 1981).

Expectations of rising inflation, exchange rate depreciation, and macroeconomic volatility provided strong incentives to shift portfolios into foreign assets. Because the government now had stopped accommodating capital flight through the sale of international reserves, this pressure was reflected in the immediate depreciation of the floating financial exchange rate to 18 percent above the commercial rate. The premium reached a high of 72 percent in November 1981, as indicated in Figure 2.2.

In December 1981, following the change in administrations forced by the intensifying economic crisis, all exchange controls were removed and the exchange rate was floated. However, the eruption of war between Argentina and the UK in April 1982 triggered a new surge of capital flight and downward pressure on the peso, prompting the reimposition of exchange controls and the re-emergence of the parallel market. In July 1982, this market was largely legitimized by the creation of a new dual rate system with a commercial rate pegged by the government for commercial transactions and a financial rate for other transactions that floated for a few weeks before being pegged as well. Restrictions on the sale of foreign exchange for imports, amortization, and external interest payments that had been imposed during the war were liberalized but not eliminated completely.

The highest priority of the economic team in mid-1982 was not the balance of payments, but the reduction of the non-financial private

Percent

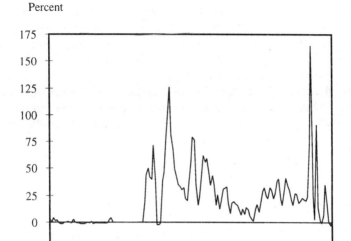

FIGURE 2.2   *Parallel market premium*
NOTES: The premium is defined as $100^*[(E_p/E) - 1]$ and E and E are the parallel and commercial exchange rates (peso/$).
SOURCE: Country case study.

sector's debt burden (Banco Central de la Republica Argentina, 1982; see also Dornbusch and de Pablo, 1989). The exchange rate guarantee scheme had largely subsidized the cost of the private sector's external debt service. To reduce the domestic debt burden, which had also grown substantially in the preceding years, in July 1982 the authorities imposed nominal interest rate ceilings upon both loans and deposits at levels below the rate of inflation. This had the effect of substantially reducing the real value of the private sector's domestic debt and thereby reducing its domestic debt burden. However, it also led to an acceleration of the flight out of local currency deposits. In consequence, the parallel market premium soared from 78 percent in June to a peak of 126 percent in August.

The Central Bank's annual report for 1982 notes that during this period, substantial international reserve losses occurred as a result of export delays motivated by expectations of future exchange rate depreciation, leakages of export receipts to the financial market, and intervention by the Central Bank in support of the financial market exchange rate (Banco Central de la Republica Argentina, 1982). In response, the authorities began to unify the two legal markets in September 1982, both by devaluing the commercial rate while keeping the financial rate fixed and by increasing the proportion of transactions conducted in the financial market, completing the process in November 1982. Because private capital flows continued to be controlled, however, the gap between the parallel market rate and the new, unified rate continued to exceed 40 percent through the end of 1982, although it had declined considerably from its mid-year level.

The Parallel Market and Disinflation Policies: 1983–9

By the beginning of 1983, a number of important adjustments to the disequilibria that developed during the pre-exchange-control period had been completed. First, the real exchange rate had been devalued to a level comparable to that in 1976, the beginning of the liberalization experiment. Second, the problem of private sector indebtedness, both domestic and external, had largely been eliminated through the interest rate policies of mid-1982, the exchange rate guarantee program, and the eventual nationalization of the private foreign debt. Finally and more speculatively, to the extent that the macroeconomic crisis of the 1980s encouraged a massive portfolio shift into foreign assets by the private sector, this process may have been largely completed by 1983; various measures of capital flight declined after 1982, as did the parallel market premium.

With the reduction in the relative importance of these considerations, the role of the exchange rate in the government's anti-inflation strategy became paramount. The use of the exchange rate as a disinflationary 'nominal anchor' was first made explicit in the Austral Plan, which was implemented in June 1985 in response to the continuing acceleration of inflation. In combination with wage and price freezes, the nominal value of the official exchange rate was frozen in order to achieve a swift reduction in inflation and inflationary expectations (see Kiguel, 1991).

The Austral Plan initially was successful both in reducing the rate of inflation, which averaged only approximately 3 percent per month for the first 6 months of the program, and in reducing the black market premium, as evidenced by Figure 2.2. The sharp reduction in inflation associated with the program, combined with the fixing of the official

Percent

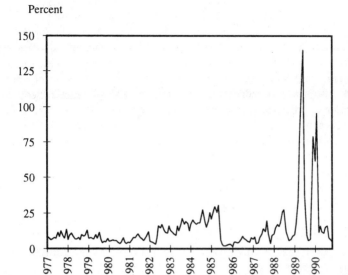

FIGURE 2.3 *Consumer price inflation per month*
NOTES: Inflation rates of 115 percent in June 1989 and 197 percent in percent in July 1989 have been omitted for scaling purposes.
SOURCE: Country case study.

exchange rate, sharply increased the rate of return on domestic assets relative to foreign assets and induced strong capital inflows. However, while the fiscal deficit declined from approximately 12 percent of GDP in 1984 to 5 percent in 1986, this was not sufficient to eliminate inflationary pressures. These pressures forced an easing of price controls and periodic devaluations of the exchange rate starting in April 1986, which led to further increases in inflation, as evidenced in Figure 2.3.

A second major disinflation program, the Plan Primavera ('Spring Plan'), was initiated in August 1988. The linchpin of the program was an agreement with private sector leaders to limit the growth of public prices, private prices, and the official exchange rate to 4 percent per month. All imports and 50 percent of industrial exports were transferred to a new, free financial market. The Central Bank auctioned foreign exchange and also tightened monetary policy, to keep the floating financial rate within 25 percent of the official rate.

Like the Austral Plan before it, the Plan Primavera initially was successful in reducing inflation and stimulating capital inflows.

However, because the inflation rate did not decline to the rate of official exchange rate depreciation, the real exchange rate appreciated substantially, leading to expectations of a corrective devaluation. These expectations were bolstered by the deteriorating fiscal situation, since the higher interest rates needed to support the exchange rate raised the costs of servicing the government's domestic debt. The expected victory of Peronist candidate Carlos Menem in the May 1989 presidential elections also was a source of concern.

These factors forced the Central Bank to intervene with increasing frequency in order to keep the financial market premium within an acceptable range. At the beginning of February 1989, faced with the depletion of its international reserves, the Central Bank floated the financial rate. This touched off the long awaited run on the austral, leading to a surge in the depreciation of the financial exchange rate, increases in the financial market premium (over the commercial rate), and an acceleration of inflation to a peak of 198 percent (monthly basis) in July 1989.

Following President Menem's inauguration in that same month, the authorities announced a stabilization program broadly similar to the Austral Plan: a freeze on public prices, private prices, and the exchange rate, coupled with long-range plans to reduce the fiscal deficit. Initially, inflation fell dramatically, precipitating a return of flight capital that reduced the black market premium essentially to zero. By October, however, the pace of fiscal reforms slowed while continued inflation appreciated the real exchange rate. Expectations of a corrective devaluation caused the parallel market premium to re-emerge, leading to a marked decline in the Central Bank's international reserves. The Central Bank tightened monetary policy to contain the parallel market premium, but as in the Plan Primavera, this raised the cost of servicing the Central Bank's debt, subsequently causing a sharp increase in monetary emission. By December 1989, the continued depreciation of the financial rate and the continued deterioration of the Central Bank's international reserve position, forced the Central Bank to float the commercial exchange rate and unify the exchange market.

The floating of the exchange rate and unification of the exchange markets neither solved Argentina's macroeconomic problems nor worsened them. After rising to 95.5 percent by March 1990, inflation declined to single-digit levels by October due to a reduction in monetary emission made possible by fiscal adjustments. A new surge of inflation in early 1991 prompted the announcement of the Convertibility Program, which committed the government to fix the exchange rate, without exchange controls, while maintaining international reserves at least equal to the value of the monetary base. Since then the inflation rate has fallen nearly to international levels. The government recognized that fiscal adjustment is the key to sustaining the disinflation program. As of this writing, notwithstanding intense financial market pressures triggered by the December 1994 devaluation of the Mexican peso, there is no serious discussion of returning to a dual exchange regime.

THE ROLE AND STRUCTURE OF THE PARALLEL MARKET IN ARGENTINA

The parallel exchange market in Argentina, as in other countries with exchange controls, played two central roles. First, it provided a basis for illicit current account transactions, serving as a source of foreign exchange for import transactions that could not be financed at the Central Bank. Second, it played a capital account function, providing a means to shift private portfolios between domestic and foreign assets.

Restrictions on these transactions were circumvented through a number of means. First, many of the same banks and exchange houses providing legal exchange services also provided illegal services 'under the counter'. The authorities were notoriously lax in their enforcement of exchange control regulations. Second, an active market in foreign exchange developed in neighboring Uruguay, which has been extremely accessible to many Argentine residents. Third, the secondary market for dollar-denominated government bonds (BONEX) provided a legal mechanism for otherwise restricted capital account transactions. Generally, it has been legal to buy and sell BONEX for both domestic currency and dollars; the relative prices of BONEX in the two currencies have therefore defined an implicit parallel market exchange rate.

Sources of the Current Account Supply and Demand for Foreign Exchange

During the exchange-control period, the primary source of illicit supplies of foreign exchange was probably export underinvoicing, the

TABLE 2.2 *Measures of misinvoicing and capital flight ($ millions)*

| | Export underinvoicing[*] | Import overinvoicing[*] | Measures of capital flight | | |
			World Bank[†]	Federal Reserve Board[‡]	Cuddington[†]
1977	630	−287	940		−618
1978	703	−1 055	1 852		1 497
1979	626	−2 917	3 128		−1 693
1980	400	−209	5 036		2 301
1981	661	−876	5 751	9 800	8 680
1982	852	−617	8 455	6 100	5 210
1983	942	−1 568	2 615	1 700	1 955
1984	1 028	−1 160	−2 617	−400	−1 635
1985	1 097	−526		500	
1986	65	−568		−1 200	

[*] Fundacion de Investigaciones Latinoamericanas (1989).
[†] Cumby and Levich (1987).
[‡] Kamin *et al.* (1989).

diversion of export receipts from the commercial market, where exporters were required to surrender their receipts, to the higher-priced parallel market. Table 2.2 presents calculations (Fundacion de Investigaciones Latinoamericanas, 1989) that compare exports reported to Argentine authorities to imports from Argentina reported to the authorities of the importing country. It indicates that during 1982–6 (the latest year calculated) export underinvoicing totaled approximately $4 billion or about 10 percent of the approximately $39 billion in reported merchandise exports in those 5 years.

Potentially, a second source of foreign exchange supply into the parallel market might have been import overinvoicing; when the parallel market premium is high, importers have a motive to declare more imports than actually purchased in order to sell their excess foreign exchange at a profit in the parallel market. As indicated in Table 2.2, however, in Argentina importers have been more likely to underinvoice than overinvoice their transactions, probably because the tariffs levied on imports more than offset the benefits to over-invoicing deriving from the parallel market premium.[3]

We now turn to the current account demand for foreign exchange in the parallel market. In countries where the commercial exchange rate is particularly overvalued and where official foreign exchange sales are tightly rationed, the black market may finance the entire range of import transactions. In Argentina, however, the parallel market probably played a less extensive role. Sales of foreign exchange for merchandise imports were much less tightly restricted in Argentina than, for example, in many African countries with exchange restrictions. At the end of 1981, when the premium of the financial rate over the commercial rate exceeded 60 percent, there was no rationing of foreign exchange in the commercial exchange market.[4] With the conflict in the South Atlantic, import restrictions became more stringent, but anecdotal evidence suggests that the parallel market generally was not a major source of financing of most merchandise imports.[5]

These considerations, along with the evidence of importer underinvoicing discussed above, suggest that most of the import transactions financed in the parallel market probably were those deliberately hidden from the authorities to evade import tariffs or quantitative barriers. During periods when tourism and other services were not permitted to be financed through the commercial market, these also would have contributed to the flow demand for exchange in the parallel market.

The Parallel Market as a Market for Foreign Assets

Considering that it probably did not play an important role in financing commercial transactions in Argentina, the parallel market's most important function may have been to facilitate private asset exchanges. In this sense, Argentina's exchange regime in the 1980s closely resembled a dual exchange market system with a pegged rate for current transactions and a floating rate for capital transactions. Figure 2.1 shows that the parallel exchange rate was far more variable than the official exchange rate during the 1980s. This is consistent with the parallel market rate's role as an asset price, equating the often volatile portfolio demand for foreign exchange with the more slowly evolving stock of dollars held by the private sector.

Various considerations point to the increasing importance of foreign exchange, particularly dollars, as a portfolio asset in Argentina. There is widespread evidence of dollarization in Argentina, ranging from the quoting of prices in dollars by retailers to the use of dollars in the purchase of automobiles, real estate, and other big-ticket items. In addition, different measures of capital flight from Argentina, while in general poorly correlated with each other, tend to agree that during 1980, 1981, and 1982, private residents exchanged domestic assets for over $15 billion in foreign assets (see Table 2.2). Estimates of the stock of flight capital outstanding by the end of the 1980s usually exceed $20 billion. By comparison, domestic monetary aggregates $M1$ and $M2$ (measured using the official exchange rate) totalled only $4.5 billion and $7.7 billion, respectively, during their mid-decade peak in December 1985.

The anecdotal evidence suggests that the authorities did not interfere significantly in the operation of the parallel exchange market. Given the importance of foreign assets in domestic portfolios, an efficient parallel market would have equated average rates of return on dollar assets to average rates of return on austral-denominated assets, to the extent that these assets were considered to be substitutable. To evaluate whether this was the case in Argentina, the following equation was estimated:

$$(1) \qquad \frac{E_{t+1}^p}{E_t^p} = \alpha + \beta\left[\frac{(1+i_t)}{(1+i_t^*)}\right] + e_t$$

where E^p is the parallel exchange rate (local currency per dollar), i is the domestic interest rates (either the deposit rate or the free loan rate, on a monthly basis), i^* is the US 1 month Treasury Bill rate (also on a monthly basis), and e is a disturbance term.

Estimates were made using both the 30 day deposit rate, which was frequently controlled by the government, and the freely determined loan rate. *A priori*, the deposit rate represents the more appropriate candidate for a rate of return variable; because it was controlled, however, the loan rate might be better correlated with the rate of return to which the major players in the financial market had access. Figure 2.4 indicates both rates to have been closely correlated during most of the sample period.

Estimates of this equation using developed-country data generally have rejected the three implications of exchange market efficiency: a β equal to one, an α equal to zero, and a non-serially correlated error term (Baldwin 1990). By contrast, the estimation results presented in Table 2.3 indicate that the Argentine parallel market performed relatively well in arbitraging rates of return between domestic and foreign assets.

The Durbin–Watson statistics in both regressions are low, indicating first-order serial correlation of the errors. As noted above, however, this problem also characterizes equations applied to markets with no exchange controls. On the other hand, the estimate of β using the deposit rate is statistically indistinguishable from unity and the intercept term in that regression is essentially zero. The estimates based upon the

Percent

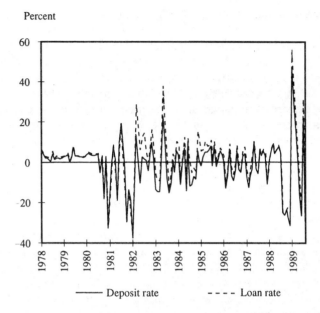

FIGURE 2.4   *Depreciation-adjusted deposit and loan rates (monthly basis)*
SOURCE: Country case study.

loan rate are less consistent with the efficient markets hypothesis, but
still confirm the significant linkage between interest rate differentials
and the depreciation of the parallel market rate in Argentina.

TABLE 2.3   *Uncovered interest parity equations, 1982.5–1988.7 (monthly):
dependent variable $E^p(+1)/E^p$*

	(1)	(2)
Constant	0.09	0.36
	(0.35)	(1.80)
(1 + deposit *i* rate)/(1 + US Treasury Bill rate)	0.95	
	(4.03)	
(1 + free loan *i* rate)/(1 + US Treasury Bill rate)		(0.67)
		(3.80)
R^2	0.17	0.15
DW	1.37	1.30

t-statistics in parentheses.

The Determination of the Parallel Exchange Rate

It is beyond the scope of this chapter to develop a full analysis of the behavior of the parallel exchange rate. Instead, we briefly discuss some of the main determinants of this rate, drawing upon the research presented in a longer version of this study (Kamin, 1991).

That research was based upon the view that in the long term, the parallel rate varied to equate the current account supplies and demands for foreign exchange described on p. 87. As such, key determinants of the long-run equilibrium parallel rate included the levels of domestic prices, foreign prices, and the commercial exchange rate. Regression analysis applied to monthly Argentine data during the 1980s confirms that these determinants, along with the parallel rate, comprised a cointegrating vector. This analysis also indicates that in Argentina, as in other countries (see Edwards, 1989; Kamin, 1993), devaluations of the commercial exchange rate led to less than proportionate depreciations of the parallel rate, thereby reducing the parallel market premium. As will be discussed in the following section, this provided the government with an important instrument with which to control the premium.

As evidenced by the residuals from the cointegrating regression described above, in practice the actual parallel rate frequently deviated from its long-term equilibrium value during the 1980s. Out of equilibrium, it is presumed that the parallel market rate moved to equate the portfolio demand for foreign assets (as described on p. 89), with the stock of these assets, which evolved in accord with the balance of current account transactions in the parallel market. Kamin (1991) uses a variant of the error-correction approach to estimate a dynamic portfolio model of the parallel market rate. The results confirm the importance of domestic monetary growth and depreciation expectations in prompting the depreciation of the parallel rate, as well as the role of the domestic interest rate in reducing the demand for foreign assets and hence appreciating the parallel rate.

Such considerations explain the most marked widenings of the parallel market premium, in mid-1982 and mid-1989. In the former episode, the imposition of deposit interest rate ceilings well below the inflation rate sharply reduced the demand for austral deposits and induced a flight into dollars (see Figure 2.4). In 1989, uncontrolled monetary emission and the prospect of hyperinflation provoked an even more dramatic run on the austral and prompted an even more rapid depreciation of the parallel exchange rate.

EXCHANGE CONTROLS AND OFFICIAL EXCHANGE RATE POLICY

The immediate rationale for exchange controls was to permit the authorities to set the commercial exchange rate in a manner that would have been unsustainable without these controls, in order to achieve the ultimate goal of stabilizing the economy. Putting off consideration of this ultimate objective until the next section, in this section we evaluate whether exchange controls were effective in their immediate goal of insulating the commercial exchange market and commercial exchange rate policy from developments in the parallel market and the financial sector. The first subsection demonstrates that increases in the parallel market premium led to significant deteriorations in Argentina's official balance of payments. The second subsection argues that monetary policy was ineffective in limiting the size of the parallel market premium and the third subsection confirms the hypothesis that the parallel market premium exerted significant influence over the setting of the official exchange rate.

The Parallel Market Premium and the Balance of Payments

Equation (2) summarizes Argentina's official balance of payments:

$$(2) \qquad dR = OX - OI + PXF + PMF + NSBAL + KA,$$

where R is the gross international reserves held by Central Bank, OX and OI are the values of official exports and official imports, PXF and PMF are the values of pre-export financing and post-import financing, $NSBAL$ is the net services balance, and KA is the capital account balance.

Based (in part) on the discussion in the previous section, there potentially have been three main points of linkage between the official balance of payments and the parallel market in Argentina: diversion of export receipts from the commercial to the parallel market, diversion of import financing from the commercial to the parallel market, and conversion of profits earned on pre-export financing through the parallel market (see below).

Exporter Underinvoicing

Equation (3) indicates that official export receipts – those surrendered in the commercial exchange market – depend positively on the volume of total exports and negatively on the degree of underinvoicing:

$$(3) \qquad\qquad OX = (1 - \phi)XP_X^*,$$

where OX is official export receipts in dollars, X is the volume of merchandise exports, ϕ is the underinvoicing ratio, and P_X^* is the dollar export price index.

Total exports should respond positively to both the parallel market rate and the tax-adjusted commercial rate, but export reporting should respond negatively to the tax-adjusted parallel premium. Increases in foreign output are assumed to raise foreign demand for exports, while increases in domestic output and hence aggregate demand are assumed to reduce the supply of goods for export. Therefore, real official exports are assumed to be determined as shown in equation (4):

$$(4) \qquad \frac{OX}{P_X^*} = ox[\,E(1 - t_X)\frac{P_x^*}{P}, \frac{E^p}{E(1 - t_X)}, Y, Y^*\,]$$

$$\qquad\qquad\qquad (+) \qquad\quad (-) \qquad (-)(+)$$

where ox is the supply of real, official exports, Y and Y^* are real GDP in Argentina and the Organization for Economic Co-operation and Development (OECD) countries, respectively, and t_x is the export tax rate.

Table 2.4 presents the estimation results for this equation using quarterly data. In developing the equation, it was determined that a measure of the real, tax-adjusted official exchange rate which uses an explicit measure of Argentine dollar export prices fitted the data less well than a measure using the US wholesale price index (WPI) as a proxy for export prices: $E(1 - t_x)P^{us}/P$. The estimated equation also incorporates a set of quarterly seasonal dummy variables.

The instrumental variables (IV) version, which instruments for the endogenous parallel premium, indicates a negative elasticity of official exports with respect to the parallel market premium of approximately 0.4, which is quite substantial. Considering that the parallel premium averaged 32 percent during the period of exchange controls in the 1980s, this implies an average loss of export receipts in the commercial market of approximately 13 percent over that period. The premium

TABLE 2.4   *Merchandise export equation (quarterly data), 1978/IV–1988/II:*
dependent variable log(OX/P_X)

	OLS	IV*
Constant	−6.06	−1.10
	(−1.16)	(−0.17)
Log $[E(1 - t_X)P^{US}/P]$	0.28	0.23
	(2.60)	(1.74)
Log $[E^p/E(1 - t_X)]$	−0.27	−0.39
	(−1.99)	(−2.06)
Log (Y)	−0.38	−1.24
	(−0.65)	(−1.46)
Log (Y^*)	0.57	0.78
	(1.67)	(1.97)
DUMQ2	0.27	0.29
	(5.68)	(5.66)
DUMQ3	0.20	0.22
	(3.85)	(3.84)
DUMQ4	−0.08	−0.02
	(−1.30)	(−0.25)
Standard error of regression	0.10	0.10
Adjusted R^2	0.74	0.72
DW	1.91	1.88

t-statistics in parentheses.
* Instruments: $\log(EP^*_m/P)$, $\log(E(1 - t_X)P^{US}/P$, $\log(E^p/E)_{-1}$, $\log(Y)$, t_X, tf_m, qr_m, $\log(Y^*)$, $\log(OI/P_m)_{-1}$, $\log(OX/P_X)_{-1}$, i_1, DUMQ2, DUMQ3, DUMQ4, constant.

rose above 60 percent in late 1981, mid-1982, and early 1989, indicating export receipt losses exceeding 24 percent of official export receipts in those periods.

Importer Overinvoicing

Equation (5) indicates the amount of legally registered imports to depend positively upon both the volume of legal merchandise imports and the degree of overinvoicing:

$$(5) \qquad\qquad OI = (1 + \delta)IP^*_M,$$

where OI is the value of officially registered merchandise imports in dollars, I is the volume of actual legal merchandise imports, δ is the import overinvoicing ratio, and P_M^* is the import dollar price index.

The volume of legal, registered imports should respond negatively to the real commercial exchange rate, as well as to increases in both tariff and non-tariff barriers. Conversely, an increase in the parallel market premium could lead to an increase in import over-invoicing to sell the exchange on the parallel market and could also induce importers financing through the parallel market in order to avoid tariffs to switch back to financing in the commercial market. These considerations suggest a relationship such as equation (6):[6]

TABLE 2.5 *Merchandise import equation (quarterly data), 1978/IV–1988/II: dependent variable* $\log(OI/P_M)$

	OLS	IV*
Constant	−4.28	−7.73
	(−0.87)	(−1.14)
Log (EP_M/P)	−0.48	−0.40
	(−3.40)	(−2.35)
Log (E^P/E)	0.04	0.01
	(0.31)	(0.09)
Log (Y)	1.07	1.36
	(2.33)	(2.16)
tf_M	0.15	0.02
	(0.36)	(0.05)
qr_M	−0.13	−0.12
	(−1.27)	(−1.26)
Log$(OI/P_M)_{-1}$	0.42	0.46
	(3.96)	(3.93)
DUMQ2	0.13	0.12
	(2.90)	(2.74)
DUMQ3	0.19	0.19
	(4.19)	(4.02)
DUMQ4	−0.10	0.08
	(1.90)	(1.34)
Standard error of regression	0.09	0.09
Adjusted R^2	0.92	0.92
DW	2.12	2.20

t-statistics in parentheses.
* Instruments: $\log(EP_M^*/P)$, $\log(E(1 - t_X)P^{US}/P)$, $\log(E^p/E)_{-1}$, $\log(Y)$, t_X, tf_M, qr_M, $\log(Y^*)$, $\log(OI/P_M)_{-1}$, $\log(OX/P_X)_{-1}$, i_1, DUMQ2, DUMQ3, DUMQ4, constant.

(6)
$$\frac{OI}{P_M^*} = oi\left(\frac{EP_M^*}{P}, \frac{E^P}{E}, Y, tf_M, qr_m\right),$$
$$(-)(+)(+)(-)(-)$$

where oi is the real, official merchandise imports, tf_M is the import tariff rate, and qr_M is the level of non-tariff import barriers.

Table 2.5 presents the results from estimating equation (6) in a manner analogous to the estimation of the export equation. While the coefficients on both the real commercial exchange rate and real GDP are of the expected sign and significantly different from zero, the coefficient on the premium is small and not significantly different from zero. To some degree, this is consistent with the evidence on the lack of import overinvoicing discussed in the previous section. It suggests that offical sales of foreign exchange were not an important source of supply to the parallel market.

Pre-export Financing

The pre-export financing facility potentially represented another means by which restrictions on capital transactions were evaded in Argentina. Users of this facility were allowed to borrow foreign exchange from external sources, convert them at the official exchange rate up to 540 days before the time of export, use the local currency proceeds to pay export expenses, and repay the external loan with the proceeds of the exports rather than surrender them to the Central Bank or its agents. Ostensibly, this facility was intended to promote exports. However, when domestic interest rates were high relative to expected exchange rate depreciation, the pre-export financing facility was an attractive method of legally repatriating capital and investing it in domestic deposits with the assurance that it could be withdrawn again legally through export sale.

We test two hypotheses below: (1) that pre-export financing was used as a means of evading capital controls and (2) that the parallel market played a direct role in the remittance of profits from this activity. We first define the dollar return to engaging in a pre-export financing arrangement. Assume that at time $t + 1$, the dollar value of exports OX will be purchased from domestic producers for local currency value $E_{t+1}OX$.[7] In the absence of pre-export financing, this sum could be raised by investing $OX/(1 + i^*)$ at time t in a foreign deposit paying interest rate i^*. Equation (7) defines the expected profits to be made by bringing in $OX/(1 + i^*)$ dollars through the pre-export financing facility at time t, converting them to local currency at the official exchange rate E_t and investing them in domestic deposits at interest rate i. Any excess of the resultant stock of austral assets at time $t + 1$ over actual export expenses $E_{t+1}OX$ are hypothesized to be converted back into dollars at the parallel rate E_{t+1}^P; alternatively, these profits might have been remitted legally as dividends at the official rate E_{t+1}, if earned by a multinational trading company or retained as local currency earnings on a local firm's balance sheet. Denoting by $_tE_{t+1}$ the expectation of E_{t+1} at time t, the return to pre-export financing, $RXPF$, can be written

$$(7) \quad RXPF = \frac{E_t OX \frac{(1+i)}{(1+i^*)} - {_tE_{t+1}}OX}{{_tE_{t+1}^P}} = OX \left(\frac{_tE_{t+1}}{E_{t+1}^P} \right) \left[\left(\frac{E_t}{_tE_{t+1}} \right) \frac{(1+i)}{(1+i^*)} - 1 \right],$$

where t is the date at which the pre-export financing is initiated and $t + 1$ the date at which the arrangement is unwound.

The term within the brackets of equation (7) indicates that pre-export financing was more profitable the greater the margin by which the domestic interest rate exceeded its uncovered interest parity level. In addition, to the extent that these profits were reconverted to dollars through the parallel market, the profitability of pre-export financing was inversely related to the future, expected parallel market premium. Based on these considerations, a reduced form for the quantity of pre-export financing is derived:

$$(8) \quad PXF = PXF \left(\frac{E_{t+1}^P}{E_{t+1}}, \frac{E_{t+1}}{E_t}, i \right).$$
$$ (-) \quad (-) \quad (+)$$

For simplicity, we ignore the rate of return on foreign assets, which in practice was small and unvarying relative to the domestic interest rate. Table 2.6 presents estimation results for the pre-export financing equation. Because pre-export financing is sometimes negative, the quantity of pre-export financing is added to merchandise exports and then expressed as a ratio to those exports before being converted to logs.[8] The explanatory variables are all endogenous – the future parallel premium, the domestic interest rate, and the expected depreciation of the official exchange rate[9] – so IV estimation was used in addition to ordinary least squares (OLS) to estimate the equation.

The estimations indicate that variations in both the deposit interest rates and the expected depreciation of the official exchange rate had

TABLE 2.6   *Pre-export financing equation (quarterly data), 1978/IV–1988/II: dependent variable* $\log((OX + PXF)/OX)$

	OLS	IV*
Constant	0.02	−0.02
	(0.27)	(−0.27)
Quarterly average of $\log(E^p_{t+1}/E_{t+1})$	−0.02	0.14
	(−0.13)	(0.68)
Deposit rate i	2.31	3.11
	(3.23)	(3.21)
Quarterly average of $\log(E_{t+1}/E_t)$	−1.57	−2.29
	(−2.88)	(−2.85)
DUMQ2	−0.05	−0.03
	(−0.75)	(−0.45)
DUMQ3	−0.20	−0.20
	(−3.18)	(−2.90)
DUMQ4	−0.06	−0.04
	(−1.05)	(−0.59)
Standard error of regression	0.13	0.14
Adjusted R^2	0.34	0.31
DW	2.05	2.08

t-statistics in parentheses.
* Instruments: $\log[E(1 - t_X)P^{US}/P]$, $\log[E(1 - t_X)P^{US}/P]_{-1}$, $\log(E)_{-1}$, $\log(E^p)_{-2}$, $\log(E^p)_{-3}$, $\log(E^p/E)_{-1}$, $\log(E^p/E)_{-2}$, $\log(E^p/E)_{-3}$, i_{-1}, i_{-2}, i_{-3}, i^*, $\log[(OX + PXF)/OX)]_{-1}$, $\log[(OX + PXF)/OX]_{-2}$, $\Delta\log(P)$, $\Delta log(P)_{-1}$, $\Delta\log(P)_{-2}$, DUMQ2, DUMQ3, DUMQ4, constant.

significant effects upon the volume of pre-export financing. Hence, the pre-export financing facility represented a loophole in Argentina's capital control regime that complemented export underinvoicing as a means of evading exchange restrictions.

The estimates do not confirm a significant direct role for the parallel premium in the determination of pre-export financing, suggesting that profits from pre-export financing probably were not remitted abroad through the parallel market. However, as will be shown on p. 100, increases in the parallel premium were associated with subsequent devaluations of the official exchange rate and through this means indirectly may have depressed pre-export finance inflows. Because the equation presented in Table 2.6 controls for the rate of official devaluation, this indirect effect is suppressed; in estimates of this equation (not shown here) that did not incorporate the official devaluation rate, the coefficient on the parallel premium is indeed negative and significant.

Monetary Policy and the Parallel Market Premium

An implication of the preceding analysis is that, all else being equal, a widening of the parallel market premium led to a weakening of the official balance of payments, threatening the government's ability to maintain a given commercial exchange rate target. As an alternative to devaluing the commercial exchange rate, one option for the government was to tighten monetary policy, thereby raising the domestic interest rate, appreciating the parallel market rate, and reducing the premium. As discussed above, this would also boost capital inflows through the pre-export financing facility.

The government attempted this strategy both in late 1988 and late 1989. However, in both cases this resulted in increased costs of servicing the government's domestic debt and a widening of the fiscal deficit. This led, subsequently, to higher rates of monetary emission and parallel exchange rate depreciation than would have been the case without the initial monetary contraction. Anticipation of this outcome caused domestic interest rates to rise still further, reinforcing the adverse fiscal effect and accelerating the government's need to monetize its debt service obligations (see Szewach, 1988, 1989).

Hence, in the presence of a large stock of domestic government debt, monetary tightening ultimately widened rather than narrowed the parallel market premium. This perverse outcome was the open-economy counterpart to the 'unpleasant monetarist arithmetic' story of inflationary bond finance in a closed economy setting (Sargent and Wallace, 1981).

The Parallel Market Premium and Commercial Exchange Rate Policy

Given the inability of monetary policy to control the parallel market exchange rate for more than short periods of time, frequently the only alternative for the Argentine government, when faced with a high parallel market premium, was to devalue the commercial exchange rate. As noted in the previous section, while this would depreciate the parallel rate, it would reduce the parallel premium.

The parallel market's influence over the commercial exchange rate is supported by the results of the simple regression shown in Table 2.7. The authorities were assumed to devalue the commercial exchange rate to achieve a particular target level of the real exchange rate

TABLE 2.7 *Commercial exchange rate determination May 1982–July 1988: dependent variable $\Delta \log (E)$*

	Monthly	*Quarterly*
Constant	1.89	6.87
	(3.04)	(3.01)
Log $(EP^{US}/P)_{-1}$	−0.21	−0.76
	(3.05)	(3.02)
$\Delta \log(P/P^{US})_{-1}$	0.89	0.85
	(7.19)	(5.29)
Log $(E^P/E)_{-1}$	0.12	0.58
	(2.36)	(3.27)
Standard error of regression	0.06	0.12
Adjusted R^2	0.50	0.67
DW	2.20	1.79

t-statistics in parentheses.

hence, a high level of the real exchange rate should have led to reduced exchange rate depreciation, while high domestic price growth should have increased the rate of devaluation. In addition, a high parallel market premium is hypothesized to have induced the authorities to step up the rate of commercial devaluation in order to reduce that gap. (Lagged values of these explanatory variables are used to avoid simultaneity problems.)

The estimation results support all three hypotheses. They suggest that the parallel market premium, which averaged 32 percent during the exchange control period, induced an additional 3–6 percent of commercial exchange rate depreciation per month, depending upon whether estimates from the monthly or quarterly regressions are used.

EXCHANGE CONTROLS AND MACROECONOMIC OBJECTIVES IN ARGENTINA

The preceeding pages demonstrate that exchange controls were not fully effective in achieving their immediate goal in Argentina, which was the insulation of the commercial exchange market and official exchange rate policy from developments in the parallel market. We now discuss the extent to which exchange controls supported progress toward the authorities' ultimate macroeconomic objectives. It should be kept in mind that fundamentally Argentina's macroeconomic problems during the 1980s stemmed from the inflationary financing of its budget deficits. Therefore, even if exchange controls had been completely successful in insulating exchange rate policy from market conditions, they could not have achieved full macroeconomic stability, but at best only have moderated Argentina's economic problems to some degree.

Moderation of Recession

While the ultimate effects of a real devaluation may be expansionary, it has often been argued that devaluation may be contractionary in the short term. Devaluations raise the cost of imported inputs, increase the domestic currency value of external debt, and redistribute income in ways which may depress aggregate demand initially. The substantial real depreciation of the commercial exchange rate probably contributed to Argentina's deep contraction in 1981 and 1982. As evidenced by Figure 2.1, however, the parallel market rate depreciated much more extensively than the commercial rate during this period. In the absence of exchange controls, the government would have had to either float the commercial exchange rate or depreciate it sufficiently to maintain its international reserves. In either case, this would have meant a steeper real devaluation of the commercial exchange rate, and probably a deeper contraction in the early 1980s, than actually occurred.

By the mid-1980s, the passage of time during which the economy could adjust to the more depreciated exchange rate, as well as the alleviation of speculative pressures on the free-market peso, largely eliminated the anti-recessionary rationale for exchange controls. This trend was reinforced by the declining effectiveness of exchange controls as a means of separating the commercial and parallel exchange markets. In 1989, when deteriorating conditions induced a massive depreciation of the parallel rate, the authorities had no choice but to follow with substantial devaluations of the commercial rate.

Protection of Firms with External Debt

One of the chief concerns of the economic team at the beginning of the exchange control period was the effect of devaluation on private sector firms with high external liabilities. To the extent that exchange controls allowed the authorities to reduce the rate of exchange rate depreciation, this reduced the increase in the domestic currency value of the firms' debt. However, the government eventually assumed the private sector's foreign currency exposure, first through the exchange rate guarantee programs of 1981 and 1982 and second, when the government could not finance up-coming maturities under the program, by the takeover of the private sector's guaranteed external debt at the end of 1982. Therefore, this rationale for exchange controls was eliminated relatively early on as well.

Reduction of Inflation

The acceleration of Argentine inflation in the early 1980s reflected, in addition to the monetization of the fiscal deficit, the inevitable devaluation of the real commercial exchange rate from its highly overvalued level in early 1981. However, as noted above, the parallel rate at times depreciated even more quickly, particularly in mid-1982. In the absence of exchange controls, a comparable increase in a unified exchange rate might have dramatically boosted inflation and inflation expectations during this period.

Subsequently, exchange controls were used to support explicitly anti-inflationary exchange rate policies. The June 1985, August 1988, and July 1989 programs were all built around a combination of exchange rate and price freezes. In all three cases, however, the lack of complementary fiscal adjustment resulted in a renewal of inflationary pressures, appreciation of the real commercial exchange rate, balance of payments problems, and eventual abandonment of the 'nominal anchor' program. Given the lack of fiscal adjustment, these programs would have failed even if exchange controls had been fully effective. However, leakages to the parallel market accelerated the process of balance of payments deterioration, thereby quickening the dissolution of these programs. Their repeated initiation and failure gave rise to the 'stop–go' pattern of inflation observed after 1985 (see Figure 2.3).

Fiscal Benefits

One benefit of exchange controls is that if the government has foreign currency obligations that exceed foreign currency revenue sources, suppressing the exchange rate below its market-clearing level will reduce the domestic currency cost of its foreign obligations (see Pinto, 1991). The external debt service obligations of the Argentine government amounted to over 5 percent of GDP per year during the 1980s. To make an approximate calculation of the fiscal benefit derived from exchange controls, assume that without these controls the commercial exchange rate would have been 30 percent more depreciated than its actual level or approximately equal to the prevailing parallel market rate. In that case, the absence of exchange controls would have meant additional (local currency) debt service obligations equal to approximately 1.5 percent of GDP annually, compared with a fiscal deficit ranging between 5 and 10 percent of GDP during the period.

This fiscal benefit, however, does not by itself justify the exchange control regime. The dual rate system imposed an implicit tax upon exporters, due to the unwillingness of the government to collect broad-based income or consumption taxes. This implicit tax, combined with explicit export taxes, has contributed to the poor performance of the export sector in Argentina during the past decade and also helped postpone the government's fundamental need to increase explicit tax collections.

Reduction of Capital Flight

There are two basic rationales for reducing capital flight: first, to protect international reserves and, second, to prevent a leakage of capital abroad that otherwise would have been invested productively within the country. As noted earlier (p. 89), most measures of capital flight show a substantial decline in capital flight after 1982, when the government stopped selling dollars without restriction to the private sector. In this sense, the former objective was certainly achieved; if the government had maintained the identical exchange rate policy without exchange controls, its reserves would have quickly disappeared.

However, there is no evidence that exchange controls helped to maintain private investment levels. During 1981, when capital flight was high as measured by any measure, private fixed investment was 11.5 percent of GDP; in 1986, when capital flight is estimated as being negative (that is, there were capital inflows), this figure had dropped to 7 percent of GDP. In their study of capital flight in developing countries, Gordon and Levine (1988) also found no correlation between investment and capital flight in Argentina, nor in most of the other countries in their sample. The imposition of exchange controls ended the financing of capital flight by the Central Bank, but did not raise the incentives for domestic investment.

CONCLUSION

As noted in the third section, the Argentine exchange regime during the 1980s essentially constituted a dual exchange rate system with a pegged rate for current transactions and a floating rate for capital transactions. The most important rationale for such a regime is to insulate commercial transactions and, by extension, the economy, from transitory, exogenous shocks affecting capital flows and deriving primarily from financial markets (see Dornbusch, 1986).

To a limited degree, exchange controls played such a role during the initial phase of the dual market system. While the rapid depreciation of the parallel market rate in 1981 and 1982 reflected various fundamental disequilibria, it also reflected tremendous but transitory uncertainties about the future economic situation. By early 1983, the resolution of the problem of private sector debt, the replacement of the economic team responsible for the 1982 interest-ceiling program, successful talks with the International Monetary Fund (IMF), and the completion of the readjustment of the real commercial exchange rate, all served to at least partially resolve these uncertainties. In consequence, as indicated by Figure 2.1, the huge run-up in the real parallel rate was substantially reversed by early 1983. Exchange controls prevented the huge, largely transitory, swing in the real parallel rate during 1982 from further destabilizing an already precarious economic situation.

By 1983, the transition from an economy with easy access to foreign exchange to one with rigid balance of payments constraints was largely completed. In consequence, many of the rationales for exchange controls – the protection of firms with external debt and the protection of aggregate demand from sharp exchange rate changes – became irrelevant. From 1983 on, the fundamental challenge facing the government was the reduction of inflation. During this period, by being used to support disinflationary exchange rate policies while inflationary fiscal pressures went uncorrected, exchange controls were forced to play a role they could not possibly fulfill. Their ability to protect the balance of payments from market forces was repeatedly undermined by developments in the parallel market.

Given these considerations, an appropriate policy for the government might have been to maintain exchange controls during the peak of the balance of payments crisis in 1981–2 and then remove these controls once the crisis had passed. In practice, however, it is very hard to dismantle controls once they are put in place. Previous experiences with exchange controls in Argentina also had been initiated by balance of payments crises and, in all those cases, controls remained long after the initial problems had been resolved. This suggests the importance of preventing the occurrence of balance of payments crises in the first place, both through fiscal balance and through an exchange rate policy geared toward keeping the exchange rate competitive.

NOTES

1. The author is a senior economist in the International Finance Division. This chapter represents the views of the author and should not be interpreted as reflecting those of the Board of Governors of the Federal Reserve System or other members of its staff. I am indebted to Pierre-Richard Agénor, Dale Henderson, David Howard, Deborah Lindner, Miguel Kiguel, Helen Popper, Andrew Rose, Enrique Szewach, and the staff at the Fundacion de Investigaciones Latinoamericanas (FIEL) for their helpful comments and suggestions. Special thanks go to Neil Ericsson for his econometrics advice, Will Melick for programming various econometric procedures, Saul Lizondo for his careful comments on an earlier draft, and Stephen Thompson for providing a constant flow of news and data from Buenos Aires. Daniel Kelley provided excellent research assistance.

2. Debate continues as to whether this appreciation was attributable to inflationary inertia and insufficient fiscal adjustment or was an equilibrium response to the heavy capital inflows taking place during this period. See Calvo (1986), Kiguel and Liviatan (1988), Sjaastad (1989) Connolly *et al* (1994) and Rodriguez and Sjaastad (unpublished).

3. These data mirror findings by Bhagwati *et al.* (1974), who applied the same methodology to a large sample of developing countries and found strong evidence of export underinvoicing but no evidence, on average, of substantial import overinvoicing.

4. There was in effect a regulation requiring importers to postpone import payments by 180 days after the purchase of merchandise (International Monetary Fund, 1982). Given the availability of supplier financing

presumably this requirement did not substantially increase the demand for foreign exchange in the dual market.

5. The relative availability of foreign exchange at the official rate for imports in Argentina should not be confused with a liberal import regime. As part of its import substitution strategy, Argentina had very high tariff and non-tariff barriers to imports in the 1980s.

6. Import tariffs are entered separately from the commercial exchange rate in the equation. Unlike the export tax, which was administered at the point of surrender of foreign exchange by the exporter, import tariffs were collected separately from foreign exchange transactions and asymmetric responses of importers to the commercial exchange rate and import tariffs are likely.

7. This price is assumed to depend on the commercial exchange rate only, since pre-export financing was most prominent in major agricultural exports where export underinvoicing probably was less pervasive.

8. Considering that asset demands usually are modeled as demands for stocks of assets, it may appear inappropriate to model the *flow* of pre-export financing. However, this financing was largely self-liquidating, since export receipts were used to cancel the original pre-export loans. Therefore, maintaining a given stock of austral assets required repeated pre-export financing, generating a correlation between the flow of pre-export financing and its expected rate of return.

9. To be most consistent with the quarterly 30 day deposit rate, the future premium and depreciation variables were calculated as the average of their *monthly* values in the second and third month of the current quarter and the first month of the subsequent quarter.

REFERENCES

Baldwin, Richard (1990) 'Re-Interpreting the Failure of Foreign Exchange Market Efficiency Tests: Small Transaction Costs, Big Hysteresis Bands', NBER Working Paper No. 3319 (Cambridge, Mass: National Bureau of Economic Research).

Banco Central de la Republica Argentina (BRCA), (various issues) *Memoria Annual* (Buenos Aires, Bank Central de la Republica Argentina).

Bhagwati, Jagdish N., Anne Krueger, and C. Wibulswasdi (1974) 'Capital Flight from LDCs: a Statistical Analysis', in J. Bhagwati (ed.), *Illegal Transactions in International Trade* (Amsterdam: North-Holland), pp. 148–54.

Calvo, Guillermo A. (1986) 'Fractured Liberalism: Argentina under Martinez de Hoz', *Economic Development and Cultural Change*, vol. 34, no. 3, pp. 511–33.

Connolly, Michael D., Alvaro Rodriguez, and William G. Tyler (1994) 'The Use of the Exchange Rate for Stabilization Purposes: an Arbitrage Model Applied to Argentina', *Journal of International Money and Finance*, vol. 13, no. 2, pp. 223–31.

Cumby, Robert and Richard Levich (1987) 'On the Definition and Magnitude of Recent Capital Flight', in Donald R. Lessard and John Williamson (eds), *Capital Flight and World Debt* (Washington, DC: Institute for International Economics), pp. 27–67.

Dornbusch, Rudiger (1986) 'Special Exchange Rates for Capital Account Transactions', *World Bank Economic Review*, vol. 1, no. 1, pp. 1–33.

Dornbusch, Rudiger and Juan Carlos de Pablo (1989) 'Debt and Macroeconomic Instability in Argentina', in Jeffrey Sachs (ed.), *Developing Country Debt and Economic Performance*, vol. 2 (Chicago: University of Chicago Press).

Dornbusch, Rudiger and Alberto Giovannini (1990) 'Monetary Policy in the Open Economy', in Benjamin M. Friedman and Frank H. Hahn (eds), *Handbook of Monetary Economics* (Amsterdam: North Holland).

Edwards, Sebastian (1989) *Real Exchange Rates, Devaluation and Adjustment: Exchange Rate Policies in Developing Countries* (Cambridge, Mass: MIT Press).

Fundacion de Investigaciones Latinoamericanas (FIEL) (1989) *El Control de Cambios en la Argentina* (Buenos Aires: Ediciones Manantial).

Gordon, David B. and Ross Levine (1988) 'The Capital Flight "Problem"', *International Finance Discussion Papers* No. 320 (Washington, DC: Board of Governors of the Federal Reserve System).

Guissarri, Adrian (1989) *La Argentina Informal.* (Buenos Aires: Emece Editores).

International Monetary Fund (various years) *International Financial Statistics.* (Washington, DC: International Monetary Fund).

Kamin, Steven B. (1991) 'Argentina's Experience with Parallel Exchange Markets: 1981–1990', *International Finance Discussion Papers* No. 407 (Washington, DC: Board of Governors of the Federal Reserve System).

Kamin, Steven B. (1993) 'Devaluation, Exchange Controls, and Black Markets for Foreign Exchange in Developing Countries', *Journal of Development Economics*, vol. 40, no. 1, pp. 151–69.

Kamin, Steven B., Robert Kahn, and Ross Levine (1989) 'External Debt and Developing Country Growth', *International Finance Discussion Papers* No. 352 (Washington, DC: Board of Governors of the Federal Reserve System).

Kiguel, Miguel (1991) 'Inflation in Argentina: Stop and Go Since the Austral Plan', *World Development*, vol. 19, no. 8, pp. 969–86.

Kiguel, Miguel and Nissan Liviatan (1988) 'Inflationary Rigidities and Orthodox Stabilization Programs: Lessons from Latin America', *The World Bank Economic Review*, vol. 2, no. 3, pp. 273–98.

Pinto, Brian (1991) 'Black Markets for Foreign Exchange, Real Exchange Rates and Inflation', *Journal of International Economics*, vol. 30, pp. 121–36.

Rodriguez, Carlos Alfredo (1994) 'Argentina: Fiscal Disequilibria Leading to Hyperinflation', in William Easterly, Carlos A. Rodriguez, and Klaus Schmidt-Hebbel (eds), *Public Sector Deficits and Macroeconomic Performance* (New York: Oxford University Press), pp. 101–66.

Sargent, Thomas and Neil Wallace (1981) 'Some Unpleasant Monetarist Arithmetic', *Federal Reserve Bank of Minnesota Quarterly Review*, Fall pp. 1–17.

Sjaastad, Larry A. (1989) 'Argentine Economic Policy, 1976–81', in Guido di Tella and Rudiger Dornbusch (eds), *The Political Economy of Argentina: 1946–83* (Pittsburgh: University of Pittsburgh).

Szewach, Enrique (1988) 'La Primavera, Las Elecciones y un Poco de Aritmetica Desagradable', mimeo (Buenos Aires: FIEL).

Szewach, Enrique (1989) 'El Verano, Las Elecciones, y un Poco Mas de Aritmetica Desagradable', mimeo (Buenos Aires: FIEL).

(Mexico)

3 Dual Exchange Rates: the Mexican Experience, 1982–7

Graciela L. Kaminsky[1]

F31 F33 F32

D19

INTRODUCTION

On 6 August 1982, after a run against the peso left the Bank of Mexico with no foreign exchange reserves, a stabilization program to deal with the balance of payments crisis was announced. One important part of this stabilization program was the institution of a dual exchange rate system. The exchange regime consisted of a 'preferential' rate and a 'general' rate. The preferential rate applied to current account transactions while the general exchange rate applied to capital account transactions. The Central Bank set the preferential rate at 49.13 pesos per dollar and announced a daily devaluation of 4 cents. In contrast, the general rate was allowed to float. Immediately after the announcement, the general rate was equal to 75.33 pesos per dollar, implying a depreciation of 54.4 percent.

Two reasons were cited by the Bank of Mexico for introducing the dual exchange rate system. First, it was claimed that a two-tier exchange rate system would improve the bank's control over its foreign exchange reserves relative to a fixed exchange rate system, since capital movements would only lead to a depreciation of the general rate. Second, it was proclaimed that the dual exchange rate system would sever the link between capital movements and domestic prices. By establishing different exchange rates for commercial and financial transactions, an increase in the demand for foreign assets would only increase the financial exchange rate. Since the commercial exchange rate did not need to change, there would be no need for domestic prices to change either.

The dual exchange rate system, as it was announced on 6 August 1982, persisted with some modifications until December 1987 when a virtual exchange rate unification was attained by a 20 percent devaluation of the peso in the 'preferential' or 'controlled' market.

The purpose of this chapter is to examine critically the Mexican experience with dual exchange rates from August 1982 to December 1987. The 1982–7 period is of special interest because in those years the Mexican economy collapsed. While between 1960 and 1981 annual output growth averaged 7.2 percent, it averaged −0.22 percent between 1982 and 1987. This dramatic decrease in growth was accompanied by an increase in inflation, from an average of 15.3 percent during the 1970s to 74 percent during the 1980s and by a dramatic increase in capital flight. The collapse in growth, the acceleration in inflation, and the increase in capital flight can undoubtedly be explained, at least in part, by the cut-off of foreign lending after the debt crisis exploded in 1982 and by the severe fall in oil prices in 1986. The object of this chapter is not to find all the determinants of this crisis. Instead, we focus on the role of dual exchange markets in contributing to (or reducing) the depth of this crisis. In particular, we will examine the role of the two-tier system in isolating domestic prices from speculative capital movements and in enhancing the Central Bank's control over its foreign exchange reserves.

The outline of the chapter is as follows. The second section describes the antecedents of the crisis. The third section examines Mexico's economic performance and exchange rate policy during the 1982–7 period. The fourth section reports the results of an econometric analysis of the effects of the dual exchange rate system on domestic prices. In order to accomplish this task, we compare the dynamics of prices in the 1976–82 period of unified exchange rates with the dynamics during the dual exchange rate period (1982–7). We first examine the univariate process followed by prices, using traditional parametric methods as in Campbell and Mankiw (1987). However, the stochastic process followed by prices may also be affected by shocks not related to the exchange rate system. To control for the effects of those shocks, we conduct a multivariate analysis of inflation dynamics in the two regimes, using the Blanchard–Bernanke structural vector autoregression analysis. The fifth section examines whether the dual exchange rate regime helped the Bank of Mexico to gain control over speculative capital movements. To test this hypothesis we use Hamilton's (1988) filter. The final section presents some concluding remarks.

ANTECEDENTS OF THE 1982 CRISIS

After the devaluation of the peso from 12.5 to 19.95 in October 1976 and after a 2 year interregnum, the Mexican economy entered a new phase of high growth spurred by an increase in government spending and investment.[2] The knowledge that Mexico's oil wealth was far greater than formerly thought was perhaps the main reason behind the increase in private and public spending.[3] Fueled by the increase in oil resources (the government's oil revenue increased from 4.8 percent of GDP in 1977 to 12.2 percent in 1980), public spending soared. Increasing oil revenues also allowed the government to reduce industry costs by setting low public sector prices and by fixing the nominal exchange rate, even though the rate of inflation was approximately 20 percent per annum (Figure 3.1 shows the monthly inflation rates for the 30 year period 1957–87). Together, the increase in government spending and the public sector pricing strategy fostered private spending. However, the substantial change in aggregate demand was also a reflection on the drastic change in the expectations of investors and managers, who had only a few months earlier held a pessimistic view of the potential of the economy. Naturally, Mexico's credit rating in

Percent

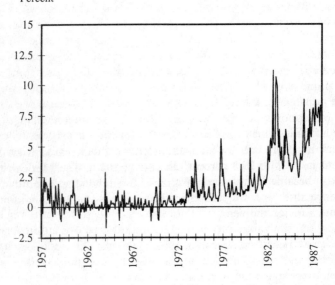

FIGURE 3.1   *Domestic inflation (monthly rate)*
SOURCE: Country case study.

Index,
1957:1=100

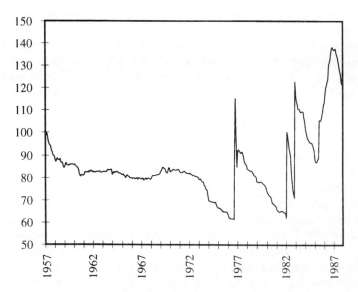

FIGURE 3.2   *Real exchange rate*
NOTES: An increase is a real depreciation.
SOURCE: Country case study.

the international financial system also improved. New funds were offered at even lower interest rates (see, for example, Table 1 in Calvo and Kaminsky, 1991). The growth rate of gross domestic product (GDP) during this period averaged 8.6 percent. The expansion in the level of economic activity was accompanied by large deficits in the trade account (which increased from 2.4 percent of GDP in 1979 to 7 percent in 1981) and by high inflation (which increased from 16.2 percent in 1978 to 29.8 percent per year in 1980). The Mexican peso quickly became overvalued (Figure 3.2 shows the monthly real exchange rate) and stagnation in the revenues of public enterprises became a major problem.

Early signs of future problems were observed by 1981. Government oil revenues reached a plateau in 1981, mainly because of falling world oil prices and the continued real appreciation of the Mexican peso. Government spending, in contrast, continued to increase at an accelerated pace. Together with an increase in world interest rates, the real appreciation of the peso had an unfavorable effect on the current account: the current account deficit was 73.7 percent higher in 1981 than in 1980. As a result, Mexican financial markets became restless. Capital flight took massive proportions in 1981. Yet even though domestic residents' expectations about the Mexican economy became gloomier in 1981, foreign credit continued to flow into the country.[4] The build up of foreign debt in 1981 was striking: external debt increased by $21 billion in that year alone. The foreign debt problem became explosive by the end of 1981 not only because of the magnitude of the debt but also because of the maturity of the loans (by the end of 1981, short-term public debt was 20.5 percent of total government foreign debt).

In 1981 the government adopted a set of corrective measures, including a 100 percent increase in the domestic price of gasoline and diesel to compensate for the deterioration of their relative price since 1976 and a 4 percent reduction of government expenditure during the second half of 1981. These policy measures could not prevent a further worsening of the public accounts. Financial markets became even more restless and capital flight intensified during the first 2 months of 1982. On 18 February 1982, the Bank of Mexico abandoned the crawling peg and allowed the exchange rate to float (although not completely freely) in order to reduce the private capital outflows. By the end of the month, the exchange rate was 45 pesos per dollar (a 67 percent devaluation).

Immediately after the devaluation, a new economic plan was announced that called for fiscal austerity and trade liberalization. In spite of the fiscal austerity plan, the government deficit persisted and, in addition, access to foreign credit started to decrease. Capital flight, together with rising inflation and the government's need to finance an increasing deficit, put extra pressure on the foreign exchange market. In August, Mexicans, anticipating another devaluation, practically bought out the Bank of Mexico's dollar reserves. As a result, during the third week of August, Mexico notified foreign creditors that its Central Bank had run out of reserves and that it would not be able to comply with previously scheduled payments on its foreign loans.

THE 1982 CRISIS AND THE DUAL EXCHANGE RATE SYSTEM

On 6 August 1982, after a balance of payments crisis, Mexico adopted a dual exchange rate system. The exchange regime consisted of a

Percent

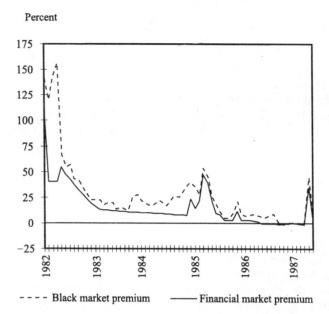

- - - - Black market premium   ——— Financial market premium

FIGURE 3.3   *Exchange rate premium 1982:8–1987:12 (percentages)*
SOURCE: Country case study.

'preferential' rate and a 'general' rate. The preferential rate applied to essential imports, petroleum export proceeds, and foreign debt repayments. The Bank of Mexico set the preferential exchange rate at 49.13 pesos per dollar and preannounced a daily devaluation of 4 cents. The general exchange rate applied to financial and all other current account transactions. The general exchange rate was allowed to float. On 6 August the general exchange rate reached 75.33 pesos per dollar, implying a depreciation of 54.4 percent. Figure 3.3 shows the monthly evolution of the financial market premium, defined as the percentage excess of the rate applicable to most financial transactions over the rate applicable to most current account transactions.

The adoption of the dual exchange rate system did not calm down the financial markets. Demand for foreign exchange continued to increase, further depreciating the general exchange rate. On 9 August 1982, the dollar in the general market reached a rate of 83.33. A few days later, on 12 August, the Bank of Mexico, unable to control speculative capital movements, closed the foreign exchange market. A day later, all foreign currency accounts in Mexican banks were converted into pesos at an unfavorable exchange rate (69.50 pesos per dollar).

When the foreign exchange market opened again on 19 August 1982, a three-tier exchange rate regime was adopted, with the 'preferential' rate for current account transactions, the 'general' rate for capital account transactions, and the 'special' exchange rate for exchange of foreign currency deposits into dollars. This last exchange rate was set at 69.50 pesos per dollar. When the exchange market reopened, the general exchange rate soared to 114.78 pesos per dollar. The Bank of Mexico, however, continued to lose reserves due to speculative capital movements, which made it impossible for Mexico to continue to service its foreign debt. Finally, the debt crisis exploded and on 22 August Mexico unilaterally declared a moratorium on its foreign loans.

On 1 September 1982, comprehensive foreign exchange controls were imposed to stop capital flight. Authorized transactions could be channeled through two different exchange markets. The 'preferential' rate, which applied to authorized essential current account transactions, was set at 50 pesos per dollar. The 'ordinary' rate, which applied to all other authorized current account transactions, was set at 70 pesos per dollar. However, these controls were difficult to enforce and the Bank of Mexico continued to lose reserves. Moreover, a black market for foreign exchange emerged, contributing to a further draining of foreign exchange reserves. The black market operated mainly in US cities close to the Mexican border; Figure 3.3 shows the premium of the black market exchange rate over the official (ordinary) rate for commercial transactions.

On 3 November 1982, to control capital flight, the peso was again devalued via the creation of an official 'free' market rate applicable within a special zone along the US border. Residents and enterprises located within that area were permitted to buy and sell dollars at a special rate controlled by the Central Bank. However, the volume of transactions in this market was very small as this exchange rate was much lower than the one in the US border cities, where the exchange rate had increased to 144.00 pesos per dollar by 16 December 1982.

On 1 December 1982, President de la Madrid took office. The new government announced a new economic program. As a part of this program, on 10 December a new system of foreign exchange controls was announced. In contrast with the comprehensive exchange controls instituted on 1 September 1982, exchange controls were imposed only on those transactions for which controls were easy to enforce. Three exchange rates were instituted: the 'controlled', the 'special', and the 'free' rates. The Bank of Mexico managed all three exchange rates. On 20 December the controlled exchange rate was set at 95.00 pesos per dollar with a preannounced daily devaluation of 13 cents. The controlled rate applied to current account transactions and payments of external loans. The special exchange rate was set at 70 pesos per dollar with a daily devaluation of 14 cents. This was the exchange rate for payment of Mexodollars contracted before 20 December. All the other transactions were channeled through the free market. When the exchange market opened on 20 December 1982, the free exchange rate was 148.50. Hence, in 1982 the Mexican peso depreciated by 268 percent in the commercial market and by 466.2 in the financial market. The economic plan also called for fiscal austerity and a number of policies to adjust domestic prices and wages. While the government deficit decreased to 8.3 percent of GDP in 1983, inflation increased to 98.9 percent in 1982 and 80.8 percent in 1983.

Since the free rate was kept basically fixed, the spread between the free and the controlled rate started to decrease, from 56 percent in December 1982 to 16 percent by the end of August 1983 (Figure 3.3), suggesting that the Bank of Mexico was planning a *de facto* unification of the dual exchange rate system. On 22 September 1983, contrary to expectations, the Bank of Mexico announced a 13 cent daily devaluation of the peso in the free market. The daily crawl in both markets increased to 17 cents on 6 December 1984.

A moderate reactivation of the economy in 1984–5 brought a new surge in inflation and a further appreciation of the peso in real terms (Figure 3.2). The real appreciation together with a deterioration of the terms of trade, led to a deterioration of the current account. By the end of 1984, Mexico's growth prospects dimmed as inflation continued to increase and the current account deteriorated. The economic outlook became bleaker as Mexico's terms of trade continued to worsen in 1985, particularly due to the fall in oil prices. This fall in oil prices also led to a further worsening of the government deficit. In 1985 the government deficit soared to 9.6 percent of GDP, in contrast to the 6.5 percent projected. These factors convinced the markets that the peso would have to be devalued against the dollar. In March 1985, the daily crawl was increased to 21 cents. It was hoped that the increased daily devaluation would stop capital flight. By then expectations of devaluation had become entrenched in the economy and were affecting foreign exchange reserves of the Bank of Mexico. For example, in June–July 1985 the Bank of Mexico lost approximately $1 billion of reserves. Furthermore, the black market exchange rate soared to 307.7 in June 1985. Finally, in July 1985 the daily preannounced devaluation policy was abandoned for a more flexible management of the exchange rate. On 25 July 1985, the peso in the controlled market was depreciated by 20 percent.

These measures proved to be insufficient to improve the current account. Oil prices plunged dramatically in 1986 (the price of Mexican crude decreasing by 46.6 percent) and so did the value of Mexican oil exports (a decline of $8.5 billion from $14.7 billion in 1985). The Mexican economy was hit hard, with an output growth rate of −4 percent.

In response to the oil shock, in 1986 the government announced a new stabilization package. The main characteristics of the new program were (1) increases in the price of public goods and services as well as in taxes on production and on income, to increase government revenues, (2) a further devaluation of the Mexican peso, and (3) in contrast to the import restriction policy followed since 1982, a reduction of import restrictions.

During the first half of 1987 the level of economic activity improved, but inflation was not controlled (Figure 3.1). The persistence of inflationary pressure and the expansion of economic activity generated expectations of devaluation, even though the real exchange rate was still high (Figure 3.2) and the current account was in surplus. These factors, together with the need for foreign exchange to repay maturing foreign loans, led to another exchange crisis in November 1987. During the months of October and November 1987 the Bank of Mexico had to sell $800 million. Finally, on 19 November 1987, the Central Bank allowed the peso to float in the free market. The peso immediately depreciated by 33 percent.

Mexico's economic performance during 1982–7, as this brief examination has shown, was dismal. The only success was the improvement in the current account. In contrast, no progress was made with respect to inflation and the government accounts were not stable. Moreover, during this period output growth was nil. Although capital flight was reduced, it was not fully controlled. During the 1982–7 period, capital outflows were approximately equal to $31 billion (using the Cuddington (1986) measure).

In December 1987 a new attempt was made to reverse the catastrophic economic performance. A new program called the 'Pacto de Solidaridad Economica' was announced in that month. The main characteristics of this program were a further reduction of the government deficit, the opening of the economy to the rest of the world, a contractionary monetary policy, and the agreement with firms and unions about price and wage controls. As a part of this program, on 14 December 1987 the peso in the controlled market was devalued by 22 percent with a virtual unification of both foreign exchange markets.

DUAL MARKETS AND DOMESTIC PRICES

The notion that capital account shocks can trigger inflation in a unified exchange rate system, strongly influenced Mexico's decision to adopt a dual exchange rate system in 1982 (see the 1982 *Annual Report* of the Bank of Mexico). At that time, the Bank of Mexico claimed that dual rates would sever the link between capital outflows and domestic prices. It was argued that by establishing different exchange rates for commercial and financial transactions, an increase in the demand for foreign assets would only increase the financial exchange rate. Since the commercial rate did not need to change, there was no need for domestic prices to change either.

However, a link between domestic prices and capital movements may still exist under dual exchange rates, since a depreciation of the financial rate may affect prices through (1) leakages between commercial and financial markets, (2) changes in interest rates and, hence, changes in investment and savings decisions, and (3) increases in the government deficit and monetary expansion.

Consider in more detail these different channels of transmission. Leakages between the commercial and financial markets exist when a depreciation of the financial rate above the commercial rate induces underinvoicing of exports or overinvoicing of imports. This in turn may affect the market prices of these goods, as was fully examined in Pitt (1981). Interestingly, in Mexico, dual exchange rates and a black market coexisted with underinvoicing of imports, presumably because of qualitative restrictions on imports (see Gulati, 1987). As a result, approximately $20 billion in imports were channeled through the black market in the 1982–5 period. This suggests that there existed a direct channel between increases in demand for foreign assets and domestic prices.

Increases in demand for foreign assets may also affect domestic prices through interest rates or the fiscal accounts. For example, an incipient capital outflow that leads to a depreciation of the financial exchange rate will generate an increase in domestic interest rates.

Changes in interest rates may affect consumption and investment. To the extent that changes in consumption and investment affect the demand for domestic goods, they will also affect domestic prices. Finally, when the government transacts in the financial and the commercial market and the exchange rate in the financial market is depreciated relative to the one in the commercial market, the budget deficit will increase if the dollar value of the net sales in the commercial market exceeds that in the financial market. The resulting quasi-fiscal deficit may be paid for by increases in money creation and thus higher inflation.

Naturally, the extent of the links between capital movements and domestic prices is strictly an empirical issue. The purpose of this section is to resolve this issue for the Mexican case. In order to test the proposition that dual rates insulate domestic prices from speculative capital movements, we will examine the stochastic process followed by domestic prices after two different stabilization programs. In the first stabilization program, announced in August 1976, Mexico adopted a unified exchange rate system. This unified exchange rate system lasted until August 1982. The second stabilization program that we will evaluate is the one announced in August 1982, which lasted until December 1987. During this period, as discussed earlier, the Bank of Mexico adopted a dual exchange rate system.

The first issue that we will examine is whether the univariate process followed by prices changed when the dual exchange rate system was implemented. This analysis will provide a preliminary assessment of the propagation mechanism of inflationary shocks in the unified and in the dual regimes. However, the univariate approach may not provide us with a complete answer about the effect of the exchange rate regime on prices, since the stochastic process followed by prices may also be affected by changes in policies or external shocks not related to the exchange rate system. In order to control for shocks extraneous to the exchange rate system we also examine the dynamics of inflation in a multivariate framework using the Bernanke–Blanchard structural vector autoregression (VAR) model.

Univariate Analysis

We estimate a variety of parsimoniously parameterized models for the Mexican consumer price index using monthly data from 1976:10 to

1987:12. Since prices follow a non-stationary process we estimate different ARMA processes for the differenced series. We consider all ARMA models for the difference of the logarithm of prices with up to two autoregressive (AR) parameters and two moving average (MA) parameters:

$$(1) \qquad \phi(L)\Delta P_t = \alpha_0 + \theta(L)\epsilon_t,$$

where α_0 is a constant, $\phi(L) = 1 - \phi_1 L - \phi_2 L^2 - \ldots - \phi_s L^s$, and $\theta(L) = 1 + \theta_1 L + \theta_2 L^2 + \ldots + \theta_q L^q$.

The estimation results are reported in Table 3.1. There we present the estimate of the constant, the coefficients of the autoregressive and moving average process, and the corresponding standard errors. We also report the Akaike and Schwarz selection criteria for each model.[5] For the 1976:10–1982:7 sample, the AR(1) model is the one selected using both criteria. Instead, for the 1982:8–1987:12 sample, the Akaike criterion selects the ARMA(1,2) while the Schwarz criterion selects the AR(1); since the difference in the Akaike criterion for the AR(1) and the ARMA(1,2) is not statistically significant, we select the more parsimonious of the two models.

Interestingly, if we just compare the autoregressive parameters of the selected models, we would conclude that the univariate process followed by prices does not seem to be affected by the adoption of a dual exchange rate regime. In contrast, the constant term (α_0) changes across regimes, from 2.06 percent per month to 5.86 percent, indicating that the adoption of a two-tier exchange rate system may result in an increase in the steady-state rate of inflation. However, we should be cautious in interpreting these results since the stochastic process followed by the different market fundamentals may have also changed. Making further progress on this issue requires including other market fundamentals in the system, so as to isolate the effect of the exchange rate system separately. This is done in the next section.

Before discussing the multivariate model, we present the impulse response function of the selected models to examine the transmission mechanism of inflation. Table 3.2 reports the impulse response functions for the logarithm of prices for the chosen models:

$$(2) \qquad p_t = (1 - L)^{-1}\phi(L)^{-1}\theta(L)\epsilon_t .$$

Both during the 1976–82 period and the 1982–7 period, the impulse response functions for inflation die out to zero but at a slow pace:

after 6 months, 20 percent of a shock is still present in inflation. After 3 years and for any foreseeable horizon, a 1 percent innovation increases prices by almost 4 percent.

TABLE 3.1 *Univariate models of inflation:*
$$\phi(L)\Delta p_t = \alpha_0 + \theta(L)\epsilon_t$$

α_0	ϕ_1	ϕ_2	θ_1	θ_2	Akaike	Schwarz
1976:10–1982:7						
2.0563	0.7152				0.6883	0.7316
(0.3458)	(0.0828)					
2.0608	0.6520	0.0930			0.7021	0.7674
(0.3873)	(0.1161)	(0.1194)				
2.1282	0.5349				0.9896	1.0519
(0.1180)	(0.1055)					
2.1590	0.6004	0.2689			0.9202	1.0058
(0.2087)	(0.1227)	(0.1229)				
2.0452	0.7766	−0.1385			0.7019	0.7672
(0.3820)	(0.0971)	(0.1590)				
2.0519	0.7157	0.0533	−0.0854		0.7215	0.8098
(0.3966)	(0.3192)	(0.2540)	(0.3391)			
2.0477	0.7884	−0.1353	−0.0340		0.7219	0.8103
(0.3928)	(0.1112)	(0.1645)	(0.1459)			
2.0609	0.6757	0.1193	−0.0241	−0.0900	0.7395	0.8511
(0.4364)	(0.3432)	(0.3071)	(0.3618)	(0.1744)		
1982:8–1987:12						
5.8603	0.7482				2.8274	3.0153
(0.8719)	(0.1133)					
6.0137	0.6592	0.1358			2.8822	3.1652
(1.1207)	(0.1519)	(0.1539)				
5.4708	0.5489				3.5018	3.7346
(0.3592)	(0.1325)					
5.4732	0.6555	0.3469			3.2383	3.5563
(0.4383)	(0.1372)	(0.1376)				
6.3998	0.9050	−0.3326			2.8510	3.1309
(1.8641)	(0.1086)	(0.1838)				
25.9096	1.5057	−0.5061	−0.8541		2.8673	3.2369
(28.5751)	(0.3365)	(0.2995)	(0.2581)			
2.5468	1.0239	−0.4501	−0.2806		2.8214	3.1851
(7.0168)	(0.0576)	(0.1525)	(0.1550)			
6.5964	0.0686	0.8556	0.4962	−0.5027	3.0132	3.4915
(4.0425)	(0.1283)	(0.1101)	(0.1757)	(0.1765)		

Standard errors are in parentheses.

TABLE 3.2   *Impulse responses of a one-unit shock on ln(price level)*

Month	1976:10–1982:7	1982:8–1987:12
1	1.000	1.000
2	1.715	1.748
3	2.227	2.308
4	2.593	2.727
5	2.854	3.040
6	3.042	3.275
7	3.175	3.451
8	3.271	3.582
9	3.340	3.680
10	3.389	3.754
11	3.424	3.809
12	3.449	3.850
13	3.467	3.881
14	3.480	3.904
15	3.489	3.921
16	3.495	3.934
17	3.500	3.943
18	3.503	3.951
19	3.506	3.956
20	3.507	3.960
21	3.509	3.963
22	3.510	3.965
23	3.510	3.967
24	3.511	3.968
25	3.511	3.969
26	3.511	3.970
27	3.511	3.971
28	3.511	3.971
29	3.512	3.971
30	3.512	3.971
31	3.512	3.972
32	3.512	3.972
33	3.512	3.972
34	3.512	3.972
35	3.512	3.972
36	3.512	3.972

A Multivariate Approach

As described in previous two sections, there are many differences in
the shocks that affected the Mexican economy in the two periods

under consideration. During the first period, the exchange rate and prices of public goods and services were basically kept constant so as to reduce inflation. During the second period, in contrast, both the exchange rate and public prices were periodically adjusted so as to maintain their relative value. External shocks also differed dramatically in the two samples. During the 1976–82 period, Mexico experienced a favorable oil shock, while in the 1982–7 period the oil shock was fully reversed.

To control for shocks extraneous to the exchange rate regime, in this section we examine the joint behavior of prices, the commercial exchange rate, the dual market premium,[6] output, the domestic interest rate, the money supply, the world interest rate, and the world price of oil. We ask whether shocks to the dual market had any effect on the price setting mechanism, commercial exchange rate policy, the money supply rule, nominal interest rates, or output. As before, we use monthly data from 1976:10 to 1987:12 to compare the transmission mechanism of inflation after August 1982 with the one during the 1976–82 period. This comparison will provide direct evidence on which shocks have played a dominant role in the substantial increase in the rate of inflation after 1982.

The Model

We assume that the economy is described by a log-linear system of six equations: an exchange rate policy equation (for the commercial rate), an output equation, a price-setting equation, a money market equilibrium equation, a money supply rule, and the financial foreign exchange market equilibrium condition. The model is represented as follows:

$$(3) \qquad AY_t = A(L)Y_{t-1} + B(L)Z_t + \mu_t$$

where the vector Y includes the six variables e (the commercial rate), y (output), p (the price level), i (the domestic nominal interest rate), m (the logarithm of money supply), and d the dual market premium. The vector Z of exogenous variables includes the logarithm of the world interest rate, i^* and the logarithm of the world price of oil, p_0^*; $A(L)$ and $B(L)$ are matrices with elements that are finite-order polynomials in the lag operator. The vector of structural disturbances μ, includes shocks to the (commercial) exchange rate policy, μ_e, shocks to output, μ_y, shocks to price setting, μ_p, shocks to money demand, μ_i, shocks to the money supply rule, μ_m, and shocks to the dual exchange market, μ_d.[7] A is a 6×6 non-singular matrix whose diagonal elements are normalized to unity. The matrix A may have arbitrary off- diagonal elements. The covariance matrix of the innovations μ is denoted by Ω and it is diagonal. Naturally, during the unified exchange rate system the model consists of only the first five equations.

Although our final goal is the estimation of the model described in equation (3), this estimation presents some problems because the system has potentially many unknown parameters. To alleviate the computational problem, Bernanke (1986) and Blanchard (1989) propose modeling the contemporaneous relationships in equation (3) by imposing restrictions on the matrix A and leaving the matrices $A(L)$ and $B(L)$ unrestricted with the exception of specifying the maximum lag length.

Premultiplying both sides of equation (3) by A^{-1} gives the reduced form associated with the structural model:

(4) $$Y_t = C(L)Y_{t-1} + S(L)Z_t + \epsilon_t,$$

where $C(L) = A^{-1}A(L), D(L) = A^{-1}B(L)$ and ϵ is the vector of reduced-form innovations $\epsilon_t = A^{-1}\mu_t$. To isolate the effects of the structural innovations on the set of variables examined we need to specify a set of restrictions on the elements of A.

Before proceeding with the estimation of the VAR model in equation (4), we specify the identification restrictions which we take to best capture the joint behavior of the market fundamentals in the Mexican economy:

$$
(5) \quad
\begin{bmatrix}
1 & 0 & 0 & 0 & 0 & 0 \\
0 & 1 & 0 & 0 & 0 & 0 \\
a_{31} & 0 & 1 & 0 & 0 & a_{36} \\
0 & a_{42} & a_{43} & 1 & a_{45} & 0 \\
a_{51} & a_{52} & a_{53} & 0 & 1 & a_{56} \\
a_{61} & 0 & 0 & a_{64} & 0 & 1
\end{bmatrix}
\begin{bmatrix}
\epsilon_e \\
\epsilon_y \\
\epsilon_p \\
\epsilon_i \\
\epsilon_m \\
\epsilon_d
\end{bmatrix}
=
\begin{bmatrix}
\mu_e \\
\mu_y \\
\mu_p \\
\mu_i \\
\mu_m \\
\mu_d
\end{bmatrix}
$$

In equation (5), innovations in the commercial exchange rate, ϵ_e, are attributed entirely to shocks to the (commercial) exchange rate policy, μ_e. This restriction implies that exchange rate innovations do not depend on innovations to output, ϵ_y, prices, ϵ_p, interest rates, ϵ_i, money supply, ϵ_m, or the dual market premium, ϵ_d. We consider that these restrictions capture the spirit of the exchange rate policy followed by the Bank of Mexico in both exchange rate regimes. We should recall that during the dual exchange rate regime, the commercial exchange rate depreciation was announced in advance and was not modified for long periods of time. Similarly, during the unified exchange rate system the exchange rate policy was mostly geared to obtaining price level stability and was only modified when the real appreciation built up to the point of a balance of payments crisis.

Innovations to output, ε_y, are assumed to respond contemporaneously to a composite shock, μ_y, that reflects both output supply shocks, such as productivity shocks, and output demand shocks, such as shocks to government spending.

The price-setting equation allows price innovations, ε_p, to depend on exchange rate innovations in both the commercial and dual foreign exchange markets, ε_e and ε_d. They also depend on the price-setting shock, μ_p, which reflects such factors as changes in mark-ups or in the prices of inputs not included in the system, such as labor costs and prices of utilities.

The money market equilibrium condition allows interest rate innovations, ε_i, to depend on money, income, and price innovations ($\varepsilon_m, \varepsilon_y$, and ε_p) as well as on shocks to money demand, such as those associated with financial innovation, that are captured in μ_i. Money supply innovations, in turn, are allowed to respond to innovations in commercial and dual exchange rates, ε_e and ε_d, in output, ε_y, and in prices, ε_p, as well as to shocks in the monetary rule of the Bank of Mexico, μ_m.

Finally, for the dual exchange rate regime, the dual market exchange rate responds contemporaneously to innovations in the commercial exchange rate, ε_e, and to shocks in the dual exchange market, μ_d, which reflect shocks to speculative capital movements. The dual market shock is a composite disturbance that reflects changes in investors' preferences as well as modifications to restrictions in international capital flows. It may also reflect investors' reactions to news about government deficits, which were not included in the system.[8]

The Reduced Form Model

In this subsection we estimate the reduced form model in equation (4) and then use the model in equation (5) to recover the structural shocks. We then examine the impulses responses and the variance decompositions to characterize the dynamic effects of the structural innovations on the endogenous variables.

Before estimating the model we have to deal with the issues of stationarity and cointegration. We performed standard tests for stationarity and we found that all the variables were integrated of order 1. In view of these results we checked for cointegration of these variables. The tests of cointegration between the eight variables show no evidence of cointegration.

These results led us to specify the system in equations (3)–(5) as a system in first differences. The model in equation (4) was estimated using the above-described variables and setting the number of lags to two.[9] Since it is very hard to interpret the coefficients of the reduced form model, we just report the marginal predictive ability of the lagged values of the different variables on the current values of the six (five for the unified exchange rate regime) endogenous variables. These statistics will provide some preliminary information on the dynamics of the model in the two different periods. Before examining those results, note that our final model excludes both oil prices and world interest rates, as tests performed on the full specification supported the hypothesis that neither variable marginally helped to predict any of the endogenous variables of the model at the 10 percent level.

The results of the estimation of the traditional VAR in equation (4) for the unified and the dual exchange rate system are contained in Table 3.3. The table reports tests of marginal predictive power of each variable for itself and the rest of the variables in the system. The table shows that the depreciation rate in the commercial market during the 1976:9–1982:7 period is marginally predicted (at the 10 percent level) by domestic inflation and money growth, suggesting some degree of accommodation by the exchange rate policy. However, we do not capture any accommodation by the commercial exchange rate policy during the dual exchange rate period. This last result may possibly be explained by the exchange rate policy followed by the Bank of Mexico after December 1982, in which the rate of the crawl in the commercial market was kept constant for long periods of time and only accommodated to changes in domestic prices when a balance of payments crisis developed.

Interestingly, the dynamics of inflation seem to have changed over time. During the first period inflation is strongly predicted level by lagged rates of inflation but no other variable has predictive power at reasonable significance levels. On the contrary, during the dual exchange rate period inflation is also marginally predicted (at the 0.05 level) by money. Finally, money seems to react passively to

TABLE 3.3 *Tests of marginal predictive power of row variables for column variables*

	e	y	p	i	m	d
1976:10–1982:7						
e	0.061	0.356	0.386	0.050	0.848	
y	0.724	0.000	0.913	9.671	0.438	
p	0.093	0.268	0.000	0.007	0.822	
i	0.380	0.073	0.374	0.000	0.669	
m	0.046	0.725	0.843	0.318	0.351	
1982:8–1987:12						
e	0.646	0.655	0.182	0.093	0.307	0.264
y	0.950	0.000	0.544	0.840	0.072	0.155
p	0.675	0.089	0.000	0.748	0.064	0.153
i	0.466	0.869	0.166	0.001	0.363	0.781
m	0.333	0.007	0.036	0.482	0.517	0.139
d	0.741	0.978	0.219	0.120	0.453	0.018

e is the pesos/dollar exchange rate in the commercial market, y is the index of industrial production, p is the consumer price index, i is the commercial banking system lending rate, m is money supply ($M1$), and d is the black market exchange rate premium. All variables are in log differences.
Entry (i, j) is the significance level of the F-test of the hypothesis that two lags of variable i can be excluded from the regression predicting variable j. A low value indicates rejection of this hypothesis.

output and inflation during the dual system, while no other variable predicts money during the unified exchange rate regime. Notably, the above results seem to support the Bank of Mexico's contention that dual exchange rates sever the links between capital outflows and prices: the dual market premium marginally predicts no other variable at any conventional significance level. However, there are some problems with this conclusion since shocks to the foreign exchange market may still have large effects on prices by contemporaneously affecting the other variables in the system.

The Structural Model

Estimated Contemporaneous Responses To test the proposition that dual rates sever the links between capital outflows and domestic prices, we first have to estimate the model in equation (5). The model was estimated using the method of moments proposed by Bernanke

(1986).[10] The results of this estimation for the unified exchange rate regime are as follows:

(6.1)
$$\varepsilon_e = \mu_e$$

(6.2)
$$\varepsilon_y = \mu_y$$

(6.3)
$$\varepsilon_p = 0.055\varepsilon_e + \mu_p$$
$$(0.013)$$

(6.4)
$$\varepsilon_i = -0.006\varepsilon_y + 0.272\varepsilon_p - 0.074\varepsilon_m + \mu_i$$
$$(0.095) \quad (0.265) \quad (0.065)$$

(6.5)
$$\varepsilon_m = 0.032\varepsilon_e - 0.238\varepsilon_y + 0.763\varepsilon_p + \mu_m$$
$$(0.066) \quad (0.173) \quad (0.533)$$

while the results for the dual exchange rate regime are as follows:

(7.1)
$$\varepsilon_e = \mu_e$$

(7.2)
$$\varepsilon_y = \mu_y$$

(7.3)
$$\varepsilon_p = 0.055\varepsilon_e - 0.031\varepsilon_d + \mu_p$$
$$(0.017) \quad (0.018)$$

(7.4)
$$\varepsilon_i = -0.109\varepsilon_y + 0.259\varepsilon_p - 0.256\varepsilon_m + \mu_i$$
$$(0.185) \quad (0.278) \quad (0.103)$$

(7.5)
$$\varepsilon_m = -0.091\varepsilon_e - 0.067\varepsilon_y + 0.597\varepsilon_p + 0.133\varepsilon_d + \mu_m$$
$$(0.054) \quad (0.207) \quad (0.371) \quad (0.053)$$

(7.6)
$$\varepsilon_d = -0.504\varepsilon_e + \mu_d$$
$$(0.101)$$

Before examining the results, note that in both periods the model is overidentified since only seven parameters are estimated for the first regime and ten for the second (from a total of ten and fifteen possible identifiable parameters, respectively). We have tested the overidentifying restrictions. The significance levels of these tests were 0.61 and 0.25, respectively, indicating that the overidentifying restrictions cannot be rejected.

Although the standard errors are generally large, indicating that some of the coefficients are estimated very imprecisely, the estimation of the model in equation (5) generates some interesting results. For the 1976–82 period (equations (6.1)–(6.5)), we find that while price innovations are positively related to commercial exchange rate innovations (as one would expect), the coefficient is quite small (a 1 percent increase in the exchange rate innovation generates an increase of only 0.06 percent in the price innovation), suggesting sluggishness in price adjustment. On the other hand, the money market equilibrium condition suggests that during the 1976–82 period the nominal interest rate was largely affected by innovations in inflation while not reacting to money innovations, suggesting that the lending interest rate during this period was a separate instrument of monetary policy. Finally, money supply innovations within a month strongly depend on innovations to output and prices. While the monetary authority seems to follow a 'leaning against the wind' type of policy with respect to the level of economic activity, reducing the money supply when output increases, it follows an accommodating type of policy with respect to inflation, increasing the money supply when prices increase.

In equations (7.1) – (7.6) we report the results for the dual exchange rate regime. The results from this estimation seem to be bad news for the hypothesis that financial exchange rates insulate the domestic economy from shocks in the foreign exchange market. For example, equation (7.1) shows that shocks to prices are marginally explained at the 10 percent level by innovations in the premium. Surprisingly, an increase in the premium leads to a decrease in domestic prices (although the contemporaneous effect is small: a 1 percent increase in the premium is translated into a 0.03 percent decrease in prices). However, increases in the premium may also have inflationary effects. For example, in equation (7.5) we note that the money supply is positively related to innovations in the premium (a 1 percent increase in the premium generates an increase of 0.13 percent in the growth rate of money). This effect may be the result of the Bank of Mexico transacting in both the commercial and financial markets. If the dollar value of the net sales in the commercial market exceeds that in the financial market, the resulting budget deficit may be paid for by increases in money creation and thus higher inflation.

There are some other interesting results. While the within-month increases in prices are positively related to innovations in the commercial exchange rate, this effect is quite small (the point estimate is 0.05) and it is identical to the effect observed for the unified exchange rate system. This suggests that the increase in the rate of crawl in the 1982–7 period (relative to the 1976–82 period) did not generate additional inflationary instability, leading only to a proportional increase in inflation. In addition, the money market equilibrium condition captures the change in monetary policy that took place in the early 1980s. We note in equation (7.4) that interest rates reacted strongly to changes in the money supply, contrary to their weak reaction during the 1976–82 period, indicating that in the 1980s the Bank of Mexico stopped using the interest rate as an independent tool of monetary policy.

Lastly, the money supply rule suggests that in both regimes the money supply accommodated changes in prices. This equation also suggests that monetary policy in both regimes was used to reduce the fluctuations of output.

Dynamic Effects of the Structural Shocks   We can now obtain the system's moving average representation or impulse response functions for the levels of the different variables rather than for the first differences. They are reported in Table 3.4. Table 3.5 presents the variance decompositions. We first discuss the results for the 1976–82 period.

Consider first the effects of exchange rate policy shocks, μ_e. Prices, interest rates, and money show a positive response to this shock. In none of the cases is the growth of the variables affected in the long term and, overall, the cumulative responses of money and prices are of a smaller order of magnitude than the cumulative changes in the exchange rate, indicating that nominal depreciations have real effects even after 3 years. In contract, shocks to the price-setting rule generate cumulative responses of similar magnitude to the initiating shock after 1 year in both prices and exchange rates, suggesting that even in the 1976–82 period the exchange rate fully accommodates changes in prices, although with a 1 year lag. Surprisingly innovations in the price-setting rule do have real effects. Nominal (and real) interest rates increase and output decreases even after 3 years.

TABLE 3.4   *Impulse responses*

	Month	e	y	p	i	m	d
1976:10–1982:7							
μ_e	1	5.958	0.000	0.327	0.057	0.438	
	12	5.867	−0.640	1.494	1.097	0.219	
	24	5.899	−0.658	1.520	1.124	0.203	
	36	5.899	−0.658	1.520	1.125	0.202	
μ_y	1	0.000	2.050	0.000	0.025	−0.487	
	12	−0.510	1.332	−0.153	−0.212	0.008	
	24	−0.514	1.335	−0.156	−0.216	0.010	
	36	−0.515	1.335	−0.156	−0.216	0.010	
μ_p	1	0.000	0.000	0.665	0.144	0.507	
	12	2.477	−1.279	2.480	2.806	−0.196	
	24	2.530	−1.313	2.527	2.853	−0.223	
	36	2.531	−1.314	2.528	2.854	−0.223	
μ_i	1	0.000	0.000	0.000	1.594	0.000	
	12	0.405	−0.810	0.692	3.426	−0.379	
	24	0.429	−0.826	0.714	3.448	−0.392	
	36	0.429	−0.827	0.714	3.448	−0.392	
μ_m	1	0.000	0.000	0.000	−0.218	2.944	
	12	−1.407	−0.388	0.234	0.791	2.256	
	24	−1.388	−0.396	0.246	0.806	2.248	
	36	−1.387	−0.396	0.246	0.806	2.248	
1982:8–1987:12							
μ_e	1	7.502	0.000	0.530	0.360	−0.870	−3.781
	12	8.629	−0.433	2.416	3.076	−0.059	−4.541
	24	10.444	−0.475	4.014	4.129	0.980	−4.756
	36	12.203	−0.514	5.566	5.142	1.988	−4.968
μ_y	1	0.000	1.513	0.000	−0.140	−0.101	0.000
	12	2.476	1.028	2.450	1.458	2.043	1.347
	24	5.795	0.958	5.375	3.376	3.948	0.953
	36	9.012	0.885	8.213	5.230	5.792	0.566
μ_p	1	0.000	0.000	0.840	0.089	0.510	0.000
	12	7.978	−0.063	7.970	4.486	5.307	−0.131
	24	16.742	−0.265	15.701	9.533	10.320	−1.195
	36	25.244	−0.456	23.201	14.429	15.191	−2.218
μ_i	1	0.000	0.000	0.000	2.206	0.000	0.000
	12	3.992	−0.308	1.494	7.049	0.484	0.003
	24	5.665	−0.339	2.946	8.053	1.437	−0.167
	36	7.267	−0.375	4.359	8.976	2.355	−0.360
μ_m	1	0.000	0.000	0.000	−0.627	2.450	0.000
	12	4.777	0.732	4.378	1.189	5.372	2.355
	24	10.712	0.602	9.614	4.610	8.780	1.660
	36	16.470	0.473	14.693	7.926	12.079	0.967
μ_d	1	0.000	0.000	−0.185	−0.223	0.683	5.962
	12	2.694	0.038	1.480	2.269	1.249	3.719
	24	4.723	−0.002	3.262	3.453	2.410	3.488
	36	6.684	−0.046	4.992	4.583	3.533	3.252

Entry (i, j) is the dynamic response of variable j to a one standard deviation shock in variable i. All entries are percent increases of the level of each variable from baseline.

TABLE 3.5 *Variance decompositions*

	Month	μ_e	μ_y	μ_p	μ_i	μ_m	μ_d
1976:–1982:7							
e	1	100.000	0.000	0.000	0.000	0.000	
	12	83.081	0.986	6.135	1.244	8.555	
	24	83.080	0.986	6.136	1.244	8.555	
	36	83.080	0.986	6.135	1.244	8.555	
y	1	0.000	100.000	0.000	0.000	0.000	
	12	4.161	85.253	4.276	5.434	0.876	
	24	4.161	85.248	4.279	5.435	0.876	
	36	4.162	85.248	4.279	5.435	0.876	
p	1	19.455	0.000	80.545	0.000	0.000	
	12	25.410	0.282	69.033	4.742	0.533	
	24	25.407	0.282	69.030	4.746	0.534	
	36	25.407	0.282	69.030	4.746	0.534	
i	1	0.123	0.023	0.789	97.249	1.815	
	12	3.861	0.899	24.842	65.205	5.195	
	24	3.863	0.899	24.846	65.199	5.193	
	36	3.863	0.899	24.846	65.199	5.193	
m	1	2.049	2.537	2.754	0.000	92.661	
	12	2.620	4.809	3.507	1.583	87.481	
	24	2.621	4.809	3.509	1.583	87.479	
	36	2.621	4.809	3.508	1.583	87.479	
1982:8–1987:12							
e	1	100.000	0.000	0.000	0.000	0.000	0.000
	12	79.908	1.532	8.446	3.950	5.043	1.121
	24	69.598	2.428	14.996	3.704	7.891	1.383
	36	62.131	3.077	19.745	3.520	9.956	1.571
y	1	0.000	100.000	0.000	0.000	0.000	0.000
	12	1.326	78.114	2.504	1.749	14.300	2.008
	24	1.327	78.013	2.584	1.751	14.314	2.010
	36	1.328	77.927	2.653	1.751	14.329	2.012
p	1	27.538	0.000	69.102	0.000	0.000	3.360
	12	7.383	6.390	60.097	2.609	20.296	3.225
	24	4.968	7.309	58.921	2.328	23.329	3.146
	36	4.177	7.610	58.531	2.239	24.320	3.122
i	1	2.373	0.357	0.146	89.013	7.202	0.909
	12	10.074	2.268	12.746	60.911	8.355	5.645
	24	8.503	3.517	22.001	48.758	12.090	5.130
	36	7.522	4.289	27.803	41.164	14.426	4.795
m	1	10.103	0.137	3.357	0.000	80.175	6.228
	12	6.499	7.440	19.625	3.055	54.461	8.919
	24	5.616	7.630	27.929	2.842	48.343	7.639
	36	5.078	7.738	33.017	2.706	44.603	6.858
d	1	28.689	0.000	0.000	0.000	0.000	71.311
	12	21.121	4.953	4.747	1.496	5.641	62.042
	24	21.078	4.960	4.872	1.497	5.686	61.907
	36	21.038	4.967	4.985	1.498	5.731	61.780

Entry (i, j) is the percentage of forecast variance of variable i at different horizons attributable to innovations in variable j.

Finally, shocks to the money supply rule do not have permanent effects on the rates of inflation, depreciation, or money growth. Interestingly, even after 3 years a monetary shock has real effects. The point estimates indicate that an increase in nominal balances results in an increase in real balances too. This may be the result of the large number of price controls introduced by the government during this period.

Table 3.5 provides some information complementary to that reported in Table 3.4. It shows the contribution of each source of innovations to the variance of the n month ahead forecast error for each endogenous variable. During this period, innovations to the exchange rate rule account for most of the variance of the forecast error at all horizons. It is however true that there is also some degree of accommodation in the exchange rate policy. Price and money innovations account for 15 percent of the variance of the exchange rate over horizons from 1 to 3 years.

In turn, innovations to exchange rate policy account for 25 percent of the variance of the 12 month ahead forecast error of prices. Even after 36 months this innovation still accounts for 25 percent of the variance. But innovations to the price-setting rule dominate both the long-term and short-term fluctuations in prices. These include innovations in wage setting and shocks to the prices of other inputs, such as utilities. Assessing the separate effects of these shocks would require the introduction of the nominal wage and prices of utilities as additional variables in the system. However, this is beyond the scope of this chapter. Lastly, it is also clear from Table 3.5 that money innovations cannot account for the variance of inflation during this period.

The propagation mechanism of inflation changes drastically during the dual exchange rate regime (Table 3.4). First, we should note that money (supply and demand) and exchange rate (commercial and financial) innovations have permanent effects on the rate of inflation. For example, one standard deviation innovations in the commercial exchange rate policy and in the financial market increase the long-term (36 month) annual rate of inflation by 1.6 and 1.8 percent per year, respectively, suggesting that dual rates could not insulate domestic prices from speculative capital movements. However, money shocks dominate the long-term path of inflation: shocks to the money supply rule increase the long-term (36 month) annual rate of inflation by 5.1 percent while money demand shocks increase the long-term (36 month) annual rate of inflation by 1.4 percent. These results are confirmed in Table 3.5, where the variance decomposition of inflation is reported. In the short term, shocks to inflation are dominated by shocks to exchange rate policy (commercial and financial) and to the price-setting mechanism. In the long term, exchange rate shocks only account for approximately 10 percent of the forecast variance of inflation. On the other hand, innovations in the money supply rule account for 24 percent of the forecast error variance of inflation after 36 months.

Finally, we should note that shocks to output had a relatively important effect on inflation. A one standard deviation shock to output led to a steady-state increase in annual inflation of 2.8 percent. Presumably this shock to output reflects a positive demand shock due to the expansionary fiscal policy followed during most of the 1982–7 period. During this period, shocks to output account for approximately 7 percent of the 36 month ahead forecast error variance of inflation. This result is in striking contrast with the results for the earlier period, in which real shocks did not have a significant effect on inflation.

Tables 3.4 and 3.5 also report the effects of shocks to speculative capital movements on the commercial exchange rate, output, interest rates, and money supply. A positive shock to the premium increases the rate of depreciation of the commercial exchange rate and the growth rate of money in both the short and the long terms. The explanation of this effect is simple enough. The premium may be responding to government announcements (not introduced in our model) about future exchange rate and monetary policies. If this is the case, it is not surprising that the increase in the premium precedes an increase in the growth rate of money and the rate of devaluation in the commercial market. The increase in interest rates due to the foreign exchange rate shocks is not unexpected either. It may simply reflect inflationary expectations generated by the government announcements. What is surprising is the strength of the effect. Interest rates increase by 4.6 percent after 36 months. This effect seems too strong given that annual inflation only increases by 1.8 percent. However, positive shocks in the financial market may also be reflecting expectations about fiscal policy. To the extent that these shocks reflect an increasing government deficit, one would expect an increasing real interest rate. Naturally, to elucidate this issue it would be necessary to include the fiscal deficit among the variables of the system.

DUAL MARKETS AND CAPITAL FLIGHT

The results of the previous section suggest that dual exchange rates did little to sever the link between capital account fluctuations and domestic prices. A second reason behind Mexico's adoption of a two-tier exchange rate system in 1982 (see the 1982 *Annual Report*, of the Bank of Mexico) was the government's desire to control capital outflows. It was argued that in a dual exchange rate system an increase in the demand for foreign assets would only lead to a depreciation of the financial rate with no loss of foreign exchange reserves by the Central Bank.

A two-tier exchange rate regime may fail to insulate reserves from capital account pressures for a number of reasons. Consider, for example, an increase in the demand for foreign assets. If the financial rate is heavily managed, as was the case in Mexico during some periods, the Central Bank will continue to lose foreign exchange reserves as in the fixed exchange rate system. This is so because the Central Bank will have to sell dollars in the financial market to keep the financial rate from depreciating. Naturally, if the Central Bank imposes foreign exchange restrictions, the loss of reserves may be avoided. This will not be possible if the restrictions are difficult to enforce. This is what happened in Mexico in September–December 1982: growing overvaluation and current account deficits fueled expectations of devaluation and capital flight that the Bank of Mexico could not prevent.

If instead the financial rate is allowed to float, an increase in demand for foreign assets does not need to be financed by a reduction in the Central Bank reserves. Still, in this case official reserves may fail to be insulated from capital outflows. A critical element is whether the Central Bank can enforce the segmentation of the foreign exchange markets. For example, if the financial rate is depreciated relative to the commercial rate, exporters have incentives to underinvoice their exports and sell the foreign exchange in the financial market. Similarly, importers will attempt to overinvoice their imports and then resell the foreign exchange so obtained in the financial market. In both cases, the leakage will result in a loss of official reserves.

In this section we examine the claim that a two-tier exchange rate system helps prevent capital flight. As we mentioned earlier, there is some indication that the two-tier regime did not completely prevent capital outflows. For example, in 1983 (using Cuddington's (1986) measure of capital flight) capital outflows were approximately

$9 billion. Perhaps this was the result of the Bank of Mexico' heavy management of the exchange rate for capital account transactions. Only in 1984 did private capital outflows start to decrease. However, this was just a transitory phenomenon. The deterioration of the current account together with the real appreciation of the peso in 1985 led investors to believe that a maxi-devaluation was imminent again stimulating incipient capital outflows. This time, however, the foreign exchange crisis that culminated in July 1985 induced the Bank of Mexico to modify the dual exchange rate system to one with a floating financial rate. Together with a large devaluation of the commercial rate, this change in the management of the financial exchange rate market seemed to have contributed to at least a transitory decrease in capital outflows. However, balance of payments problems proved difficult to overcome, particularly in the face of Mexican inflation that continued to exceed targets. In 1987, the persistence of inflationary pressure and the improvement of the level of economic activity generated expectations of devaluation. Market confidence deteriorated and a new exchange rate crisis erupted in November 1987. In October and November 1987 alone, the Bank of Mexico lost $800 million. As in other foreign exchange crises the Bank of Mexico let the peso float in the financial market to mitigate the loss of foreign exchange reserves.

Summarizing, there is some preliminary evidence that the two-tier exchange rate regime seemed to have contributed, at least over brief periods, to a reduction in capital flows. However, the extent of this effect is still unclear. It is also clear that there were only a few episodes in which the Bank of Mexico was willing to accept a large spread (and a truly floating financial rate) so as to reduce the severity of speculative capital outflows. But we do not know whether the modification of the dual exchange rate regime to one with a flexible rate in the financial market immediately prevented the acceleration of capital flight. To test these different propositions we need to estimate the stochastic process followed by capital outflows and examine whether it was affected by the adoption or modification of the two-tier system.

The Model

The stochastic process followed by capital flight is estimated using Hamilton's (1988) non-linear filter to evaluate endogenously whether there was a regime change in August 1982 (when the dual rates were introduced) or when the financial rate was allowed to float (for example, in July 1985 or in November 1987). The model estimated is described in equations (8) and (9).

(8) $cf_t = \alpha_0^i + \alpha_1 cf_{t-1} + \epsilon_t,$ $i = 0, 1$ $\epsilon_t \sim N(0, \sigma_i^2)$

(9) $\lambda_{ij} = \text{Prob}(R_t = j \mid R_{t-1} = 1),$ $i = 0, 1.$

In equation (8), cf_t is capital flight in period t, $\alpha_0^i + \alpha_1 cf_{t-1}$ is expected capital flight in period t if and only if regime i occurs ($R_t = i$) and ϵ_t is an independently and identically distributed shock. In equation (9), λ_{ij} is the (time invariant) probability of switching from regime i to regime j.

We refer to regime 0 as a 'low-capital flight regime' ($\alpha_0^0 < \alpha_0^1$) and to regime 1 as a 'high-capital flight regime'. The null hypothesis that the dual exchange rate regime can prevent capital flight will not be rejected if the period 1982:Q3–1987:Q4 can be identified as regime 0 or a low-capital flight regime. If instead only those episodes with a flexible financial rate prevented capital flight we should be able to identify those episodes with regime 0. Lee and Porter (1984) showed that the rule that minimizes the probability of misclassification is the one that assigns observation t to regime 1 if the estimated probability of being in regime 1 in period t (using all the information known in period t) is larger than 0.5. In our case this rule implies that the observation in period t belongs to a high-capital flight regime if Prob $(R_t = 1 \mid cf_t, \ldots, cf_1) \geq 0.5$.

Since there is no presumption that the dual exchange rate regime performs well, the estimation procedure is based on the assumption that the regime is not observed directly but it must be inferred based on the observation of current and past values of capital flows. The optimal forecast of this process, as analyzed in Hamilton (1988), can be thought of as the following sequences of steps. For any period t, we can use the transition probabilities in equation (9) to calculate a prior probability of being in regime 1 or 0 based on past information about capital flight:

(10) $\text{Prior}(R_t = 1) = (1 - \lambda_{10}) \text{Post}(R_{t-1} = 1) + \lambda_{01}[1 - \text{Post}(R_{t-1} = 1)],$

where $\text{Prior}(R_t = 1) = \text{Prob}(R_t = 1 \mid cf_{t-1}, \ldots, cf_1)$ and $\text{Post}(R_t = 1) = \text{Prob}(R_t = 1 \mid cf_t, \ldots, cf_1)$. We then calculate the conditional density function of cf_t:

$$(11) \quad f(cf_t \mid cf_{t-1}, \ldots, cf_1) = f(cf_t \mid R_t = 1)\text{Prior}(R_t = 1) \\ + f(cf_t \mid R_t = 0)[1 - \text{Prior}(R_t = 1)],$$

where equation (8) gives us $f(cf_t \mid R_t = 1) = ((1/2)\pi\sigma_i^2)^{-1/2} \exp(-1/2 (cf_t - \alpha_0^i - \alpha_i cf_{t-1})^2/\sigma_i^2)$. Finally, we update our predictions using Bayes' formula:

$$(12) \quad \text{Post}(R_t = 1) = \frac{f(cf_t \mid R_t = 1)\text{Prior}(R_t = 1)}{f(cf_t \mid cf_{t-1}, \ldots, cf_1)}.$$

We update repeatedly over the entire sample using equations (10)–(12).

The estimation procedure is simple enough. We start at $t = 1$ with the unconditional probability p_1, which we set equal to the limiting probability of being in state 1 of the Markov process in equation (9): $p_1 = \lambda_{01}/(\lambda_{01} + \lambda_{10})$. Using equations (10)–(12), we construct the sample log likelihood

$$(13) \quad \ln f(cf_t, cf_{t-1}, \ldots, cf_1) = \sum_{t=1}^{T} \ln f(cf_t \mid cf_{t-1}, \ldots, cf_1),$$

which can be maximized numerically with respect to the unknown parameters $\alpha_0^0, \alpha_0^1, \alpha_1, \sigma_0^2, \sigma_1^2, \lambda_{01}$, and λ_{10}.

Empirical Results

Estimates of capital flight, using Cuddington's (1986) measure (that is, the sum of errors and omissions plus other short-term capital movements), are reported in Table 3.7. We use quarterly data from the IMF's *Balance of Payments Statistics* for the period 1975:1 to 1987:4.

In Table 3.6 we report estimates of the model. Interestingly, the estimates imply substantial differences across regimes. In regime 0 α_0^0 is approximately \$271 million, while in regime 1 it increases to \$2.2 billion. Moreover, regime 1 is identified with large volatility ($\sigma_1^2 = 3.9$), in strong contrast to regime 0 ($\sigma_1^2 = 0.5$), which might be referred as a 'tranquil times' regime.

From the estimation we can also obtain the probability of being in regime 1 (the high-capital flight regime). These estimated probabilities are reported in Table 3.7. Using past and current information on capital outflows, the shift in regime in the fourth quarter of

TABLE 3.6 *Maximum likelihood estimates of the model in equations (8) and (9)*

Variable	Coefficient	t-statistic
α_0^0	0.271	1.970
α_0^1	2.145	2.949
α_1	0.161	1.014
λ_{10}	0.034	0.956
λ_{01}	0.115	1.179
σ_0^2	0.538	3.788
σ_1^2	3.883	1.801

1981 is fairly convincing: $Post(R_{1981:Q4} = 1) = 1.00$. It is in this period that capital outflows using Cuddington's measure increase to almost \$4 billion. This level of capital flows persists well into 1984. Using Lee and Porter's (1984) rule we can classify the 1981:Q4 to 1984:Q2 period as belonging to the high-capital flight regime.

TABLE 3.7 *Probabilities of being in regime 1 (high-capital flight regime)*

Date	Priors	Posteriors	Capital flight
1975:2	0.229	0.067	251.07
1975:3	0.091	0.024	398.52
1975:4	0.055	0.017	629.47
1976:1	0.048	0.011	123.66
1976:2	0.043	0.024	1 048.54
1976:3	0.054	0.030	1 192.15
1976:4	0.059	0.025	1 032.73
1977:1	0.055	0.013	22.86
1977:2	0.045	0.011	305.34
1977:3	0.044	0.010	159.41
1977:4	0.043	0.029	1 178.82
1978:1	0.059	0.014	91.10
1978:2	0.046	0.015	−708.16
1978:3	0.047	0.011	95.49
1978:4	0.044	0.035	1 248.16
1979:1	0.064	0.015	12.28
1979:2	0.047	0.012	−436.77
1979:3	0.044	0.011	231.37
1979:4	0.043	0.014	673.93

1980:1	0.046	0.012	526.21
1980:2	0.045	0.020	−876.50
1980:3	0.051	0.012	−428.11
1980:4	0.045	0.011	−431.86
1981:1	0.043	0.010	−264.88
1981:2	0.043	0.106	1 691.4
1981:3	0.124	0.232	1 925.46
1981:4	0.231	1.000	3 936.80
1982:1	0.885	0.852	−634.74
1982:2	0.760	1.000	3 952.59
1982:3	0.885	1.000	4 609.99
1982:4	0.885	1.000	5 527.86
1983:1	0.885	0.999	3 804.03
1983:2	0.885	0.631	688.12
1983:3	0.571	0.401	1 097.02
1983:4	0.376	0.996	3 203.71
1984:1	0.882	0.975	2 481.97
1984:2	0.864	0.603	681.50
1984:3	0.547	0.265	695.49
1984:4	0.260	0.124	951.72
1985:1	0.140	0.051	844.89
1985:2	0.078	0.020	−202.32
1985:3	0.051	0.144	1 760.96
1985:4	0.157	0.067	1 092.47
1986:1	0.091	0.048	−870.25
1986:2	0.075	0.049	975.51
1986:3	0.075	0.024	−507.62
1986:4	0.055	0.018	−811.41
1987:1	0.050	0.014	−677.37
1987:2	0.046	0.015	534.64
1987:3	0.047	0.013	−391.11
1987:4	0.045	0.331	2 106.50

Capital flight is defined using the Cuddington (1986) measure (the sum of errors and omissions plus other short-term capital movements).
SOURCE: International Monetary Fund, *Balance of Payments Statistics*, various issues.

These results suggest that the adoption of a two-tier exchange rate system could not, in general, prevent capital outflows. One possible reason for this failure, as emphasized earlier, is that during most of the 1982–7 period the financial exchange rate was heavily managed. It is important to note that restrictions on capital movements, such as those implemented in September 1982, were not successful either. Only when the daily crawl was abandoned for a more flexible management of the exchange rate, as in July 1985 or November 1987, were expectations of devaluation not reflected in massive capital outflows.

CONCLUSIONS

This chapter has examined whether the dual exchange rates system is useful in (1) limiting speculative capital flows and (2) insulating domestic prices from capital flows. Our results suggest that Mexico was not very successful in restricting capital flows. Only by the end of 1984 did capital outflows decrease to an average of $900 million. The inability of the Bank of Mexico to gain control over capital outflows was due to the fact that only very seldom did the Central Bank allow the financial exchange rate to float freely. Foreign exchange restrictions, such as those imposed in September 1982, were difficult to enforce and largely ineffective.

On the other hand, the dual exchange rate system did not completely buffer domestic inflation from capital outflows. The results on p. 121 suggest that the adoption of a dual exchange rate system may result in an increase of the steady-state rate of inflation. However, as we mentioned before, this conclusion may be misleading since the increase in the rate of inflation may be due to shocks extraneous to the exchange rate system, such as a more expansionary fiscal policy. To account for these other shocks to the market fundamentals, we estimated a multivariate structural VAR for both exchange rate regimes. The results from this estimation suggest that the increase in the steady-state rate of inflation was primarily explained by shocks to the price-setting rule and by monetary shocks. Together these two shocks can explain approximately 83 percent of the 36 month forecast variance of inflation. Even if the increase in the rate of inflation can be explained primarily by money and price-setting shocks, we cannot conclude that the dual exchange rate system severs completely the link between speculative capital shocks and domestic prices. For example, a 6 percent increase in the dual market innovation generates a 5 percent increase in prices after 36 months.

NOTES

1. I am grateful to Guillermo Calvo, Michael Dooley, Alain Ize, Miguel Kiguel, Leonardo Leiderman, Saul Lizondo, Nancy Marion, Steve O'Connell, Carmen Reinhart, Patricio Rojas, Aaron Tornell, and seminar participants at the International Monetary Fund, New York University and the World Bank for helpful discussions and comments on an earlier version.
2. During the early part of this period, international competitiveness was assisted by the adoption of a 'controlled' floating exchange rate system.

3. See Buffie (1989) for a detailed analysis of the effect of oil discoveries on macroeconomic policy after 1978.
4. See Ize and Ortiz (1989) for an explanation of the simultaneity of private capital flight and public foreign borrowing using the 1981–2 Mexican experience as illustration.
5. The Akaike (1973) and the Schwarz (1978) criteria involve choosing the parameterization with the minimum residual sum of squares after imposing different penalties for the number of estimated parameters.
6. Although we want to examine the effect of speculative capital movements on prices, we could not obtain monthly series on this variable. Since capital outflows are translated into a depreciation of the financial rate, we decided to introduce the exchange rate premium as another variable in the system. In this case capital outflows are identified with increases in the premium.
7. The commercial exchange rate, prices, and money supply series are taken from the *International Financial Statistics*, IMF (Lines ae, 64, and 34, respectively). Output is proxied using the index of industrial production from *Economic Indicators*, Bank of Mexico. The domestic interest rate is the commercial banking system lending rate from Arias and Guerrero (1988). The dual market premium is the ratio of the black market over the commercial market exchange rate. The black market rate series is taken from the *World Currency Yearbook*. Finally, the world interest rate is the 30 day return on US Treasury Bills and the price of oil is the Saudi Arabia price; both were obtained from the Data Bank of the Board of Governors of the Federal Reserve System.
8. New information about investors' preferences or restrictions on capital flows, as summarized in the shocks to the dual market, μ_d, is assumed not to be correlated with financial innovations in the money market, μ_i. This assumption does not say that fluctuations in interest rates are not affected by speculative shocks to the capital account. Note that in equation (5) shocks to the dual market affect the dual market premium, which in turn affects the pricing rule and the domestic interest rate. Admittedly, we could have imposed a direct effect of μ_d on the domestic interest rate. In this case, the money market equilibrium condition would have been equal to $a_{42}\varepsilon_e + a_{43}\varepsilon_p + \varepsilon_i + a_{45}\varepsilon_m = \mu_i + \alpha\mu_d$.
9. To ensure stationarity and take seasonality into account, we have regressed each variable on a constant and 11 seasonal dummies. The variables in the VAR are the residuals from these first step regressions.
10. Through this method the coefficients in equation (5) are obtained by equating population moments implied by the theory with the sample moments of ε,

$$\hat{\Omega} = A^{-1}\left[\sum_t (\boldsymbol{\varepsilon}_t \boldsymbol{\varepsilon}_t')/T\right](A^{-1})'.$$

The number of estimated parameters must not exceed the number of distinct covariances in $\varepsilon\varepsilon'$ which is equal to $n(n+1)/2$ where n is the number of elements in the vector ε. Thus, for the unified exchange rate regime we will be able to identify 15 parameters (5 for the diagonal elements of Ω and 10 for the non-zero elements of A) while for the dual exchange rate system we will be able to identify 21 parameters (6 for the diagonal elements of Ω and 15 for the non-zero elements of A).

REFERENCES

Akaike, H. (1973) 'Information Theory and the Extension of the Maximum Likelihood Principle', in B. N. Petrov and F. Csaki (eds), *2nd International Symposium on Information Theory* (Budapest: Akademiai Klado), pp. 267–81.

Arias, L. and V. Guerrero (1988) 'Un Estudio Econometrico de la Inflacion en Mexico de 1970 a 1987', mimeo (Mexico City).

Bernanke, Ben, S. (1986) 'Alternative Explanations of the Money–Income Correlation', in Karl Brunner and Allan Meltzer (eds), *Carnegie-Rochester Conference Series on Public Policy* 25, (Amsterdam: North-Holland), pp. 49–99.

Blanchard, Olivier (1989) 'A Traditional Interpretation of Macroeconomic Fluctuations', *American Economic Review*, vol. 79, pp. 1146–64.

Buffie, Edward (1989) 'Economic Policy and Foreign Debt in Mexico', in Jeffrey Sachs (ed.), *Developing Country Debt and Economic Performance* (Chicago: University of Chicago Press for the National Bureau of Economic Research), pp. 393–551.

Calvo, Guillermo, A. and Graciela Kaminsky (1991) 'Debt Relief and Debt Rescheduling: the Optimal Contract Approach', *Journal of Development Economics*, vol. 36, pp. 5–36.

Campbell, John and N. Gregory Mankiw (1987) 'Are Output Fluctuations Transitory', *Quarterly Journal of Economics*, vol. 102, pp. 857–80.

Cuddington, John T. (1986) 'Capital Flight: Estimates, Issues, and Explanations', *Princeton Studies in International Finance* No. 58 (Princeton, NJ: International Finance Section, Department of Economics, Princeton University).

Gulati, S. (1987) 'A Note on Trade Misinvoicing', in Donald Lessard and John Williamson (eds), *Capital Flight and Third World Debt* (Washington, DC: Institute for International Economics), pp. 68–78.

Hamilton, John (1988) 'Rational-expectations Econometric Analysis of Changes in Regime: an Investigation of the Term Structure of Interest Rates', *Journal of Economic Dynamics and Control*, vol. 12, pp. 385–423.

International Monetary Fund (various years), *Balance of Payments Statistics* (Washington, DC: International Monetary Fund).

International Monetary Fund (various years), *International Financial Statistics* (Washington, DC: International Monetary Fund).

Ize, Alain and Guillermo Ortiz (1989) 'Fiscal Rigidities, Public Debt, and Capital Flight', in Mario Blejer and Ke-young Chu (eds), *Fiscal Policy, Stabilization and Growth in Developing Countries* (Washington, DC: IMF), pp. 50–71.

Lee, L. and Porter, R. (1984) 'Switching Regression Models with Imperfect Sample Separation Information – with an Application on Cartel Stability' *Econometrica*, vol. 52, pp. 391–418.

Pitt, Mark (1981) 'Smuggling and Price Disparity', *Journal of International Economics*, vol. 11, pp. 447–58.

Schwarz, G. (1978) 'Estimating the Dimension of a Model', *Annals of Statistics*, vol. 6, pp. 461–4.

4 Adoption, Management, and Abandonment of Multiple Exchange Rate Regimes with Import Control: the Case of Venezuela

Ricardo Hausmann[1]

F13
F32
F33
F31
019

INTRODUCTION

In February 1983 Venezuela adopted a multiple exchange rate regime as part of a package designed to deal with a balance of payments crisis. The idea was to ease the process of adjustment to a lower level of oil income and financial flows, so as to avoid more drastic measures. Initially, the program generated a rapid improvement in the current account while maintaining relatively low inflation, but it produced a surprisingly high and growing exchange premium. On two occasions, in February 1984 and in December 1986, the government was forced to devalue the official rate, not because of insufficient reserves, but due to the unsustainable level of the exploding premium. In February 1989, after 6 years of experimentation – in which the parallel exchange rate depreciated by a factor of 10 – and in the midst of a new balance of payments crisis, the government decided to abandon the regime and adopt a unified floating arrangement. This change was followed by a 9 percent drop in GDP and by a 60 percent jump in the price level.

Multiple exchange rate systems are usually adopted by countries as part of policy packages designed to improve external imbalances. They are often designed to stop or slow down capital outflows by forcing these transactions to take place in a parallel market. Although multiple rates produce obvious inefficiencies in resource allocation, the failure of these regimes has most often been attributed to the inability of governments to control the flow of foreign exchange and trade, given the incentives to overinvoice imports and to underinvoice or smuggle exports. It is argued that these leakages tend to undermine the control of the capital account while the system is no substitute for official devaluations and contractionary fiscal and monetary policies as mechanisms to improve the current account. Given this, it is tempting to use the exchange control system to restrict the volume of imports directly and thus take control of the trade balance.

In this respect, the Venezuelan experience provides important lessons about the perils of multiple rate regimes, even when control of capital flows and smuggling is adequate.[2] It highlights the implications of using administrative allocations of foreign exchange for imports to seize control of international reserve levels. Introducing import controls in the standard descriptive framework leads to a model with a globally unstable region.[3] Identifying the path the economy will follow requires additional assumptions as to how the government will alter the policy regime to make it consistent. If agents anticipate that eventual adjustment will rely mainly on devaluations without sufficient fiscal correction then the system falls into a cyclic *leaping peg* regime, with large and sporadic official rate devaluations accompanied by a smooth depreciation of the parallel rate.

One result of the framework is that, contrary to the predictions of the Kiguel and Lizondo (1990) model, adoption of the dual exchange system can lead to very significant improvements in the current account but at the cost of a high and exploding premium, which is itself produced by a money overhang problem endogenous to the system. Another result is that official rate devaluations affect the economy mainly through their effect on the fiscal accounts and the flow supply of money and not through the balance of payments or the price level. If the fundamental policies are viable, devaluation may allow the economy to reach an otherwise unattainable equilibrium. If the fundamentals are not in place, a devaluation will temporarily reduce the premium and the real stock of money, but the economy will return to an explosive path. These disparate properties appear to capture important differences between the devaluations of 1984 and 1986 in Venezuela.

An anticipated abandonment of the regime from a situation of import controls will be preceded by a period in which both the dollar value of the stock of money calculated at the official rate and the exchange premium will be rising. Once abandonment takes place, financial wealth and domestic spending will collapse, the current account will improve, and there will be private capital outflows.

The main policy lesson is that major short-term balance of payments improvements can be obtained through the use of import rationing and dual rates. This can allow the government to get by with a slower or otherwise insufficient adjustment of the fundamentals. However, these improvements come at the cost of a major monetary disequilibrium expressed in a large and exploding premium which will eventually force the government to act. In the end, the postponement of adjustment will come at a significant cost as the 1989 Venezuelan experience suggests. In addition, it suggests that when governments rely on import controls to protect the level of international reserves, there is less pressure to use contractionary monetary policy and high interest rates, thus aggravating the control of the premium and the costs of abandonment.

The chapter consists of four sections. The second section introduces import controls into the standard descriptive model of multiple exchange rate systems and analyzes the dynamics of adoption and devaluation. The third section narrates and interprets the Venezuelan experience with adoption in 1983, devaluations in 1984 and 1986, and abandonment in 1989. The final section derives the main macroeconomic and policy lessons and indicates further research issues.

INTRODUCING IMPORT CONTROLS IN THE STANDARD FRAMEWORK

In this section we will develop a descriptive model with import controls for an oil-exporting economy. We start by presenting the standard model of dual exchange rates, following the Kiguel and Lizondo (1990) model closely but introducing the effects of the oil industry on the fiscal, external, and monetary accounts. We use the resulting model as a benchmark with which to compare the impact of binding import controls. We then study a model that encompasses both regimes.

The Standard Model for an Oil-exporting Country

Assume three sectors of production with exogenously given outputs. The oil sector is solely owned by the government and is its only source of revenue. We label its output as z. The non-oil economy is composed of two sectors: a (non-oil) tradeable sector with output x_T and a non-tradeable sector with output x_N. For simplicity, z is measured in units of (non-oil) tradeables since we are not interested in distinguishing between changes in real oil income caused by variations in output and those caused by changes in the terms of trade.

Tradeables are freely exchanged, making their price equal to world prices P^* calculated at the official exchange rate E. We assume there is no world inflation and normalize international prices to unity. Hence, $P_T = P^*E = E$. Wealth a is composed of domestic money M and foreign assets k. Its real value measured in units of tradeables is given by

$$(1) \qquad a = \frac{M}{E} + \frac{Fk}{E} = m + \pi k,$$

where F is the floating parallel rate and $\pi = F/E$ is (one plus) the exchange premium.

Households spend out of wealth and have Cobb–Douglas utility functions where α is the share of tradeables in consumption and β is the propensity to spend. Hence, demand for tradeables c_T and non-tradeables c_N is given by

$$(2) \qquad c_T = \alpha\beta(m + \pi k)$$

$$(3) \qquad c_N = (1 - \alpha)\beta q(m + \pi k),$$

where $q = P_T/P_N$ is the real exchange rate.

Demand for non-tradeables must equal domestic supply:

$$(4) \qquad x_N = c_N + g_N,$$

where g is public consumption of non-tradeables. This determines the real exchange rate:

$$(5) \qquad q = \frac{x_N - g_N}{(1 - \alpha)\beta(m + \pi k)}.$$

Since imports are demand determined at the official exchange rate, the trade balance, tb, is given by

$$(6) \qquad tb = x_T + z - c_T - g_T.$$

Oil is the government's only source of revenue. Hence, the fiscal deficit in units of tradeables, fd, is equal to

$$(7) \qquad fd = g_T + \left(\frac{g_N}{q}\right) - z.$$

Notice that a real depreciation reduces the fiscal deficit by increasing the purchasing power of oil revenue in terms of non-tradeables. This is a consequence of the fact that the public sector has a deficit in its exchange with the non-tradeable sector. Hence, changes in the real exchange rate act as a shift in the government's terms of trade with the rest of the economy. As we shall see in the third section, this phenomenon is of great macroeconomic significance for Venezuela. It is also crucial in determining the dynamics of the model.

Money is passively supplied by the Central Bank and is equal to the level of reserves plus the domestic credit to the government. We assume that the exchange regime restricts private capital flows completely, so that the change in reserves is determined solely by the trade balance. Real domestic credit varies with the fiscal deficit. Hence, assuming that the official exchange rate is fixed, the change in the real domestic money supply is given by

$$\dot{m} = tb + fd = x_T - c_T + \left(\frac{g_N}{q}\right).$$

Substituting for c_T and q and rearranging terms, we obtain

$$(8) \qquad \dot{m} = x_T - \beta(m + \pi k)\left[\frac{\alpha x_N - b_N}{x_n - g_n}\right].$$

Setting this equation to zero defines the $\dot{m} = 0$ schedule in the π versus m space. Since there is a unique level of wealth consistent with stationary real money balances, this schedule has a negative slope equal to $-1/k$ (see Figure 4.1). Above (below) the line, wealth and spending are too large (small), causing a trade deficit (surplus) and a loss (rise) in reserves, thus generating a decline (increase) in the money supply. Stability requires that $g_N < \alpha x_N$, so that $\dot{m}$ depends negatively on $m + \pi k$.

We can also derive an expression for the schedule along which reserves are constant. This can be obtained by setting the trade balance tb to zero (equation (6)) and substituting equation (2):

$$(9) \qquad \dot{r} = z + x_T - g_T - \alpha\beta(m + \pi k) = 0.$$

Again there is a unique level of wealth consistent with balanced trade, so the $\dot{r} = 0$ schedule is parallel to the $\dot{m} = 0$ schedule and below (above) it by a distance which is proportional to the fiscal deficit (surplus) (see Figure 4.1). At any point on the $\dot{m} = 0$ schedule, the loss of reserves equals the fiscal deficit, leaving the money supply

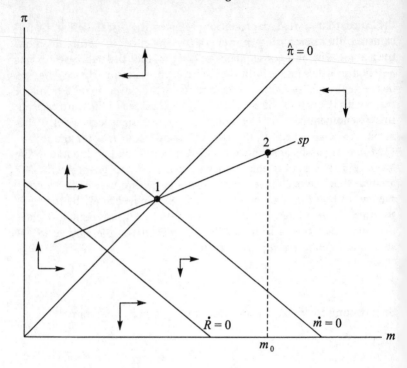

FIGURE 4.1   *The standard model*

NOTES: Adjustment from point 2 to point 1 occurs along the saddle path *sp*.

SOURCE: Country case study.

constant. This implies that if there is a fiscal deficit, points on the $\dot{m} = 0$ schedule will not be sustainable.

It will be useful to define the level of private imports $c_T - x_T$ along the $\dot{m} = 0$ schedule, which we label i^*. Using equations (2) and (8) we find this to equal[4]

$$(10) \qquad\qquad i^* = \frac{x_T g_N (1 - \alpha)}{\alpha x_N - g_N} \quad .$$

The level of imports consistent with $\dot{m} = 0$ is therefore an increasing function of government spending on non-tradeables, g_N. Intuitively, a rise in g_N worsens the fiscal deficit, causing money balances to grow unless the trade balance worsens by an equal amount.

The model is closed by the portfolio behavior of households. Agents choose a portfolio structure depending on the expected depreciation of the parallel rate, F. Given that the official rate is fixed, this is just the same as the rate of change of the premium, $\hat{\pi}$, where the symbol '‸' over a variable indicates its percentage rate of change. Thus,

$$\left(\frac{Fk}{m}\right) = \left(\pi\frac{k}{m}\right) = g(\hat{\pi})$$

or, alternatively,

(11) $$\hat{\pi} = h\left(\frac{\pi k}{m}\right),$$

where $h = g^{-1}$ and $h' > 0$. The schedule $\hat{\pi} = 0$ is a positively sloped ray: since k is fixed, a rise in m requires an increase in π in order to maintain a constant portfolio structure.

Equations (8) and (11) describe a system of differential equations, with state variables m and π. Equilibrium is achieved when both variables remain stationary, that is when $\dot{m} = \hat{\pi} = 0$; this occurs at point 1 in Figure 4.1. The model exhibits saddle path stability with an upward sloping manifold, sp. Along this path, wealth changes monotonically and with it the real exchange rate q (equation (5)) and the fiscal deficit (equation (7)). Since π is free to jump, a perfect foresight path starting from an initial level of real balances m_0 involves an immediate vertical jump (or drop) onto the saddle path (at point 2), followed by a gradual adjustment along that path to the equilibrium point.

Notice that the equilibrium point does not depend on either z or g_T. A fall in the first variable or a rise in the second will generate a balance of payments deficit compensated by a fiscal deficit, leaving a constant money supply. Notice also that the equilibrium point does not depend on the official exchange rate E, so that devaluations have only transitory effects. A devaluation reduces m and π on impact, lowering wealth and improving both the trade balance and the fiscal accounts. But the economy then returns to the original equilibrium through the stable manifold.

However, the equilibrium point is affected by g_N, since an increase in this variable appreciates the real exchange rate and deteriorates the fiscal deficit, without having a direct impact on the trade balance. The $\dot{m} = 0$ schedule shifts up, producing a new equilibrium with higher wealth and imports and a faster fall in reserves to compensate for the increased deficit. Under the fixed exchange rate, changes in g_N are in fact the only way of generating a long-term equilibrium with constant international reserves.

Introducing Import Controls

The previous subsection assumed that imports at the official rate were demand determined. Moreover, it established that if there is a fiscal deficit, there will be a loss of reserves at the equilibrium point. In fact, Kiguel and Lizondo (1990) show that an unanticipated adoption of the dual exchange rate system will not improve the current account which will actually deteriorate.

However, dual rates are usually adopted in the context of a balance of payments crisis when it is not possible to allow reserves to fall any further. Usually, one reason for adopting exchange controls is the presumption that they will allow adjustment to take place with a smaller correction in fiscal and exchange rate policies than would otherwise be required. In fact, if the change in fundamentals had been sufficient, it is unlikely that capital outflows would take place, thus negating the usefulness of capital controls. Hence, with sufficient adjustment, the demand for imports is likely to exceed the level that makes the balance of payments viable, prompting the government to adopt quantitative restrictions. In particular, in the Venezuelan case the exchange control system was supposed to allot an import 'budget' on a case by case basis, designed to target a given level of reserves.

In this subsection we will develop a model which assumes that the allotted foreign exchange budget is insufficient to satisfy import demand. A model that encompasses the two regimes is presented in the following subsection.

A binding import constraint will make the trade balance exogenous. We will assume, for simplicity, that the public sector imports g_T directly[5] and specifies a fixed quota i on imports by the private sector. The trade balance is then

$$(12) \qquad tb = z - g_T - i,$$

which can be zero if i is set equal to the public sector's balance of payments surplus $z - g_T$. The private demand for tradeables c_T must therefore be equal to available resources. The domestic price of tradeables P_T will adjust to clear the tradeable market at a level higher than the border price E. Otherwise, the import constraint will not bind. It is convenient to define $\rho = P_T/E$ as the ratio of the domestic to the border price of tradeables. Consumption demands are then given by

$$(13) \qquad c_T = \alpha\beta(m + \pi k)/\rho$$

(14) $$c_N = (1 - \alpha)\beta q(m + \pi k)/\rho,$$

and market clearing for tradeables and non-tradeables determines q and ρ simultaneously:

(15) $$q = \frac{\alpha}{1 - \alpha}\left(\frac{x_N - g_N}{x_T + i}\right)$$

(16) $$\rho = \alpha\beta\left[\frac{m + \pi k}{x_T + i}\right].$$

Notice that q does not depend on private wealth but only on the ratio of the availability of non-tradeables $(x_N - g_N)$ to that of tradeables $(x_T + i)$. This implies that, in contrast with the previous model, q will not be changing in the space π versus m. Notice also that ρ depends only on the ratio of wealth calculated at the official rate $(m + \pi k)$ to the availability of tradeables. In this sense, ρ can be interpreted as the factor by which wealth must be reduced so that demand for tradeables matches available resources.

Setting $\rho = 1$ in equation (16) allows us to study the frontier between the two regimes. Figure 4.2(a) and (b) shows this line in the space π versus m. To the left of the curve, the standard model is valid since import demand is smaller than the allotted quota i. The present model explains the behavior to the right of the line, where the trade balance is exogenous and wealth in units of tradeables a is constant and equal to $a = (m + \pi k)/\rho = (\alpha\beta)^{-1}(x_T + i)$. Given the new equation for the trade balance (equation (12)) and the definition of the fiscal deficit, $\dot{m}_R$ can be written as

(17) $$\dot{m}_R = (P_N/P_T)(P_T/E)g_N - i = (\rho/q)g_N - i$$
$$= \left(\frac{(1 - \alpha)\beta g_N}{x_N - g_N}\right)(m + \pi k) - i,$$

where the subscript 'R' indicates that this equation is valid only when the import quota i is a binding restriction.

Equation (17) for $\dot{m}_R$ states that there is a unique level of financial wealth at which real money balances (measured in foreign exchange at the official exchange rate) are constant. The equation has an unstable root, however: a rise in m increases the domestic price level relative to the official exchange rate, worsening the fiscal deficit and, since there is no offsetting deterioration of the trade balance, money balances rise further. Import rationing has removed the principal stabilizing mechanism in the fixed exchange rate regime, namely the link between the balance of payments and the money supply. The system also lacks the stability of a flexible exchange rate regime, because any constant rate of domestic inflation – which would help to finance the fiscal deficit through the inflation tax – implies an ever-increasing parallel premium. The result is that the steady state in (m, p) space is globally unstable (recall that the portfolio balance equation, which is unchanged, already has an unstable root).[6] Since m cannot jump instantaneously, the import-rationing system does not return to the stationary equilibrium if it does not start there.[7]

In what follows, we 'close' the model by recognizing three possibilities: first, an import quota that is initially binding may become non-binding at some point, so that a smooth transition takes place from the explosive, import-constrained dynamics to the well-behaved dynamics we studied in Figure 4.1. Second, an immediate (and unanticipated) policy change can move us from an unstable situation to one that eventually converges on the unconstrained equilibrium. Finally, an anticipated future policy change may allow the economy to evolve on an explosive path for the period preceding the policy change and then to converge, once policies are changed to sustainable levels, to the equilibrium appropriate to the new policy settings. To make these points we unify the two models into a single 'encompassing' model whose local behavior depends on whether the import quota binds.

The Encompassing Model

It is convenient to analyze the relative position of the three schedules $\dot{m} = 0, \dot{m}_R = 0$, and $\rho = 1$. Solving equations (8), (12) and (16) we obtain

$$(18) \qquad \pi_u = -\frac{m}{k} + \frac{x_T}{\beta k} \left(\frac{x_N - g_N}{\alpha x_N - g_N} \right)$$

$$(19) \qquad \pi_R = -\frac{m}{k} + \frac{i}{k} \left(\frac{x_N - g_N}{(1 - \alpha)\beta g_N} \right)$$

$$(20) \qquad \pi_\rho = -\frac{m}{k} + \frac{x_T + i}{\alpha \beta k},$$

where the subscripts U and R refer to the unrestricted (standard) and import-restricted models, respectively and ρ refers to the boundary between the two regimes.

As can be seen by inspection, all functions are parallel straight lines with slope $-1/k$. It can further be established that the relative position of the three curves depends solely on whether the import quota i fixed by the government is greater or less than the level of imports i^* demanded along the $\dot{r} = 0$ schedule in the unrestricted model – or equivalently, if i is chosen to prevent international reserves from changing, whether or not there is a balance of payments deficit along $\dot{m} = 0$. The two possible configurations of the encompassing model are presented in Figure 4.2(a) and (b).

Case a: $i > i^*$

Suppose that $i > i^*$, so that the quota that would produce constant reserves (if it were binding) is above the level of imports that would be demanded in an unconstrained monetary equilibrium. In this case, the fiscal fundamentals are 'consistent' with a fixed exchange rate in the sense that there is actually a fiscal surplus – giving rise to an equal balance of payments surplus – along the $\dot{m} = 0$ schedule. The $\dot{m} = 0$ schedule lies below the $\dot{m}_R = 0$ schedule, with the $\rho = 1$ schedule between the two. Above the $\rho = 1$ schedule, the quota is binding and the dynamics for m lead away from the $\dot{m}_R = 0$ schedule. Below $\rho = 1$, the quota is not binding and the dynamics for m lead towards the $\dot{m} = 0$ schedule.

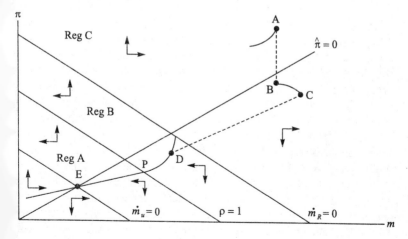

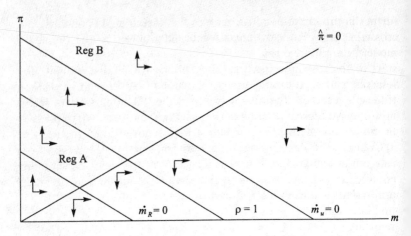

FIGURE 4.2 (a) *The encompassing model with $i > i^*$. (b) The encompassing model with $i < i^*$*

SOURCE: Country case study.

The actual path followed by the premium and money balances now depends on the initial level of real balances, m_0. If m_0 is small enough that a vertical jump can place the economy on the saddle path in region A, this jump determines the initial premium and the adjustment takes place along the saddle path. If m_0 is larger than this, but small enough that a jump can place the economy at a point like D on an unstable manifold that cuts through the B region and intersects the $\rho = 1$ schedule precisely where the saddle path in the A region intersects it, then the initial premium is determined by this vertical jump. Subsequent adjustment takes place first along the unstable path and then, once the $\rho = 1$ schedule is reached, along the saddle path. Since the entire path is anticipated, perfect foresight rules out a jump in the premium at the time the quota becomes non-binding. This requirement selects the unique manifold in the constrained region that is consistent with smooth convergence to the unconstrained equilibrium.

It is important to notice that the behavior of the economy through the manifold of region B is quite different from that along the saddle path of region A. In the former, the level of imports, real wealth (in units of tradeables), and the real exchange rate are constant. The value of financial assets calculated at the official exchange rate will be falling, since the fiscal surplus exceeds the balance of payments surplus. This will require a fall in ρ to keep wealth constant. Such a decline will further improve the fiscal accounts and reduce m. Once the border is crossed at point P, the dynamics will be determined by the unrestricted model: the import quota will no longer bind, the trade balance will start to improve, the fiscal surplus will exceed the accumulation of reserves, and m will keep falling. To maintain equilibrium in the non-tradeable market, the real exchange rate will depreciate, further improving the fiscal accounts. The system will converge to the equilibrium point E defined by the unrestricted model.

Complications emerge when the initial level of m is large enough to rule out a smooth adjustment to E, since in this case the short-term equilibrium is indeterminate in the absence of a policy change. One approach is to adjust the fundamentals further (though they are already 'in place' in the sense that a locally viable steady state exists at E) by reducing g_N. This reduces the fiscal deficit and shifts both the $\dot{m} = 0$ and $\dot{m}_R = 0$ schedules to the right, so that the initial level of money balances becomes consistent with adjustment to the new unconstrained equilibrium. A second way of restoring consistency is through a nominal devaluation. A devaluation reduces m on impact and a sufficient devaluation can clearly move the economy into the region where a smooth adjustment to E takes place. We will see below that devaluation alone is inadequate to restore adjustment to equilibrium when $i < i^*$.

Anticipated changes in fiscal policy or the nominal exchange rate can also work. Figure 4.2(a) shows the evolution of the economy when the private sector correctly anticipates that the authorities will devalue by a known amount at some known future date. Starting at a point like A in region C, the anticipation of a future devaluation of known date and magnitude causes an immediate jump to point B on an unstable manifold. The devaluation is implemented at point C and moves the economy (along a ray from the origin) to point D, from which adjustment takes place to the equilibrium at E.

It is worth noting that in regions B and C, $\rho < \pi$, so that the domestic price of tradeables is below the parallel exchange rate. This can be seen from the fact that under the $\rho = 1$ schedule, ρ equals unity and $\pi > 1$. Above the $\rho = 1$ schedule, π and ρ increase at the same rate, so that ρ never catches π. Import smuggling through the parallel market is therefore unprofitable.

Case b: $i < i^*$

Figure 4.2(b) looks at the case in which the fundamentals are *not* in place, in the sense that the unrestricted equilibrium would imply a permanent loss of reserves. In this case, $i < i^*$: the import quota that is required to protect reserves is below what would be demanded in an unconstrained equilibrium. Since the unconstrained steady state is unreachable under the quota restriction, the $\rho = 1$ schedule is now below the $\dot{m} = 0$ schedule. The $\dot{m}_R = 0$ schedule, in contrast, now lies in the non-binding region, below the $\rho = 1$ schedule; this follows from the fact that while the trade balance is zero along $\rho = 1$ (since the quota is just binding), the fiscal deficit is positive (since money balances would be rising in the absence of a quota). The constrained steady state is therefore also unreachable. Figure 4.2(b) shows the dynamics. Above $\rho = 1$, the quota is binding and the dynamics of m are governed by the $\dot{m}_R = 0$ schedule; below $\rho = 1$, the quota is non-binding and the dynamics are governed by the $\dot{m} = 0$ schedule. The trade surplus therefore systematically exceeds the fiscal deficit measured at the official exchange rate in the quota regime, so that nominal money balances – and therefore real balances, when measured at the official exchange rate – inevitably rise, whatever their current value.

The absence of an equilibrium point means that eventually an adjustment policy will have to be adopted. Notice that a devaluation in and of itself will not be sufficient to reach equilibrium since such a point does not exist. Hence, other changes would need to take place. What is required is adjustment of the fiscal fundamentals, in the form of a reduction in g_N or an increase in i. For the latter policy to work without further losses of reserves, the government's balance of payments must be improved through a reduction in g_T that is sufficient to raise i above i^*. We are then back to Figure 4.2(a), where adjustment can take place to point E (with an initial devaluation if required).

THE MULTIPLE EXCHANGE RATE SYSTEM IN VENEZUELA (1983–9)

This section narrates the adoption, management, and abandonment of the multiple exchange rate system that was in effect in Venezuela from February 1983 to February 1989 and interprets its outcome. We will deal with the reasons that prompted the authorities to adopt the system, the interaction between results and further changes to the system, and the causes and consequences of abandonment. The results of policies in each period are analyzed through the use of the models presented in the previous section. A summary of the exchange regime, of policies, and of macroeconomic results is presented in Table 4.1.

Some Background

Venezuela, a major oil exporter, traditionally had a policy regime based on four major principles: a fixed and unified exchange rate, fixed and rather rigid interest rates, fiscal discipline, and a protectionist trade policy.[8] This regime appeared to guarantee high growth and a very low inflation rate (1.9 percent for the period 1950–70). Fiscal balance implied that the exchange rate was viable and interest rates were fixed above world levels, thus securing demand for the instruments offered by the rapidly expanding financial system.

When the first oil shock occurred in 1973, policy discussions dealt almost exclusively with the issue of what to do with the additional fiscal resources. The newly elected government of Carlos Andrés Pérez[9] initially decided to sterilize the windfall revenue abroad 'until profitable investments appeared locally'. However as the 5 year presidency progressed, expenditures, mainly on public sector companies, rose very quickly and oil revenues declined so that fiscal balance was reached in 1976 and a deficit of 14 percent of GDP developed by 1978. Growth initially accelerated to over 10 percent in 1975 and then began to fall reaching 3.5 percent in 1978, as shortages of labor and infrastructure became dominant.[10]

By early 1979, the newly elected government faced a rapidly falling reserve level, an exploding foreign debt, and repressed inflation due to severe overheating. It did not foresee the second oil shock which occurred just a few months later. Hence, it adopted a policy of fiscal cutbacks, mainly on imported goods, and it freed most prices.[11] The economy went into a recession led by a contraction in the construction sector and by a fall in import-competing output, the latter resulting from the rise in real wages and rapidly appreciating real exchange rate associated with the gradual return of the overheated economy to its natural rate of unemployment. Moreover, political difficulties in adjusting the controlled local interest rates to the jump in international rates led to some capital outflows.

TABLE 4.1 *Summary of events, policies, and results*

Event/variable	Adoption 1983	Devaluation 1984	Devaluation 1986	Abandonment 1989
Context	Negative external shock. Large current account and fiscal deficits (1982). Inventory accumulation, capital flight	Stable but lower oil revenue. Large balance of payments surplus but with huge premium. Repressed inflation, severe price controls, lowered but still important fiscal deficit. Four exchange rates: 4.3, 6.00, 9.90 and free	Expansionary fiscal policy in the context of a major decline in oil revenues. Rising premium. Rapidly growing economy with an external real appreciation but an internal real depreciation (that is, rising). Balance of payments deficit but with no expansion in imports in spite of larger demand	Critical level of reserves, large external and fiscal deficits, repressed inflation and financial repression. Stable oil revenues
Exchange rate policy	Strategy: to go from 4.30 to 6.00 in 3 years, as in 1960. Implementation: exchange control office established to give prior approval to each import permit. One-third of imports sent to 6.0. Parallel rate initially free through auctions. However, as rate exceeded the ceiling of 10 Bs. per $, the Central Bank of Venezuela (BCV) decided to create a special market where it alloted $30 million a week to banks at the rate of 9.90. Since there was excess demand in this market, another exchange market developed and was allowed to operate under a floating arrangement. Import allocations by company decided on a historical basis. Non-traditional exports allowed at parallel rate	Strategy: increase credibility. End of the 9.90 rate. New official rate at 7.50. A transitory program of $2 billion in imports left at 4.30 to be completely eliminated by December 85. Private sector debt recognized at 4.30	Devaluation of the official exchange rate to 14.50. A list of priority imports left at 7.50. Some floating rate transactions sent to 14.5, especially non-traditional exports and Margarita freeport. Increasing limitations on parallel rate market participants. Imports must be financed for 180 days. This produces 'forced' capital inflows which will reach US$ 6 billion by 1988. Imports in the pipeline recognized at old exchange rate	Abandonment of the exchange control mechanism. Unified float

Commercial policy	Long list of import prohibitions and of imports reserved to government, but which can be delegated	System maintained. Given other changes, official rate import quota had less bite	Import allocations negotiated through the Chambers of Commerce, with budgets decided by sector	Radical trade liberalization. Import prohibitions eliminated. Import permit requirements reduced except for some agricultural products. Tariffs made more uniform and lowered
Monetary policy	Interest rates float freely. Money supply mainly endogenous. BOP surplus and fiscal deficit produce excess supply of money. Only monetary instrument is rediscounts, which fall	BCV takes control of interest rates and lowers them. Fiscal surplus reduces monetary growth	Interest rate controls are binding. Central Bank tries to sterilize excess liquidity, but must do so at rates that exceed maximum lending rate. A parallel interest rate develops	Interest rates are allowed to move within wide bands. Additional instruments created. After some time interest rates are allowed to float freely
Fiscal policy	Mainly restrictive but insufficient to reduce the deficit completely. Important fiscal benefits of adoption, but large deficit remains (4.6 percent)	Government spending reduced. Large fiscal surplus mainly because of the revenue increasing effects of devaluation	Fiscal spending expands, financed through money creation. Fiscal benefits of devaluation dampened by recognition of imports in pipeline at old exchange rate	Cut in capital spending and subsidies. Large fiscal benefit of devaluation. Deficit reduced from 11.6 to 2.7 percent of non-oil GDP
Price policy	Tight price controls. Agricultural prices frozen. Companies must ask for approval before raising prices	Big adjustment in controlled prices: meat, sugar, cereals, milk, and gasoline. After November 1984, price controls relaxed	Price controls tighten up again	Price controls abandoned
Macro-economic results	Growth: −3 percent. Very little inflation. Huge BOP surplus with fiscal deficit. Huge money supply growth. Falling interest rates. Exploding premium	Growth:−1.2 percent in 84 and 3.4 percent in 1985. Inflation: surprisingly low. Wage settlements low. Huge BOP and fiscal surplus. Low money growth. Stable and lower premium	Growth remains strong. Inflation accelerates. Balance of payments and fiscal deficits large, leaving moderate monetary expansion. Real interest rates become strongly negative	Collapse in GDP. Big jump in price level. Large surplus in balance of payments. Interest rates become positive after the jump

Adoption of the Multiple Exchange Rate System

The Collapse of the Fixed Exchange Rate System

By the end of 1980, the government had already gone through 2 years of spending cutbacks (1979–80) which had produced a prolonged recession. Furthermore, it assumed, as in fact most analysts did at that time, that the second oil shock was permanent. The generally optimistic view of oil income, which was supposed to increase by 12 percent per year, prompted the government to adopt an expansionary fiscal policy for 1981.

As the policy got under way, oil revenues declined in 1982 by 25 percent of projected levels, generating large current account and fiscal deficits. The real exchange rate tended to appreciate in spite of a major adverse external shock. The public reacted with a massive attack against the currency: international reserves declined by $8.2 billion in 1982, of which $6.5 billion can be traced to capital flight (Table 4.2). Given the fixed exchange rate regime, the government had very limited recourse to inflationary finance. In fact, the nominal value of base money declined in 1982 by $0.8 billion. To stem the capital outflow the Central Bank abandoned interest rate controls, but the expansionary monetary effects of fiscal policy sterilized the impact of the falling reserves level on liquidity. In February 1983, after liquid international reserves reached critical levels, the Central Bank decided to abandon the traditional unified and fixed exchange rate system and adopt multiple rates.

The Policy Mix

The policy package adopted in February 1983 was similar to that adopted in Venezuela in 1960, when the country faced its only other balance of payments crisis since 1903. At the time, the end of the 1956–7 Suez Canal crisis caused a fall in oil revenues in the context of a fiscal expansion. The government adopted a contractionary fiscal policy, a protectionist trade policy and a multiple exchange rate regime. Three and a half years later, in 1964, the country returned to a unified and fixed exchange system after a cumulative devaluation of only 35 percent.[12]

The policy proposed (see Table 4.1) was pretty much a carbon copy of this experience. Just as in 1960, there was to be a 3 year transition

TABLE 4.2 *Macroeconomic Performance 1981-9*

	1981	1982	1983	1984	1985	1986	1987	1988	1989
External indicators (billions of US$)									
Current account	4.0	-4.3	4.4	4.8	3.6	-1.6	-1.3	-4.2	2.4
Oil exports	19.1	15.7	13.7	14.6	13.1	7.6	9.1	8.2	9.8
Imports	-12.1	-13.6	-6.4	-7.3	-7.5	-7.9	-8.8	-11.6	-7.2
Capital flight*	-3.6	-6.5	-1.7	-0.0	-0.6	-1.7	-0.6	0.0	0.0
International reserves	16.3	8.1	8.4	10.3	12.0	8.2	7.3	2.4	2.5
Yearly change	0.5	-8.2	0.3	1.9	1.7	-3.8	-0.9	-4.9	0.1
Fiscal Indicators (percent of non-oil GDP)†									
Surplus or deficit		-11.2	-4.6	5.3	-0.2	-9.4	-5.6	-11.6	-2.7
Oil revenue		20.6	18.0	28.5	25.7	12.6	16.8	13.5	26.1
Exchange profits		0.0	3.6	4.2	4.3	1.6	-2.1	-2.9	-2.7
Consumption and investment		-39.8	-32.4	-21.4	-24.0	-25.4	-24.2	-23.9	-21.8
Other spending (net)		8.0	6.2	-6.0	-6.2	1.8	3.9	1.7	-4.3
Monetary indicators (billions of US$)									
Dollar value of base money‡									
At commercial rate	7.4	6.6	7.6	5.4	6.0	3.9	4.1	4.6	2.3
At floating rate	7.4	6.6	3.1	3.0	3.1	2.2	2.0	1.9	2.3
Yearly changes in dollar value of base money									
At commercial rate	1.0	-0.8	1.0	-2.2	0.6	-2.1	0.2	0.5	-2.3
At floating rate	1.0	-0.8	-3.5	-0.1	0.1	-1.0	-0.2	-0.1	0.4
Seniorage§	1.0	-0.8	0.9	-0.1	0.6	0.2	0.4	0.4	0.6

TABLE 4.2 (Continued)

	1981	1982	1983	1984	1985	1986	1987	1988	1989
Macroeconomic indicators (percentages)									
Non-oil GDP growth	0.4	1.8	-3.7	-1.2	3.4	5.9	5.4	5.7	-9.7
Absorption growth	3.0	-20.2	6.5	1.0	4.1	6.7	9.0	-20.9	-20.9
Domestic savings	40.7	28.0	22.3	31.0	28.2	22.3	27.6	23.7	26.4
Fixed investment	34.6	32.0	24.1	21.0	21.9	23.0	25.4	26.1	22.4
Inventories	-2.1	2.3	-9.2	1.9	1.5	0.6	4.3	5.9	-5.4
Foreign savings	-8.3	6.3	-7.5	-8.1	-4.8	1.3	2.2	8.3	-9.4
CPI inflation	16.0	9.7	6.3	12.2	11.4	11.6	40.1	36.7	80.4
Non-oil GDP deflator	15.2	7.4	8.4	13.1	10.5	10.9	26.3	24.2	66.8
Exchange premium¶	0.0	0.0	147.6	81.4	92.3	81.4	102.7	146.7	0.0

* Private short-term capital flows plus errors and omissions.
† Consolidated public sector accounts. Data before 1984 are not comparable.
‡ End of year stocks calculated at closing exchange rate. Commercial exchange rate is average rate for imports.
§ Change in the nominal stock of base money divided by average floating rate of the year.
¶ Percentage difference between the parallel rate and the average commercial rate for imports.
SOURCES: IMF and Banco Central de Venezuela.

period to 6.00 Bs. per US$ (implying a cumulative devaluation of 39.5 percent), with one-third of import items being transferred to the new rate each year. Access to foreign exchange at the official rate was to be managed by an exchange control office on the basis of *ex ante* case by case authorizations, which were supposed to allocate a given import 'budget'. Traditional exports (oil and iron ore) were left at the 4.30 rate. Non-traditional exports, most invisibles, and new capital flows were allowed to take place at a parallel floating rate which was expected to fluctuate some 20–40 percent above the new official rate. A long list of import prohibitions was announced and 50 percent of allowed imports were subject to a system of import permits (delegaciones). In addition, cuts were announced in public investment projects and wide price controls were imposed. The average exchange rate for imported goods, including those traded at the parallel rate, reached 5.21 Bs. per US$ by December 1983, implying a nominal devaluation of 21.2 percent with respect to the pre-crisis unified rate (see Table 4.3).

The parallel rate was to be instrumented through the stock market, with the Central Bank auctioning some $30 million a week. Very quickly, the exchange rate started to depreciate, breaking the 'psychological barrier' of 10 Bs. per US$ in late May 1983. The Central Bank then changed the system, cancelling the auctions and offering $30 million a week to banks at the rate of 9.90 Bs. per US$ to be sold to their clients at 9.95 Bs. per US$, but with no rationing system. Given that demand exceeded the allotted amount, another floating rate appeared which depreciated to 17.2 Bs. per US$ by July, but then stabilized and strengthened, reaching 12.9 Bs. per US$ in December. Fiscal policy became contractionary in 1983, with the fiscal deficit falling from 11.2 to 4.6 percent of non-oil GDP, an improvement of 6.6 percent.

Main Macroeconomic Results

The two most dramatic early results were the drastic depreciation of the currency in the parallel market and the improvement of the current account. The premium between the parallel rate and the average commercial exchange rate reached 230 percent in July 1983 before declining to 148 percent by December. The current account switched from a deficit of $4.2 billion in 1982 to a surplus of $4.4 billion, in spite of a fall in oil exports of $3.0 billion (Table 4.2). The

TABLE 4.3   *Basic macroeconomic indicators*

	Dec. 82	Mar. 83	Jun. 83	Sep. 83	Dec. 83	Mar. 84	Jun. 84	Sep. 84	Dec. 84	Mar. 85	Jun. 85	Sep. 85	Dec. 85	Mar. 86
Exchange rates (Bs. per US$)														
Official	4.30	6.00	6.00	6.00	6.00	7.50	7.50	7.50	7.5	7.5	7.5	7.5	7.5	7.5
Average commercial	4.30	4.83	5.01	5.51	5.21	6.84	6.88	6.79	7.00	7.2	7.5	7.7	7.8	8.2
Parallel	4.30	7.50	10.10	17.25	12.90	14.20	14.00	12.00	12.70	13.1	14.0	14.6	14.9	19.1
Premium														
Parallel versus official	100.0	125.0	168.3	287.5	215.0	189.3	186.7	160.0	169.3	174.7	186.7	4.7	8.7	254.7
Parallel versus commercial	100.0	155.3	201.6	313.1	247.6	207.6	203.5	176.7	181.4	181.4	187.9	0.4	2.3	233.8
Base money														
Billions of Bs	28.4	29.0	31.8	36.1	39.6	35.5	33.5	33.6	38.1	38.8	43.1	40.9	46.4	42.4
Billions US$ (commercial rate)	6.6	6.0	6.4	6.5	7.6	5.2	4.9	4.9	5.4	5.4	5.8	5.3	6.0	5.2
Billions of US$ (parallel rate)	6.6	3.9	3.2	2.1	3.1	2.5	2.4	2.8	3.0	3.0	3.1	2.8	3.1	2.2
External indicators (billions of US$)														
Imports	3.1	2.1	1.2	1.4	1.7	1.8	1.8	2.0	2.2	1.8	2.0	2.1	2.2	1.9
Exports	4.8	3.5	3.4	3.6	3.5	3.8	4.1	4.2	3.9	3.7	3.2	3.7	3.9	2.5
Trade balance	1.7	1.3	2.1	2.2	1.8	2.0	2.3	2.2	1.7	1.9	1.2	1.6	1.6	0.6
Foreign exchange reserve	5.4	4.0	4.7	5.9	6.4	6.3	7.1	7.5	7.7	8.3	8.7	8.5	8.9	8.6
Domestic government spending														
Billions of Bs	19.9	18.5	17.6	17.1	12.0	14.8	16.5	18.1	20.6	17.1	22.0	18.0	25.6	18.3
Billions US$/ (commercial rate)	4.6	3.8	3.5	3.1	2.3	2.2	2.4	2.7	2.9	2.4	3.0	2.4	3.3	2.2
Relative prices														
RER (border prices)*		100.0	101.1	108.6	101.1	128.7	123.6	112.7	111.0	109.4	110.2	110.5	108.9	106.5
WPI versus CPI		100.0	101.5	102.7	102.8	106.1	105.8	107.3	107.5	111.6	112.5	112.3	111.9	114.5
$\rho^{\dagger}$		100.0	99.0	92.1	98.9	77.7	80.9	88.7	90.1	91.4	90.7	90.5	91.8	93.9

* Average commercial exchange rate multiplied by the US WPI and divided by the CPI.
† Venezuelan WPI divided by commercial exchange rate multiplied by the USWPI.
SOURCE: Central Bank of Venezuela.

December 1982 to December 1989

Jun. 86	Sep. 86	Dec. 86	Mar. 87	Jun. 87	Sep. 87	Dec. 87	Mar. 88	Jun. 88	Sep. 88	Dec. 88	Mar. 89	Jun. 89	Sep. 89	Dec. 89
7.5	7.5	14.5	14.5	14.5	14.5	14.5	14.5	14.5	14.5	14.5	36.0	37.2	38.2	43.8
8.4	8.8	13.0	13.2	14.1	14.9	15.1	15.2	15.4	15.7	15.9	19.9	37.2	38.2	43.8
17.6	20.5	23.6	23.1	27.9	31.7	30.5	29.7	33.2	37.0	39.3	36.0	37.2	38.2	43.8
234.7	273.3	162.8	159.3	2.4	218.6	210.3	204.8	229.0	255.2	271.0	100.0	100.0	100.0	100.0
209.8	233.8	181.4	174.9	7.6	213.0	202.7	196.0	215.9	235.2	246.7	181.1	100.0	100.0	100.0
50.2	49.2	50.9	48.4	50.2	51.2	61.0	59.1	62.1	60.7	73.9	71.5	68.1	81.9	98.6
6.0	5.6	3.9	3.7	3.6	3.4	4.1	3.9	4.0	3.9	4.6	3.6	1.8	2.1	2.3
2.9	2.4	2.2	2.1	1.8	1.6	2.0	2.0	1.9	1.6	1.9	2.0	1.8	2.1	2.3
2.3	2.1	2.2	1.8	2.2	2.7	3.0	2.7	3.1	3.2	4.3	4.1	1.6	1.6	1.6
2.1	2.0	2.0	2.4	2.6	2.9	2.7	2.3	2.7	2.6	2.7	2.7	3.4	3.2	3.8
−0.2	−0.1	−0.1	0.6	0.4	0.2	−0.3	−0.4	−0.4	−0.6	−1.6	−1.4	1.9	1.6	2.3
7.8	6.5	5.0	4.7	4.4	4.7	4.5	3.9	3.8	3.5	3.0	3.2	3.0	3.7	4.1
28.3	23.9	24.9	24.8	31.5	35.0	49.9	35.7	41.8	40.5	40.8	35.9	53.0	55.6	68.2
3.4	2.7	1.9	1.9	2.2	2.3	3.3	2.4	2.7	2.6	2.6	1.8	1.4	1.5	1.6
104.3	105.2	148.3	126.8	124.3	123.9	121.1	122.1	122.2	120.2	115.1	97.8	139.0	140.2	159.0
116.0	116.9	117.8	132.8	131.9	130.3	124.3	127.1	121.2	116.2	106.9	127.0	135.9	127.5	121.8
95.9	95.1	67.4	78.9	80.5	80.7	82.6	81.9	81.8	83.2	86.9	102.2	71.9	71.3	62.9

main cause of this result was a decline in imports from $13.6 billion to
$6.4 billion and of travel and tourism by $1.9 billion. This improvement represented 13.5 percent of GDP, over half of which is explained
by an increase in private sector financial savings. However, the
increase in private financial savings was not due to a rise in gross
savings, which in fact declined by 8.9 percent, but mainly to a negative
inventory swing of 11.4 percent.

The growth in liquidity accelerated drastically, due mainly to the
accumulation of international reserves at the Central Bank. By the end
of the third quarter of 1983, base money was 42.5 percent above the
level reached in the same quarter of 1982, having grown by only 3.8
percent in the previous 12 month period. The increase in base money
caused Central Bank net lending to the banking system to go from
15.9 percent of base money in the fourth quarter of 1982 to -17.0
percent in the third quarter of 1983. Prompted by this swing in the
money market, interest rates fell from 15.1 percent at the end of 1982
to 13.0 percent in the third quarter of 1983.

The increase in base money amounted to 4 percent of GDP and
implied that its dollar value calculated at the average commercial rate
(our *m*) had increased from $6.6 billion in December 1982 to $7.6
billion a year later, in spite of the devaluation of the commercial rate
(see Table 4.3). However, calculated at the parallel rate base money
declined to $3.1 billion, an indication that the nominal increase was
not desired by the public.

Output dropped significantly, with non-petroleum GDP falling 3.7
percent. The 12 month inflation rate reached only 7 percent by
December, in spite of the parallel rate depreciation of 200 percent.
Absorption slumped by 20.2 percent of non-oil GDP[13] (Table 4.2).
This reduction, which is much greater than the drop in output, was
concentrated in tradeables (21.4 percent), since non-tradeables
declined only by 0.3 percent of non-oil GDP. This result would be
consistent with an expenditure-switching effect that follows a major
depreciation. However, there is little evidence of significant domestic
relative price shifts and tradeable output actually declined. Why did
the structure of absorption change so dramatically?

Although our model cannot deal with this issue, we shall advance
an explanation that further elaborates on the consequences of import
controls. Suppose that agents anticipate the adoption of multiple
rates. This will lead to a speculative inventory accumulation before
the collapse of the fixed exchange regime. Given this behavior, the
anticipated cut in the official supply of foreign exchange for imports

will be compensated by a reduction in inventories, as agents smooth out the consumption of tradeables. This implies that the effective supply of these goods is enhanced through destocking, limiting the domestic price increase in spite of the increase in border prices. This effect is strengthened when inventories have a high rate of depreciation, so that they must be consumed quickly after rationing is imposed.

Interpretation

Kiguel and Lizondo (1990) showed that when imports are demand determined, adopting a multiple exchange rate regime will not improve the trade balance. The Venezuelan experience stands in sharp contrast: there the amelioration reached 13.5 percent of GDP! Can this be explained by policies other than the switch to an exchange regime with binding import controls? No: money increased drastically, the official exchange rate was devalued only modestly in comparison, and there was a significant though smaller fiscal deficit. The dollar value of base money at the average commercial rate actually increased by approximately 15 percent between December 1982 and December 1983. Why would demand for imports collapse?

Moreover, a look at the quarterly structure of the adjustment (Table 4.3) suggests that imports declined abruptly before any of the other contractionary measures took place. They reached a minimum in the second quarter of 1983 and grew slowly thereafter, while the money supply ballooned. Fiscal adjustment came mainly in the fourth quarter. These observations are consistent with the assumption that the improvement in the trade balance was exogenous and that it explains the jump in the flow supply of money.

In the restricted model, the adoption of a multiple exchange rate system with import rationing may lead to either a stable or an unstable scheme depending on the configuration of the $\dot{m} = 0$ and $\dot{m}_R = 0$ schedules, as shown in Figures 4.2(a) and (b). It can be shown that for the system to fall into the stable framework, government spending, g_N, should be less than a critical value, g_N^*, given by

$$(21) \qquad g_N^* = \frac{\alpha x_N i}{i + x_T (1 - \alpha)}$$

Notice that a cut in the import quota i requires a reduction in g_N so as to avoid an unstable configuration. We can use this expression to find a lower bound on how much g_N should be reduced to accompany a reduction in i. This is given by the elasticity of g_N relative to i, ϵ_g^i:

$$(22) \qquad\qquad \epsilon_g^i = \frac{(1 - \alpha)x_T}{i + x_T(1 - \alpha)}$$

In 1982 the share of tradeables in absorption (that is, our α) was 0.45, x_T measured at current prices reached Bs. 77.6 billion and i equaled Bs. 69.1 billion. This leads to an estimated value for ϵ_g^i equal to 0.38. This implies that since i was reduced by 53 percent, g_N should have fallen by at least 20.2 percent, in order to avoid the system becoming unstable. However, government spending in non-tradeables g_N actually increased by 1 percent of non-oil GDP in 1983 since the cut in public absorption affected mostly tradeables.

Given this, the economy was left on an explosive path in which the money supply (calculated at the commercial rate), m, grew continuously. In Figure 4.2(b), m and the premium π move along an unstable manifold which is pinned down by expectations of the date and nature of the inevitable policy adjustment.[14] The fact that elections were to be held in December 1983 and that the opposition party Acción Democrática was expected to win by a wide margin meant that a new government would have the ability to impose adjustment, making the date of its implementation known. Furthermore, during the second semester of 1983 public spending was cut and the import quota relaxed, anticipating the nature of future adjustment and reducing money supply growth, thus explaining the reduction in the premium which took place during that period.[15]

Thus, the improvement in the current account and the explosive path followed by the money supply and the premium are consistent with the insights provided by our model, when the import restriction is binding and the import quota is inconsistent with fiscal policy.

THE 1984 AND 1986 DEVALUATIONS

The reaction of the economy to a devaluation will depend also on whether or not there is a stable equilibrium, as described in Figure 4.2(a) and (b). If the economy is in region C of Figure 4.2(a), a devaluation will cause it to move towards the origin along a ray. If it is large enough so that it passes the $\rho = 1$ schedule, it will continue along the stable manifold where both the money supply and the premium are falling. If it is insufficient, it will return to an explosive path. An explosive result will also be obtained if the economy is in a situation such as that described by Figure 4.2(b), where the lack of a stable equilibrium will mean that the money supply and the premium will grow without bound after the devaluation.

The Venezuelan case provides two experiences of devaluation with remarkably different results. Our model will allow us to explain the difference.

The 1984 Devaluation and Policy Mix

After the December 1983 election, a new government took office in February 1984. Facing a large premium and judging that the original plan of unifying the exchange rate at 6 Bs. per US$ by 1986 was not viable, the authorities decided to make a credible devaluation. They created an official exchange rate of 7.50 Bs. per US$ for most commercial transactions and for debt service (see Table 4.1). A subsidized market at the old exchange rate of 4.30 Bs. per US$ was left for food and medicine imports and for repayment of principal on registered debt contracted before February 1983. The 9.95 Bs. per US$ exchange rate was eliminated and a single floating parallel rate market was created. The value-added portion of non-traditional exports was left in this market, together with tourism, services, additional imports, and new financial flows. By December 1984, the average exchange rate for imports had devalued by 34.1 percent (see Table 4.3). The policy also included a relaxation of price controls which had been established in 1983.

On the fiscal side, further adjustment measures were carried out. Current and investment spending were cut by an additional 2.3 percent of GDP. However, the devaluation increased the domestic value of debt service so interest payments increased by 2.6 percent of GDP (Table 4.3). Given the lack of change in domestic tax revenues, these measures would have added up to a small increase in the fiscal deficit. However, the devaluation had other more important effects on the public sector accounts.

The operating profits of Petroleos de Venezuela Sociedad Anonima (PDVSA, the national oil monopoly) increased by 6.4 percentage points of GDP, even though export revenue in real dollars rose by only 1.8 percent of GDP. The difference is explained by the increase in the domestic value of the surplus, through devaluation. Moreover, the elimination of the 9.90 Bs. per US$ exchange rate and the intervention of the Central Bank in the higher parallel market allowed exchange profits to increase, in spite of the fact that the Central Bank was now buying foreign exchange from PDVSA at a much higher exchange rate.[16] In total, the fiscal accounts went from a deficit of 4.6 percent of GDP in 1983 to a surplus of 4.8 percent in 1984, a swing of 9.4 percent of GDP.

Monetary policy remained passive, but interest rate controls were reimposed at the levels prevailing at the time, which were influenced by the excess supply of money generated in 1983. However, these ceilings did not have much effect.

Main Macroeconomic Results

The contractionary fiscal policy and the reduction in private spending associated with devaluation translated into a further cut in aggregate consumption and investment of 4.5 percent. However, the overall absorption increased by 6.5 percent because of the swing in inventories, which represented 11 percent of GDP (Table 4.2). The nominal devaluation of 34.1 percent between January and December 1984 translated into a real depreciation of 14 percent, measured at border prices. Non-oil GDP fell by an additional 1.2 percent but growth started in tradeables as would be expected after a real depreciation. Inflation accelerated but remained remarkably moderate (20.6 percent by December) considering the devaluation and the new price policy.

In spite of the significant real depreciation, the cut in consumption and investment spending, and the increase in oil exports of $1.1 billion, the current account did not show a significant improvement ($0.3 billion) with respect to the already large surplus of 1983. In fact, imports actually increased by $0.8 billion. The small change in foreign savings masks important changes in the financial savings behaviour of both private and public sectors. The end of destocking and the rise in private fixed investment (mostly in tradeables) meant that private financial investment fell by over 11 percent of GDP. By contrast, the changes in fiscal policy mentioned above caused public financial savings to increase by a similar amount. Thus, were it not for the fiscal adjustment, the inventory cycle could not have been accommodated.

As opposed to 1983, when the accumulation of reserves was financed through seigniorage, in 1984 the fiscal surplus sterilized the balance of payments surplus causing nominal base money to fall by 4.3 percent (0.5 percent of GDP; Table 4.2). However, demand for nominal balances increased, with $M2$ rising by 10.3 percent. The system reacted through a decline in net excess reserves of some 21.7 percent of base money. The dollar value of base money calculated at the official rate declined from $7.6 billion in December 1983 to $5.4 billion in December 1984, mainly because of the devaluation, while its value calculated at the parallel rate remained stable at $3 billion. All these developments imply a significant reduction in the excess supply of money and translated into a decline in the premium of 83 percentage points (Tables 4.2 and 4.3). Moreover, the fact that imports increased even though the dollar value of the money supply decreased implied that import rationing was reduced or may have actually disappeared.

Background to the 1986 Devaluation

There were few changes in economic policy in 1985. Oil revenues declined by $1.5 billion, causing the operating surplus of PDVSA to fall by 2.8 percent of GDP. Moreover, public investment was increased by 24.4 percent in real terms or 2.6 percent of GDP and the import quota was maintained. This caused both the fiscal and the balance of payments surpluses to decline. However, while the fiscal accounts reached equilibrium, the current account remained in surplus by $3.3 billion (4.8 percent of non-oil GDP) and international reserves increased by $1.7 billion (see Table 4.2). The economy started to grow by 3.2 percent, led by the tradeable sector, while unemployment stayed high at 12.1 percent.

Feeling that macroeconomic balance had been established, the government designed a fiscal expansion package for 1986 that was aimed at reducing unemployment through investment in infrastructure. Just as the spending plans got under way in early 1986, however, the price of oil collapsed. Export revenues to fell by $5.5 billion and PDVSA's operating surplus declined by 8.2 percent of GDP. The fiscal accounts went into a deficit of 8.7 percent of GDP (Table 4.2).

Absorption increased by 4.1 percent of GDP, mainly in non-tradeables since the real supply of tradeables was limited as the government tried to defend the level of reserves by clamping down on import authorizations. Thus, domestically produced tradeables increased by 1.9 percent of GDP while real imports declined by 0.8 percent of GDP. The domestic price of tradeables increased as can be shown from the fact that the ratio of the wholesale price index (WPI) to the consumer price index (CPI) rose by 4 percent. This happened in spite of the fact that the exchange rate calculated at border prices exhibited some appreciation. This implied a rise in ρ by 4.5 percent between December 1985 and September 1986 (Table 4.3).

The non-oil economy grew by 5.9 percent and inflation accelerated only marginally to 12.7 percent. International reserves fell by $3.9 billion, but their contractionary monetary effect was more than compensated by the rising fiscal deficit. Hence, base money increased by 20.3 percent in the year to September 1986. Between January and November the exchange premium doubled to 170 percent (Table 4.3). Regime collapse was perceived as imminent and excess demand for durable goods and for dollars at the official rate caused severe problems.[17] Demand for credit expanded as anticipated inflation meant that real interest rates had become strongly negative. In December 1986, after losing almost half of its operating reserves ($3.9 billion) the government finally decided to act.

The 1986 Devaluation and Policy Mix

The policy package of December 1986 was based on a 93 percent devaluation of the official exchange rate (from 7.50 to 14.50 Bs. per US$). Such a large change was deemed necessary so as to give credibility to the new exchange rate policy, given that the parallel rate had reached 26 Bs. per US$ in November. As in 1984, a list of food, agricultural inputs, and medicines was left at a preferential rate which, as before, was fixed at the previous official rate (7.5 Bs. per US$). Imports already in the regulatory pipeline were left at the rate at which they were contracted. Since the Central Bank would only sell dollars 6 months after goods had entered the country, this meant that until June 1987 most foreign exchange sales were made at the previous exchange rates (Table 4.1). In contrast, however, inflows, mainly from the oil industry, were connected at the new exchange rate causing exchange losses at the Central Bank of 2.1 percent of non-oil GDP (Table 4.2).

Given the size of the devaluation, the government decided not to accompany it with other harsh measures. Hence, the fiscal expansion that was planned before the collapse remained on course and nominal interest rate ceilings remained fixed at 14 percent for commercial loans

Main Macroeconomic Results

Oil exports rose in 1987 by $1.5 billion or 1.7 percent of GDP but declined in 1988 by $1 billion. PDVSA's operating surplus in 1987 increased by 4.3 percent of non-oil GDP because the 93 percent devaluation raised the real domestic value of its income by 2.6 percent of GDP, but it fell in 1988 by 2.9 percent of GDP given the decline in the terms of trade and the absence of new devaluations. However, much of that additional revenue of 1987 was compensated by exchange losses at the Central Bank caused by the recognition of previous import commitments at the old exchange rate.[18] Exchange profits declined by 3.7 percent of GDP in 1987, leaving no net fiscal benefits from the devaluation, in contrast with the 1984 experience.

Given the increase in oil exports and the short-term cash-flow alleviation provided by forced trade financing,[19] the government was able to increase its exchange allocation for new imports. As in 1984, imports increased by $1 billion in 1987 and by $3.2 billion in 1988, in spite of the massive devaluation. In 1988, facing elections, the government financed the increased import allocation with $4.9 billion in reserve losses.

Different measures of the real exchange rate point towards an initial real depreciation. The average nominal commercial exchange rate depreciated by 72.9 percent in the year following the devaluation, while CPI inflation reached only 39.4 percent, leaving a real depreciation of 35.3 percent. The ratio of the WPI to the CPI increased by 6.3 percent.

The lack of fiscal adjustment in the context of a forced reduction in reserve losses meant that base money increased at a 20 percent rate in the year to December 1987 and by 21 percent in 1988. This meant that the value of base money calculated at the commercial exchange rate, which had declined from $5.6 to 3.6 billion between September 1986 and March 1987 (because of devaluation), rose to $4.1 billion by December 1987 and to $4.6 billion by December 1988.

As monetary claims on the dwindling international reserves increased, the premium between the official and the parallel rate, which had fallen from 173 percent in September 1986 to 59.3 percent by March 1987, went back to 110 percent by December 1987 and to 171 percent in December 1988. The value of base money calculated at the parallel rate therefore declined throughout the period (Table 4.3). Inflation, which had remained remarkably low from 1983 to 1986 in spite of significant macroeconomic imbalances, shot up to approximately 40 percent in 1987 and 36.7 percent in 1988. The Central Bank tried to design new instruments to absorb liquidity and found that it could only place them in the market at interest rates that were more than double the maximum rate on commercial loans. This started to undermine the interest control mechanism and parallel interest rates started to make their appearance in the money market.

Interpreting the 1984 and 1986 Devaluations

Both the 1984 and the 1986 devaluations show that when imports are rationed, devaluations in a dual exchange rate system have very little impact on the balance of payments. While fiscal spending was cut in 1984, money supply was curtailed in nominal terms, and the official exchange rate was devalued by an average of 32 percent, imports actually increased by US$0.8 billion, given the expanded official allocation. However, the devaluation was quite important in improving the fiscal accounts and removing the money market excess liquidity,[20] thus putting downward pressure on the parallel exchange rate. A remarkably stable period ensued in 1984 in which the premium remained steady at much lower levels and m declined after being cut through devaluation. This contrasts with the extreme volatility of the parallel rate in the previous year.

In terms of our model, a cut in g_N reduces i^*, while an increase in i makes it more likely for $i > i^*$. Hence, if the economy was initially in an unstable situation such as region B in Figure 4.2(b), this policy change will move the $\rho = 1$ and $\dot{m}_R = 0$ schedules outward and the $\dot{m} = 0$ schedule inwards, generating a picture such as Figure 4.2(a). If no stable region existed before the policy shift, explaining the extreme volatility of m and π in 1983, these changes in fundamental variables may have created that region.

Given the changes in g_N and i, the devaluation, by instantaneously cutting m, π, and $\dot{m}$, moved the economy towards the stable regions A or B in Figure 4.2(a). The dynamics observed in Venezuela resemble the path described by the indicated points in the figure, as explained above.

It is interesting to ask whether the combination of devaluation and adjustment of the fundamentals placed the economy in region A or B. In this respect, the fact that imports did not fall suggests that the economy may have still been constrained by the import quota i. This is so because if i is constant and the economy crosses the $\rho = 1$ line imports should fall, but they did not. Hence, we suspect the economy to have remained in region B, as shown. Furthermore, in region B m is falling, not because of an endogenous decline in the level of reserves r as in region A, but because the fiscal surplus is greater than the exogenously decided accumulation of reserves. This surplus is endogenous, in the sense that the devaluation reduces ρ, thus improving the fiscal accounts. Furthermore, since the saddle-path has a positive slope, the fall in m entails a decline in π. As mentioned before, this is exactly our set of observations for 1984.

It is important to point out that the internal price of tradeables had not risen to the level of the parallel rate, in spite of ample evidence of rationing. Hence, as shown in the model, $\rho < \pi$. In addition, the inflation rate dropped below 10 percent after the first few months of 1984, in spite of a relaxation in price controls. Hence, large premia may not have significant direct effects on the price level or the inflation rate, provided the economy is in a stable region.[21]

Developments in 1985 were broadly consistent with what would be expected of a fiscal expansion in the unconstrained model. The increase in g_N moves the $\dot{m} = 0$ schedule to the right, causing the saddle path to move upward. Both π and m increase, as observed.

The collapse of oil income in 1986 in the context of a fiscal expansion implied a decline in i and an increase in g_N. These developments may have shifted the curves sufficiently to make the model globally unstable as in Figure 4.2(b), causing the premium to jump initially and then to continue on an unstable manifold. In that process, m increased in spite of the fall in reserves, making the situation unsustainable. The expansion in the money supply was clearly undesired by the public as can be seen from the fall in its dollar value measured at the parallel rate.

As the import constraint becomes stronger, the real exchange rate measured at domestic prices depreciates and ρ increases even though at border prices there appears to be real appreciation (Table 4.3), thus increasing the rents obtained by importers and further deteriorating the fiscal accounts.[22]

In contrast with 1984, the December 1986 devaluation was not accompanied by a change in policy fundamentals that would render the model stable. Obviously, m, π, and ρ were cut instantaneously by the nominal devaluation (Table 4.3), thus improving the fiscal situation endogenously, but only transitorily. Since the economy was in a configuration such as Figure 4.2(b), the absence of a stable equilibrium meant that the economy would enter an explosive manifold.

This result contrasts markedly with the aftermath of the 1984 devaluation when $\dot{m}$ became negative, thus prompting a period of stable and falling premia.

THE 1989 ABANDONMENT OF THE MULTIPLE EXCHANGE RATE SYSTEM

The 1986–8 expansion left the newly elected government with four major disequilibria. First, an external imbalance expressed in a large current account deficit, a very low level of liquid international reserves (US\$ 300 million), an exploding foreign exchange premium, short-term central bank dollar liabilities (recognized official rate letters of credit) of US\$ 6.3 billion (of which over US\$ 1 billion were overdue), and no international financing plan for 1989.

Secondly, the fiscal deficit, which had reached 11.6 percent of GDP in 1988, was projected to rise further due mainly to the impact of increasing explicit and implicit subsidies on goods, such as fertilizers, milk, feed grains, electricity, and petroleum products. More importantly, while the monetary impact of the 1988 deficit was partly offset by reserve losses, the projected deficit for 1989 would have had to be financed through the inflation tax.

Thirdly, repressed inflation was causing serious shortages of basic products and massive speculative inventory accumulation.[23] This situation was generated not only by growing pressures on controlled prices, but also by the general perception that a major devaluation was imminent.

Fourthly, inflationary expectations in the context of controlled interest rates generated severe financial repression. Very strong demand for credit emerged, which was generally used to finance inventory accumulation or capital flight. For the first time ever, a parallel interest rate appeared which hovered around 30 percent when the official ceiling on commercial loans was set at 13 percent.

These four macroeconomic imbalances can be characterized as implying excess demand for goods, foreign exchange, and credit while money is in excess supply. Since the expansion left the economy very close to full employment,[24] this situation also implied real exchange rate misalignment in the sense that, at prevailing relative prices, external balance and full employment could not be achieved simultaneously.

The Policy Mix

The new policy adopted by the government (Table 4.1) was based on the abandonment of the multiple exchange rate mechanism and the adoption of a unified float. Pressured by an unsustainable balance of payments and by strong expectations of devaluation, policy makers had to decide on a way of devaluing the currency. Obviously, with an exchange premium of almost 200 percent, only a major adjustment of the official rate could be credible. However, the wrong guess would require future adjustments which were likely to erode credibility. With a low level of reserves, there is very little room for defending any particular peg. This makes a floating arrangement, even a temporary one, an expedient way of solving the problem.[25]

The adjustment program adopted in 1989 also included a major cut in the fiscal deficit through a reduction in subsidies and investment and through the impact of devaluation on the fiscal accounts. Interest rates were increased and new instruments were designed to get liquidity out of the system. Prices were freed and import controls and prohibitions scrapped. A 3 year extended financing program was agreed with the International Monetary Fund.

Main Macroeconomic Results

When the exchange mechanism was unified in March 1989, equilibrium was achieved at a rate close to that of the parallel market. This outcome produced a major depreciation of the commercial rate, which increased by 168 percent between January and December 1989. Prices jumped by 51 percent between March and May, but increased at an annual rate of only 31 percent in the second semester of 1989, implying a cumulative inflation for the January–December period of 88.7 percent. These developments implied a major real depreciation: the real commercial exchange rate increased by 53.3 percent. Compared with the previous parallel rate, this implied an appreciation of 36.2 percent.

The real depreciation increased the domestic value of the oil surplus by 10.7 percent of GDP; with export revenues increasing by $1.7 billion in 1989, PDVSA's operating surplus rose by 13.8 percent of GDP. This was the main force behind a cut in the fiscal deficit of 9.3 percent of GDP (Table 4.2).[26]

The current account improved by $8.3 billion (17 percent of GDP), due mainly to a shift in the trade balance as imports fell by $4.9 billion (41 percent) and non-oil exports increased by $1.1 billion (51 percent). This swing, which was much larger than the improvement in the fiscal accounts, implied a large increase in private financial savings, which was generated mainly by negative swings in inventories, investment, and consumption of 10.1, 4.7, and 5.1 percent of GDP, respectively. Overall, real absorption declined by 20.9 percent of GDP. Given such a drastic fall in demand, output suffered its worst decline ever, with non-oil GDP falling 9.8 percent.

Interpreting the 1989 Unification

The Venezuelan experience of 1989 fits rather neatly into the theoretical framework developed by Kiguel and Lizondo (1990). In this approach, the dual exchange system allows the market for tradeables to clear at one price while portfolio balance is achieved at another.[27] Exchange unification implies the elimination of a price from the system, namely the premium π. Unification will occur at a level close to the parallel rate because that is the price that generates portfolio balance. However, the market for tradeables under multiple rates with import controls clears at a much lower price.[28] Hence, exchange unification will cause a jump in the price level and a related fall in the real value of financial wealth. Agents will react to this by increasing savings in order to restore wealth to levels close to those observed previously. This accumulation will take the form of both domestic and foreign assets. The latter will require a trade surplus, meaning that absorption will fall more than output.

As predicted, unification took place close to the parallel rate and implied a once and for all shock to the economy, with the price level jumping in March–May by over 50 percent. This prompted a collapse in the real value of domestic and foreign assets as m fell by more than half and π reached unity (Table 4.3). The collapse in real financial wealth produced by unification severely cut spending, causing the massive contraction in economic activity and the great improvement in the current account. This was a consequence both of the massive transfer of resources to the government through devaluation and of the attempt of the private sector to replenish their financial assets: in spite of the fall in income, private financial savings amounted to 6.5

percent of non-oil GDP. As on previous occasions this increase is mostly explained by inventory reductions.

It is important to reflect on the causes of the drastic fall in output in 1989, by comparing them with those that affected the economy when the multiple exchange regime was adopted. In both cases, absorption fell by approximately 20 percent of non-oil GDP. However, in 1983 the drop in output was only approximately one-third of the decline in 1989, while the improvement in the current account was more pronounced.

This difference illustrates the importance of inventory cycles in the process of adoption and abandonment of multiple exchange regimes. If adoption with import controls is expected, agents will tend to accumulate imported goods while they can. As import controls take effect, agents will use up their inventories: this decline in absorption will translate directly into an improvement in the current account, thus explaining the facts observed in 1983.

In contrast, when the system is about to be abandoned, agents know that the real value of all financial assets, both domestic and foreign, is about to collapse. The best asset to hold is real goods. However, as import controls are still in effect, agents will not be able to increase their holdings of foreign goods and will instead hoard domestically produced storable goods. While this process is going on, demand for domestic output is brisk, as was the case in 1987–8. However, as soon as the system is abandoned and the price level jumps, agents will attempt to convert goods into financial assets in order to replenish their depleted real holdings. Companies reduce stocks and pay back liabilities, making banks face a major decline in the demand for credit.[29] Households retire temporarily from the goods market and run down their inventories. This will be measured again as an inventory-led decline in absorption, only now it is demand for domestically produced storable goods that will feel the brunt. Hence, the decline in output will be greater and the improvement in the current account much smaller than after adoption.

SOME CONCLUSIONS AND FURTHER RESEARCH ISSUES

This chapter has analyzed the adoption, management, and abandonment of the multiple exchange rate system that was implemented in Venezuela between 1983 and 1989. To capture some of the stylized

facts of the macroeconomy we incorporated import controls. This led
to a model with an unstable region which depended on the relationship between the import quota and fiscal spending. When faced with
instability, economists tend to alter the model in order get rid of it.
Instead, we followed a different route. Convinced that the instability
in the model captured an important aspect of the exchange regime, we
proceeded to derive solution paths by assuming agents had expectations about the eventual adjustment required.

We attributed the unusually explosive path followed by the economy in 1983 to the inherent instability of a system in which the
balance of payments was improved exogenously through import controls, but without the accompanying fiscal and exchange rate policies
that would make this improvement sustainable. We analyzed the
impacts of devaluation and noted that if the fundamentals are in
place, as in 1984, devaluation may move the economy towards an
otherwise unreachable but stable equilibrium. By contrast, if the
regime is in its unstable mode, as in 1986–8, a devaluation will only
reduce the premium and the growth in the money supply temporarily.
In neither case will a devaluation improve the current account, unless
it is of sufficient magnitude to make import controls redundant.

The dynamics of abandonment appear to be well captured by the
model. Financial wealth collapses as the premium disappears, causing
the price level to jump. Given that most output has become non-
tradeable, the ensuing reduction in absorption causes a major decline
in economic activity.

One interesting aspect not captured by the model is the importance
of inventory swings. As shown, stocks of goods play an important
part in the macroeconomic dynamics of both adoption and abandonment. This should not be surprising. With restrictions on trade and
capital flows, regime changes may make real goods the best available
reserves of value. Incorporating them formally into the model appears
to be an important extension.

Our analysis also suggests that policy uncertainty may play a major
role in exchange rate volatility under multiple rates. Given that the
level of the premium is tied down by expectations of future policy
change, variations in opinion about what this may be will translate
into sudden and large changes in the premium. Incorporating uncertainty formally into the model may also lead to interesting results.[30]

From a long-term policy perspective, it is difficult to see the advantages of a multiple exchange regime. The system has an impressive
capacity to isolate the goods market from variations in the parallel

rate. This is clear from the fact that inflation in Venezuela was surprisingly low when the regime was adopted and surprisingly high when it was abandoned. It is also clear that import controls may permit current account improvements with little effort on the fiscal, monetary or exchange rate front. The Venezuelan experience suggests, however, that such an approach will generate a money overhang problem that will come to haunt policy makers in the form of recurrent crises that are caused not by insufficient reserves but by an unsustainable exchange differential. In the end, the degrees of freedom obtained through adoption of the system will have to be paid back – and with a premium (so to speak) – at the time of abandonment.

NOTES

1. I would like to thank Roberto Rigobon for extensive assistance and very valuable substantive contributions and comments. I am also indebted to Miguel Kiguel, Stephen O'Connell, and Jose Saul Lizondo for detailed comments on an earlier draft. I also benefited from comments received from participants at the World Bank Seminar on Parallel Exchange Rates.
2. Since most exports are carried out by the state-owned companies in oil, aluminum, iron ore, and steel the government has direct control over the principal source of foreign exchange.
3. The literature on multiple exchange rates can be classified into descriptive and optimizing models. A comprehensive non-technical review is presented in Lizondo (1990). The standard descriptive models have been popularized in Dornbusch (1986) and Edwards (1989). Optimizing models include Adams and Greenwood (1985) and Park and Sachs (1987). Since we will deal mostly with issues of adoption and abandonment, this chapter will follow closely Lizondo (1987) and Kiguel and Lizondo (1990). See also Obstfeld (1986) and Chapter 1 of the present volume.
4. Notice that along the $\dot{m} = 0$ schedule as well as along any line with slope equal to $-1/k$, wealth is constant. This translates into a constant level of imports and of the real exchange rate.
5. As we shall see, the domestic price of tradeables P will be greater than the international price calculated at the official rate E. This assumption implies that the government buys its tradeables at the cheapest price and hence has a smaller fiscal deficit. For the points we will make in this section, this constitutes a conservative hypothesis.
6. Pinto (1991) and O'Connell (1992) study models in which the official trade balance is exogenous but smuggling and misinvoicing allow the accumulation of (illegal) foreign assets over time. Steady states have the property that the supply of illegal foreign exchange from misinvoicing and export smuggling is balanced by the flow demand generated by a

binding import quota and in these equilibria, $\rho \geq \pi$ (= π if there are no costs to import smuggling). We argue below that in our model such a situation is never achieved. Although imports at the parallel rate were legal in Venezuela, they remained very small given the large premium.

7. This means that the short-term equilibrium is indeterminate, if we assume that the economy remains in the import-constrained regime. An alternative interpretation of the indeterminacy here can be obtained by looking at variables deflated not by the (fixed) commercial exchange rate but by the (endogenous) domestic price of traded goods. Defining new variables m' and π' as $m' = M/P_T$ and $\pi' = F/P_T$, money growth takes the form

(*) $$\dot{m}' = \frac{g_N}{q} - \frac{E}{P_T}(z - g_T) - \mu m',$$

where μ is the rate of inflation of P_T (which equals domestic inflation since $q = P_T/P_N$ is fixed) and the portfolio balance condition is

(**) $$\frac{\pi' k}{m'} = g(\hat{F}) = g(\hat{\pi}' + \mu).$$

A stationary state in this new system would involve $\hat{\pi}' = 0$ and $\dot{m}' = 0$. As P_T goes to infinity, the term $(E/P_T)(z - g_T)$ in the fiscal deficit goes to zero and equations (*) and (**) give us two equations in m, π, q, and μ. Two additional equations are supplied by the non-tradeables market-clearing condition and the binding import constraint. But in this 'steady state' (which is never reached in finite time) the quota rent $(P_T/E) - 1$ and the parallel premium $(F/E) - 1$ would both be rising forever, providing massive incentives for illegal transactions that we are not modeling here. This problem would not arise if the government allowed the official exchange rate to crawl along with domestic inflation, so that E/P_T was constant.

8. Venezuelan policy in this period has been analyzed by Baptista (1989) and Hausmann (1990, Chapter 10).

9. Presidential elections take place in Venezuela in early December every 5 years. The new government takes office in the first quarter of the following year. The reader should keep in mind the recurring coincidence of the political and economic cycles: 1979, 1984, and 1989 are years in which newly elected governments take over and also periods in which stabilization programs are adopted.

10. On the impact of the oil windfall see Pazos (1979), Rodriguez (1987a) Bourguignon and Gelb (1989), and Hausmann (1990, Chapter 5).

11. Even though total real public sector spending increased by only 0.5 percent in 1979–80, expenditures on non-tradeables rose by 5.1 percent while those on tradeables fell by 11.1 percent. Consequently, the policy alleviated the balance of payments more than it did the internal imbalance.

12. See Hausmann (1990, Chapter 8).

13. This and all other similar ratios are measured in relation to non-oil GDP, since variations of nominal oil GDP were large during the period

because of changes in world petroleum prices and in the exchange rate applied to the oil sector. Hence, even when we do not point it out, we will always refer to non-oil GDP.

14. In fact, point D in Figure 4.2(a) is determined by expectations of the date and nature of the eventual adjustment which the government will have to undertake in order to make the economy viable. This policy must include a devaluation and a change in the relative size of i and g to make them consistent.

15. One contributing reason for the radically explosive path followed initially by the premium is the fact that Central Bank sales of foreign exchange to the parallel market took place not at the rate determined in that market but at the fixed rate of 9.90 Bs. per US$. This meant that the contractionary monetary impact of these sales did not increase with depreciation, thus eliminating one stabilizing mechanism in the money supply process.

16. In other words, profits from sales at the parallel rate of approximately 7 Bs. per US$ exceeded losses at the subsidized rate of Bs.3.20 per US$ by an amount equal to 4.2 percentage points of GDP.

17. Waiting lists for consumer durables made their appearance and delivery dates became ever farther away. In August 1986, the exchange control office RECADI, swamped by a flood of demands for import allocations, decided to scrap all applications and ask for new ones.

18. In addition, its profits from sales as the parallel market declined because of a fall in the premium.

19. Import credits to the private sector increased by $2.2 billion in 1987.

20. This effect was enhanced by the fact that the supply of foreign exchange at the rate of 9.90 Bs. per US$ was stopped and those dollars were sold at the higher freely floating exchange rate.

21. These observations are also consistent with our model in the sense that the internal price of tradeables is too low to allow imports to be profitably supplied through the parallel market.

22. Even though our model does not treat output explicitly, we propose the following conjecture: the explosive path tends to accelerate domestic output growth as the binding import constraint makes all non-oil activity become non-tradeable at the margin, thus making the expansionary demand push affect mainly domestic output, not the balance of payments.

23. As shown in Table 4.2, inventory accumulation averaged 5 percent of GDP in 1987–8.

24. The rate of unemployment reached 6.9 percent in the second semester of 1988. This clearly signals a situation very close to full employment since it was the lowest rate in 9 years and was also below the 1967–82 average of 7.3 percent.

25. Blanco and Garber (1986) and Obstfeld (1986) show that a viable fixed exchange rate after a collapse has to be higher (more devalued) than a floating rate, where the latter assumes no reserve change. Hence, floating may lead to the lowest viable exchange rate.

26. Real government spending declined by 2.4 percent, but the real domestic value of interest payments increased by 3.1 percent of GDP. This

27. means that part of the resources extracted from the private sector by the government through devaluation were transferred abroad.

27. Portfolio balance determines π and tradeables clear at the commercial rate in the unrestricted model and at ρ in the restricted model.

28. For Kiguel and Lizondo (1990) the price of tradeables is the official exchange rate, implying $\rho = 1$. In our restricted model, ρ exceeds unity but is less than π. In either case, unification will cause a major jump in the price level.

29. A contractionary effect of devaluation analyzed in the literature is the fall in real credit and its effects on supply (see van Wijnbergen, 1986; Montenegro, 1989). In Venezuela during 1989 the stock of net real bank credit to the private sector fell by 37.8 percent. This may suggest that excess demand for credit would appear given the large rise in working capital requirements given the rise in the price level. Instead, the credit market during most of the year was characterized by excess supply, with bank liquid reserves rising quickly. The inventory cycle helps explain this anomaly.

30. Obstfeld (1986) shows that it may cause the collapse of an otherwise viable fixed exchange regime. Froot and Obstfeld (1988) further extend work on policy uncertainty for flexible exchange regimes.

REFERENCES

Adams, Charles and Jeremy Greenwood (1985) 'Dual Exchange Rate Systems and Capital Controls: an Investigation', *Journal of International Economics*, vol. 18, pp. 43–63.

Baptista, A. (1989) 'Tiempo de Mengua: Los Años Finales de una Estructura Económica', in Cunill-Grau *et al.* (eds), *Venezuela Contemporánea 1974–1989* (Caracas: Fundación Mendoza).

Blanco, Herminio and Peter M. Garber (1986) 'Recurrent Devaluation and Speculative Attacks on the Mexican Peso', *Journal of Political Economy* vol. 94, no. 1, pp. 148–66.

Bourguignon, Francois and Alan Gelb (1989) 'Venezuela', in Alan Gelb (ed.) *Oil Windfalls: Blessing or Curse?* (Oxford: Oxford University Press), pp 289–325.

Dornbusch, Rudiger (1986) 'Special Exchange Rates for Capital Account Transactions', *World Bank Economic Review*, vol. 1, no. 1, pp. 1–33.

Edwards, Sebastian (1989) *Real Exchange Rates, Devaluation and Adjustment Exchange Rate Policies in Developing Countries* (Cambridge, Mass: MIT Press).

Froot, Kenneth and Maurice Obstfeld (1988) 'Exchange Rate Dynamic Under Stochastic Regime Shifts: a Unified Approach', *Journal of International Economics*, vol. 31, nos 3–4, pp. 203–29.

Hausmann, Ricardo (1990) *Shocks Externos y Ajuste Macroeconómico* (Caracas: Banco Central de Venezuela).

Kiguel, Miguel and J. Saul Lizondo (1990) 'Adoption and Abandonment of Dual Exchange Rate Systems', *Revista de Análisis Económico*, vol. 5, no. 1, pp. 2–23. (Previously *Development Research Department Discussion Paper* No. 201, (Washington, DC: World Bank).)

Lizondo, J. Saul (1987) 'Unification of Dual Exchange Rate Markets', *Journal of International Economics*, vol. 22, nos 1/2, pp. 57–77.

Lizondo, J. Saul, (1990) 'Multiple Exchange Rates and Black Market Exchange Rates: a Non-technical Survey', mimeo, (Washington, DC: IMF).

Montenegro, S. (1989) 'External Shocks and Stabilization Policy in Developing Economies', DPhil thesis, St Antony's College, University of Oxford, Oxford.

Obstfeld, Maurice (1986) 'Capital Controls, the Dual Exchange Rate and Devaluation', *Journal of International Economics*, vol. 20, pp. 1–20.

O'Connell, Stephen A. (1992) 'Short and Long Run Effects of an Own-funds Scheme', *Journal of African Economies*, vol. 1, No. 1, pp. 131–50.

Park, Daekeun and Jeffrey Sachs (1987) 'Capital Controls and the Timing of Exchange Regime Collapse', *NBER Working Paper* No. 2250 (Cambridge, Mass: National Bureau of Economic Research).

Pazos, Felipe (1979) 'Efectos de un Aumento Súbito en los Ingresos Externos: La Economía de Venezuela en el Quinquenio 1974–1978', mimeo, (Caracas: Banco Central de Venezuela).

Pinto, Brian (1991) 'Black Markets for Foreign Exchange, Real Exchange Rates and Inflation', *Journal of International Economics*, vol. 30, pp. 121–36.

Rodriguez, Miguel (1987a) 'La Estrategia del Crecimiento Económico para Venezuela', *Academia Nacional de Ciencias Económicas, Cuaderno No. 19* (Caracas).

Rodriguez, Miguel (1987b) 'Consequences of Capital Flight for Latin American Debtor Countries', in Donald R. Lessard and John Williamson (eds), *Capital Flight and Third World Debt* (Washington, DC: Institute for International Economics).

van Wijnbergen, Sweder (1986) 'Exchange Rate Management and Stabilization Policies in Developing Countries', in Sebastian Edwards and Liaquat Ahamed (eds), *Economic Adjustment and Exchange Rates in Developing Countries* (Chicago, Ill: University of Chicago Press), pp. 17–38.

5 Macroeconomic Aspects of Multiple Exchange Rate Regimes: the Case of Ghana

Yaw Ansu[1]

INTRODUCTION

In April 1983 Ghana began a series of exchange rate policy reforms that by 1988 had transformed the exchange rate regime from one in which a rigidly fixed official exchange rate operated alongside a thriving black market to one in which market forces determined exchange rates on an official auction and on legalized foreign exchange bureaus. Concurrent with the exchange rate reforms, controls on imports were progressively removed, culminating in 1989 in the abolishing of import licensing, which had operated in Ghana since 1961. The black market for foreign exchange, while not completely eradicated, is now a shadow of its former self, confined to the fringes of the foreign exchange bureaus and motivated more by a desire on the part of dealers to avoid taxes rather than exchange and trade controls.

This chapter reviews the exchange regimes in the period before the reforms (1970–82) and also in the reform period from 1983 to 1989. In both periods dual or multiple exchange rates prevailed. In the first period an official rate existed together with a black market rate, which though illegal governed a significant volume of economic transactions. In addition, periodically the official exchange rate was supplemented with taxes on foreign exchange for services and advance deposit requirements for goods imports, which *de facto* transformed even the official exchange regime into a multiple rate system. In the second period, there has been a gradual attempt to convert the official rate into a market-based system with the importance of the black market rate receding. However, at various times since 1983, there has been more than one official exchange rate. This chapter seeks to answer the following questions. What were the key economic reasons leading to the emergence or adoption of the various exchange rate regimes? What have been the macroeconomic – balance of payments, fiscal, monetary, inflation, and GDP growth – impacts of the various exchange rate regimes and, in turn, how have macroeconomic factors affected developments in the exchange regimes?

During the 1983–9 period, exchange rate reforms were part of a broader reform effort which is still in progress. One therefore has to be careful in attributing any macroeconomic responses during the period to exchange rate actions *per se*. However, it is not the aim of this chapter to evaluate the whole reform program that Ghana has been implementing since 1983; the focus is exchange rate regimes and as far as possible only aspects of the overall reform program that have direct bearing on exchange rates will be discussed.

The structure of the chapter is as follows. The second section discusses exchange rate policy in the period from 1970 to 1982, the reasons for the increasing importance of the black market for foreign exchange, and the resulting macroeconomic effects as well as the government's policy response. The third section describes the exchange reforms implemented since 1983 and in particular the workings of the auction and forex markets. The fourth section traces the major macroeconomic impacts of the exchange reforms taking into consideration the reforms that have been implemented concurrently in trade, monetary, and taxation policies. The final section provides a summary and policy conclusions. Econometric estimates of the determinants of the black market premium and its effects on cocoa exports are provided in an appendix.

EXCHANGE RATE POLICIES BEFORE REFORMS (1970–82)

On 27 December 1971 the Ghanaian currency – the (new) cedi – was devalued by 78 percent against the US dollar (that is, from 1.02 cedis per US$ to 1.82).[2] This devaluation was part of a slow, halting, but nevertheless discernible process of trade liberalization that had started in 1966. By the time of the devaluation, although imports were regulated by licensing and the importation of as many as 80 items was either restricted or banned, there was an open general license (OGL) system that allowed registered importers to freely import most chemicals, spare parts, fertilizers, certain electrical machinery, mineral manufactures, paper and paperboard, certain foodstuffs, and pharmaceutical products.[3] Unregistered importers could also import under the OGL system after paying a fee of 25 cedis a year. In addition, individuals with their own foreign currency were issued with special unnumbered licenses (SULs) that permitted the importation, in noncommercial quantities, of all imports not on the OGL system and not restricted or banned. Prior to the devaluation, there was an export bonus scheme under which exporters received a bonus of 25 percent of the value of exports expressed in cedis. The scheme covered all exports, except cocoa beans, minerals, and primary metals in the case of exports to African countries and, in the case of exports to outside Africa, also timber and cocoa products. Tourists cashing foreign currency or travelers checks were also given a 25 percent bonus. On the imports side, a 'temporary' surcharge ranging from 5 to 75 percent was in place and a 10–25 percent tax was levied on service payments as well as remittances out of Ghana. With the devaluation, the bonus on foreign exchange inflows and the surcharges on outflows were abolished.

In January 1972, 3 weeks after the devaluation, the civilian government was overthrown through a military coup. On 7 February the cedi was moved back from 1.82 per US$ to 1.28, a revaluation of approximately 29 percent. It was widely believed at the time that resentment of the December 1971 devaluation was one of main reasons for the coup. True or false, that belief became so strong within policy-making circles in Ghana that it exercised a powerful influence on the course of the exchange rate and trade policies in Ghana throughout the 1970s. In February 1973 when the US$ was devalued, the cedi retained its par value in gold and thus appreciated against the dollar by approximately 10 percent (that is from 1.28 cedis per US$ to 1.15 cedis). The exchange rate stayed fixed until June 1978 when a new military government, emerging from a internal putsch, floated it for 6 months and fixed its value at 2.75 cedis per US$ in December 1978. The rate remained at 2.75 until April 1983 – three governments later – when the current exchange rate reforms began. Meanwhile the consumer price index (1977 = 100) increased from 16 in 1972 to 173 in 1978, and to 1062 by the end of 1982; the average annual inflation rates were 46 percent in 1972–8 and 63 percent in 1978–82. The real effective exchange rate, using the official exchange rate, appreciated by 289 percent from 1973 to 1978 and by another 187 percent from 1978 to 1982 (see Figure 5.1).

In addition to revaluing the cedi, the government that came to power in 1972 also promptly canceled certain pre-1966 suppliers

Index,
1980=100

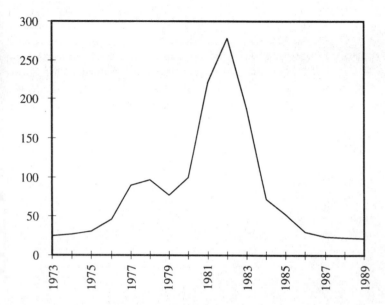

FIGURE 5.1   *Real effective exchange rate*
SOURCE: IMF. Increase=appreciation.

credits that it considered were fraudulent. It also renounced the terms of the debt rescheduling agreements of 1966, 1968, and 1970 and suspended moratorium interest under those agreements. It declared that all medium-term loans were to be repaid over 50 years, including 10 years of grace.[4] Hence, not only were incentives for exports and other foreign exchange inflows reduced, access to trade credits and new loans was severely curtailed.

Although the government tried some steps to attract more foreign exchange inflows, on the whole its response was to tighten the exchange and import control regimes. Among the measures taken to gain more foreign exchange were the reintroduction of the export bonus system in 1973; the voucher system, introduced in 1976, under which a visa or an entry permit could be issued to a traveler into Ghana only after they had purchased in foreign exchange vouchers amounting to US$50 plus US$20 for each day of their stay in Ghana; and the retention scheme under which exporters in the mining and timber sectors, as well as exporters of non-traditional products could retain 20 percent of their export proceeds for approved imports. On the side of import restrictions, the scope of the OGL was initially reduced to the importation of trade samples, personal effects, and gifts and in 1974 the OGL as well as the SUL systems were abolished.[5] Levies on import licenses were increased and mandatory advance cash deposits for imports, except crude oil and fertilizers, introduced. From 1974 until 1981 when they were abolished, the advance cash margins ranged from 50 to 25 percent for industrial raw materials, chemicals, spare-parts, building materials, and medical supplies; 75 to 50 percent for machinery and equipment, and 100 to 65 percent on all other goods. In 1982 these margins were abolished and replaced with a 20 percent tax on letters of credit.

The immediate impact of the increasing restrictions was an almost 50 percent drop in the volume of imports in 1972 compared with 1971.

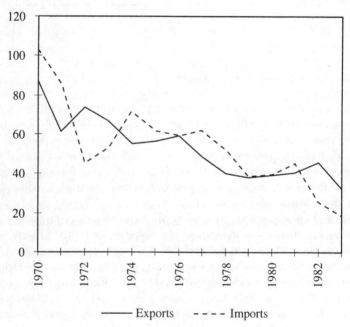

FIGURE 5.2 *Exports and imports volume index*
SOURCE: Country case study.

However, by 1974 real imports had recovered to approximately 80 percent of the level in 1971, due to increased availability of foreign exchange arising from a higher international price of cocoa. The higher cocoa price ensured that Ghana's external terms of trade increased by approximately 25 percent in 1973 and by 12 percent in 1974 despite the oil price shock. After 1974, however, import volumes began a steady downward trend and by 1983 the index of real imports was down to a quarter of that in 1974 or to a fifth of the level in 1971 (see Figure 5.2).

A consequence of the decreasing supplies of imports and the tightening of trade and exchange controls was an increase in the black market premium on foreign exchange and in parallel economic transactions, including the smuggling of imports and exports. The black market premium increased steadily from 50 percent in 1974 to over 2100 percent in 1982 (that is, from a black market rate which was 1.5 times the official exchange rate in 1974 to one that was over 22 times in 1982). Although producer prices of cocoa in Ghana from 1974 to 1982 were generally higher than those in neighboring Togo and the Ivory Coast in terms of official exchange rates, the situation was quite the reverse in terms of the black market exchange rates.[6] The result was significant smuggling of cocoa from Ghana to Togo and the Ivory Coast. The foreign exchange earned from export smuggling helped finance imports either directly by the cocoa smugglers themselves or indirectly through its sale in the black market for foreign currency.[7]

By its very nature, the size of black market transactions is difficult to measure. However, rough estimates put the amount of cocoa smuggled out of Ghana from 1974 to 1980 at between 10 and 20 percent of official purchases. One econometric study estimated the size of the parallel market economy in Ghana indirectly through estimates of the amount of money generated by cocoa smuggling. Using this approach, the parallel market economy was estimated to have grown from approximately 0.5 percent of GDP in 1974 to approximately 32 percent in 1982.[8] While one might question these estimates, the increasing importance of black or parallel market transactions in the Ghanaian economy over this period was unmistakable, so much so that in 1977 the Ghanaian government publicly accused Togo of economic sabotage through the running of a black market in the cedi and of smuggling from Ghana.[9] Of course, demand factors also influenced the black market rate and the volume of transactions on that market. These are covered in the next section.

MACROECONOMIC CONSEQUENCES OF EXCHANGE RATE POLICY AND THE BLACK MARKET

This section reviews some of the key linkages between the foreign exchange black market and exports, the fiscal accounts, money growth, and domestic price formation in Ghana over the pre-reform period.

Exports

We have already referred above to how the smuggling of cocoa out of Ghana was encouraged by the fact that producer prices in Ghana compared quite unfavorably with those in neighboring Togo and the Ivory Coast at the black market exchange rates. With the official exchange rate fixed over most of the period from 1972 to 1982, the producer price for cocoa could not be increased appreciably without imposing large trading losses on the parastatal Cocoa Marketing Board (now CocoBod). The low producer prices reduced incentives for production, which were only partly relieved by the opportunities for smuggling. Cocoa production fell from an average of 427 000 tons in 1970–2 to an average of 220 000 tons in 1981–3. Over the 14 year period, both production and exports fell by an average of 3.5 percent a year.[10]

Fiscal Performance

The ratio of domestic revenue (that is, government revenue excluding external grants) to GDP, which had climbed from 16 percent in 1970 to 19 percent in 1971, fell to 15 percent in 1972 and to 11 percent in 1973.[11] It subsequently climbed back up to 15 percent in 1975 and then began a steady fall for the next 8 years, reaching 5.2 percent in 1982. What role did exchange rate policy and the increasing scope of black market transactions play in this fall? One of the most important sources of government revenue in Ghana in the early 1970s was cocoa; 7 percent of GDP or 37 percent of revenues in 1971. After some fluctuations from 1972 to 1975, the ratio of cocoa revenue to GDP began a steady fall, reflecting the declining volumes of production and exports. It reached zero in 1981 and 1982. Further, the low official exchange rate meant low (residual) revenue going to the government at any level of official export volumes and international prices. The ratio of import duties to GDP also followed the same declining trend as that of cocoa revenues (and export duties in general). From 3.3 percent of GDP in 1971, import duties had fallen to 0.9 percent by 1982, an average annual fall of approximately 12 percent. A simple decomposition exercise shows that this 12 percent annual average fall in the import duty to GDP ratio breaks down into an 11 percent fall in import volumes and a 23.7 percent decrease in the real exchange rate,[12] which were compensated partially by a 14.5 percent increase in the foreign prices of imports, a 0.4 percent fall in real GDP, and a 7.7 percent increase due to contributions from discretionary import tax measures (for example, increasing duty rates and imposing surcharges) and possible measurement error in the data. From this exercise, the falling real exchange rate emerges clearly as the biggest drag on the import duty to GDP ratio. In fact if the real exchange rate had stayed constant, instead of falling by almost 24 percent a year, then even without the discretionary import tax measures and possible measurement error (that is, disregarding the 7.7 percent yearly increase due to these factors), the import duty to GDP ratio would have increased by an average of 3.9 percent a year from 1971 to 1982 and the ratio in 1982 would have been 5.0 percent instead of 0.9. In addition, given the heavy dependence of Ghanaian industry on imported inputs, the falling volumes of imports, necessitated in part by the falling exports, led to reduced production and, consequently, to declines in domestic indirect taxes as well as income taxes.

The budget, which had shown a small surplus (before foreign grants) of 0.5 percent of GDP in 1971 went into a deficit in 1972. Except for 1974, the ratio of the deficit to GDP increased every year, up to almost 14 percent in 1976. Subsequently, despite reductions in the expenditure to GDP ratio, deficits remained high – an average of around 7 percent of GDP a year – due to falling revenues (see Figure 5.3). The bulk of the deficits were financed from the banking system, primarily the Central Bank. Data from government sources and from the International Monetary Fund (IMF) indicate that an average of 60 percent of the budget deficit (including net lending) was financed by the Bank of Ghana from 1974 to 1977. From 1979 to 1981, however, government sources put the share at an average of 37 percent, while IMF sources put it at an average of 68 percent.[13]

Percent of GDP

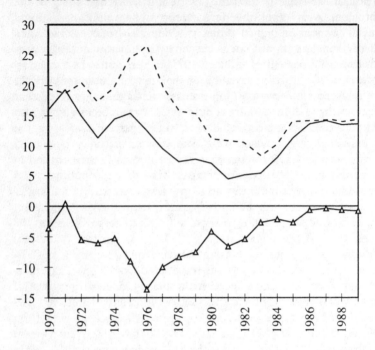

——— Domestic revenue - - - -Total expenditure —△— Budget deficit

FIGURE 5.3   *Fiscal performance*

SOURCE: Country case study.

Money Growth

Whatever the actual size of budgetary deficit finance from the Bank of Ghana and from other banks for that matter, the monetary data clearly indicate heavy government borrowing from the banking system. From 1972 to 1982 the central government took on average approximately 69 percent of the annual flow of net domestic credit from the banking system. Only in 3 of those 11 years did the government's share of credit fall below this average – 20 percent in 1973, 67 percent in 1974, and 15 percent in 1982. The private sector received an average of approximately 10 percent of the credit, cocoa financing 19 percent, and the rest of the public sector 2 percent. Since net domestic credit expansion averaged approximately 110 percent of the annual increase of $M2$ over the 1972–82 period, it means the central government alone was responsible for at least two-thirds of the annual monetary expansion, which averaged around 39 percent a year. This rate of monetary expansion occurred despite periodic increases in commercial bank reserve requirements and demonetization exercises in March 1979 and February 1982. In the first exercise, currency notes were replaced with new ones at a rate of exchange that was less than par, resulting in an approximately 15 percent reduction in the money stock. In the 1982 exercise, 50-cedi notes were demonetized and holders issued with receipts, which were not legal tender. This led to an approximately 12 percent fall in currency.[14] Since currency during this period made up approximately half of $M2$, the impact of the exercise on money supply was an approximately 6 percent reduction.

Inflation

The high rate of monetary expansion in a situation where the compression of import volumes and falling production levels had produced acute shortages of goods contributed to a high rate of inflation in the consumer price index (CPI) and to rapid increases in the black market premium. From under 10 percent in both 1971 and 1972, inflation began climbing in 1973, culminating in 116 percent in 1977 and again in 1981. The average inflation rate over 1973–82 was 55 percent. The black market premium, which had been falling from 1970 to 1972 began rising after 1972. From 27 percent in 1972, the premium reached 2142 percent in 1982. In the face of the high inflation, nominal interest rates were kept at low levels producing negative deposit interest rates throughout the period. The average real deposit rate on savings during 1972–82 was −42 percent a year. The negative deposit rates together with the uncertainty introduced by the arbitrary demonetization exercises greatly discouraged the channeling of savings through the banking system.

EXCHANGE RATE POLICIES AFTER 1982

Beginning in April 1983, Ghana began a series of macroeconomic policy reforms which have helped reverse the deterioration in many of the macroeconomic indicators reviewed in the previous section. Central to these reforms were the gradual move of the exchange rate to a market-determined system and the liberalization of foreign trade.

From Bonuses and Surcharges to a Crawling Peg

On 21 April 1983 a system of bonuses and surcharges on the official exchange rate of 2.75 cedis per US$ was instituted.[15] Foreign exchange receipts from cocoa, gold, timber, and other traditional export products received a bonus equivalent to 750 percent of the official exchange rate (that is, an effective exchange rate of 23.375 per US$). All other receipts, including those from invisibles and capital, received a bonus of 990 percent or an effective exchange rate of 29.975 per US$. Payments were also split into two categories: payments for imports of crude oil, essential raw materials, capital goods, and basic foodstuffs, as well as transfers in respect of official commitments were subject to a surcharge of 750 percent; all other payments were subject to a surcharge of 990 percent. The weighted effective rate under this official multiple exchange rate system was 24.692 per US$. After 6 months of operation, the system was unified by moving the official exchange rate to 30 cedis per US$ and removing the bonuses and surcharges. From the second quarter of 1984 to the first quarter of 1986, the authorities moved to a crawling peg system, under which they pursued a policy of small and regular devaluations, approximately one to two per quarter, with the average devaluation per quarter being around 15 percent. This put the rate at 90 in February 1986, where it remained for a year.

The Exchange Rate Auction

In the meantime, a weekly exchange rate auction was introduced in September 1986. In the first auction, all successful bidders paid the marginal rate (that is, the rate at which bids or demands exhausted the available supply – the English auction); subsequently all successful bidders paid their bidding rates, with the marginal rate being paid only by the marginal bidder(s) (that is, the Dutch auction). The exchange rate established at the auction was applicable to all transactions, including those ineligible for finance from the auction, except for receipts from exports of cocoa and residual oil and payments for petroleum products, essential drugs, and service of government debt contracted before 1 January 1986.[16] These items continued to use the fixed official rate of 90 cedis until February 1987 when the fixed official exchange rate was dropped and they were transferred to the auction. The auction rate, which started at 132.9 cedis per US$ in September 1986, had climbed to 150.6 by the time the fixed official rate was discontinued.[17]

Foreign Exchange Bureaus (Forex Market)

In February 1988, the government made it legal for any person or institution licensed by the Bank of Ghana to operate a foreign exchange bureau on which foreign currencies could be bought and sold freely. The requirements for a license were a deposit of $500 and maintenance of a balance of not less than $2500 in a bank account in Ghana. The only informational requirements on the bureaus were that each of them should clearly display its buying and selling rates and report sales and purchases to the Bank of Ghana on a monthly basis.[18] All bona fide imports and services were eligible for funding through the forex bureaus.

Trade Liberalization

Concurrent with the gradual evolution of the exchange and payments regime towards a market-based system was a gradual relaxation of import controls. With the introduction of the auction, imports were grouped into three categories – A, S, and G – for the purposes of import licensing. Category A included drugs and producer goods (that is, raw materials, spare parts, capital goods, and intermediate goods) and holders of this license could bid at the auction.[19] Category S imports comprised all goods not prohibited for non-trade reasons, except for beers, stout, cigarettes, asbestos or fiber cement pipes, and roofing sheets. Holders of this license could not bid at the auction, but just like the old SULs, the holders could use their own foreign exchange to import goods. However, advance income tax payment equivalent to 20 percent of the value of the license was collected when it was issued. Category G licenses were reserved for imports by government organizations. Foreign exchange for these imports was allocated outside the auction. Following the unification of the official rate with the auction in February 1987, the scope of the auction was progressively broadened to include items covered by the S license, a process that was completed by February 1988 when the forex market was introduced. In January 1989, the whole import licensing system was abolished and importers were required only to file an import declaration form at the commercial banks.

On the exports side, the retention scheme under which exporters of minerals, timber, and non-traditional exports had been allowed to retain 20 percent of their export earnings continued. Cocoa exports were added to the list at 10 percent in 1984, but in 1985 reduced to 2 percent. With the introduction of the forex market, all exporters of non-traditional exports were allowed to sell the balances in their retention accounts on the bureaus. The large exchange rate changes also allowed substantial increases in producer prices for cocoa, which increased in real terms by approximately 50 percent between 1987 and 1989.

Characteristics of the Foreign Exchange Markets in the Reform Period

The exchange rate policy changes begun in 1983 meant that from 1983 to September 1986 the exchange regime consisted of an official crawling rate and a black market; from September 1986 to February 1987, it consisted of a fixed rate, an auction, and a black market; from February 1987 to April 1988, an auction and a black market; and from April 1988 onward, an auction and a forex market on which rates are determined daily, with the black market diminished in importance.[20]

The Auction Market

The supply of funds on the auction increased from an average of US$2.9 million a week (with an average excess demand of US$1. million) in the first 6 full months of operation to US$7.9 million week (with an average excess demand of US$0.4 million) in the months ending July 1990. On an annual basis, the US$2.9 million week from October 1986 to March 1987 represented approximately 16 percent of merchandise imports, while the US$7.9 million a week in 1990 would represent approximately 38 percent of imports in 1989. The number of bidders on the auction increased from an average of 66 a week in the first 6 full months of the auction to an average of 173 in the 6 months ending 16 March 1990. In April 1990, the auction was converted into a wholesale auction, on which commercial banks and other authorized dealers bid on behalf of their clients.

The spread between the highest and the lowest bids for the dollar fell from 65 cedis in the first auction to 29 in the second and then to 12 in the third. It then stayed at or below 10, except in August–September 1988 when it rose to 25 and February–April 1989 when it rose to 40. The changeover from the English to the Dutch auction did not have any appreciable effect on the premium, contrary to what one would expect. The large drop in the spread in the first 2 months of the auction was caused mainly by decreasing demand, resulting in part from a drop in the number of bidders. The switch to the wholesale auction in April 1990 does not appear to have had any marked impact on the spread. As a percentage of the (marginal) auction rate, the spread has been around 5, except in the months mentioned above.

Since the marginal auction rate is the lower bound of the rates paid by successful bidders, the government or the Bank of Ghana derives a surplus – akin to the traditional 'consumer surplus' – from the operation of the auction. A rough approximation of this surplus by the 'triangle method'[21] gives an average of 78 million cedis a month or a rough total of 3.8 billion cedis from the inception of the auction to the second week of August 1990.

The Forex Market

Most of the forex bureaus operate in Accra. Access to the bureaus is quite free, in particular for selling and buying small amounts of foreign currency. For buying large amounts of currency, there are unconfirmed reports that bureaus tend to develop special relationships with particular clients, giving them preferential access. Despite its higher price for foreign currency compared with the auction, the forex market is used by importers, particularly small traders, because of its lower transactions costs and also because many small traders do not finance their importation through the banking system.[22]

Figure 5.4 shows the volume of transactions in cedis on the forex market from April 1988 to May 1990. Both sales and purchases by dealers (or demand and supply by the public correspondingly) followed an upward trend, from a little over 0.5 million cedis in the first month of operation to between 12 and 14 million cedis a month in the last 6 months ending in May 1990. The figure also shows the monthly excess demand for foreign currency by the public (that is, sales minus purchases by dealers). Dealers have no access to foreign exchange supply on either the domestic or foreign financial markets; the predominant source of supply is purchases from the public – travellers to Ghana and remittances. This would suggest that dealers cannot support significant and sustained (positive) excess demands. In addition, barring strong reasons to hoard for speculative purposes, the profit motive would rule out significant and sustained excess supply, imply-

Cedi (millions)

———— Sales - - - - Purchases —△— Excess demand

FIGURE 5.4   *Transactions on the forex market (monthly) (sales=demand;*
purchases = supply)

NOTES: Excess demand is defined as sales minus purchases
SOURCE: Country case study.

ing that the monthly excess demands should fluctuate within a narrow band around zero. This is more or less confirmed by the data. The excess demands were all within 2 million cedis, except for 2 months when they exceeded +2 and −2 million cedis by slight amounts. As a percentage of the supply, excess demands have ranged between 3.5 and 18.9 in absolute values. However, the period from October 1988 to June 1989 did experience sustained excess demand, but even then, only in 6 of those 9 months was the excess demand more than 5 percent of the supply and only in 2 months was it more than 10 percent.[23]

The spread between the buying and selling rates ranged from 2.4 to 12.2 percent of the buying rate. The average spread over the period from April 1988 to August 1990 was 5.7 percent but falling, suggesting increasing efficiency of the market. The spread stayed below 4 percent in the last 4 months of the period (that is, May to August).

Exchange Rates in the Reform Period

The Forex and Black Market Rates

Figure 5.5 shows the rates on the various markets from January 1982 to August 1990. The black market rate has been below the forex rate since the latter was established. One reason for this may be the fact that the black market rate used here is the average of the buying and selling rates, while the forex rate is the selling rate (that is, selling by dealers to the public).[24] However, there is a possible economic reason. A major reason why black market dealers have been able to coexist with the forex is that they offer slightly better rates: a marginally higher rate than the forex on the buying side and a marginally lower rate on the selling side, which means that an average of the black market buying and selling rates would be lower than the forex selling rate. The black market dealers are able to offer slightly better prices than the forex dealers because they have no fixed overhead costs and also do not pay income tax on their earnings, unlike the forex bureaus which have to pay the company income tax of 55 percent.

The Black Market and Official Rate

When the bonus surcharge exchange rate system was introduced in April 1983, the black market rate had been falling for 3 months – from

Cedi/US$

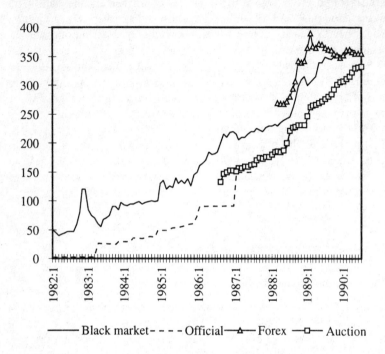

FIGURE 5.5   *Foreign exchange rates*

SOURCES: Country case study; black market rate from International Currency Analysis, Inc., *World Currency Yearbook*.

120 cedis per US$ in December 1982 to 70 in March 1983.[25] With the effective devaluation of the official rate of approximately 798 percent (from 2.75 to 24.69) in April, the black market rate fell further to 60. The black market premium therefore fell dramatically, from 2446 percent in March to 143 percent in April. It continued to follow a downward trend as the black market rate continued to fall, reaching 24 percent by the time the forex market started operating in April 1988.

The Forex Market and the Official (Auction) Rate

Figure 5.6 shows the average monthly rates on the forex and auction markets and also the percentage premium of the forex rate over the

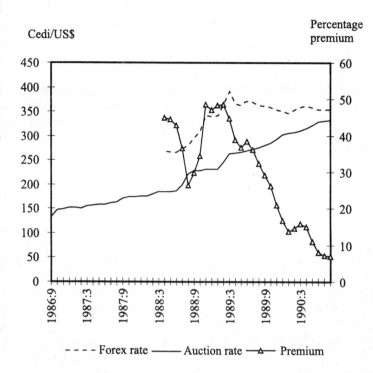

FIGURE 5.6   *Auction and forex rates and premium*
NOTES: Premium is defined as the percentage excess of the forex rate over auction rate.
SOURCE: Country case study.

auction rate. The forex market began operation with a 45 percent premium over the auction rate, followed by a gradual decline over the subsequent 4 months to 27 percent in August 1988. However the premium started rising in September, peaking at 49 percent in February 1989, before gradually falling to below 7 percent in August 1990. The first year of the operation of the forex was marked by large fluctuations in the rates. After June 1989, however, changes were quite small, mostly negative, resulting in a slight, but steady decline in the rate. The auction rate increased sharply in the first 3 months following the introduction of the forex, probably due to the increased liberalization of imports. By early 1989, the rate was generally increasing by modest amounts, which given the slowly decreasing forex rate, resulted in the decreasing premium.

MACROECONOMIC IMPACTS OF EXCHANGE REFORMS

The Balance of Payments

Between 1984 and 1989, real exports grew at an annual average rate of 13 percent. Cocoa exports grew by an average of 11 percent. Certainly all of this increase cannot be attributed directly to the changes in the exchange rate regime. However, the changes in the exchange rate enabled the government to increase producer prices in real terms, at an average annual rate of almost 16 percent over 1983–9. The black market premium, which as shown in the Appendix is an important determinant of official cocoa exports, has been reduced because of the exchange rate reforms and also because there have been more imports in the system – an average annual growth of 11 percent in import volumes from 1984 to 1989. The increase in import volumes has in a large part been financed by foreign grants and loans made possible by the whole economic reform program, of which the exchange reforms were central and also by greater inflows of remittances encouraged by the import decontrol process and the forex system.

Foreign grants averaged US$138.7 million a year in the 7 years from 1983 to 1989; in contrast, in the 7 years preceding 1983 they averaged only US$68 million.[26] Similarly, whereas net private transfers were negative in each of the 7 years prior to 1983, averaging US$−3.8 million a year, in 1983–9 they were positive in each year, averaging US$110 million a year. The increase in net private transfers was particularly strong following the acceleration of import liberalization in 1987 and the introduction of the forex market; the annual average over 1987–9 was US$192 million.

Fiscal Performance

The ratio of domestic revenues to GDP followed an upward trend beginning in 1983 (recall Figure 5.3), averaging some 11.4 percent in the 7 years ending in 1989 (13.7 percent in the last 4 of those years), compared with 7.7 percent over 1976–82. Although cocoa revenues have recovered from the negligible levels to which they had fallen in 1981 and 1982, their ratio to GDP, approximately 2.4 percent, is not appreciably different from the levels in the mid-1970s. This is most probably the result of the policy of increasing the producer price in real terms and also the falling world price of cocoa. The ratio of import duties to GDP has, on the other hand, almost doubled compared with the pre-reform ratios of the mid-1970s and early 1980s. From 1984 to 1989 the ratio increased by an average of almost 20 percent annually.[27] A decomposition exercise similar to that done for the 1971–82 period (see note 12) shows that this 20 percent average annual increase in the ratio was made up of a 10 percent increase due to the rising volume of imports, a 0.4 decrease from a fall in the international price of imports, a 12.5 percent increase in the real exchange rate,[28] a 5 percent fall due to rising real GDP (which reduces the ratio, other things being equal), and a 3.2 percent increase which may be attributed to the net impact of tax rate changes and efforts to improve the efficiency of collection. In fact tariff rates have tended to fall, reflecting the decision by the authorities not to pass the full effect of exchange rate changes into prices.

The rising revenue effort has permitted expenditures also to rise while at the same time improving the overall fiscal situation. In the 4 years ending in 1989, the expenditure ratio averaged 14.3 percent of GDP a year while domestic revenues were around 13.7 percent, leaving a small deficit which has been more than amply covered by foreign grants averaging a little over 1.0 percent of GDP. Hence, overall, the budget registered a surplus (before repayment of debts) averaging 0.4 percent of GDP over 1986–9. In fact a surplus of 0.1 percent of GDP in 1986 was the first such occurrence since 1971. This achievement was maintained and improved upon in the subsequent 3 years.

A major concern often expressed about large exchange rate devaluations (or depreciations) of the sort that have occurred in Ghana is the likely increase in the domestic cost of servicing government foreign debt.[29] This issue is usefully examined under three headings: interest payments, amortization, and clearance of arrears, where they exist. In the case of Ghana, foreign interest payments from the budget have increased from an average of approximately US$25 million a year over 1976–82 to approximately US$29 million a year over 1983–9. However, due to the exchange rate changes these payments expressed as a percentage of GDP have greatly increased, from approximately 0.1 percent to 0.5 percent. They have also increased as a percentage of total budgetary expenditures, from 1.0 to 3.6 percent. However, since the exchange rate changes also increased revenues and helped attract foreign grants, a more meaningful measure would be the ratio of interest payments to government revenues including grants (that is, total budgetary resources). Using this measure, the burden of foreign interest payments on budgetary resources increased from an average 2.1 percent in the first period to 3.7 percent, representing an approximately 76 percent increase compared with the 16 percent increase in the dollar value of the interest payments. This suggests that the exchange rate changes resulted in an approximately 60 percent increase in the burden of foreign interest payments on budgetary resources. In the case of net inflows of external loans to finance the budget, the situation was reversed: average annual net inflows decreased from approximately US$51 million over 1976–82 to approximately US$22 million over 1983–9,[30] but the depreciation in the exchange rate compensated for almost all of this fall; the ratio in terms of GDP was practically the same – from 0.22 to 0.20 percent.

Perhaps the most relevant comparison is the one that holds the dollar values of the flows constant over the two periods in order to isolate the exchange rate effect. If the dollar inflows during 1983–9 had stayed the same as in the 1976–82 period (that is averaging US$51 million a year, instead of falling to US$22 million), then they would have amounted to an average of 0.99 percent of GDP a year compared with the 0.22 percent over 1976–82 (a gain of 0.77 percent of GDP a year). Similarly, if annual interest payments in 1983–9 had stayed at the same dollar levels as in 1976–82 (that is, an average of US$25 million instead of rising to US$29 million), then they would have amounted to 0.45 percent of GDP a year compared with the 0.13 percent in 1976–82 (that is, a loss of 0.32 percent of GDP a year). Hence, considering both net inflows of loans and interest payments together and holding the dollar values constant (at the 1976–82 flows), the budget seems to have gained an average of 0.45 percent of GDP per annum during 1983–9 as a result of the exchange rate changes. To this must be added the positive impact of the exchange rate changes on foreign trade taxes.

While exchange rate changes have had a positive net impact on the budget, their impact on the Treasury's indebtedness on account of outstanding arrears to external creditors has been quite severe. These arrears are from the Treasury's own foreign borrowing as well as government-guaranteed foreign borrowing of the private sector. As the Central Bank began to clear the arrears with external creditors, the cedi amounts needed to balance the transaction increased rapidly, since the new highly depreciated exchange rate was used. The Central Bank created an accounting entry, the revaluation account, in its asset column to bring about the required balance. From approximately

8.5 billion cedis at the end of 1983, this account had grown to approximately 270 billion cedis by the end of 1989. However, up to the end of 1989 it was not clear whose liability the revaluation account was since the Treasury had not yet formally accepted responsibility for it. In 1990 the Treasury formally accepted responsibility for these debts and they were converted into a long-term debt owed to the Bank of Ghana.

In summary, the overall impact of the large exchange rate changes on the budget was most probably positive in flow terms: revenues from international trade rose and the net effect on repayments of current maturities (interest and amortization) and new inflows was beneficial once the dollar flows are adjusted to make them equal before and during the exchange rate reforms. It has not been possible to analyze the impact of exchange rate changes on other components of government expenditure (for example, government imports) in addition to debt service, but it is unlikely that taking them into account would reverse the direction of the overall budgetary impact of the exchange rate changes. However, the story might have been different if the Treasury had been made to absorb on a current basis the impact of the exchange rate changes on its stock of arrears on foreign debt. First, Central Bank net lending would have been shown as increasing concurrently with exchange rate changes while the arrears remained. Unless this was explicitly recognized in the government's program with the IMF, either the credit ceilings would have been breached or the government's scope for actual borrowing would have been correspondingly reduced. Second and perhaps more importantly, treating the revaluation account as debt of the Treasury implies annual debt service from the budget. At the average Treasury bill rate of 19.8 percent in 1989, interest alone on the 270 billion cedis in the revaluation account would have amounted to 53.5 billion cedis, approximately a quarter of total revenues (including grants) in 1989. It is possible that had the Treasury been required to make regular provisions in the budget for this impact, there would have been severe pressure to slow down the pace of or even discontinue the exchange rate reforms. By waiting a number of years and then converting the accumulated impacts into long-term debt owed to the Central Bank, the government could ensure that the budget was not unduly burdened. Perhaps the same effect could have been achieved more cleanly by anticipating the problem at the start of the exchange reforms and making explicit allowance for it in the design of the macroeconomic programs. Given that this was not done, the pragmatic approach actually pursued was very helpful in containing the problem.

Money and Credit

Money supply ($M2$) grew at an average nominal rate of 48 percent a year over 1983–9, compared with 42 percent a year over 1976–82.[31] However, due to lower inflation over the 1983–9 period, real $M2$ growth has been higher – an average of 6 percent a year, compared with a negative 28 percent a year during 1976–82. On the whole, the government was a source of liquidity to the banking system during 1983–9, in contrast to the earlier period. Net credit outstanding from the banking system to the central government declined by an average of 60 percent a year in real terms (by approximately 33 percent to the public sector as a whole, not counting cocoa financing). Credit to the private sector, on the other hand, increased at a real rate of 39 percent a year over 1983–9. However, if one looks only at the 3 year period 1987–9, credit to the private sector declined by an average of 13 percent a year in real terms. When one considers the fact that a substantial portion of credit to the private sector during this period was in the form of rolled-over, non-performing loans, then the credit squeeze on the private sector was even more severe. To tie this to exchange rate developments, credit to the private sector in foreign exchange terms (that is, credit deflated by the official exchange rate) fell at an annual average rate of 30 percent over 1983–9. This imposed a considerable burden given the dependence of Ghanaian industry on credit to finance imported inputs. This was the complaint voiced most often by the private sector regarding the exchange rate reforms. In addition, the large changes in the exchange rate without corresponding revaluation in the assets of firms meant that firms found it difficult to qualify for foreign exchange loans. By the end of the 1980s several commercial banks were in financial trouble due not only to their own inefficiencies and bad loan decisions, but also to the effect of the real credit squeeze on otherwise viable clients. Thus, while the exchange rate changes through their positive fiscal impact have reduced government reliance on the banking system for deficit financing and consequently helped restrain money growth and inflation, they have nevertheless led to a credit squeeze in real terms on the private sector. This squeeze may have held back growth in manufacturing and further weakened the financial sector.

Inflation

Ignoring the initial year of reforms (1983), the average rate of inflation (that is, over 1984–9) was 28.5 percent, compared with averages of 70 percent in 1976–82 and 55 percent in 1973–82. The available data did not permit a complete and satisfactory econometric estimation of the determinants of inflation for the period since the introduction of the auction and forex bureaus. An early version of this chapter, however (Ansu, 1991, Appendix 3), reports econometric results suggesting that the rate of inflation has not been affected in any significant way by changes in either the auction or forex bureau exchange rates. With the fall in the inflation rate, it has been possible to gradually liberalize interest rates.

SUMMARY

Ghana went through a period of macroeconomic deterioration from approximately 1973 to 1983. This deterioration manifested itself particularly in declining exports, declining government revenues, rising inflation, and decreasing real output. An important cause underlying all these trends was the increasingly overvalued exchange rate, which discouraged production and exports, necessitated increasing controls on imports, encouraged smuggling, and spawned a thriving black market in foreign currencies. In 1983, the government began pursuing a more realistic exchange rate policy which by 1989 had resulted in the exchange rate being put on a market-determined basis. Correspondingly, the deteriorating trends in many of the macroeconomic indicators were reversed or arrested. Although the government simultaneously implemented reforms in areas other than the exchange rate front, the exchange rate reform clearly contributed to the turnaround. Moreover and in this context more important, the fears of higher inflation and government budget deficits (on account of foreign debt payments) often expressed about exchange rate reforms, which in countries starting from Ghana's condition in 1983 must of necessity involve massive devaluations or depreciations, have not materialized. The tight stabilization program pursued in conjunction with exchange rate reform no doubt helped control inflation. In addition, the adverse impact of exchange rate changes on government expenditures and ultimately on the deficit and inflation was to some important extent avoided by postponing having to deal squarely with the impact of exchange rate devaluations/depreciations on the cedi obligations corresponding to arrears on foreign debts most of which were either owed or guaranteed by the government. Up to 1990, the government's budget was protected from this impact by the expediency of the Central Bank creating a nebulous 'revaluation account', to offset it. Further, contrary to the fears often expressed, the move to a market-determined exchange rate has not led to explosions in the rate. After rising at an average monthly rate of 3 percent in the first 8 months of its operation (that is, in 1988), the forex bureau rate became very stable, rising by an average of only 0.2 percent from January 1989 to August 1990. Meanwhile, the auction rate climbed gradually towards the forex bureau rate at an average monthly rate of 2.1 percent (that is, 2.8 percent between April 1988 and December 1989 and 1.8 percent between January 1989 and August 1990), resulting in a differential of approximately 7 percent between the two rates in August 1990 (compared with 45 percent when the forex bureaus first began operating in April 1988). The moderation experienced in the rate of change in the exchange rates has no doubt been helped by the moderate inflation rates made possible by the tight stabilization program.

The successful exchange rate reforms have not been without macroeconomic costs, however. The tight monetary control needed to control inflation and to sustain the exchange reforms combined with the large exchange devaluations to cripple several of the import-dependent firms in the industrial sector, not all of whom were economically inefficient, and in the process further weakened banks which had loans outstanding to the firms. It must be stressed, however, that the financial sector in Ghana did have serious structural problems which were merely compounded by the exchange rate reform and the supporting monetary policy.

NOTES

1.   The author is a Senior Economist, Africa Region, the World Bank. He gratefully acknowledges the research assistance of Mr Sam Ankrah and the cooperation of Ms P. Jones, Mr T. Long, and the Ghanian Authorities. The views expressed here are not necessarily those of the World Bank or affiliated organizations.

2. The Ghanaian cedi, introduced in July 1965, was renamed the new cedi in February 1967 after a change in the par value from 0.857 cedis to a dollar to 0.714 cedis to a dollar. In February 1972 the prefix, 'new' was dropped and the name reverted to the cedi. In this paper, any references to cedi(s) prior to February 1972 apply to the new cedi.

3. International Monetary Fund, *Exchange Arrangements and Exchange Restrictions* (1972).

4. International Monetary Fund, *Exchange Arrangements and Exchange Restrictions* (1973). Ghana's medium-term debts were subsequently rescheduled again in 1974.

5. The SUL system was reintroduced in 1975.

6. See Franco (1981) and Ansu (1984).

7. Cocoa smuggling was the dominant source of inflow of foreign exchange to the black market from exports. Comparison of export and import values reported by Ghana and those reported by Ghana's trade partners over 1970–83 revealed no clear evidence of either underinvoicing or overinvoicing.

8. See May (1985).

9. Economist Intelligence Unit (1977, no. 4 p. 6).

10. Using least-squares growth rates. The cocoa production data are most likely based on official sales (to the marketing board), and may therefore overstate the extent of production decline, given the significant increase in cocoa smuggling.

11. From 1970 to 1981, the fiscal data are on a 1 July to 30 June fiscal year basis. From 1982 onwards, the fiscal year corresponds to the calendar year. Reference to a year in the period 1970–81 applies to the fiscal year ending 30 June that year. The GDP data used in the denominator of the ratios are on calendar year basis; they have not been adjusted by averaging 2 adjacent years.

12. For the decomposition exercise, data on total import duties in domestic currency terms are used to compute R_m, the ratio of import duties to nominal GDP. R_m is then expressed as $R_m = tEP_mM/PY$, where t is the effective tariff rate, P_m is the foreign price of imports, E is the official exchange rate, M is the volume of imports, P is the GDP deflator, and Y is real GDP. Taking logs then gives

$$(^*) \qquad \log R_m = \log P_m + \log(E/P) + \log M - \log Y + residual$$

Year-to-year differences in each of the variables in equation (*) were averaged over the period to obtain the results reported in the text. Changes in the 'residual' reflect changes in statutory tax rates as well as in collection effort. The real exchange rate was defined here as the ratio of the official exchange rate to the GDP deflator, E/P.

13. Central Bureau of Statistics of Ghana, *Quarterly Digest of Statistics* (March 1984, December 1987), and IMF, *Government Finance Statistics Yearbook* (1981, 1986). The IMF's GFS does not have data on Bank of Ghana financing of the budget in 1978, but the Central Bureau of Statistics data put Bank of Ghana's financing of the deficit at 82 percent.

14. The currency in circulation at the end of March 1982 (1 month after the exercise) was 12 percent lower than that at the end of January 1982, just prior to the exercise.

15. This description of the system of bonuses and surcharges is based on the World Bank (1984), Annex A.

16. This description of the auction is taken from the World Bank (1989), Annex D.

17. The monthly rates given here are averages of the weekly rates weighted by the volume of sales.

18. As of 1991, currencies traded at the bureaus are the US dollar, the pound sterling, the Deutschmark, the Japanese yen, the Swiss franc, the French franc, the CFA franc, and the Canadian dollar.

19. International Monetary Fund, *Exchange Arrangements and Exchange Restrictions* (1987).

20. Although the forex market was legally introduced in February 1988, actual operation began in April, when the first bureau opened for business in Accra.

21. This assumes that bids are uniformly distributed between the highest and the marginal rate.

22. Transactions costs on the auction were estimated by some officials in the Bank of Ghana to be around 2.75 percent.

23. Under-reporting of transactions volumes, possibly in order to minimize tax liability, cannot be ruled out entirely. The extent of this incidence is not known.

24. The black market rate was obtained from International Currency Analysis, Inc. New York. Separate buying and selling rates were not provided; just a single series. In oral communications, a representative of the company pointed out that the series was the average of buying and selling rates.

25. This fall was most likely the reflection of the return of approximately 1 million Ghanaians resident in Nigeria to Ghana. The exchange of the Nigerian naira and other foreign currencies (since some of the Ghanaian workers were paid partly in dollars or sterling) for the cedi on the black market could very well have depressed the black market premium. The naira was at that time the currency of choice for the small traders who used it to buy goods from Nigeria to sell in Ghana.

26. These figures include only outright grants and exclude the grant element of concessional loans.

27. In fact, except for 1987 when it fell due to poor collection effort, the ratio increased in each year from 1984 to 1989 (Provisional National Defence Council, 1988).

28. Ratio of the nominal average exchange rate to the GDP deflator.

29. See, for example, Pinto (1989).

30. These net inflows do not include rescheduling and other forms of debt relief.

31. For the whole 1970–82 period, the growth rate was 38 percent.

REFERENCES

Ansu, Yaw (1984) Monetary and Exchange Rate Policies for an Economy with Parallel Markets: The Case of Ghana (Unpublished Ph.D. Dissertation, Stanford University).

Ansu, Yaw (1991) 'Macroeconomic Aspects of Multiple Exchange Rate Regimes: the case of Ghana', mimeo (Washington, DC: World Bank).

Central Bureau of Statistics of Ghana (various issues) *Quarterly Digest of Statistics* (Accra: Government Printer).

Economist Intelligence Unit (1977) *Report #4* (London: The Economist).

Franco, Robert G. (1981) 'The Optimal Producer Price of Cocoa in Ghana', *Journal of Development Economics*, vol. 8, no. 1, pp. 77–92.

International Monetary Fund (various years) *Exchange Arrangements and Exchange Restrictions* (Washington, DC: International Monetary Fund).

International Monetary Fund (various years) *Government Finance Statistics Yearbook* (Washington, DC: International Monetary Fund).

May, Ernesto (1985) 'Exchange Controls and Parallel Market Economies in Sub-Saharan Africa: Focus on Ghana', *PPR Working Paper* No. 771 (Washington, DC: World Bank).

Pinto, Brian (1989) 'Black Market Premia, Exchange Rate Unification, and Inflation in Sub-Saharan Africa', *World Bank Economic Review*, vol. 3, no. 3, pp. 321–38.

Provisional National Defence Council (1988) Budget Statement and Economic Policy for 1988 (Accra: Government Printer).

World Bank (1984) *Ghana: Managing the Transition* (Washington, DC).

World Bank (1989) *Ghana: Structural Adjustment for Growth* (Washington, DC: The World Bank).

APPENDIX: ECONOMETRIC ESTIMATES

This appendix models and estimates the black market premium and official cocoa exports in the period 1971 to 1989 using annual data.

The Black Market Premium

The black market premium is derived from the market-clearing condition for the demand and supply of foreign exchange. The total demand for foreign exchange comprises the demand for trade and services through the official channel (D_O), the demand for trade and services through the black market (D_B), and the demand for portfolio investment or simply capital flight (D_F). The supply of foreign exchange comes from two parts: inflows through the official channel (S_O) or the black market (S_B). The market-clearing condition is then

$$(A5.1) \quad \frac{D_O(e,y) + D_B(\rho,y) + D_F(r)}{++ \quad\quad -+ \quad\quad +} = \frac{S_O(X,P_x,\theta,\rho) + S_B(X,P_x,\theta,\rho)}{++-- \quad\quad ++++}$$

The demand for foreign exchange for trade and services, D_O, depends positively on the general price level, CPI, deflated by the official exchange rate, E. This ratio, denoted e, is a measure of the real official exchange rate. The higher the ratio, the more overvalued the official exchange rate is and, hence, the greater the demand for foreign exchange through the official window for imports. Demand through the official channel is also positively influenced by the level of income in foreign currency terms, y (GDP divided by the official exchange rate). Foreign exchange demand on the black market for imports of goods and services, D_B, depends negatively on the ratio of the black market foreign exchange rate to the official exchange rate, ρ, referred to here as *the premium*. The demand on the black market for imports is also assumed to be positively related to y. The financial demand, D_F, is channeled only through the black market. It depends positively on r, the ratio of foreign to domestic deposit interest rates taking into account the expected depreciation of the black market exchange rate:

$$r_t = \left(\frac{1 + i_t^{UK}}{1 + i_t^{GH}}\right) \left(\frac{\xi_{t+1}}{\xi_t}\right) \left(\frac{\phi_{t+1}}{\phi_t}\right)$$

I use the deposit rate in the UK, because of the historical business ties between that country and Ghana. The conversion to cedis was first through the official sterling/dollar exchange rate, ξ and, second, through the black market exchange rate between the dollar and the cedi, ϕ. The expected rate of depreciation term, $(\xi_{t+1}/\xi_t)(\phi_{t+1}/\phi_t)$, was replaced by the realized rate of depreciation in the most recent period, $(\xi_t/\xi_{t-1})(\phi_t/\phi_{t-1})$.

Inflows of foreign exchange through official channels, S_O, depend positively on exports through official channels, which in turn depend positively on the total volume of export production, X and on the foreign prices of exports, P_x. They are affected negatively by the volume of cocoa smuggled out of Ghana. Since the Ivory Coast was the main destination for cocoa smuggling, I assume that smuggling increases directly with the ratio of the producer price of cocoa in the Ivory Coast to that in Ghana, where the Ivory Coast producer price is converted to Ghanaian cedis using the official CFA franc to dollar rate and the black market rate of the dollar in cedis. The ratio can be expressed as the product of the ratio of the producer prices using the official exchange rate for the cedi, θ and the black market premium, ρ. Both θ and ρ therefore simultaneously reduce S_O and increase foreign exchange inflows through the black market, S_B. Black market foreign exchange inflows are also positively affected by the volume of export production and the foreign price of exports.

Under the mild assumption that a rise in the premium increases the net supply of foreign exchange (the demand for foreign exchange unambiguously falls and while the supply of foreign exchange may fall as well (see below), this is the result of opposing influences whose net effect is likely to be smaller), we can linearize equation (A5.1) and solve for the premium to obtain

$$(A5.2) \qquad \rho = C + s_1 X + s_2 P_x + s_3 \theta + d_1 e + d_2 y + d_3 r,$$

$$s_1, s_2 < 0; s_3, d_1, d_2, d_3 > 0.$$

The expected signs of the coefficients are all unambiguous with the exception of s_3, the coefficient on θ. It is reasonable to assume, however, that the diversion of a unit of exports from official to parallel channels reduces the foreign exchange coming into Ghana. This follows from the fact that the producer price in the Ivory Coast was generally below the international price (which would have been received by the cocoa marketing authorities in Ghana) and that cocoa smugglers may have had to take a discount on this price in order to move the cocoa through Ivorian middlemen. It follows that s_3 is positive (and also that a rise in the premium reduces the total inflow of foreign exchange from exports).

Table (A5.1) shows estimates of equation (A5.2) using annual data from 1971 to 1989. Since there are no reliable data on the volume of export production, as distinct from the volume of reported exports, the variables X and P_x were replaced by the dollar value of reported exports, *EXPTUSD*. The method of estimation was two-stage least squares, since the CPI in the variable e, the volume of export production, and GDP in the variable y are endogenous. The instruments used are the one-period lags of e, y, r, and *EXPTUSD*. Table A5.1 presents the results of the estimation. In the table, y is denoted by *GDPEX* (GDP divided by the official exchange rate), e, the real exchange rate variable, by *CPIEX* (the CPI divided by the official exchange rate), r by *IRATIOUK* (the UK to Ghana deposit interest ratio), and θ by *ICTOGHPR* (the Ivory Coast to Ghana producer price ratio for cocoa at the official exchange rate). The second column of estimates corrects for serial correlation using the Cochrane–Orcutt procedure

TABLE A5.1 *Determination of black market premium (annual data 1972–88): dependent variable B/E*

	1	2	3
Constant	−4.73	−4.85	−1.14
	(−0.87)*	(−10.39)	(−0.48)
GDPEX	−2.31E−05	−2.14E−05	−4.74E−05
	(−0.31)	(0.28)	(0.70)
CPIEX	3.96	4.00	3.00
	(2.59)	(2.46)	(4.4)
IRATIOUK	4.25	4.23	4.29
	(1.88)	(1.83)	(1.86)
EXPTUSD	−0.003	−0.003	−0.002
	(−0.86)	(−0.82)	(−0.65)
ICTOGHPR	3.29	3.41	–
	(0.72)	(0.71)	
Standard error of Regression	1.84	1.93	1.87
Adjusted R^2	0.88	0.87	0.88
DW	1.95	1.96	2.35
Serial correlation correction?[†]	No	Yes	No

The dependent variable is the ratio of the black market exchange rate to the official exchange rate. The method of estimation was two-stage least squares. The instruments used were the constant, *ICTOGHPR*, and the one-period lags of *GDPEX*, *CIPEX*, *IRATIOUK*, and *EXPTUSD*.

[*] Numbers in parentheses are *t*-statistics.
[†] Correction for serial correlation was by the Cochrane–Orcutt method.

and the third column reduces the chances of serial correlation by dropping *ICTOGHPR*, which was not significant in either of the two previous regressions. The results are similar in all the regressions. All of the signs, except the one on real income, are those expected. Only the real exchange rate and the interest ratio are significant, the former at 3 percent and the latter at 9 percent. The results indicate that both overvaluation (an increase in *CPIEX*) and an increase in foreign interest rates relative to the domestic savings deposit rate are likely to increase the black market premium.

Cocoa Exports

Another equation was developed for estimating cocoa exports through official channels. The volume of official cocoa exports was assumed to depend on the volume of cocoa production and the ratio of the producer price of cocoa in the Ivory Coast to that in Ghana using the black market exchange rate to convert the Ivory Coast price into cedis. Again, this ratio can be decomposed into the product of the price ratio at the official exchange rate and the black market premium. Thus,

$$
(A5.3) \quad COCOEXP = b_0 + b_1 COCOPRO + b_2 ICTOGHPR + b_3 PREMIUM,
$$
$$
\text{where } b_1, b_2, b_3 > 0
$$

Since the cocoa production data are unreliable the cocoa production variable ($COCOPRO$) was replaced in the estimation with the lagged value of the official cocoa exports variable ($COCOEXP(-1)$). Two-stage least squares was used since the black market premium is also an endogenous variable. The instruments used were the black market premium and the real producer price of cocoa in Ghana, each lagged one period. Table A5.2 presents the estimation results. In the first column, the only variable that is significant is the lagged export variable. The premium variable is of the right sign but insignificant, while the producer price ratio at the official exchange rate is of the wrong sign and insignificant. It is perhaps not surprising that the producer price ratio (Ivory Coast to Ghana) at official exchange rates

TABLE A5.2   *Determination of official cocoa exports (annual data 1971–89): dependent variable COCOEXP*

	1	2	3
Constant	48.31	117.87	70.95
	(0.37)*	(2.48)	(2.44)
$COCOEXP(-1)$	0.71	0.64	0.76
	(4.80)	(4.54)	(8.61)
Premium	−2.21	−6.92	−4.43
	(−0.28)	(−1.96)	(−2.40)
$ICTOGHPR$	31.21	–	–
	(0.46)		
Standard error of regression	35.19	39.96	33.58
Adjusted R^2	0.76	0.71	0.78
DW	–	–	–
Serial correlation correction?[†]	No	No	Yes

The method of estimation was two-stage least squares. The instruments were the constant, $ICTOGHPR$ and the one-period lags of $COCOEXP$, Premium, and the real producer price of cocoa in Ghana.
  Numbers in parentheses are *t*-statistics
  Correction for serial correlation was by the Cochrane–Orcutt method.

should be positively correlated with official exports: from 1977 to 1985, a period that spans the most significant decline in cocoa exports, the ratio was significantly below one for each year, except for 1980 and in several years it was falling. The producer price in Ghana was therefore higher than that in the Ivory Coast at official exchange rates and was becoming increasingly so. However, in the years since 1985 when cocoa exports in Ghana were gradually recovering, the ratio has been above one. This suggests that it was the black market premium, rather than the producer price ratio at the official exchange rate that exerted the predominant influence on smuggling, and hence on the volume of official exports. In the second column of estimates on Table A5.2, the price ratio (at official exchange rates) variable is dropped. This greatly improves the coefficient estimate for the premium, which becomes significant at the 7 percent level. Correction for serial correlation further improves the estimates and the premium variable becomes significant at the 3 percent level. According to the estimates, therefore, the black market premium had a strong negative effect on official cocoa exports.

6 The Parallel Market Premium for Foreign Exchange and Macroeconomic Policy in Sudan

Ibrahim A. Elbadawi[1]

O11   F32

F31   F33

F40

O19

INTRODUCTION

The last two decades in Sudan have witnessed the emergence and subsequent expansion of an active parallel economy. Parallel economic activities have been primarily concentrated in the foreign sector of the economy, in the form of misinvoicing and smuggling of exports and imports and diversion of remittances from Sudanese nationals working abroad (SNWA) to the parallel market for foreign exchange. Foreign exchange transactions in this market have taken place at a freely determined parallel exchange rate.

The parallel foreign exchange market in Sudan has coexisted with an official system of fixed exchange rates, exchange controls, and varying degrees of import rationing. Major episodes in the two markets are detailed in Table 6.1. Table 6.2 shows the long-term evolution of the average annual premium (measured as the ratio of the parallel exchange rate B to the official rate E, both measured in Sudanese pounds (LS) per US\$) during 1970–90. The premium averaged over 170 percent for the subperiod 1970–87 and over 500 percent for 1988–90.

Because of the large volume of transactions in the parallel market[2] and the extent of the rationed demand for imports, the parallel market rate is in fact the marginal price for imports and for foreign exchange. Furthermore, its rate of change reflects the opportunity cost of holding domestic currency rather than assets denominated in foreign exchange. The parallel market is therefore strongly linked to the rest of the macroeconomy. The (endogenous) parallel market premium

TABLE 6.1   *Exchange markets in the Sudan*

Period	Official exchange rate	Regulated parallel rate	Rate for worker remittances	Free market rate	Illegal market rate (picks)
Exchange control (1955–August 1979)					
1955–May 1978	0.35	–	–	–	–
1972	0.35	0.40	–	–	0.61
July 1973	0.35	0.40	0.45	–	0.61
January 1974	0.35	0.40	0.56	–	0.60
July 1976	0.40	0.40	0.57	–	0.55
March 1979	0.40	0.40	0.67	–	0.67
Initial liberalization attempt (September 1979–June 1981)					
September 1979	0.50	0.80	–	–	1.00
September 1980	0.50	0.80	–	–	1.10
June 1981	0.50	0.80	–	–	0.90
Legalized free market (July 1981–April 1983: January 1984–January 1985)					
July 1981–April 1983					
July 1981	0.50	0.80	–	1.08	0.94
November 1981	0.90	–	–	1.10	1.25
June 1982	0.90	–	–	1.13	1.41
August 1992	1.30	–	–	1.75	1.43
November 1982	1.30	–	–	1.75	2.17
February 1983	1.30	1.75	–	1.85	1.69
March 1983	1.30	1.75	–	–	1.75
May 1983–December 1983 (brief suspension)					
May 1983	1.30	1.75	–	–	1.72
June 1983	1.30	1.80	–	–	1.75
December 1983	1.30	1.80	–	–	2.00
January 1984–January 1985					
January 1984	1.30	1.80	–	–	2.04
June 1984	1.30	1.80	–	2.00	2.63
October 1984	1.30	2.10	–	–	2.50
January 1985	1.30	2.10	–	3.60	3.03
Quasi-legalized free markets (February 1985–June 1989)					
February 1985	2.50	3.30	–	–	4.35
March 1986	2.50	4.00	–	–	7.69
April 1987	2.50	4.00	–	–	6.25
October 1987	4.50	4.50	–	–	7.69
October 1988	4.50	11.30	–	–	14.29
June 1989	4.50	12.10	–	–	25.00

Policy reversals (July 1989–December 1990)

July 1989	4.50	12.10	–	–	16.67
September 1989	4.50	12.10	–	–	12.50
December 1989	4.50	12.10	–	–	20.00
February 1990	4.50	12.10	–	–	33.33
December 1990	4.50	12.10	–	–	50.00

acquires importance not only from these direct linkages, but also as an important indicator of inconsistency between macroeconomic policy and the foreign trade and exchange rate regime; this signaling role is likely to feed back into macroeconomic outcomes by influencing government policy and private sector expectations of such policy (for example, expectations of devaluation).[3]

TABLE 6.2   *Exchange rates in the Sudan*

Year	E	B
1970	0.35	0.67
1971	0.35	0.61
1972	0.35	0.52
1973	0.35	0.59
1974	0.35	0.61
1975	0.35	0.67
1976	0.35	0.60
1977	0.35	0.60
1978	0.39	0.67
1979	0.45	0.74
1980	0.50	0.98
1981	0.60	1.01
1982	1.00	1.54
1983	1.30	1.82
1984	1.30	2.47
1985	2.50	3.53
1986	2.50	6.51
1987	3.00	6.48
1988	4.50	11.91
1989	4.50	17.18
1990	4.50	50.00

E and *B* are the official and parallel market exchange rates in Sudanese pounds per US$.
SOURCES: *E* is from International Monetary Fund, *International Financial Statistics*; *B* is from *World Currency Yearbook* (various years).

In a survey of exchange rate regimes in sub-Saharan Africa (SSA), Pinto and van Wijnbergen (1987) argued that parallel market and dual regimes are not only common in Africa, but that 'a key insight is that part of the current macroeconomic instability in SSA may be due to a failure to adjust policy for the existence of parallel markets' (Pinto, 1987, p. 2).[4] In addition to the often-cited efficiency costs associated with the dual regime, a high and persistent parallel market premium can substantially undermine the allocational role of the real exchange rate in the economy by exposing the credibility problem of macroeconomic policy. Even under the unlikely scenario of a depreciated parallel market rate leading to real depreciation in the export sector for example,[5] it does not necessarily follow that investment and other resource flows into this sector will be enhanced. This is because of the increased business risk created by the perceived declining credibility of policy.[6] According to this literature, therefore, successful and sustainable unification of the parallel market rate with the official rate should be a prime objective of economic reforms in those countries, Sudan included.

Exchange rate unification, however, requires explicit consideration of the endogeneity of the premium and the sequencing of policy reforms. More precisely, Pinto (1987, 1989, 1991) has argued for the primacy of fiscal policy and the need to design the pace of exchange rate policy to be consistent with fiscal reform. The driving idea behind this prescription is that if the public sector is a net buyer of foreign exchange, a policy of unifying the exchange rates (for example, through an accelerated crawl of the official rate) before the fiscal deficit is sufficiently reduced may lead to unsustainable post-unification inflation as the authorities find themselves forced to rely exclusively on increases in the inflation tax to replace foregone implicit revenue derived from the taxation of exports through the premium.

Along the lines of the above discussion, we study in this chapter the macroeconomic implications of the parallel market for foreign exchange and the extent to which the presence of such a sizable market interferes with macroeconomic management in Sudan. The second section provides an overview of major macroeconomic developments and the evolution of policies in the areas of exchange rate(s) and foreign trade. The structure of the foreign exchange market is described and analyzed in the third section. The fourth section studies the interactions between the premium and other major macroeconomic indicators and includes an econometric analysis of the effects of the premium on key macroeconomic variables. A more rigorous analysis of the flow and asset-market determinants of the premium is conducted in the fifth section based on an empirical, forward-looking model of the parallel premium. Finally, the last section draws on some implications of the chapter's findings for economic reform and adjustment in Sudan.

AN OVERVIEW OF EXCHANGE RATE AND FOREIGN TRADE REFORM, 1970–90

Sudan, the largest country in Africa, has experienced sharply declining economic fortunes from the mid-1970s to the present. Despite its enormous natural resource base and relatively skilled labor force, per capita GDP has declined by 11 percent over the last 14 years. According to a recent World Bank study, the country's share of merchandise exports fell by 46 percent over the 1980s and Sudan's outstanding external debt reached US$13.9 billion in 1989.[7]

The 1970s marked the beginning of an era characterized by expansive macroeconomic policies aimed at supporting a massive economic development program. With government revenues barely meeting current expenditure and no financial markets available, the authorities relied heavily on currency issue and external financing. For example, the broad money supply increased from LS 2.8 million in 1970–1 to a staggering LS 877 million in 1978–9.

On the other hand, the Sudanese foreign trade and payment regime has been one of full exchange control and highly regulated current account transactions since before the country's independence in 1956. In addition, the exchange rate was fixed at LS 0.35 per US$. Clearly this arrangement was not consistent with the expansive macroeconomic policies of the 1970s and the oil price shocks of the mid- and late 1970s. In an attempt to limit the adverse consequences of these policies for inflation and the real exchange rate, particularly for official non-traditional exports and SNWA remittances, the authorities augmented the control regime by introducing a dual exchange rate system and special foreign trade schemes as early as the second half of the 1970s.

The limited exchange rate and foreign trade reforms could not keep pace with the vastly deteriorating macroeconomic conditions and the elaborate ensemble of economic controls achieved nothing but to pave the way for the development of a sizable parallel economy. The severe rationing of import demand generated a linkage between the current account and the parallel market for foreign exchange. After 1973 Sudan had developed into a major labor exporting country, with remittances sent by Sudanese nationals working abroad accounting for more than three times the foreign exchange earnings from exports. The large capital inflows and excessive monetary expansion that permitted the massive spending spree during the second half of the 1970s created substantial real appreciation and thus facilitated the expansion of the parallel market; by the late 1970s, the economic situation started to assume crisis proportions. In September 1979 an agreement with the International Monetary Fund (IMF) was concluded, marking the beginning of a series of IMF-style stabilization and liberalization programs that dominated virtually the entire decade of the 1980s.

The central policies emphasized by the package were twofold: successive devaluation and continuous shifting of imports (and to some extent exports) from the official market to the 'legalized' free parallel market. This way, it was envisaged that exchange rate unification would ultimately be achieved and the parallel market integrated into the regular economy or perhaps squeezed into a 'side show' role. Unfortunately, the quest for liberalization in Sudan was a dismal failure and the parallel market continued to expand as economic conditions deteriorated even further as indicated above.

The analysis of this chapter covers the period up to December 1990. More recently the authorities have undertaken substantial policy initiatives. In October 1991, the official exchange rates were devalued from LS 5.4 and LS 12.3 per US$ to LS 15 and LS 30 per US$. The most sweeping reforms, however, came on 2 February 1992, when the authorities announced a package of measures that included the adoption of a free float for the Sudanese pound (starting with a unified rate at LS 90 per US$), complete liberalization of the foreign exchange and trade systems, product and factor market liberalization including the abolition of price controls for almost all goods and services, substantial liberalization of investment procedures, and an opening up of further opportunities to the private sector. Unfortunately, despite these unprecedented and deep liberalization programs, macroeconomic policy – especially fiscal policy – remains out of control. The combination of expansive fiscal and monetary policies, political uncertainty, reduced external finance, and low credibility resulted in unsustainable rates of domestic inflation, with the free rate depreciating at very high rates. This prompted the authorities to attempt to manage the float, leading to a re-emergence of the spread. The main thesis of this chapter therefore remains valid for Sudan today, despite the sweeping liberalization of 1992.

THE FOREIGN EXCHANGE MARKET IN SUDAN

The previous section provided a brief review of the policies involved in the areas of foreign trade and payment regime. In this section, we discuss the structure of the foreign exchange market and its current account links to SNWA remittances and the market for goods and services. An analysis of the structure of the foreign exchange market that assesses the extent of its competitiveness and the nature of its sources and uses is essential both for our subsequent analysis formalizing the interaction between this market and the macroeconomy and for the design of policies aimed at improving resource allocation through better macroeconomic management. Given the importance of the parallel market in Sudan, the parallel premium becomes an indicator with important macroeconomic significance. A formal assessment of this link to the macroeconomy will be addressed in the next two sections.[8,9]

The Structure of the Market

The free foreign exchange market in Sudan is composed of two main channels: the private and public commercial banks and the private licensed and unlicensed dealers. The commercial banks, being subject to government-imposed maximum selling and buying rates (see Table 5.1), effectively operate in a managed or a moving peg environment. The main supply of foreign exchange through the banking system is provided by the proceeds from non-traditional exports. As for SNWA remittances, the main source of foreign exchange,[10] only approximately 20 percent is believed to flow through official channels on average (including the banking system), leaving private dealers with approximately 80 percent.

The structure of the free market by currency composition shows a large share for the dollar, averaging more than 70 percent for buying transactions and more than 80 percent for selling transactions. The other major currency, the Saudi Rayal, comes a distant second. In terms of dealer concentration, the number of authorized dealers during legalization was large and was increasing, particularly during 1984. Many of these dealers had a very small share of the market.[11] This may be explained by the homogeneous product (the dollar) and the relatively lenient conditions for entry and exit from the market (when it was legal).

The foreign exchange market, however, is still judged not to be fully competitive. While dealers tend to be well informed about market conditions (using telephone communications among themselves), the large number of small primary suppliers and some of the end users were usually less informed. This is a factor that explains the observed discrepancies in the daily prices across dealers. As we noted above, the lack of full market information also partially explains the reliance on 'street dealers' by the more established traders in the market. The market also may sometimes 'lapse into buying oligopsony and selling monopoly' because of the seasonality that characterizes supply and demand and also because some dealers have relatively larger shares than others. In general, however, the market has been regarded as competitive enough to ensure the uniformity of quoted rates among dealers (de Macedo, 1985; USAID, 1985).

The Current Account Link, Capital Flight, and the Role of SNWA Remittances

The importance of SNWA remittances as a source of foreign exchange is reflected by the ratio of remittances to relevant indicators in the economy such as exports, imports, and GDP. Even though remittances transferred through official channels comprised only approximately 20 percent of total remittances, these inflows have maintained an average ratio of 48 percent with respect to commodity exports, 23.4 percent with respect to imports, and 4.2 percent with respect to GDP since 1980–1. The remainder (approximately 80 percent of total SNWA remittances) is available to meet the flow and asset demand for foreign exchange in the free foreign exchange market (see Table 2 of Elbadawi, 1992). The share of imports financed through the free market was high even before the September 1979 liberalization. After legalization of the free market in 1981, the free market financed an average of 39.4 percent of total imports.[12]

The size of remittance flows to the free market tends to be consistently larger than the value of imports financed through this market. For example, imports financed through the free market averaged less than 70 percent unrecorded remittances over the 1981/2–1988/9 period (Table 3 of Elbadawi, 1992). This is consistent with the general view that despite the possibility of market thinness at times of high seasonal demand or when liberal import policies were pursued, there were more frequent surpluses than not in the private current account in Sudan. This story is also consistent with the estimates of capital flight from Sudan.

For example, according to the estimates contained in Table 4 of Elbadawi (1992),[13] the ratios of capital flight to the change in the stock of debt and to GDP averaged approximately 163 and 15 percent, respectively, over the 1980–8 period. The undesirable macroeconomic and development consequences of capital flight have been convincingly explored in Dornbusch (1986) and Cuddington (1986) and have been further elaborated by Ali (1988) for the case of Sudan and by Pastor (1990) for Latin America. It is clear from these ratios that capital flight may have substantially damaged the economic fortunes of Sudan. The impact of domestic investment may be particularly costly in growth terms given the presumably high social rate of return to investment in a developing, agrarian economy lacking basic physical and human infrastructure. Consequences that may be applicable in the Sudanese case include erosion of the tax base, a negative impact on domestic investment, and an increased marginal cost of foreign borrowing. It is possible that if the authorities in Sudan had been able to contain this phenomenon during the 1970s and 1980s, for example, the current debilitating debt problem would not have materialized.

Given the very extensive capital flight that occurred in Sudan and the high costs just enumerated, the most critical question is what role, if any, trade and financial liberalization played in accelerating capital flight in Sudan. As a second question, should exchange control be considered a remedy? We address these issues in the next section in the context of a set of simple econometric models analyzing the role of the premium in the determination of key macroeconomic indicators, including capital flight.

THE PARALLEL MARKET PREMIUM AND
MACROECONOMIC PERFORMANCE

The declining economic fortunes of the country paved the way for the implementation of the fiscal/monetary stabilization and the exchange rate, trade, and financial liberalizations that started after September 1979. The rate of growth of domestic credit continued to be quite high, however. During the 1978–87 period, the rate of growth in real domestic credit declined to the still high 28 percent and during the most recent period (1988–9) it rose to approximately 35 percent, matching the levels set for the 1974–7 period. Under the exchange rate policy pursued during liberalization, such monetary and fiscal policies are certainly inconsistent with the objective of reducing the parallel premium and achieving ultimate exchange rate unification. The high and rising premium ensured a continued deterioration in the *reported* external accounts and rising capital flight, as a sizable share of SNWA remittances continued to flow through unofficial channels.

For the remainder of this section we discuss the results of simple econometric models emphasizing the role of a high and rising premium – such as experienced in Sudan – in the determination of capital flight, official exports, and tax revenues on foreign trade.

Table 6.3 contains the results of the econometric estimation. Starting with foreign trade tax revenue (which accounts for over 60 percent of total tax revenue in Sudan on average), I estimated two models, one with real tax revenue on foreign trade *(FTAXP)* as the dependent variable and the other with the ratio of foreign trade tax revenue to GDP *(FTAXY)* as the dependent variable. For both variables, the period 1983–7 was one of low fiscal effort due to the dramatically reduced share of the official (reported) economy in Sudan over this period. The results show a significant and negative effect for the premium in both cases. A high and rising premium leads to declining officially sanctioned exports and consequently official imports decline as official foreign exchange proceeds fall; if, in addition, officially sanctioned imports do not rise by enough to compensate for this decline, the tax base on foreign trade shrinks. The official real exchange rate $(RER = E/CPI$, where E and CPI are the official exchange rate and consumer price index, respectively) has a negative effect on *FTAXP* which indicates that the import-reducing effect of real depreciation outweights its export-expanding effect, leading on balance to a smaller tax base and tax revenue. On the other hand the *RER* has exactly the opposite effect on *FTAXY*. In both cases

TABLE 6.3   *The parallel premium and macroeconomic performance (OLS: 1970–88)*

Regressors	Dependent variable				
	FTAXP	*FTAXY*	*KFLT*	*KFLTDEBT*	*EXPGDP*
Constant	1859.76	0.07	–	–	0.28
	(3.15)	(2.33)	–	–	(1.58)
log *GDP*	62.17	0.002	–	–	–
	(1.03)	(0.63)	–	–	–
log *(B/E)*	–971.20	–0.04	461.26	133.36	–0.16
	(–2.91)	(–2.44)	(1.09)	(3.88)	(–2.77)
log *RER*	–505.16	0.03	–	–	–
	(1.34)	(1.44)	–	–	–
WIRATE	–	–	87.15	5.00	–
	–	–	(3.01)	(1.96)	–
P_X/P_N	–	–	–	–	1.22
	–	–	–	–	(3.25)
GDP/Trend GDP	–	–	–	–	–0.11
	–	–	–	–	(–2.29)
DUM (83–7)	–312.30	–0.01	–	–	–
	(–2.09)	(1.44)	–	–	–
DUM 85	–	–	–	204.26	–
	–	–	–	(5.50)	–
DUM 87	–	–	1724.80	–	–
	–	–	(4.24)	–	–
DUM 88	–	–	–484.94	–	–
	–	–	(–1.11)	–	–
DUM (73–88)	–	–	–	95.62	–
	–	–	–	(4.74)	–
R^2	0.55	0.55	0.70	0.75	0.84
Adjusted R^2	0.45	0.42	0.63	0.69	0.81
DW	1.79	2.21	1.40	1.30	1.50

FTAXP, real taxes on foreign trade; *FTAXY*, ratio of foreign trade tax to GDP; *KFLT*, capital flight in 1980 fixed US$; *KFLDEBT*, capital flight as a ratio to GDP; *EXPGDP*, export ratio to GDP; *B/E*, parallel market premium; *WIRATE*, world interest rate; P_X/P_N, ratio of price of exports to non-traded goods prices.

however, the *RER* effect is only marginally significant. For the *FTAXY* model, we could not reject the plausible hypothesis of a unitary elasticity for real output. The income effect is also positive in the *FTAXP* model but is only marginally significant.

A closely related macroeconomic performance indicator which is estimated in Table 6.3 is the ratio of official merchandise exports to

GDP (*EXPGDP*). The reason why we decided to consider exports rather than official trade or current account balances is that official imports are by and large determined by foreign exchange availability. The results show a strong and significant negative effect for the premium (*B/E*, where *B* is the black market exchange rate) on official exports, with a 10 percent rise in the premium leading to a 1.6 percent decline in the official export : GDP ratio. The real exchange rate relevant for official exports, on the other hand (P_X/P_N, where P_X and P_N are the prices of exports and non-traded goods, respectively), has a significant and appreciably positive effect: a real depreciation in (P_X/P_N)[14] of 10 percent raises the official export : GDP ratio by 12.2 percent. Finally, an increase in current income relative to its trend leads to an increase in exports in absolute terms, but to a reduction in the export : GDP ratio.

The final macroeconomic indicator estimated in Table 6.3 is capital flight, measured in 1980 US\$ (*KFLT*)[15] and as a ratio to change in the stock of foreign debt (*KFLTDEBT*). In each case, the premium has a positive effect. In the case of the *KFLT* model, the premium effect is only marginally significant, however. The inadequacy of domestic interest rate policy[16] is reflected in the positive and significant influence of the world interest rate (*WIRATE*)[17] in both models. The subperiods 1973–6 and 1985 witnessed unusually high *KFLTDEBT* ratios, as reflected in the positive coefficients on the two corresponding dummies. The first period may simply reflect initial reactions to the onset of worsening economic conditions in Sudan while the country's indebtedness was still quite low. The 1985 spike in the *KFLTDEBT* ratio seems to be precipitated by the authorities' aggressive attempts to enforce exchange controls beginning in February of that year or by the increasing political instability that ultimately led to the March–April popular uprising and the change of government on 6 April. The absolute level of capital flight (*KFLT*), on the other hand, which had been rising steadily over the period, took a steep rise in 1987 – the year that witnessed the last devaluation in the Sudan – before declining sharply in 1988.

At the conclusion of the previous section, we discussed the potential negative effects of capital flight on the Sudanese economy and asked (1) what role, if any, trade and financial liberalization played in accelerating capital flight in Sudan and (2) whether exchange control should be considered a remedy. The results discussed above provide strong support for the view that inadequate or incredible reform – such as Sudan's IMF-type stabilization programs beginning in

September 1979 – is responsible for capital flight, through its influence on the premium (a view echoed in Ali (1988) and Pastor (1990)). Sudan's emphasis on exchange control as a remedy for capital flight, however, is rather dubious as argued in Ali (1988). Capital flight in fact rose significantly when the authorities attempted to tighten the enforcement of exchange controls. As long as macroeconomic conditions are conducive to capital flight, it appears to be extremely difficult to stop capital flight from occurring in Sudan, given the potential for offshore market dealings in the receiving countries of SNWA.

AN EMPIRICAL MODEL FOR THE PREMIUM

In this section, I estimate a linearized, forward-looking version of the dual exchange rate model.[18] The economic environment in question, as described above, is one of a sizable parallel market for foreign exchange, in which 'illegal' albeit relatively riskless currency substitution takes place at a premium rate. This market is assumed to be strongly linked to the rest of the economy, specifically to the money market and the foreign trade sector. The specification of the premium for which I solve in this model will be consistent with the equilibrium in both the asset market and the current account balance. Starting with the asset market, we posit the following relative asset demand equation:

$$(1) \qquad \log \frac{m_t}{q_t f_t} = a_0 - a_1 \hat{B}^e_{t+1},$$

where E and B are, respectively, the official and parallel market exchange rates, $q = B/E$ is the premium, $m = M/E$ is the real money stock (measured in foreign exchange at the official rate), and f is the stock of foreign money held by the private sector. We also have $\hat{B}^e$, the expected rate of depreciation in the parallel market:

$$(2) \qquad \hat{B}^e_{t+1} = \hat{q}^e_{t+1} + \hat{E}^e_{t+1}.$$

We will assume that expectations are rational, so that the subjective expectations $\hat{q}^e_{t+1}$ and $\hat{E}^e_{t+1}$ correspond to the mathematical expectations of the rates of changes in q and E, given available information. For the purposes of the model, we use the continuous approximation to the discrete rates of change, so that

$$(3) \qquad \hat{q}^e_{t+1} = {}_t\Delta \log q_{t+1} \qquad \text{and} \qquad \hat{E}^e_{t+1} = {}_t\Delta \log E_{t+1},$$

where Δ is the difference operator and a preceding subscript 't' denotes a mathematical expectation conditional on information available at time t.

The above set of equations suffices for asset market equilibrium. For the current account, I assume that the official (reported) balance is zero, that is, $\dot{R} = 0$.[19,20] I model unreported exports, X_u and unreported imports I_u, using the following generic formulations:

$$(4) \qquad X_u = X_u(e, \frac{B}{E(1 - t_x)}; z),$$
$$\qquad\qquad (+) \;\; (+) \qquad (-)$$

$$(5) \qquad I_u = I_u(e, \frac{B}{E(1 + t_m + t_{QR})}; v) * (\frac{m}{q} + f),$$
$$\qquad\qquad (-) \qquad (-) \qquad\qquad (-)$$

where $e = E/P$ is the real official exchange rate, t_x and t_m are the tax rates of exports and imports, respectively, and t_{QR} reflects the scarcity rents on imports implied by quantitative restrictions (QRs). Equation (4) specifies unreported exports to depend positively on the official real exchange rate, e, which influences the allocation of resources between the broad tradeable and non-tradeable sectors. X_u is also positively influenced by the ratio of the parallel market rate to the tax-adjusted official rate. The parameter, z, the share of exports required to be surrendered and transacted through the official market, will have a negative effect on X_u. The determinants of I_u also have similar interpretations: e discourages excessive importing in general and the term $B/[E(1 + t_m + t_{QR})]$ reflects an arbitrage condition relating the premium and the tax rate on imports inclusive of the implicit tax due to QRs. The shift parameter v is the share of imports allowed through the official market; this reflects trade liberalization. Finally, I_u is proportional to real wealth $(m/q) + f$, where nominal financial wealth is deflated by B, which serves as the marginal price of imports.

From equations (4) and (5), we can write the following unreported current account balance:

$$(6) \qquad \dot{f} = X_u(e, \frac{q}{(1 - t_x)}; z) - I_u(e, \frac{q}{(1 + t_m + t_{QR})}; v) * (\frac{m}{q} + f).$$
$$\qquad (+) (+) \quad (-) \qquad (-) \quad (-) \qquad (-)$$

By assuming equilibrium in the unreported current account balance ($\dot{f} = 0$) and imposing the monetary rule $\dot{R} = 0$,[21] equations (1)–(3) and a linearized version of equation (6) can be used to derive a forward-looking expression for the equilibrium level of the premium in equation (8) below.

To state the expression in concise form, define the vector $\delta = (\delta_0, \delta_1, \ldots \delta_6)$ and the corresponding set of fundamentals

$$(7) \quad F_t \equiv (1, \hat{E}_{t+1}^e, \log m_t, \log e_t, \log(1 - t_x)_t, \log(1 + t_m + t_{QR})_t, H(z_t, v_t)),$$

and obtain the following expression for the steady state level of the premium for a given stationary set of the fundamentals, F^*:[22]

$$(8) \quad \log q_t^* = \sum_{j=0}^{\infty} \lambda^j (\delta'_t F_{t+j}^*),$$

which leads to the following expression:

$$(9) \quad \log q_t^* - \left(\frac{1}{1 - \lambda}\right)\delta' F_t^* = \sum_{j=1}^{\infty} \left(\frac{\lambda^j}{1 - \lambda}\right) (\delta'_t \Delta F_{t+j}^*).$$

If q_t and F_t are first-difference stationary, then the right-hand side of equation (9) is $I(0)$ and the left-hand side of the equation defines a cointegration of q and F with cointegrating vector $[1/(1 - \lambda)]\delta$. Table 6.4 reports the Dickey–Fuller tests for cointegration. According to the results of the tests, we found the variables to be cointegrated.[23]

TABLE 6.4 *Cointegration test for the parallel market exchange rate premium for Sudan (including a time trend)*

Variable	DF	ADF[4]	Difference	DF	ADF[4]
log (q)	−3.09	−0.63	dlog (q)	−9.68	−4.25
log (m)	−1.95	−1.51	dlog (m)	−9.39	−4.62
log (1−tx)	−2.10	−1.80	dlog (1−tx)	−8.49	−4.35
log (1+tm)	−2.54	−2.84	dlog (1+tm)	−8.20	−3.60
log (e)	−3.20	−1.97	dlog (e)	−10.06	−4.39
log(Z)^e	−4.02	−2.32	dlog (Z)	−9.56	−4.11
Cointegration					
residual (w/o tax)	−4.91	−2.96			

q, parallel market rate/official exchange rate; m, broad money/official exchange rate; tx, export tax rate; tm, import tariff; e, real exchange rate (official exchange rate × US WPI/domestic CPI: where WPI and CPI are wholesale and consumer price indexes; Z, the expected rate of devaluation.

The long-term cointegrating relationship of equation (9) gives rise to an error-correction specification of the form (Engle and Granger, 1987)

(10)
$$\Delta \log q_{t+1} = a\left(\frac{1}{1-\lambda}\delta' F_t - \log q_t\right) + \sum_{i=0}^{R_1} b_i \Delta_t F_{t+1-i}$$
$$+ \sum_{i=0}^{R_2} c_i \Delta \log q_{t-i} + d(L)\epsilon_t,$$

where ϵ_t is white noise process and $d(L)$ is a finite polynomial in the lag operator L.[24] While the cointegrating equation gives the long-term (or stationary) equilibrium determination of the premium, the error-correction equation provides the short-term dynamic specification compatible with the long-term equilibrium relationship.

Estimation and Interpretation of the Model

Equations (9) and (10) require a proxy for the expected rate of devaluation, $\hat{E}^e$. For this purpose I use the fitted values from a linear forecast equation in which the logarithm of the official exchange rate is specified as a function of its own lag and past levels of the premium and rates of change in the stock of money (Elbadawi (1992) provides the full specification and estimation results from this forecast equation).

Equations (9) and (10) were estimated sequentially using quarterly data for the period from 1970:Q1 to 1989:Q4. The results are reported below in equations (11) and (12) (with t-statistics in parentheses):

(11)
$$\log q_t = 0.10 - 0.17 \log e_t + 0.3 \hat{E}^e_{t+1}$$
$$(9.66) \ (-1.68) \qquad (3.87)$$
$$- 0.05 \, DUM(79Q3 - 81Q2) \ - 0.13 \, DUM(81Q3 - 83Q1)$$
$$(-1.76) \qquad\qquad\qquad (-4.10)$$
$$- 0.12 \, DUM(83Q2 - 83Q4) \ + 0.08 \, DUM(85Q1 - 89Q2)$$
$$(-2.91) \qquad\qquad\qquad (3.69)$$
$$R^2 = 0.52, \bar{R}^2 = 0.47, \ DW = 1.21$$

$$\Delta \log q_t = 0.47[(1 - \lambda)^{-1} \delta' F_t - \log q_t] + 0.60 \Delta \log m_{t+1} + 0.33 \Delta \hat{E}^e_{t+1}$$
$$(4.19) \qquad\qquad\qquad (4.60) \qquad\qquad (6.09)$$
$$- 0.18 \Delta \log e_t + 3.87 \log(1 - t_x)_t + 0.58 \log(1 + t_m + t_{QR})_t$$

(12) $(-1.80) \qquad (2.10) \qquad\qquad (1.60)$

$$- 0.25 \Delta \log q_{t-2} - 0.18 \Delta \log q_{t-3}$$
$$(-3.19) \qquad\qquad (-2.26)$$
$$R^2 = 0.68, \; \bar{R}^2 = 0.65, \; DW = 1.98$$

With regard to the first equation, even though the tax policy terms appear to be non-stationary (Table 6.4), they were not found to be significant and the model was still cointegrated when I dropped them out. The tax policy effect is found to be significant and consistent with the predictions of the model, however, in the error-correction equation.

First, let me consider error-correction equation (12), which gives the short-term dynamic behavior of the premium. The attraction of the premium to its long-term equilibrium value is captured by the positive (but less than one) and significant coefficient on the error-correction term. If the fundamentals in the previous period call for a higher premium than observed (that is, $[\delta' F_t / (1 - \lambda)] - \log q_t > 0$), then since the coefficient is positive, the level of the premium in the following period will increase. The results also show substantial and significant short-term influences for changes in the expectations of future devaluation and in the stock of money. As predicted by the model, a higher tax on exports[25] reduces the premium in the short term, while a higher import tax causes the premium to rise. Real depreciation, on the other hand, has a negative short-term effect on the premium. Finally, changes in the premium are shown to display a lag structure extending up to the fourth quarter.

Now turning to the long-term specification of equation (11), we start with the effects of commercial policy and other policy-related regime shifts. The commercial policy term $H(z, v)$ which accounts for the effect of trade liberalization, is represented by *DUM* (79Q3–81Q3) and *DUM* (81Q3–83Q1), while policy reversals are represented by the other two dummies. As mentioned earlier, trade liberalization in Sudan has involved a successive transfer of imports to the free market where imports are financed by 'own resources' obtained through the black 'free' market; for exports, however, liberalization has generally been slow and largely confined to marginal exports.

This effect of such trade policy, which will be to exert an upward pressure on the stationary level of the premium, should be balanced with other aspects of trade liberalization that may lead to an enhanced flow of remittances and imports and, hence, a reduction in scarcity rents on the latter. These effects should cause the premium to decline. The negative coefficients for the first two dummies of equation (11) above show that the net effect of trade liberalization has been to reduce the long-term level of the premium. *DUM* (83Q2–83Q4) represents a brief interlude of renewed exchange controls between the two liberalization periods (1981Q3–1983Q1 and 1984Q1–1985Q1) during which the parallel market was fully legalized (see Table 6.1). As the results show, the temporary nature of this suspension was correctly anticipated by agents in the economy and therefore it did not alter the negative influence of liberalization on the premium. After February 1985, however, when the authorities began to slow down the liberalization drive and then started drifting systematically towards more tightened levels of exchange controls, the long-term level of the premium experienced a rise, as reflected by the coefficient of *DUM* (85Q1–89Q2).

The other long-term determinant that reflects current account conditions is the official real exchange rate, which has an elasticity of -0.17. This effect shows the importance of real exchange rate overvaluation in explaining the persistence of the high premium in Sudan. This implies that bringing down the level of the premium in the long run requires more than just a nominal devaluation; rather, it is the effectiveness or the efficiency of that devaluation that matters. The long-term effect of real wealth, as reflected by the coefficient of $\log m_t$ in equation (12), is slightly smaller at 0.10 but much more significant.

The long-term influences of the asset market provide for some interesting interpretations with regard to the influence of the fiscal deficit, $g - t$ (measured in foreign exchange at the official exchange rate) on the premium. Assuming that seigniorage is the only source of government financing and that the growth in real money demand is zero, the government's budget constraint states that $m = (g - t)/\pi$, where m (as before) is real money balances measured in foreign exchange at the official exchange rate and π is the rate of depreciation of the official exchange rate.[26] Taking logs in this expression, substituting for $\log m$ in equation (11) and then imposing the steady-state condition $\hat{E}^e = \pi$, we obtain an expression of the form $\Delta \log q = 0.1 \Delta \log(g - t) + (0.3 \log \pi_a - 0.1) \Delta \log \pi + \Delta z$, where π_a is the average rate of official depreciation (used to convert the parameter of 0.3 into an elasticity) and z contains all variables on the right-hand side of equation (11) other than $\hat{E}^e_{t+1}$ and $\log m$. The average rate of expected depreciation over the 1980s was approximately 25 percent. Using this value, we find the following relationship across long-term equilibria:

$$(13) \qquad \Delta \log q + 0.025 \Delta \log \pi = 0.1 \Delta \log(g - t) + \Delta z.$$

Holding the rate of crawl constant, therefore, an increase in the deficit drives up the premium with an elasticity of 0.1, by increasing domestic money balances measured at the official exchange rate. However, the increased seigniorage requirement can also be met by an increased rate of crawl, provided (as these estimates imply) the elasticity of money demand with respect to expected depreciation is below unity.

Equation (13) is suggestive of the fiscal trade-off between the premium and the rate of crawl (or of domestic inflation) analyzed by Pinto (1991). Pinto (1991) argued that this trade-off exists when the elasticity of money demand with respect to expected inflation is below unity – so that increases in the inflation rate increase seigniorage revenue – and the private sector is a net seller of foreign exchange to the central bank at the official exchange rate – so that a higher parallel premium acts like a net tax on the private sector. In this view, the tightening of exchange controls during the 1980s effectively substituted for (at least part of) the increase in inflation that would otherwise have been required to finance the higher fiscal deficits of the period.

The econometric evidence in favor of a trade-off should be interpreted cautiously, however. The calculations underlying equation (13), for example, do not allow for any effect of the premium on the fiscal deficit itself. They also do not allow for changes in the elasticity of money demand over the course of the sample, although increases in the average inflation rate and ongoing financial innovation may well have increased this elasticity over time (see Chapter 1 of this volume for further discussion of these issues). The direct evidence for Sudan suggests that intrasample developments may in fact be important. The fiscal deficit increased from 5.8 percent of GDP to a staggering 12.9 percent between 1974–7 and 1978–87, with seignorage revenue correspondingly increasing from 2.8 percent of GDP in the first period to 5.4 percent in the second.[27] The premium, however, remained fairly stable at approximately 178 percent during each of these two periods (Table 6.5). The opposite occurred between 1988 and 1989: the fiscal deficit increased only slightly, from 12.9 to 15.9 percent of GDP, while seigniorage revenue declined to only 3 percent of GDP. Meanwhile the premium soared to above 300 percent. Thus, while a trade-off may have existed until the late 1980s, dramatic increases in inflation

TABLE 6.5 *Exchange rates and domestic inflation (quarterly averages)*

	1970–3	1974–7	1978–87	1988–90
Official exchange rate, E	0.348	0.348	1.334	4.500
Parallel market exchange rate, B	0.598	0.619	2.179	24.717
Parallel market premium, B/E	1.719	1.778	1.777	5.493
Black market depreciation (%)	1.049	0.530	9.135	21.282
Official devaluation (%)	0.000	0.000	8.417	0.000
Domestic inflation (%)	3.289	3.752	6.583	14.842

Domestic inflation is based on the consumer price index.

thereafter probably moved the economy to a point at which the inflation tax was a revenue sink on the margin and a trade-off between the premium and inflation no longer existed.

SOME CONCLUDING REMARKS AND IMPLICATIONS FOR FUTURE ECONOMIC REFORM

This chapter has focused on the macroeconomics of multiple exchange rates and the parallel market for foreign exchange in Sudan. The objectives of the study were to understand the economic forces and policy decisions that gave rise to the system, the determinants of the parallel market premium, the extent to which the presence of a parallel market may have interfered with macroeconomic management of the economy, and, finally, the lessons that can be drawn for the design of future policy.

In addition to enhancing export performance, the main objective of the post-1979 reform program was to achieve a significant increase in the share of SNWA remittances brought through 'legal' channels. Discrete maxi-devaluations of the exchange rate and a gradual trade liberalization were employed with the aim of achieving exchange rate unification and the ultimate integration of the parallel market into the regular economy. To uncover the reasons behind the failure of these reforms, we studied the determinants of the parallel premium using an empirical linearized version of a standard dual exchange rate model. The model emphasizes the role of expectation and the distinction between long-term flow determinants of the premium and short-term dynamic influences coming from the asset market.

Real exchange rate depreciation was found to have a significant negative effect on the premium in both the short and long term. This finding points to the key role real depreciation can play in improving the current account balance and consequently in raising the stock of foreign money held by both the official and private sectors. Expectations of future devaluations were shown to have a strong and significant positive effect on the premium, suggesting that flight from domestic money has been an important source of demand for illegal foreign exchange. Real money balances were shown to have a significant, positive long-term effect on the premium; invoking the direct link assumed in the model between the real fiscal deficit and monetary emission establishes a direct link between the fiscal deficit and the stationary level of the premium. When its indirect effect through expectations is considered as well, the net effect of the fiscal deficit on the premium can be quite substantial. Finally, the effect of trade liberalization – proxied by a dummy variable – was negative and significant. The rather asymmetric nature of this policy, which emphasized liberalization on the import side as opposed to the export side, should exert an upward pressure on the premium, but this appears to have been more than outweighed by the effects of the policy on the availability of imported goods and the supply of remittances, both of which work in the opposite direction.

The main conclusion from this analysis is that a lack of strong commitment to fiscal retrenchment has been the main cause behind the failure of economic reform in the Sudan. Because the steady-state level of the parallel premium depends critically on the size of the fiscal deficit, a devaluation policy by itself will not reduce the premium in the long term unless it is either preceded or accompanied by a serious fiscal adjustment. Furthermore, when a large fiscal deficit persists and credibility is low, aggressive devaluation and trade liberalization policies aimed at exchange rate unification and integration of the parallel market run the risk of leading to expectations of further devaluation, large-scale currency substitution, and a rising premium.

According to the analysis in the fourth section, a rising premium has negative impacts on official exports and foreign trade taxes and a positive effect of capital flight. A rising premium and expanding parallel market may therefore have serious fiscal and commercial policy implications by squeezing the tax base in foreign trade transactions and expanding the opportunities for large-scale rent-seeking activities. A high premium also aggravates the debt problem and the foreign exchange constraint through its effects on capital flight and the recorded current account balance.

The Sudanese experience underscores the key role of fiscal policy in stabilization and exchange rate unification, a lesson potentially relevant in understanding similar experiences in Sierra Leone, Zambia, and other countries. While the effect of the fiscal deficit on the premium through the supply of domestic money is familiar from the literature on foreign exchange parallel markets (for example, Pinto, 1987, 1989, 1991), this paper has emphasized a second channel for the deficit, operating through expectations of a devaluation of the official exchange rate. When underlying fiscal problems are not addressed, expectations of future devaluation may lead to flight from domestic money, raising the premium and reducing revenue from the inflation tax regardless of how aggressively the authorities devalue the official rate. It follows that under conditions of large fiscal deficits and low credibility, expectations of future devaluation may pre-empt the intended effects of exchange rate devaluation, even before such a devaluation actually happens. This finding substantially strengthens the case for effecting structural reform aimed at the fiscal sector at an early stage of the stabilization program.

NOTES

1. The author is indebted to A. A. Ali, R. Dornbusch, G. Kaminsky, M. Kiguel, S. Lizondo, and particularly S. O'Connell for helpful comments. The author acknowledges able research assistance from Nita Ghei and Ayda Kimemia.
2. The size of just one source of foreign exchange for the black market (non-official remittances by Sudanese nationals working abroad) averaged more than $1 billion per annum throughout the 1980s (Table 3 in Elbadawi, 1992).
3. de Macedo (1985), for example, argued that the importance of the black market for macroeconomic management in Sudan during the period derives from the role played by the premium as a relative price signal for lack of credibility on the part of government policies or economic reform. The above description fits the example of many countries from sub-Saharan Africa that have experienced deteriorating economic conditions during the 1980s and in most cases aborted or incredible attempts at economic reform as well (see Pinto, 1987).
4. This notion has been formalized and elaborated upon in a series of papers by Pinto (1987, 1989, 1991).
5. Devarajan and Weiner (1990) develop a model that predicts real appreciation as a result of a rising premium even if exports are sold at the free

rate, provided that the marginal cost of labor is determined at the free market.

6. This effect is what Pinto (1987) refer to as reducing the 'informational content' of the real exchange rate.

7. Furthermore, Sudan has had more than its share of political instability. Since its independence in 1956, the country has experienced a civil war in its Southern region except for 12 years (1972–83) during which a peace agreement was in effect.

8. In an extended version of this paper (Elbadawi, 1992) I analyze the statistical characteristics of the premium (and the free rate) and their non-economic determinants such as seasonal factors and bubbles.

9. As we saw from the previous section, trading in foreign exchange (whether legalized or not, inside the country or in the offshore markets) has basically continued unimpeded for most of the last two decades, even though it was only after the IMF-inspired liberalization of September 1979 that the market expanded rapidly to become a major sector in the economy. We will therefore interchangeably use the terms 'black' or 'free' to refer to the same thing.

10. For example, the size of the total SNWA remittances is estimated to average $1.6 billion per annum for the 1980/1–1988/9 period (see Table 2 of Elbadawi, 1992).

11. de Macedo (1985) computed a measure of concentration based on the Herfindhal index, obtaining a value of 5.6 for 1984. In comparing this finding to similar computations obtained for US auto firms (for example, Dixit, 1988), he concluded that this shows a degree of competition in the Sudanese foreign exchange market that is far greater than generally believed.

12. If the years 1985–6 and 1986–7 were excluded, this share would rise to 52.5 percent.

13. The methodology adopted by Elbadawi (1992) for computing capital flight is based on Dornbusch (1986) and is adapted to account for SNWA flows through the unofficial market and own-funds imports.

14. Where P_N is the price of non-tradeables. The data for P_X and P_N were obtained from Elbadawi (1987, 1989).

15. The estimates for capital flight are from Table 4 of Elbadawi (1992).

16. Interest rates were abolished in the Sudan effective 1984 and although they have reappeared in various guises since then, real rates have been substantially negative.

17. WIRATE is equal to the annualized London Interbank Offer Rate (LIBOR) on 3 month US$ deposits.

18. Variants of the above simple model constitute a common framework of analysis in the dual exchange rate literature. See, for example, Dornbusch *et al.* (1983), Dornbusch (1986), Lizondo (1987a, b), Pinto (1987, 1989, 1991), Kiguel and Lizondo (1990), and Chapter 1 of the present volume.

19. To keep matters tractable, we impose the condition that $dR/dt = 0$. For the case of Sudan, this seems a perfectly realistic assumption since the average change in official reserves during the period under consideration (1970–89) was a minuscule US$0.23 million per quarter (though the change varied considerably during the period).

20.   Equating the official current account balance to the change in reserves clearly abstracts from external debt accumulation. For the case of the Sudan, such an assumption may be difficult to justify, particularly over the last half of the 1980s. Since we intend to estimate this model using quarterly data, however, we cannot make use of the change in debt term for lack of data.

21.   The condition $dR/dt = 0$ is referred to as a monetary rule in terms of its implications for the stationary level of the stock of real money, $m^*(= (g - t)/\pi$, where π is the rate of depreciation of the official exchange rate; see the section on estimation and interpretation of the model below), but in fact it amounts to a trade policy rule whereby an import 'quota' enforced through foreign exchange rationing is equal to current official export revenue.

22.   The level of foreign assets, f, is unobservable. However, the steady-state value of f can be solved in terms of the other variables, so that the vector of fundamentals includes only observable variables and the expected rate of official depreciation. For a full derivation that contains a dynamic martingale intermediate equation, see Elbadawi (1992).

23.   This test also supports the no bubble solution of equation (10) (see Kaminsky, 1988). Cointegration implies that while the daily or weekly premium may be influenced by seasonals or transitory bubbles, the quarterly and annual premium is determined by the economic fundamentals.

24.   In fact, strict application of the cointegration model of equations (8) and (9) yields an error-correction equation with only the error-correction term $[\delta' F_t/(1 - \lambda) - \log q_t]$ on the right-hand side of equation (11). The general representation of $\Delta \log q_{t+1}$ in equation (11), therefore, provides a test of this strict interpretation of the model. By including lagged dependent variables, the above specification also accounts for the existence of important moving average (MA) components in the disturbance term process.

25.   *A priori*, the export tax effect could go either way since it may also reduce the overall level of exports and hence the portion that goes into smuggling.

26.   The latter equation can be derived from the central bank balance sheet $DC + ER = M$, where DC and R are domestic credit to the government and international reserves, respectively. We assume that $dR/dt = 0$ and that the government finances its deficit solely by borrowing from the central bank, so that $d(DC)/dt = (g - t)E$.

27.   Strictly speaking, seigniorage revenue is not in general equal to the revenue from the inflation tax (except when $dm/dt = 0$).

REFERENCES

Ali, A. Ali (1988) 'On Reform Policies and Capital Flight', mimeo (in Arabic) (Kuwait: Conference on Reform Policies and Development in the Arab World).

Cuddington, John T. (1986) 'Capital Flight: Estimates, Issues, and Explanations', *Princeton Studies in International Finance* No. 58 (Princeton, NJ: International Finance Section, Department of Economics, Princeton University).

de Macedo, Jorge Braga (1985) 'The Free Foreign Exchange Market in Sudan: Description and Analysis'. Department of Economics, Princeton University.

Devarajan, Shantayanan and R. Weiner (1990) 'Why the Sandinistas Lost: Coffee, Hyperinflation, and the Black Market for Foreign Exchange in Nicaragua', presented at the North-East Development Economic Conference (New Haven, CT: Yale University).

Dixit, Avinash (1988) 'Optimal Trade and Industrial Policies for the US Automobile Industry', in Robert C. Feenstra (ed.), *Empirical Methods for International Trade* (Cambridge, Mass: MIT Press), pp. 141–65.

Dornbusch, Rudiger (1985) 'External Debt, Budget Deficits and Disequilibrium Exchange Rates', in G. W. Smith and J. T. Cuddington (eds), *International Debt and The Developing Countries* (Washington, DC: World Bank).

Dornbusch, Rudiger (1986), 'Special Exchange Rates for Capital Account Transactions', *World Bank Economic Review* vol. 1, no.1, pp. 1–33.

Dornbusch, Rudiger, Daniel V. Dantas, Clarice Pechman, Roberto Rocha, and Demetri Simoes (1983) 'The Black Market for Dollars in Brazil', *Quarterly Journal of Economics*, vol. 98, pp. 25–40.

Elbadawi, Ibrahim (1987) 'Foreign Trade and Exchange Rate Policy and Their Long-term Impact on Sudanese Agriculture', prepared for the USAID/SUDAN.

Elbadawi, Ibrahim (1989) 'The Extent and Consequences of Direct and Indirect Taxation of Sudanese Agriculture', prepared for the United States Agency for International Development.

Elbadawi, Ibrahim (1992) 'Macroeconomic Management and the Black Market for Foreign Exchange in Sudan', *Policy Research Working Paper Series* No. 859 (Washington, DC: World Bank).

Engle, Robert and Clive Granger (1987) 'Co-integration and Error-correction: Representation, Estimation, and Testing', *Econometrica*, vol. 55, pp. 251–76.

International Currency Analysis, Inc. (Various years), *World Currency Yearbook* (Brooklyn, NY: International Currency Analysis. (Formerly *Pick's Currency Yearbook*).

International Monetary Fund (various years), *International Financial Statistics* (Washington, DC: International Monetary Fund).

Kaminsky, Graciela (1988) 'The Real Exchange Rate Since Floating: Market Fundamentals or Bubbles?', mimeo (San Diego: University of California at San Diego).

Kiguel, Miguel and J. Saul Lizondo (1990) 'Adoption and Abandonment of Dual Exchange Rate Systems', *Revista de Análisis Económico* vol. 5, no. 1, pp. 2–23. (Previously *Development Research Department Discussion Paper* No. 201 (Washington, DC: World Bank).

Lizondo, J. Saul (1987a) 'Exchange Rate Differential and Balance of Payments Under Dual Exchange Markets' *Journal of Development Economics*, vol. 26, no. 1, pp. 37–53.

Lizondo, J. Saul (1987b) 'Unification of Dual Exchange Rate Markets', *Journal of International Economics*, vol. 22, nos 1/2, pp. 57–77.

Pastor, Manuel, Jr (1990) 'Capital Flight from Latin America', *World Development*, vol. 18, no. 1, pp. 1–18.

Pinto, Brian (1987) 'Exchange Rate Unification and Budgetary Policy in Sub-Saharan Africa', mimeo (Washington, DC: World Bank).

Pinto, Brian (1989) 'Black Market Premia, Exchange Rate Unification, and Inflation in Sub-Saharan Africa', *World Bank Economic Review*, vol. 3, no. 3, pp. 321–38.

Pinto, Brian (1991) 'Black Markets for Foreign Exchange, Real Exchange Rates and Inflation', *Journal of International Economics*, vol. 30, pp.121–36.

Pinto, Brian and Sweder van Wijnbergen (1987) 'Exchange Rate Regimes in Africa', mimeo (Washington, DC: World Bank).

USAID (1985) 'The Free Foreign Exchange Rate Market in Sudan', United States Agency for International Development (USAID/SUDAN).

7 Exchange Controls and the Parallel Premium in Tanzania, 1967–90

Daniel Kaufmann and Stephen A. O'Connell[1]

F31
F32
F33
019

INTRODUCTION

Developments in Tanzania's parallel foreign exchange market have mirrored the evolution of macroeconomic policy in that country since its independence in 1961. At independence, Tanzania operated a relatively open trade and payments regime supported by conservative monetary and fiscal policies. These policies survived the introduction of the Tanzanian shilling in 1965, but the Arusha Declaration of 1967 generated a fundamental reorientation under the rubric of self-reliance and African socialism. In the two decades following the Arusha Declaration, the exchange rate in Tanzania's illegal parallel foreign exchange market rose at a rate of nearly 2.5 percent per month, more than three times as rapidly as the official exchange rate. By early 1986, the parallel rate exceeded the official rate by more than 800 percent.

Trade and exchange rate reforms formed the centerpiece of the 1986 Economic Recovery Program and its successors, with the result that the country moved gradually but determinedly over the next 8 years towards a unified foreign exchange market. By early 1990, the premium had fallen to approximately 50 percent. In early 1992, the government introduced foreign exchange bureaus, allowing these entities to transact in foreign exchange at freely determined exchange rates for current account transactions. The spread between the parallel market rate and the bureau rate quickly narrowed to below 10 percent and over the subsequent year the spread between the official exchange rate and the bureau rate gradually fell, reaching approximately 10 percent in mid-1993. During 1993 the government liberalized nearly all remaining restrictions on foreign exchange transactions for current account purposes and late in that year the official and bureau markets were officially unified. At the time of writing (early 1995), a vestigial parallel market remains, with a small premium reflecting the operation of residual capital controls, the financing of illegal activities, and tax evasion.

This chapter focuses on the development and evolution of the parallel foreign exchange market in Tanzania during its 'heyday', in the period from 1967 to 1990. While parallel foreign exchange markets are common in developing countries, the Tanzanian case is particularly interesting given the size and persistence of its premium. We use the Tanzanian case to shed light on issues that are important not only for Tanzania but also for other countries with extensive exchange controls.[2] The first half of the chapter characterizes the macroeconomic sources and consequences of the parallel market both during its long expansion and in the subsequent move towards convertibility on the current account. While the parallel market was variously dismissed by the policy authorities as a nuisance or as the domain of a small group of economic saboteurs, we argue instead that it played a central macroeconomic role throughout most of the 1970s and 1980s and that the dynamics of the parallel exchange rate followed those of the free rate in a well-functioning dual exchange market. The second half of the chapter then focuses particularly on the fiscal implications of exchange rate unification.

The chapter is organized as follows. The second section provides an overview of macroeconomic developments from 1967 to 1990, focusing particularly on the external sector and the parallel foreign exchange market. In the third section, we specify and estimate an empirical model for the parallel premium. The empirical results indicate that portfolio determinants have an important influence on the premium in the short term and that trade balance determinants are dominant in the longer term. We extend the basic model by endogenizing the real exchange rate and find limited evidence of a long-term effect of aid flows, the terms of trade, and other determinants of the trade balance. A further extension leads to the somewhat paradoxical theoretical presumption that Tanzania's own-funds scheme implemented in 1984 should have raised the premium; the empirical results provide some support for this view.

The fourth section takes up the more narrow question of the fiscal effect of the premium. Our main concern here is to assess the possibility, raised by Pinto (1989, 1991), that exchange rate unification may require a simultaneous fiscal contraction in order to avoid an increase in money growth and inflation. We generalize Pinto's (1989, 1991) theoretical analysis and provide estimates that suggest that the opposite was true for Tanzania: for much of the sample and particularly beginning in the late 1980s, more aggressive moves towards unification would have provided a fiscal bonus and a reduction in inflation. The fifth section concludes the chapter.

EMERGENCE AND GROWTH OF THE PARALLEL MARKET, 1967–90

Foreign exchange black markets arise in response to restrictions on the convertibility of domestic assets into foreign exchange. Although such restrictions may be imposed with microeconomic goals in mind (such as a reduction of luxury imports), they become important at the macroeconomic level when used as a mechanism to offset sustained pressure on the balance of payments. In Tanzania, balance of payments pressures first emerged in the early 1970s, in response to capital flight and expansion of the public sector. The situation was exacerbated by a

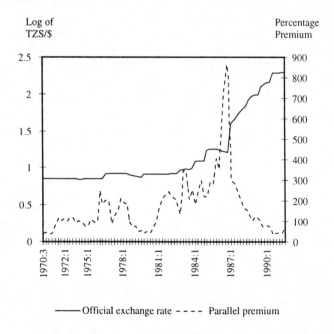

FIGURE 7.1   *Official exchange rate and parallel premium, 1970:3–1990:4*

SOURCES: IMF, *International Financial Statistics*; International Currency Analysis, Inc., *World Currency Yearbook*; and Kaufmann & O'Connell (1991).

combination of drought and the first Organization of Petroleum Exporting Countries (OPEC) oil shock in 1974–5. Figure 7.1 shows the official exchange rate and the parallel premium from 1970 to 1990.

Exchange controls, which had been in place since the introduction of the Tanzanian shilling in 1965, were tightened in response to the 1970–1 balance of payments 'mini-crisis' and supplemented by the introduction of an administrative scheme for the allocation of foreign exchange (Green *et al.*, 1980).[4] They were then tightened further in response to the more severe crisis in 1974–5. The external situation was dramatically improved by the arrival of the coffee boom in 1976, but by this time the parallel premium was over 200 percent.

The foreign exchange inflows associated with the coffee boom helped reduce the premium to 100 percent by the end of 1977, but the government chose to use the windfall to initiate the Basic Industrial Strategy (BIS), a major public investment program whose introduction had been deferred in response to the 1974–5 crisis. Increases in public sector spending under the BIS at least partially offset the reduction in monetary financing that might otherwise have accompanied the coffee boom. The presence of an underlying balance of payments disequilibrium was dramatically revealed in 1978 when the government loosened import controls in response to its comfortable reserves position (see Figure 7.2). Reserves fell by 63 percent in 1978, to less than a month of imports (approximately the crisis level before the coffee boom) and controls were reimposed.

The war with Idi Amin began in late 1978. Government expenditures approximately doubled in 1979 as a share of GDP, to nearly 20 percent. The accompanying compression of parastatal and private sector imports helped initiate a period of macroeconomic collapse (Bevan *et al.*, 1989, 1990). The premium rose rapidly, exceeding 200 percent between 1981 and 1984; the devaluation of 1984 brought it down only momentarily and it reached 800 percent at the time of adoption of the crawling peg exchange rate regime and a major structural adjustment program in early 1986.

In retrospect, it is clear that a key missing element in the Tanzanian policy package up to the mid-1980s was exchange rate adjustment. A bias against devaluation had emerged in Tanzania as early as 1967, when the government decided not to follow the 14.3 percent devaluation of sterling. Arguments were based on the belief that import and export volumes would respond only weakly to changes in the real exchange rate; a devaluation was therefore unlikely to improve the external balance. Compounding this elasticity pessimism was the view that a nominal devaluation would in any case lead to a general increase in wages and prices, undercutting any desired real devaluation. Finally, opponents of devaluation argued that capital flight was motivated primarily by fears of expropriation rather than by exchange rate expectations and the Bank of Tanzania viewed existing exchange controls as sufficient to contain any speculative pressure that might emerge in the immediate aftermath of the sterling devaluation.[5]

The decision not to devalue in the face of balance of payments pressures led inexorably to the need for direct balance of payments controls and increasingly severe convertibility restrictions. These restrictions enabled the authorities to maintain an increasingly overvalued real exchange rate, as indicated in Figure 7.2. An important side-effect of this overvaluation was to exacerbate the secular decline

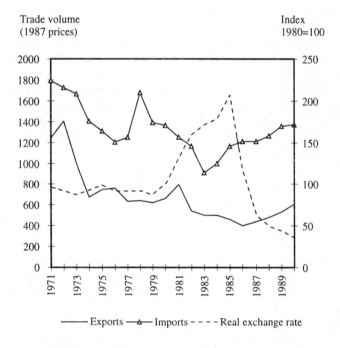

FIGURE 7.2 *Trade volumes and real official exchange rate, 1971–90*
NOTES: Trade volume on left scale, real exchange rate (increase=appreciation) on right. The real exchange rate is the ratio of Tanzania's consumer price index to a trade weighted index of wholesale price indexes for Tanzania's eight largest trading partners, each converted using the relevant bilateral official exchange rate.
SOURCES: World Bank; IMF.

in exports that had begun as early as the collapse in world sisal markets in the late 1960s. The decline in measured or official exports shown in Figure 7.2. was even more dramatic than the decline in export production, since it was the joint effect of deteriorating incentives for export production (for example, the worsening real exchange rate for exports) and an increasing incentive, embodied in the rising parallel premium, to divert export proceeds away from official channels.

The steady decline of official export revenues, punctuated only briefly by the coffee boom, meant a steady tightening of import restrictions, the results of which are apparent in the declining import volume in Figure 7.3. Since price controls had been imposed in 1974, the response to import compression beginning in the mid-1970s was a combination of limited increases in official prices and increased reliance on direct rationing of goods. Shortages of intermediate imports and of both imported and domestically produced consumer goods, which began to emerge in the 1974–5 crisis only to subside during the coffee boom and subsequent import liberalization, re-emerged strongly beginning in 1979. Shortages of consumer goods were particularly severe in rural areas, where they led to a reduction in peasant labor supply, leading to further declines in export production in a vicious circle of output decline and declining availability of goods (cf. Bevan *et al.*, 1989, 1990; O'Connell, 1995).

The import compression of the late 1970s was insufficient to prevent the emergence of arrears in 1978 and the onset of an increasingly difficult confrontation between Tanzania and its external creditors and donors over the issue of devaluation and macroeconomic adjustment.[6] Aid flows fell in the early 1980s, further contributing to the cycle of import compression and output reduction. The collapse of the early 1980s began to be reversed only with the reforms of 1984, which included a 36 percent devaluation, removal of price controls on a number of goods, and implementation of an 'own-funds' (OF) import license scheme. Under the OF scheme, individuals with access to their own foreign exchange were granted import licenses without having to purchase the corresponding amount of official foreign exchange. By divorcing the government's import licensing function from its foreign exchange allocation function, this amounted to a legalization of what would previously have been import smuggling. Moreover, goods imported through the OF window, some of which still carried controlled prices if purchased from official sources, could be sold at market-clearing prices.

Although the OF scheme produced a substantial import liberalization (Figure 7.2), with favorable effects on output in the short term, it represented an asymmetric liberalization of foreign exchange controls, lowering the cost of import 'smuggling' relative to export smuggling. It may well have contributed, along with expectations of a further maxi-devaluation, to the increase in the parallel premium that occurred between 1984 and the initiation of the major structural adjustment program in 1986.

From the perspective of the parallel foreign exchange market, the key elements of the 1986 structural adjustment program were the maxi-devaluation and adoption of a crawling peg, large inflows of external assistance (Figure 7.3), and a commitment to public sector reform with the objective, among other things, of reducing the government's overall borrowing requirement. The OF scheme was broadened and the process of price decontrol gradually proceeded until by mid-1988 only 12 commodities remained under control. The premium fell dramatically with the maxi-devaluation of early 1986

Percent of GDP

Current account balance   - - - - Net capital inflows
—△— Official transfers   —■— Change in reserves

FIGURE 7.3   *Current account and financing, 1971–90*
NOTES: The current account is before official transfers. Net Capital inflows include errors and omissions.
SOURCE: World Bank.

and continued to fall with the subsequent smaller adjustments in the official exchange rate. Full unification of the exchange rate for current account purposes was achieved in the early 1990s, in a sequence of steps that began with the licensing of private foreign exchange dealers in 1992 and the introduction of a weekly Central Bank auction to registered dealers and commercial banks in 1993 and culminated with the removal of remaining payments restrictions on the current account (for example, export remittance requirements) in late 1993. In 1994, the move to a market-determined exchange rate was completed with the elimination of the Central Bank auction and its replacement with a daily interbank foreign exchange market as the mechanism for determining the official exchange rate (Bank of Tanzania, 1994).

In summary, the Tanzanian experience indicates the difficulties that can emerge if the burden of external adjustment is placed on exchange controls and concessional financing rather than on the exchange rate itself or on policies affecting aggregate demand. Such a policy is economically sustainable as long as the shocks in question are sufficiently small and short-lived that they can be absorbed (as in the early 1970s) by a combination of temporary aid inflows, a tightening of import controls, and a modest rise in the premium. Exchange controls are significantly less successful when used to maintain an overvalued official exchange rate in the face of systematic internal demand pressures. In this case, growing resource misallocations and macroeconomic difficulties associated with the exchange control regime eventually lead to a reversal of the government's stance with respect to the official exchange rate; in Tanzania, policy since 1986 has been geared towards achieving a more competitive real exchange rate and restoring convertibility at the official exchange rate for current account purposes. Lasting reductions in the parallel premium required a restoration of consistency between aggregate demand and the exchange rate or effectively between fiscal policy and exchange rate policy. Reductions in the primary deficit, increases in external aid and increases in the rate of crawl of the official exchange rate all contributed to the Tanzanian success in this endeavor.

How Large was the Parallel Market?

Since the parallel foreign exchange market is illegal, there are no direct measures of the stock of privately held foreign exchange or the flow of foreign exchange through the parallel market. Here we report two sets of evidence on the size of market flows in the 1980s. The best single estimate is the volume of imports brought in through the OF scheme. The proportion of import licenses allocated to the OF window rose from 19 percent in 1984 to an average of 36 percent between 1985 and 1988. The share of actual imports financed by own funds is almost certainly greater; unofficial estimates suggest a share exceeding one half.[7] This would imply that as of the late 1980s, some $500 million of imports were being financed through the parallel foreign exchange market.

For the economy as a whole, there are two sources of foreign exchange for OF imports. The first is decumulation of private net foreign assets. Individuals with assets abroad can repatriate their dollars, either by selling them on the parallel foreign exchange market (where they can be recycled to individuals using the OF window) or by purchasing own-funded imports directly. Individuals without access to foreign balances can bring in own-funded imports by borrowing foreign exchange from relatives or associates abroad or by purchasing the required foreign exchange on the parallel market.[8] In all of these cases, the net result is a decumulation of net foreign exchange holdings by the private sector, that is the reverse of capital flight.

The second source of foreign exchange for own-funded imports is the flow supply of foreign exchange generated by illegal exports (for example, gold smuggling or illegal sale of housing services to expatriates) and overinvoicing of officially financed imports. What proportion of OF imports were financed by illegal trade? Since the OF program undoubtedly led to a net repatriation of flight capital, the magnitude of OF imports provides an upper bound on the value of gross foreign exchange inflows from illegal trade. However, adjustments in private foreign exchange stocks would be expected to play themselves out fairly rapidly, even taking into consideration the possibility of a gradual response as market participants assess the credibility of the 'no questions asked' provision.[9] Therefore, although it is likely that reverse capital flight was an important source of own-funded imports early in the program, we would expect the stock adjustment in response to the OF opportunity to have been largely completed by 1987 or 1988. The magnitude of OF imports in the late 1980s should therefore be a good indication of the flow supply of foreign exchange into the parallel market from various illegal trade channels.

Table 7.1 draws upon three detailed studies (Bagachwa *et al.*, 1989; Maliyamkono and Bagachwa, 1990; Mshomba, 1993) to give some

TABLE 7.1 *Disaggregated estimates of unrecorded exports*

Export	Source	Annual amount ($ millions)	Period of Estimate
Minerals (mainly gold)	Maliyamkono and Bagachwa (1990)	10	1985–8
Gold	Bagachwa et al. (1989)	14	1988
Diamonds	Bagachwa et al. (1989)	1	1988
Tourist expenditure	Maliyamkono and Bagachwa (1990)	36	1980–5
	Bagachwa et al. (1989)	69	1988
Private expatriate housing	Maliyamkono and Bagachwa (1990)	43	1988
	Bagachwa et al. (1989)	34	1988
Illegal tusks and rhino horns	Bagachwa et al. (1989)	148	1988
Coffee arabica	Mshomba (1993)	8	1969–85
		26	1984–5

indication of the primary categories of illegal exports and the associated magnitudes in the latter half of the 1980s. The largest suspected sources of illegal foreign exchange earnings were gold exports, unrecorded tourist expenditures, expatriate housing services, illegal ivory and rhino horns, and coffee. The total estimated foreign exchange inflow from these activities is in the order of $275 million in 1988; this accounts for somewhat more than half of the illegal trade suggested by the OF approach. The discrepancy is presumably accounted for by some combination of other illegal exports, reverse capital flight, and overinvoiced imports.

MACROECONOMIC DETERMINANTS OF THE PARALLEL PREMIUM[10]

The preceding discussion suggests that one should be able to account for movements in the parallel premium using a combination of trade and portfolio factors. In this section, we estimate a simple version of the Dornbusch et al. (1983) stock-flow model, which incorporates both portfolio and trade determinants of the parallel premium (see Chapter 1). The portfolio determinants are the stock of domestic monetary assets measured in dollars at the official exchange rate

$(M2/E)$ and the relative yield on unofficial foreign exchange and domestic monetary assets (or 'interest parity differential', IPD). A rise in the domestic money stock measured in foreign exchange implies an excess relative supply of domestic assets (denominated in Tanzanian shillings) and a rise in the parallel premium; a rise in the relative yield on unofficial foreign exchange implies an excess demand for foreign exchange and also raises the premium.

As an overall proxy for the trade determinants, we use the official real effective exchange rate ($REER$): a real appreciation reduces overall exports and therefore unofficial exports as well, given the value of the premium; at the same time, it increases the smuggling of imports by leading to a tightening of foreign exchange rationing controls and an increase in domestic price premia on imports. The net effect of a real official appreciation is therefore to worsen the unofficial trade balance for any given level of the parallel premium; equivalently, for any given value of the unofficial trade surplus, a real appreciation raises the value of the parallel premium.[11]

Since the unofficial trade balance does not depend on the portfolio factors, the requirement that it approaches zero in the long term implies that the parallel premium is determined only by trade factors in the long term and not by portfolio factors. To allow for differences in the short- and long-term effects of the various determinants, we estimate the following autoregressive distributed lag equation for the parallel premium:

$$
\begin{aligned}
\ln z_t = a_0 &+ a_1[(M2/E)_t - (M2/E)_{t-1}] + a_2(IPD_t - IPD_{t-1}) \\
&+ a_3(REER_t - REER_{t-1}) + a_4(M/E)_{t-1} \\
&+ a_5 IPD_{t-1} + a_6 REER_{t-1} + a_7 \ln z_{t-1}
\end{aligned}
$$

(1)

The coefficients a_1, a_2, and a_3 capture the short-term effects of the three determinants of the parallel premium; they give the immediate impact of a one-unit increase in each of the determinants. The coefficients a_4, a_5, and a_6 (divided by $1 - a_7$) give the long-term effects. The hypothesis that portfolio factors matter only in the short term is given by $a_4 = a_5 = 0$.[12]

Table 7.2 gives the results of estimating equation (1) using annual data from 1967 to 1988. The results are very satisfactory, particularly given the short sample and the uncertain quality of the data.[13] They give strong support to the conclusion that both trade and portfolio factors are at work in determining the premium on unofficial foreign exchange in Tanzania. All variables enter with the expected signs: a

TABLE 7.2   *Determinants of the parallel premium: dependent variable, parallel premium (PPREM)*

	OLS		IV*	
	1967–88		1968–88	
	1	2	3	4
CONSTANT	−191.38	−259.94	−195.95	−285.31
	(−2.27)	(−2.69)	(−1.39)	(−2.47)
$PPREM_{t-1}$	0.38	0.45	0.71	0.40
	(1.49)	(2.03)	(1.41)	(1.60)
$d(M2/E)_t$	0.19	0.24	0.22	0.27
	(2.58)	(2.82)	(1.55)	(2.32)
$d(IPD)_t$	2.45	1.20	1.91	0.89
	(2.16)	(1.09)	(0.76)	(0.58)
$d(REER)_t$	3.32	0.80	6.13	0.48
	(2.24)	(0.69)	(2.03)	(0.37)
$(M2/E)_{t-1}$	−0.05	–	−0.12	–
	(−1.40)		(−1.60)	
IPD_{t-1}	3.63	–	4.97	–
	(3.03)		(2.74)	
$REER_{t-1}$	2.46	3.08	2.56	3.17
	(2.78)	(3.09)	(1.84)	(4.26)
Adjusted R^2	0.86	0.79	0.80	0.78
$Q(11)^†$	14.73	16.76	8.67	14.78
	$(0.20)^‡$	$(0.12)^‡$	$(0.56)^‡$	$(0.14)^‡$

t−statistics are in parentheses.

$PPREM = 100 \times (U - E)/E$ is the end of year parallel premium in percentage points, with the unofficial and official exchange rates U and E taken from Kaufmann and O'Connell (1991, Table 2.1). $M2/E$ is end of year $M2$ in TShs (source: IMF, *IFS*), deflated by the official exchange rate.

$IPD = 100 \times [(1 + i^*)(E_{t+1}/E_t) - (1 + i)]$ is the uncovered interest parity differential, with i^* given by the London Eurodollar deposit rate (source: *IFS*) and i by the saving deposit rate in Tanzania (source: Bank of Tanzania). $REER$ is the ratio of the Tanzanian CPI to a trade-weighted average of WPIs of eight major developed country partners (source: World Bank). *TAXCINV* is the ratio of the producer price for coffee to the f.o.b. export price in TShs (sources: 1966–79, Bank of Tanzania, *Twenty Years of Independence*, Table 24; 1980–8, our calculation using data from the Tanzania Marketing Development Board, *Annual Review of Coffee*, 1988). *TOT* is the terms of trade (sources: UNCTAD and World Bank). *AID* is net official resource transfers in millions of US$ (sources: 1966–84, Collier (1991); 1985–8, World Bank).

* Instruments for $d(REER)_t$ and $d(IPD)_t$ are $M2_{t-2}$, $REER_{t-2}$ and IPD_{t-2} (along with the other right-hand side variables, which are assumed to be

predetermined; note that in the case of $PPREM_{t-1}$, this is only valid if the disturbances are serially uncorrelated).
[†] Q is the Box–Pierce statistic for testing general serial correlation. For columns 3 and 4, the statistic reported is $Q(10)$.
[‡] This is the marginal significance level for the Q-statistic.

rise in the interest parity deviation or an increase in the real value of domestic financial assets leads to portfolio substitution towards unofficial foreign exchange, raising the premium; a real appreciation (which is an increase in *REER*) shifts incentives away from export smuggling and towards import smuggling, raising the premium. Moreover, we cannot reject the null hypotheses that a_1 and a_2 are zero, using standard *F*-tests. The results therefore support the prediction of the model that portfolio factors influence the parallel premium in the short term only and that the premium is determined by flow factors in the long term.

The parameter estimates in Table 7.2 also support the conclusion that nominal devaluations are capable of lowering the parallel premium to the degree that they lower the foreign exchange value of domestic financial assets or depreciate the real exchange rate. In both cases, the need for complementary macroeconomic policies is clear, to ensure that a nominal devaluation is not offset by increases in money supply or domestic prices. While the underlying mechanisms driving the domestic money supply and the domestic price level are left implicit, a more sophisticated analysis would give a central role to the public sector deficit (including parastatal borrowing from the banking sector) in monetary growth and inflation. This would in turn imply that control of the public sector deficit is a fundamental requirement for achieving a lasting reduction in the parallel premium.

Extending the Basic Model

While equation (1) captures a large share of the variation in the parallel premium, the extremely simple form of the equation obscures some of the underlying forces at work in determining the parallel premium. In this section we report the results of estimating an extended form of the model that captures the trade determinants more carefully as well as key features of the exchange control regime. Along with the portfolio factors, we explore the role of the following determinants: (1) the (inverse of the) direct tax on coffee exports, measured by the ratio of the domestic producer price of coffee to the f.o.b. export price converted to Tanzanian shillings $(TAXCINV)$[14] (2) the terms of trade (TOT), (3) the net official resource transfers in dollars (AID), (4) the OF scheme $(OWNFUNDS)$, and, finally (5) $D83$, a dummy variable capturing the 1983 crackdown on 'economic saboteurs' during which a large number of businessmen were jailed (Maliyamkono and Bagachwa, 1990).

As outlined in Kaufmann and O'Connell (1991), the extended model is derived in four steps. First, the unofficial trade balance equation is specified more carefully. This allows for the introduction of a range of 'trade' determinants of the parallel premium, including the tax on coffee exports, the domestic price premium on imports, the intensity of the enforcement effort, and the real exchange rate for exports. Second, the domestic price premium on imports and the real exchange rate for exports are modeled directly as functions of the overall expenditure and the official allocation of foreign exchange. Third, official foreign exchange allocations are modeled as a function of official foreign exchange availability, thus capturing the endogenous trade liberalizations and import compressions that accompanied balance of payments fluctuations in the 1970s and 1980s. Finally, the overall expenditure is modeled as a function of the terms of trade and other variables determining income and desired aggregate saving. The resulting reduced form replaces the real exchange rate in equation (1) with an unrestricted linear function of $TAXCINV$, TOT, AID, $OWN-FUNDS$, and $D83$.

The theoretically predicted signs on these variables are generally not unambiguous. Given the parallel premium, a rise in $TAXCINV$ has two opposing effects on the premium: the real exchange rate for coffee exports improves, increasing aggregate coffee supply and thus increasing coffee smuggling, but the share of exports diverted onto unofficial channels also rises, reducing the premium. The net effect on illegal exports and thus on the premium is an empirical question.

TOT enters in a number of ways: (1) through the endogenous trade liberalization that follows an improvement in the balance of payments, (2) through a direct valuation effect on the illegal trade deficit, (3) through resource movements in favor of exports and away from imports, and (4) through effects on aggregate demand, depending on the savings response. The first three of these would be expected to lower the parallel premium, while the third would raise it, to an extent depending on the savings response. Overall, we expect a net negative effect.

A rise in *AID* should lower the premium both through direct increases in illegal export flows (for example, aid flows may serve as a proxy for the demand for expatriate housing services) and through the endogenous trade liberalization effect; it should raise the premium to the degree that it raises aggregate demand. Again, we expect a negative effect on balance, although the aggregate demand effect might be rather strong given that changes in aid have a strong permanent component.

OWNFUNDS is a dummy variable for the years 1984 and 1985, during which the OF scheme was in operation (due to data availability limitations, the sample only extends to 1985). As argued in O'Connell (1992), an OF scheme reduces the cost of what was previously import smuggling, leading to a rise in the volume of imports financed at the parallel rate; unless the import liberalization gives rise to a strong aggregate export supply response, the parallel premium must rise to bring forth the required increase in export smuggling. We therefore expect *OWNFUNDS* to have a positive effect on the premium, given the values of the other variables.

D83 has a theoretically ambiguous effect. From the illegal trade side, a crackdown simultaneously affects the supply and the demand for illegal foreign exchange, with an uncertain net result. Effects operating through the portfolio side are clearer, since a crackdown impairs the liquidity of foreign exchange assets and reduces their expected yield; these effects tend to reduce the premium.

The results are in Table 7.3. Most of the variables have the expected signs. Both portfolio and flow determinants enter significantly, with magnitudes generally close to those found in Table 7.2. Of the flow determinants, however, only the *TOT* comes in strongly, with the lagged *TOT* exerting a strong negative effect on the premium (as observed, for example, during and after the coffee boom). Lagged aid inflows also lower the premium, although the effect is not estimated precisely. The effect of lagged terms of trade and lagged aid is consistent with a substantial endogenous trade liberalization in response to balance of payments improvements; this corroborates evidence from the import equations in Ndulu and Lipumba (1988).

The coefficient on the coffee tax variable is consistently negative but insignificant, implying that any smuggling response is more than offset by an aggregate coffee supply response in the opposite direction. While this finding does not rule out a macroeconomic role for coffee smuggling in determining the parallel premium, it suggests that the elasticity of smuggling supply is low in the coffee sector, at least over the horizon of a year.

TABLE 7.3   *Determinants of the premium: extended model: dependent variable*
parallel premium (PPREM) 1967–88

	OLS		IV*	
CONSTANT	369.06	285.57	381.13	226.83
	(1.33)	(1.19)	(1.33)	(0.73)
$PPREM_{t-1}$	0.51	0.66	0.60	1.12
	(2.08)	(3.01)	(1.78)	(2.66)
$d(M2/E)_t$	0.19	0.29	0.16	0.55
	(1.85)	(2.98)	(1.50)	(2.54)
$d(IPD)_t$	3.33	2.28	3.46	0.58
	(2.83)	(2.08)	(2.22)	(0.28)
$TAXCINV_{t-1}$	−1.00	−1.01	−1.02	−0.40
	(−0.48)	(−0.57)	(−0.47)	(−0.17)
TOT_{t-1}	−2.42	−1.68	−2.60	−1.72
	(−1.30)	(−1.03)	(−1.35)	(−0.83)
AID_{t-1}	−0.12	−0.24	−0.14	−0.42
	(−0.82)	(−1.83)	(−0.89)	(−2.01)
OWNFUNDS	157.46	203.93	160.81	232.26
	(2.59)	(3.68)	(2.58)	(3.18)
D83	–	222.07	–	315.10
		(2.41)		(2.32)
$RBAR^2$	0.73	0.81	0.72	0.68
DW	1.39	1.78	1.54	2.79
$Q(10)^\dagger$	5.49	12.05	5.92	16.86
	$(0.86)^\ddagger$	$(0.28)^\ddagger$	$(0.82)^\ddagger$	$(0.08)^\ddagger$

t-statistics are in parentheses.
For definitions of variables see Table 7.2.
* Instruments for $d(IPD)_t$ are $(M2/E)_{t-2}$, $TAXC_{t-2}$, TOT_{t-2}, and $D83$, along
with the other right-hand side variables.
† Q is the Box–Pierce statistic for testing general serial correlation. For
columns 7 and 8, the statistic reported is $Q(9)$.
‡ This is the marginal significance level for the Q-statistic.

   The OF scheme appears to have raised the premium, *ceteris paribus*,
as predicted by the model in the absence of a strong aggregate export
supply response. The magnitude of the increase, between 150 and 240
percentage points, is impressive and suggests that the low elasticity of
export smuggling indicated in the coffee case may be a more general
phenomenon in Tanzania. More obviously, the results suggest that the
lowering of the parallel premium since 1986 has been a function of
other developments in policy and external conditions, such as (1)
cumulative depreciations of the official exchange rate that reduced

the real stock of domestic money and (2) large inflows of foreign aid, and not of the OF scheme itself.

The 1983 crackdown also appears to have raised the premium, holding other variables constant; this suggests that the crackdown had a particularly strong effect on export smuggling.

These results must be viewed as provisional, given the short sample and the limited set of variables that we were able to incorporate. Nonetheless, they do shed some light on the particular forces at work in determining the parallel premium in Tanzania.

FISCAL EFFECTS OF UNIFICATION

One of the goals of Tanzanian policy since the mid-1980s has been to restore the central role of commercial policy considerations in the granting of import licenses, a role usurped by constraints on overall foreign exchange availability since at least the late 1970s. For the remainder of the chapter, we consider the fiscal implications of 'unifying' the official and parallel exchange markets for current account purposes, by which we mean achieving and sustaining full convertibility of the shilling for imports (subject to commodity-specific tariffs and/or quotas). We model a movement towards unification as a sustained fall in the parallel premium that is achieved through simultaneous liberalization of import licensing at the official exchange rate and exchange rate adjustments designed to facilitate this occurring without excessive losses in international reserves. The theoretical literature on dual exchange rate systems suggests that required adjustments in the exchange rate may be accomplished either through an 'overnight' float of the exchange rate or through an appropriate combination of changes in the level and possibly rate of crawl of the official rate.[15] Capital controls are assumed to remain in place; this implies that the parallel market will not disappear altogether, since any situation of portfolio disequilibrium will give rise to a premium (which may be negative) and illegal trade flows. However, in the absence of convertibility restrictions on the trade account, the premium will be zero in a steady state.

The effects on government revenue of central bank transactions at multiple official exchange rates are well known (for example, Sherwood, 1956; Easterly *et al.*, 1995). Recent work on parallel markets has emphasized that exchange controls have important 'shadow' fiscal

264 *Parallel Exchange Rates*

implications even when all transactions of the central bank take place at a single exchange rate. In particular, Pinto (1989, 1991) argued that if the government is a net seller of foreign exchange to the private sector, exchange rate unification imposes a fiscal shock that will raise money growth and inflation in the long run unless the policy package includes contractionary fiscal measures.

As indicated in Figure 7.4, Tanzania appears to have avoided any trade-off between inflation and the parallel premium during its move towards unification, enjoying a simultaneous reduction in both variables in the second half of the 1980s. Part of this may be associated with an improvement in inflationary expectations associated with the reduction in fiscal deficits in the first half of the decade (from 20 percent in 1979 to 7.5 percent in 1985) and the improvements in overall fiscal management obtained under the reform program. Moreover, the direct cost-push effect of nominal devaluations undertaken in the mid-1980s was minimized by the fact that domestic prices were determined at the margin largely by the parallel exchange

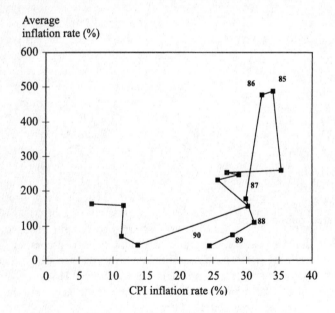

FIGURE 7.4 *Inflation and the parallel premium, 1976–90*

Sources: CPI and official exchange rate from IMF, *International Financial Statistics*; parallel exchange rate from International Currency Analysis Inc., *World Currency Yearbook* and Kaufmann and O'Connell (1991).

rate rather than the official exchange rate. However, the fiscal fundamentals made little direct contribution in the second half of the decade, as central government deficits fluctuated between 6 and 10 percent of GDP and off-budget losses of the public sector grew over the period (Mans, 1994). The relatively favorable outcome for inflation during the unification process therefore raises the possibility that the longer-term fiscal effect of the parallel premium was negative over the period in question, so that reductions in the premium – holding the fiscal deficit constant – had the direct effect of reducing the underlying rate of monetary growth and inflation.[16] In this section, we explore this possibility by providing rough counterfactual estimates of the fiscal effect of exchange rate unification from 1976 to the present. We begin by generalizing Pinto's (1989, 1991) theoretical analysis of the inflationary effect of exchange rate unification.

Some Steady-state Accounting[17]

The effect on inflation of a reduction in the parallel premium ultimately depends, given the growth in real money demand, on its effect on monetary expansion. We therefore require an expression for the flow supply of domestic monetary assets.

The consolidated public sector in Tanzania incorporates central and local governments, parastatals, and a banking system that until recently consisted of the Bank of Tanzania and a single nationalized commercial bank. Since the banking system did very little lending to the private sector and there was virtually no domestic government bond market in the period under study, the flow supply of broad money is approximately equal to the domestic financing of the consolidated public sector:[18]

$$\begin{array}{ccccc} \dot{M} & = & D & - & E(a^* - \dot{r}^*), \\ \text{Domestic} & = & \text{Public} & - & \text{Foreign} \\ \text{financing} & & \text{sector} & & \text{financing} \\ & & \text{deficit} & & \end{array}$$

(2)

where M and D are the broad money supply and the consolidated public sector deficit and r and a are international reserves and foreign inflows in the form of aid and loans. The superscript "*" denotes a quantity denominated in foreign currency and a dot over a variable denotes a time derivative.

Using the balance of payments identity $\dot{r}^* = b^{*g} + b^*$, where b^{*g} and b^* are the government and private sector balances of official foreign exchange transactions with the banking system, equation (2) can be written $\dot{M} = D - E(a^* - b^{*g}) - Eb^*$. However, since all foreign exchange transactions by the public sector are mediated through the banking system, the quantity $E(a^* - b^{*g})$ is simply the foreign currency component of the public sector deficit. What is left over after subtracting this from the overall deficit is the domestic currency component, D^d, giving us the following alternative to (2):

$$(3) \qquad \dot{M} = D^d + Eb^*.$$

In real terms, equations (2) and (3) imply

$$(4) \qquad \dot{M}/P = \dot{m} + \pi m = d - e^{-1}(a^* - \dot{r}^*) = d^d + e^{-1}b^*,$$

where P is the domestic price index, $m \equiv M/P$ is real money balances, $\pi \equiv \dot{P}/P$ is the rate of inflation, and $e \equiv P/E$ is the (official) real exchange rate. The flow supply of domestic money balances can therefore be calculated either as the consolidated public sector deficit net of foreign financing or as the sum of the domestic currency component of the deficit and net purchases of foreign exchange from the private sector.

Turning to the demand side, the empirical evidence in the previous section is consistent with a model in which domestic monetary assets and foreign exchange are imperfect substitutes in private portfolios and asset transactions take place at the parallel exchange rate. An asset demand formulation that captures these features can be written $m = h(\dot{U}/U)w$, where $w \equiv (M + U \cdot f)/P$ is real wealth and $\dot{U}/U$ is the expected rate of depreciation of the parallel exchange rate (which is equal to the actual under perfect foresight). A rise in expected depreciation increases the opportunity cost of holding wealth in the form of domestic monetary assets, so that $h' < 0$.[19] Since all nominal variables must grow at the same rate in a steady state, we have $\dot{U}/U = \pi$ and the following relationship holds between long-term values of the variables

$$(5) \qquad \pi h(\pi)w = d - e^{-1}a^* = d^d + e^{-1}b^*.$$

Equation (5) helps tie down the inflation rate in the long term by requiring that the domestic financing requirement be fully covered by the inflation tax. More importantly for our purposes, to the degree that the variables in equation (5) are jointly determined with the

parallel premium, it provides a long-term relationship between inflation and the premium that can help determine the inflationary effects
of exchange rate unification. These effects are complex in principle,
since all of the variables in equation (5) are jointly determined with the
parallel premium in general equilibrium. In the following limiting
case, analyzed by Pinto (1989), the effect of unification on inflation
comes down to a question of whether the private sector is a net buyer
or seller of foreign exchange to the government.

Proposition 1 (Pinto, 1989): Suppose (1) that the domestic financing
requirement $d - a^*$ is positive, (2) that the private sector consumes only
imports and that these are priced at the parallel exchange rate ($P = U$),
(3) that the elasticity of the function h is between zero and -1, (4) that
real wealth (w) and private sector net sales of foreign exchange to the
banking system (b^*) are constant with respect to the parallel premium
across steady states, and (5) that the real domestic currency component
of the public sector deficit (d^d) is also constant with respect to the
parallel premium across steady states. Then exchange rate unification
will cause a rise (fall) in inflation if and only if the private sector is a net
seller (buyer) of foreign exchange *vis-à-vis* the government.

To prove proposition 1, let $z \equiv U/E$ be (one plus) the parallel
premium and define $\theta \equiv e^{-1}b^*/(d^d + e^{-1}b^*) = e^{-1}b^*/(d - a^*)$ as the
ratio of the private sector official balance of payments to the overall
financing requirement. Log differentiate equation (5) under the stated
assumptions to obtain $d\ln\pi/d\ln z = \theta e_z/(1 + h_\pi)$, where we use subscripts to denote elasticities (for example, h_π is the elasticity of the
function h with respect to π). Since $P = U$ by assumption, we have
$e = 1/z$ and $e_z = -1$. This implies

$$(6) \qquad d\ln\pi/d\ln z \equiv \pi_z = -\theta/(1 + h_\pi).$$

Since $\theta > (<)0$ if and only if $b^* > (<)0$, the reduction in z that
accompanies unification will raise inflation if and only if $b^* > 0$ and
reduce it if and only if $b^* < 0$.

Although the Pinto analysis would appear to rely on an impossibly
restrictive set of assumptions, it is worth being precise about where these
assumptions are weakest in describing the Tanzanian case. Assumptions
(1)–(3) are in fact plausible approximations of reality for Tanzania and
for many other countries with parallel markets. Assumption (1) is confirmed for Tanzania by column 3 of Table 7.4, where the growth of
broad money typically exceeds 5 percent of GDP. Assumption (2) is
simply an extreme version of our earlier argument that domestic prices

are closely linked to the parallel exchange rate in an exchange control regime with severe import rationing; what is actually required here is the weaker (and highly plausible) assumption that a sustainable exchange rate-led unification must be accompanied by a real depreciation (so that $e_z < 0$). Assumption (3) is more questionable; it is equivalent to the requirement that the inflation rate be below the rate that maximizes inflation tax revenues. Measured inflation has never exceeded 40 percent in Tanzania and we will proceed under the assumption that the rates experienced are below the revenue-maximizing rate.[20]

Assumption (4) abstracts from general equilibrium effects. We loosen this assumption in the following subsection to allow changes in the parallel premium to be reflected in trade flows and private sector wealth. For the remainder of this section, however, we focus on assumption (5), which restricts the base for the tax/subsidy scheme represented by the parallel premium to private sector net sales of foreign exchange to the banking system. The underlying assumption is that net domestic currency flows in the public sector are fixed in real terms. This is a troublesome assumption in the Tanzanian case, since a number of important flows, including customs duties and parastatal purchases of the export crop, are more closely linked to the official exchange rate than to the overall price level. The following proposition generalizes the earlier result in a way that will be useful for our subsequent calculations, by identifying domestic currency flows that are indexed to the official exchange rate.

Proposition 2: Suppose that assumptions (1)–(4) of proposition 1 hold and that assumption (5) is replaced by the assumption that an amount x^* (measured in dollars at the official rate) of the overall deficit consists of domestic currency flows indexed to the official exchange rate. All remaining domestic currency flows $(d^d - x^*)$ continue to be fixed in real terms. Define $\theta' \equiv e^{-1}(x^* + b^*)/(d^d + e^{-1}b^*) = e^{-1}(x^* + b^*)/(d - a^*)$ as the ratio of such indexed flows to the overall domestic borrowing requirement. Then exchange rate unification will cause a rise (fall) in inflation if and only if $\theta' > (<)0$.

To prove this proposition, simply log differentiate equation (5) as before to obtain $\pi_z = -\theta'/(1 + h_\pi)$.

In the Pinto (1989, 1991) analysis, unification tends to be inflationary when governments rely on net purchases of foreign exchange from the private sector to finance official imports (including debt service). According to proposition 2, this tendency can be overturned if domestic currency flows that are closely linked to the official exchange rate are in sufficient surplus.

General Equilibrium Complications

The results of the previous section indicate that indexation of the domestic currency budget can be extremely important in determining the inflationary impact of exchange rate-led unification. In this sub-section we ask about the appropriateness of assumption (4), which abstracts from general equilibrium complications. The discussion suggests that the likelihood of a favorable impact of reductions of the premium on inflation is even stronger than indicated in the previous section.

The first general equilibrium complication arises from the linkage between export supply and real wealth that emerges from the require-ment of a balanced overall current account in the long term. If aggregate export supply is negatively correlated with the parallel pre-mium across steady states, as suggested by the Tanzanian experience reviewed in the first section, a move towards unification will raise export supply and thereby increase the level of real wealth consistent with the current account balance. This in turn increases the base for the inflation tax (see equation (5)), allowing a reduction in the required inflation tax rate.

The second complication works through the effects of the premium on official trade volumes. Pinto's (1989, 1991) analysis and our cal-culations both assumed that the private sector's net sales of foreign exchange to the banking system were uncorrelated with the premium across steady states. In reality, a reduction in the steady-state pre-mium will be associated with an increase in official trade volumes, as aggregate exports respond to real depreciation and exports that would previously have been smuggled are channeled through the official market. The effect on the private sector's net sales of foreign exchange is likely to be negligible, since changes in export revenues are passed on directly to increased import allocations in an exchange control regime of the Tanzanian style; however the increase in import volumes brings a customs revenue boom. This revenue boom reduces the domestic currency component of the consolidated public sector deficit, reducing monetary emission and inflation in the steady state.

Calculating the Fiscal Effect

In this section we apply the logic of proposition 2 to Tanzanian data by (1) using balance of payments data to approximate private sector net sales of foreign exchange to the banking system and (2) splitting domestic currency expenditure and revenue flows of the consolidated public sector into flows that are (to a first approximation) indexed fully to the official exchange rate and flows that are (to a first approximation) indexed to the domestic price level. We ask a simple question: viewing the parallel premium as an implicit tax on individuals who surrender foreign exchange receipts at the official exchange rate (or receive payments indexed to the official rate) and an implicit subsidy to individuals who receive foreign exchange at the official rate (or make payments indexed to the official rate), what are the direct effects on monetary emission of this 'shadow' tax/subsidy scheme? We will see that there is a close relationship between this calculation, which is a generalization of familiar calculations of the revenue impact of multiple exchange rates, and the inflationary impacts of unification studied in the previous section.

Define the *direct monetary effect* (*DME*) of the premium as the reduction in monetary emission consequent on pricing foreign currency flows (and indexed domestic currency flows) at the official rather than the parallel rate, holding underlying real quantities (measured in dollars) fixed. From equation (3), this can be written

$$(7) \qquad DME \; = \; (U - E)x^* \; + \; (U - E)b^*.$$

Domestic	Central
budget	bank
balance	profits
effect	effect

The change in money growth has two components. Given our indexation assumptions, $(U - E)x^*$ is simply the change in the domestic currency component of the deficit that would occur if the official exchange rate were devalued by the amount $U - E$ and this was translated fully into a real devaluation (in this case, the domestic price level is unchanged; since we are assuming that the remainder of the domestic currency budget is fixed in real terms, there are no further effects on monetary expansion from domestic currency flows). The second term, $(U - E)b^*$, has a direct analogy in the fiscal gain enjoyed by the public sector in a multiple exchange rate system when the central bank buys and sells foreign exchange at different rates (cf. Sherwood, 1956; Dornbusch, 1986a, b); we therefore call it the 'central bank profits' effect.

Equation (7) applies to an economy in which money growth is quite clearly a 'fiscal' phenomenon; indeed, the monetary effect can also be written as $DME = DFE - (U - E)(a^* - \dot{r}^*)$, where $DFE = (U - E)(x^* + a^* - b^{*g})$ is the (analogously defined) *direct fiscal effect* of the premium. The monetary effect is therefore simply the fiscal effect corrected for the implicit revaluation of net foreign financing implied by the premium. For a given value of *DFE*, a larger level of foreign financing reduces the monetary benefits of the premium, since it implies a reduction in the private sector's net sales of foreign exchange to the banking system. In effect, the government is implicitly passing on a larger net subsidy to the ultimate recipient – the private sector – of these foreign inflows.

Not surprisingly, the *DME* has a close relationship with the parameter θ' governing the inflationary impact of exchange rate-led changes in the parallel premium across steady states. Denoting the parallel premium by $\phi \equiv z - 1 = (U - E)/E$ and noting that $\theta' = E(x^* + b^*)/\Delta M$, we have

$$(8) \qquad\qquad DME/\Delta M = \phi\theta'$$

where ΔM is the monetary emission that would occur under the counterfactual of no change in the parallel premium.[21]

The implementation of equation (7) is made difficult by the fact that the fiscal and balance of payments accounts do not identify flows associated with the large Tanzanian parastatal sector. Data on the foreign exchange cash flow of the banking system, which would allow direct measurement of at least b^*, are also unavailable. We therefore approach equation (7) by making a set of adjustments to the standard fiscal and balance of payments accounts in order to separate the parastatal sector from the private sector. We also require a set of assumptions regarding the indexation of the underlying flows; the assumptions regarding indexation are in Table A 7.2 in the Appendix. A thorough description of the calculations, which we summarize here, is also in the Appendix.

The Central Bank Profits Effect

Calculating private sector net sales of foreign exchange to the banking system requires two adjustments to the balance of payments data on trade flows. The first is to remove the influence of the public sector, including parastatals. On the export side, we subtract from total exports traditional exports (coffee, cotton, and other traditional crops), which are marketed through parastatals; we also subtract the 15 percent of non-traditional exports that we assume are produced by parastatals. The remainder is private sector exports, x_o^p. On the import side, we use 1990 data to identify the share of the total import bill going to the consolidated public sector in that year; we then extrapolate backwards, making changes in the share to reflect our best assessment of the net impact of factors affecting the public share. We then multiply the implied private sector share by total imports to get official private imports, q^p.

The second adjustment to the balance of payments data is to eliminate own-funded imports, q_{own}, starting in 1984; these enter the official statistics but are not mediated through the banking system. Finally, private sector capital flows, which are illegal, are assumed to take place only in the parallel market. The central bank profits effect is therefore given by $(U - E)b^* = (U - E)(x_o^p - q^p + q_{own})$.

The Domestic Budget Balance Effect

Our task here is made simpler by the fact that we only have to identify public sector flows that are denominated in domestic currency but to a first approximation indexed to the official exchange rate. Among these we include marketing board purchases of traditional exports, in dollar amount x^m; using $m_x \equiv 1 - (P_x^m/E)$ to denote the margin imposed by parastatal export marketing boards between the world price and the domestic producer price of the crops purchased from peasants and assuming this margin to be fixed with respect to the official exchange rate, the amount actually paid to peasants (measured in dollars at the official rate) is $(1 - m_x)x^m$.[22] Also included are marketing board sales of imports, q^m and taxes – primarily customs duties – directly indexed to the official exchange rate, τ.[23] All other domestic currency flows of the public sector are assumed to be indexed fully to the domestic price level. Under these assumptions, the domestic budget balance effect can be written $(U - E)$ $[(1 - m_x)x^m - q^m - \tau]$.

Baseline Results

Equation (7) can now be written

$$(9) \quad DME = (U - E)[(1 - m_x)x^m - q^m - \tau] + (U - E)(x_o^p - q^p + q_{own}).$$

Domestic budget
balance effect

Central bank
profits effect

Column 4 of Table 7.4 shows the estimated *DME* relative to current GDP for 1976–93. The calculations through to 1989 are based on actual fiscal and balance of payments data; for 1990–3 we use our own projections of the underlying flows. Table 7.5 and Figure 7.5 decompose this overall effect into its two major components, the domestic budget balance effect and the central bank profits effect.

Several conclusions can be drawn from the data. First, the *DME* is often large; it exceeds 5 percent of GDP in magnitude for half of the observations in the sample. The *DME* remains substantial in many years even under the conservative assumption that the parallel rate overstates the appropriate shadow rate by 40 percent of the observed premium (column 5 of Table 7.4). Second, the *DME* shows a substantial amount of persistence, so that it is possible to distinguish at least two and perhaps three distinct regimes in the sample. The sample begins in 1976, the first year of the coffee boom and the monetary effect makes a rapid transition from 7.5 percent of GDP to −4.1 percent in 1978. This is the joint effect of the collapse of the coffee boom, which improved the domestic budget balance by drastically reducing outlays for purchases of coffee by the marketing board and the temporary import liberalization of 1978, which dramatically reduced private sector net sales of foreign exchange to the banking system.

After the 1976–8 transition, the *DME* fluctuated around zero for the period from 1979 to 1985, notwithstanding an increase in the parallel premium to over 230 percent by 1981 and a subsequent increase to nearly 500 percent in 1985. Both the domestic budget balance effect and the central bank profits effect are small for most of this period, a development driven by a reduction in export proceeds remitted to the banking system and the onset of severe rationing of foreign exchange for imports. The private sector's net purchases of foreign exchange hover near zero for most of the period, suggesting that the low and falling export receipts were being channeled directly to private sector imports, while official imports were largely financed through aid and increases in arrears. As indicated in the further decomposition in Table 7.5, the contraction in trade reduced the revenue base for customs duties and export taxes, roughly offsetting the net contractionary effect of other indexed items in the domestic budget balance.

TABLE 7.4 *Direct monetary effect of the parallel premium**† *(percent)*

Year	Actual			Estimates of DME/Y			
				Baseline		Alternative scenarios (using U-E)	
	Parallel premium	ΔM/M$_{-1}$	ΔM/Y	Using U-E	Using 0.6(U-E)§	Small/efficient public sector	Large/inefficient Public Sector
1976	161	25.1	5.7	7.5	4.5	3.0	14.5
1977	159	20.2	4.9	0.5	0.3	-4.0	7.4
1978	70	12.6	3.3	-4.1	-2.5	-6.5	-1.0
1979	46	46.9	12.2	-0.2	-0.1	-1.9	2.0
1980	156	26.9	8.9	0.4	0.2	-5.2	7.4
1981	233	18.1	6.5	4.1	2.5	-2.5	12.8
1982	251	19.5	6.9	-1.6	-1.0	-7.4	5.9
1983	255	17.8	6.3	0.6	0.4	-3.9	6.6
1984	266	3.7	1.2	-0.4	-0.2	-5.7	6.7
1985	477	30.3	7.3	-2.2	-1.3	-13.7	5.5
1986	405	27.9	7.1	-12.4	-7.4	-21.9	2.0
1987	180	32.1	7.3	-8.3	-5.0	-15.1	-0.7
1988	111	32.1	7.1	-7.3	-4.4	-10.6	-0.7
1989	77	29.5	6.6	-6.8	-4.1	-8.0	-0.7

1990‡	78	42.1	12.1	-9.0	-5.7	-7.8	-3.2
1991‡	71	26.1	8.1	-10.6	-6.2	-14.0	-5.7
1992‡	19	38.9	12.0	-9.3	-2.0	-4.4	-1.9
1993‡	2	28.4	9.6	-8.3	-0.2	-0.5	-0.2

* See Table 7.5 for a decomposition of the results in column 4 and Table A7.2 for a full description of the assumptions underlying the simulations in columns 4–7.

† Y is current year GDP.

‡ Based on authors' projections of fiscal and balance of payments data. See note on sources.

§ This assumes that the parallel exchange rate overestimates the shadow equilibrium real exchange rate by 40 percent of the premium.

SOURCES: 1976–89: monetary, fiscal and balance of payments data are from the World Bank. Black market exchange rates from the *World Currency Yearbook*, various years, supplemented by the survey conducted by Maliyamkono and Bagachwa (1990); see Kaufmann and O'Connell (1991) for details. Official exchange rates are from the IMF. Parallel premium is the average of monthly figures. 1990–3: actual monetary and GDP data (columns 2 and 3) are from Bank of Tanzania, *Economic Bulletin*, September 1994. Balance of payments flows underlying columns 4–7 are based on authors' projections rather than actual data. Parallel premiums are based on end of year figures from *World Currency Alert* and the IMF.

TABLE 7.5 Decomposition of baseline case (shares of GDP)

Year	x^*	b^*	Components of x^*			Components of b^*		
			$+(1-m_x)x^m$ export crop outlays	$-\tau$ trade tax revenue	$-q^m$ sales of imports	$+x_o^p$ private sector exports	$-q^p$ private sector imports	$+q_{own}$ own-funded imports
1976	2.0	2.7	8.3	-3.8	-2.5	9.7	-7.5	0.5
1977	0.8	-0.5	7.8	-4.5	-2.5	5.6	-6.5	0.4
1978	-2.5	-3.3	4.8	-4.3	-3.0	5.9	-9.5	0.4
1979	-3.1	2.7	4.0	-3.8	-3.3	7.8	-5.4	0.3
1980	-2.0	2.3	3.7	-2.6	-3.2	7.9	-5.9	0.3
1981	0.3	1.4	4.4	-1.6	-2.5	6.7	-5.5	0.3
1982	-0.2	-0.4	3.1	-1.3	-2.0	3.9	-4.5	0.2
1983	0.1	0.2	2.9	-1.3	-1.6	3.4	-3.4	0.2
1984	0.2	-0.3	3.5	-1.6	-1.7	3.5	-4.5	0.7
1985	-1.0	0.5	2.4	-1.9	-1.5	3.7	-5.3	2.2
1986	-1.8	-1.2	4.4	-4.0	-2.2	3.1	-8.6	4.3
1987	-5.4	0.8	3.7	-5.8	-3.3	6.5	-13.3	7.5
1988	-5.6	-0.9	3.1	-5.1	-3.6	7.0	-16.1	8.2
1989	-6.4	-2.4	3.6	-5.8	-4.2	8.7	-22.1	11.0

1990*	−5.9	−6.3	4.9	−6.4	−4.4	12.2	−29.4	10.8
1991*	−5.4	−9.1	5.4	−6.5	−4.4	13.9	−32.8	9.9
1992*	−5.2	−11.7	6.5	−7.0	−4.7	18.5	−40.8	9.8
1993*	−4.4	−12.9	7.0	−6.7	−4.8	22.0	−43.7	8.8

* Results for 1990–3 are based on authors' projections of fiscal and balance of payments data.

SOURCE: Underlying fiscal and balance of payments data are from the World Bank and the authors' projections. This is a decomposition of column 4 in Table 7.4. The data in that column are given by $DME/Y = [(U - E)/E](x^* + b^*)$, where $[(U - E)/E]x^*$ and $[(U - E)/E]/E]b^*$ are the 'domestic budget balance effect' and the 'central bank profits effect', respectively. The quantities in x^* and b^* are dollar flows converted to TShs using the official exchange rate and then deflated by nominal GDP.

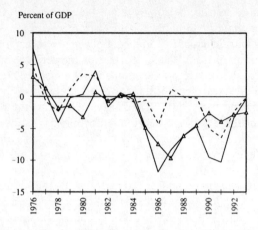

FIGURE 7.5   *Decomposition of the monetary effect of the parallel premium*
SOURCE: Authors' calculations, summarized in Table 7.5.

A clear break occurs in 1986, a year in which the figures suggest
that unification would have converted monetary growth of 7 percent
of GDP into monetary contraction of over 5 percent. From 1986 on,
the monetary effect is consistently negative and above 6.5 percent of
GDP. On the domestic budget balance side, this dramatic change is
largely the result of a customs revenue boom (Table 7.5). A strong
contribution is also made by increases in the private sector's net
purchases of foreign exchange from the banking system. Both developments were decisively influenced by the large inflows of external aid
that became available starting in 1986. A large portion of this aid was
channeled to the private sector, in line with the government's liberalization and structural adjustment priorities. The customs revenue
boom was further propelled by the expansion of aggregate imports
brought about by the introduction of the OF window in 1984 and its
rapid expansion starting in 1985.

Two Alternative Scenarios

Table 7.4 reports two further calculations using alternative assumptions about the size and efficiency of the public sector. The underlying
assumptions are given in Table A7.2 in the Appendix. Relative to the

baseline, a large/inefficient public sector is assumed to take a 15 percent higher share of imports and to lose to corruption a share of the marketing margin equal to 15 percent of the producer price paid to peasant producers of traditional exports. For the period from 1991 to 1993, the large/inefficient public sector also collects lower import duties and sales taxes on imports (lowering the term τ in equation (7) by 2.6, 6.5, and 9 percent, respectively, relative to the baseline in 1991, 1992, and 1993), due to laxity in enforcement. A more efficient public sector takes a 15 percent smaller share of imports and collects higher trade taxes (by 5.1, 11, and 13.6 percent relative to the baseline in 1991, 1992, and 1993).

These differences in size and/or efficiency of the public sector affect the *DME* by changing the base for both the domestic budget balance effect and the central bank profits effect. Under the large/inefficient scenario, we attribute a large share of total imports to the public sector and thus implicitly assume a larger private trade surplus; we simultaneously assume an increase in the government's deficit in items indexed to the official exchange rate, through a combination of corruption and laxity in enforcement. For both reasons, the direct monetary effect of the premium and thus the temptation to maintain an overvalued official exchange rate, is greater than under the baseline case. In the efficient case, we implicitly assume a larger private trade deficit and a smaller public sector deficit in items indexed to the official exchange rate. Both assumptions weaken the incentive for containing monetary growth through an overvalued exchange rate; exchange rate unification would have tended for most of the sample to reward the efficient government with a *reduction* in monetary growth.

These calculations underscore the fundamentally fiscal impetus behind the maintenance of overvalued exchange rates and hence the adoption of exchange controls. They also give some sense of the sensitivity of our calculations to some of the underlying assumptions; while the magnitude of the *DME* is sensitive to these assumptions, there remains a clear reduction in the estimated *DME*s in the mid-1980s, suggesting a turning point in favor of a positive fiscal effect of exchange rate unification. Rodrik (1989) applies a simple test to policy reforms that are ultimately guided by efficiency considerations but take place under conditions of macroeconomic instability and potentially low credibility: 'does the proposed reform directly contribute to the goals of macroeconomic stability and fiscal retrenchment?' (p. 10). Our calculations suggest a resounding 'yes' for exchange rate unification by the mid-1980s.

CONCLUSIONS

Our first aim in this chapter was to characterize the macroeconomic forces underlying the emergence and growth of the parallel market and the premium in Tanzania. We have found that both portfolio and trade flow determinants played important roles and that the premium responded to these variables as predicted by the theory. We trace the rising premium between 1966 and 1986 to a growing inconsistency between macroeconomic policies and the exchange rate regime; the premium was brought down definitively starting in 1986 when the authorities instituted a maxi-devaluation, adopted a crawling peg, and entered upon a major structural adjustment effort generously supported by external donors.

Our second aim was to investigate the fiscal impact of the parallel premium in an exchange control regime. We have shown that while a long-term trade-off between inflation and the parallel premium will prevail if inflation rates are moderate and the real deficit and foreign financing flows are exogenous, an exchange rate-led unification brings a variety of macroeconomic mechanisms into play that reduce the likelihood of a *highly* inflationary long-term outcome and may even produce a reduction in inflation. In the Tanzanian case, our calculations of the short-term outcome under plausible assumptions regarding the indexation of public sector revenues and expenditures suggest that starting in the mid-1980s, more aggressive depreciation of the official exchange rate would have delivered a substantial fiscal bonus, reducing monetary growth and therefore moderating inflationary pressures.

NOTES

1. The authors are a Senior Economist, Eastern Europe Region, World Bank and Associate Professor of Economics, Swarthmore College. The authors are grateful to Saul Lizondo for many helpful discussions, to Paul Collier for comments on work in progress, and to Varga Azad, Jon Isham, and David Ko for research assistance. The views expressed are solely those of the authors.
2. This chapter draws on earlier work of the authors, including Kaufmann and O'Connell (1991) and O'Connell (1990, 1992).
3. A more extensive account appears in Kaufmann and O'Connell (1991). See also Green *et al.* (1980) and Bevan *et al.* (1987, 1990). Mans (1994)

provide an excellent overview of the Economic Recovery Program (ERP) period.

4. Before the introduction of the Tanzanian shilling in 1965, Tanzania was part of the sterling area and thus effectively subject to exchange controls prevailing in Britain. In June 1965, Tanzania adopted its own tighter set of controls, exempting only Kenya and Uganda. These controls were extended to Kenya and Uganda in March 1971, after having been temporarily extended to these countries in the 4 months following the Arusha Declaration of February 1967. See Mtei (1973).

5. See Bank of Tanzania, *Economic Report* (December 1967, June 1968) and particularly the address by Mtei (1968) in the *Economic Report*. While capital flight was reasonably well contained in 1967, the adequacy of exchange controls was called into question by intensified capital flight in 1970–1, leading to the tightening of controls referred to above and to an increase in the enforcement powers of the exchange control authorities (Mtei, 1973).

6. Loxley (1989) provides a thorough analysis of the degree to which 'the single issue of the exchange rate dominated the rift between Tanzania and the IMF in the years 1981 to 1983' (p. 32).

7. The import license data are from the Bank of Tanzania. Ndulu and Hyuha (1989) gave three reasons why the share of licenses may underestimate the true import share: (1) OF consignments of under 10 000 Tanzanian shillings ($50) do not require licenses, (2) the utilization rate of OF licenses is considerably higher than that of licenses accompanied by official foreign exchange, and (3) the incentive to underinvoice OF imports to avoid customs duties is much stronger than for officially financed imports (which may even be overinvoiced).

8. Note that of these alternatives, only the direct repatriation in the form of own-funded imports is legal. It is still illegal to acquire or sell foreign exchange.

9. Note that fears of a reversal of the policy have two opposing effects on the rapidity of the stock adjustment: fears of legal reprisals would slow down the adjustment, and fears of a reversal of the program would speed it up.

10. This section draws on O'Connell (1990) and Kaufmann and O'Connell (1991).

11. These effects are the conventional ones suggested by the theoretical literature on parallel foreign exchange markets; Lizondo (1990) and Agénor (1992) review the literature.

12. Equation (1) is a standard autoregressive distributed lag (ADL) specification with one lag. Parameter estimates and t-statistics from this equation are numerically identical to those from the error-correction model $\Delta \ln z_t = a_0 + a_1 \Delta \ln(M2/E)_t + a_2 \Delta IPD_t + a_3 \Delta REER_t - (1 - a_7) \ln z_{t-1} + a_4 (M/E)_{t-1} + a_5 IPD_{t-1} + a_6 REER_{t-1}$. The latter specification accommodates the possibility that the variables are non-stationary and cointegrated, with cointegration vector $[1, -a_4/(1 - a_7), -a_5/(1 - a_7), -a_6/(1 - a_7)]$ (see Banerjee *et al.*, 1993).

13. There are potential simultaneity problems in the ordinary least squares (OLS) results. First, we assume rational expectations and therefore use

the actual rate of depreciation of the parallel exchange rate, in the interest parity variable. This introduces an error in variables problem because actual depreciation incorporates a forecast error that is correlated with other variables in the current period. The real exchange rate is also jointly endogenous with the parallel premium. To handle these problems, we re-estimated the equations using instrumental variables. The *IPD* variable becomes statistically insignificant, but the results do not otherwise change substantially. One reason for the weaker results for *IPD* may be that we do not have good instruments for the increase in expected depreciation in 1985–6.

14.   We use an average ratio for arabica and robusta, calculated by taking the ratio of payments to producers for the two types of coffee to the total f.o.b. export value of the two types. For data availability reasons, we use the advance price for coffee.

15.   See for example Kiguel and Lizondo (1990) and the references therein. For a cautionary note, see Morris (1995).

16.   See also Morris (1995), who independently derives steady-state results similar to ours and reaches the same conclusion about unification and money growth for Uganda in the late 1980s. His calculations differ in some key respects from ours; in particular, they include credit to the private sector (assumed to be zero in our analysis) and are imbedded in a model in which unification has no implications for trade flows. His paper incorporates a full discussion of the short-term dynamics; in his model, the sign of what we call the 'direct monetary effect' of the premium (see below) affects not only the steady state but also the stability properties of the model.

17.   Table A7.1. in the Appendix contains a full list of variable names and descriptions.

18.   As emphasized by Collier and Gunning (1991), the National Bank of Commerce, Tanzania's sole commercial bank until recently, has essentially operated as a government finance agency, channeling private sector deposits into loans to the public sector. Loans to the private sector constituted less than 9 percent of commercial bank assets on average between 1980 and 1988 (Bank of Tanzania, *Economic and Operations Report* (30 June 1989), Table 10). Thus the entire stock of broad money constituted 'outside' money in Tanzania, as implied by equation (2).

19.   Since *m* refers to broad money, the opportunity cost of holding *m* rather than *f* should include domestic and foreign interest rates as well as the rate of expected depreciation, as in the empirical work reported in the second section. We omit these for notational convenience.

20.   This is not uncontroversial. Adam *et al.* (1996) estimate dynamic money-demand equations for Ghana, Kenya, and Tanzania, and conclude on the basis of point estimates that Tanzanian inflation rates were above the revenue-maximizing rate for most of the 1970s and 1980s. However, the Tanzanian results are the weakest econometrically, due to the difficulty of capturing the determinants of the huge fall in velocity associated with rationing in the goods market in 1979–84 (see Bevan *et al.*, 1990); in fact, for most years, it is difficult to reject the null

hypothesis that the economy is on the good side of the inflation tax Laffer curve. See also Easterly *et al.* (1995) for an argument that more flexible functional forms for the money-demand equation tend to produce significantly higher revenue-maximizing inflation rates for developing countries.

21. It is important to emphasize that the results of the section on steady-state accounting are based on steady-state comparisons. Not surprisingly, unification is not typically attempted from a position of steady state. One must therefore use caution in using equation (8) to work backwards from the *DME*s estimated below – which use the *actual* gap between the parallel and official rate in each year – to conclusions about the precise long-term inflationary impact of unification.

22. These assumptions are approximations to what would occur under a counterfactual policy of exchange rate unification. In actual practice, producer prices were determined on a cost-plus basis and maxi-devaluations were often not passed along to peasant producers in the form of increased prices paid by the marketing boards. Our assumption is that pass through would have been substantial under a determined policy of exchange rate unification, as it has generally been in the post-1985 period.

23. We are assuming that $m_q \equiv (P_q^m/E) - 1$, the before-tax mark-up on world import prices charged by the import marketing parastatals, is zero or, equivalently, that the after-tax margin consists of customs duties and sales taxes that are already counted in τ.

REFERENCES

Adam, Christopher S., Benno Ndulu, and Nii Kwaku Sowa (1996) 'Liberalization and Seigniorage Revenue in Kenya, Ghana and Tanzania', *Journal of Development Studies*, vol. 32, no. 4, pp. 531–53.

Agénor, Pierre-Richard (1992) 'Parallel Currency Markets in Developing Countries: Theory, Evidence, and Policy Implications', *Princeton Essays in International Finance* No. 168 (Princeton, NJ: International Finance Section, Department of Economics, Princeton University).

Bagachwa, M.S.D., N.E. Luvanga, and G.D. Mjema (1989) 'Tanzania: a Study on Non-traditional Exports (Preliminary Draft)', (Dar es Salaam: Economic Research Bureau, University of Dar es Salaam).

Banerjee, Anindya, Juan Dolado, John W. Galbraith, and David F. Hendry (1993) *Co-integration, Error Correction and Econometric Analysis of Non-Stationary Data* (Oxford: Oxford University Press).

Bank of Tanzania (1967) *Economic Report*, December (Dar es Salaam, Government Printer).

Bank of Tanzania (1968) *Economic Report*, June (Dar es Salaam, Government Printer).

Bank of Tanzania (1981) *Tanzania: Twenty Years of Independence (1961–1981)* (Dar es Salaam: Government Printer).

Bank of Tanzania (1989) *Economic and Operations Report for the Year Ended 30th June, 1989* (Dar es Salaam: Tanzania Printers Limited).

Bank of Tanzania (1994) *Economic Bulletin for the Quarter Ended 30th June, 1994*, vol. 23, no. 2 (Dar es Salaam: Tanzania Printers Limited).

Bank of Tanzania (1994) *Economic Bulletin for the Quarter Ended 30th September, 1994* (Dar es Salaam: Tanzania Printers Limited).

Bevan, David, Paul Collier, and Jan W. Gunning (1987) 'East African Lessons in Economic Liberalization', *Thames Essays* No. 48 (London: Trade Policy Research Centre).

Bevan, David, Paul Collier, and Jan W. Gunning with Arne Bigsten and Paul Horsnell (1989) *Peasants and Governments: An Economic Analysis* (Oxford: Oxford University Press).

Bevan, David, Paul Collier, and Jan W. Gunning with Arne Bigsten and Paul Horsnell (1990) *Controlled Open Economies: A Neoclassical Approach to Structuralism* (Oxford: Oxford University Press).

Collier, Paul (1991) 'Aid and Economic Performance in Tanzania', in Uma Lele and Ijaz Nabi (eds), *Transitions in Development: The Role of Aid and Commercial Flows* (San Francisco: ICS Press).

Collier, Paul and Jan Willem Gunning (1991) 'Money Creation and Financial Liberalization in a Socialist Banking System: Tanzania 1983–88', *World Development*, vol. 19, no. 5, pp. 533–8.

Dornbusch, Rudiger (1986a) 'Multiple Exchange Rates for Commercial Transactions', in Sebastian Edwards and Liaquat Ahamed (eds), *Economic Adjustment and Exchange Rates in Developing Countries* (Chicago, Ill: University of Chicago Press), pp. 143–65.

Dornbusch, Rudiger (1986b) 'Special Exchange Rates for Capital Account Transactions', *World Bank Economic Review*, vol. 1, no. 1, pp. 1–33.

Dornbusch, Rudiger, Daniel V. Dantas, Clarice Pechman, Roberto Rocha, and Demetri Simoes (1983) 'The Black Market for Dollars in Brazil', *Quarterly Journal of Economics*, vol. 98, pp. 25–40.

Easterly, William, R., Paolo Mauro, and Klaus Schmidt-Hebbel (1995) 'Money Demand and Seignorage Maximizing Inflation', *Journal of Money, Credit, and Banking*, vol. 27, no. 2, pp. 583–603

Green, R. H., D. G. Rwegasira, and B. Van Arkadie (1980) *Economic Policy Making: Tanzania in the 1970s.* (The Hague: Institute of Social Studies).

International Currency Analysis, Inc. (various years) *World Currency Yearbook* (formerly Pick's Currency Yearbook) (Brooklyn, New York: International Currency Analysis, Inc.).

International Currency Analysis, Inc. (various issues) *World Currency Alert* (Brooklyn, New York: International Currency Analysis, Inc.).

Kaufmann, Daniel and Stephen A. O'Connell (1991) 'The Macroeconomics of the Unofficial Foreign Exchange Market in Tanzania', in Ajay Chhibber and Stanley Fischer (eds), *Economic Reform in Sub-Saharan Africa* (Washington, DC: World Bank), pp. 50–65.

Kiguel, Miguel and J. Saul Lizondo (1990) 'Adoption and Abandonment of Dual Exchange Rate Systems', *Revista de Análisis Económico*, vol. 5, no. 1, pp. 2–23. (Previously *Development Research Department Discussion Paper* No. 201 (Washington, DC: World Bank).)

Lizondo, J. Saul (1990) 'Multiple Exchange Rates and Black Market Exchange Rates: A Non-technical Survey', mimeo (Washington, DC: IMF).

Loxley, John (1989) 'The Devaluation Debate in Tanzania', in Bonnie Campbell and John Loxley (eds), *Structural Adjustment in Africa* (New York: St Martins), pp. 1–36.

Maliyamkono, T. and M.S.D. Bagachwa (1990) *The Second Economy in Tanzania* (Oxford: Oxford University Press).

Mans, Darius (1994) 'Tanzania: Resolute Action', in Ishrat Husain and Rashid Faruqee (eds), *Adjustment in Africa: Lessons from Country Case Studies* (Washington, DC: World Bank), pp. 352–426.

Morris, Stephen (1995) 'Inflation Dynamics and the Parallel Market for Foreign Exchange', *Journal of Development Economics*, vol. 46, pp. 295–316.

Mshomba, Richard E. (1993) 'The Magnitude of Coffee Arabica Smuggled from Northern Tanzania into Kenya' *Eastern Africa Economic Review*, vol. 9, no. 1, pp. 165–75

Mtei, E.I.M. (1968) 'Recent Developments in Tanzania's Economy and Central Bank Policies', address to a Conference of Managers of the National Bank of Commerce, 9 May. (Excerpted in Bank of Tanzania, *Economic and Operations Report* (June 1968).)

Mtei, E.I.M. (1973) 'Exchange Control', in Bank of Tanzania, *Economic and Operations Report*, June (Dar es Salaam: Government Printer).

Ndulu, Benno and Mukwanason Hyuha (1989) 'Inflation and Economic Recovery in Tanzania: Some Empirical Evidence', *Uchumi*, vol. 2, no. 1.

Ndulu, Benno and Nguyuru H.I. Lipumba (1988) 'International Trade and Economic Development in Tanzania', mimeo (Dar es Salaam: Department of Economics, University of Dar es Salaam).

O'Connell, Stephen A. (1990) 'The Parallel Foreign Exchange Market in Tanzania', mimeo (Dar es Salaam: Bank of Tanzania).

O'Connell, Stephen A. (1992) 'Short and Long Run Effects of an Own-funds Scheme', *Journal of African Economies*, vol. 1, no. 1, pp. 131–50.

O'Connell, Stephen A. (1995) 'Monetary Adjustment and Policy Compatibility in a Controlled Open Economy', *Journal of African Economies*, vol. 4, no. 1, pp. 52–82

Pinto, Brian (1989) 'Black Market Premia, Exchange Rate Unification, and Inflation in Sub-Saharan Africa', *World Bank Economic Review*, vol. 3, no. 3, pp. 321–38.

Pinto, Brian (1991) 'Black Markets for Foreign Exchange, Real Exchange Rates and Inflation', *Journal of International Economics*, vol. 30, pp. 121–36.

Rodrik, Dani (1989) 'Credibility of Trade Policy Reform: a Policymaker's Guide', *The World Economy*, vol. 12, no. 1, pp. 1–16.

Sherwood, Joyce (1956) 'Revenue Features of Multiple Exchange Systems: Some Case Studies', *IMF Staff Papers*, vol. 5, pp. 74–107.

Tanzania Marketing Development Board (1988) *Annual Review of Coffee, 1988* (Dar es Salaam: Government Printer).

APPENDIX: DERIVING EQUATION (9) IN THE TEXT

Decomposing central government expenditures into wages ($W \cdot L^c$), consumption of non-traded goods and imports (G_n^c and q^c), and grants to parastatals (V_s) and revenues into general taxes (T), *ad valorem* duties at rates t_q and t_x on private sector imports and exports (q_o^p and x_o^p), and a domestic sales tax at rate s_q on imports, the central government's deficit can be written

$$(A7.1) \quad D^c = WL^c + P_n G_n^c + Eq^c + V_s + i_g C + Ei^* k^g - E\tau - T,$$

where $\tau \equiv (t_q + s_q)q_o^p + t_x x_o^p$ is total revenue from trade taxes and sales taxes on imports, measured in dollars at the official exchange rate and where we have assumed (for expositional purposes only) that all official external borrowing is done by the central government. Note that all trade volumes (q^c, q_o^p and x_o^p) are measured in foreign currency (definitions of the variables appear in Table A7.1).

We need to keep track of three types of non-bank parastatal in Tanzania: (1) export marketing parastatals, which purchase an amount x^m of the export crop from peasant producers and sell it on world markets, (2) import marketing parastatals, which purchase an amount q^m of imports and resell them to the private sector, and (3) producing parastatals, which produce amounts Y_n^s and y_x^s of home goods and exports, respectively (with y_x^s in foreign exchange). Letting L^s be the total labor input of the non-bank parastatal sector and q^s be parastatal imports that are not resold to the private sector, the deficit of the non-bank parastatal sector is given by

$$(A7.2) \quad \begin{aligned} D^s &= WL^s + Eq^s + i_g C^s + [(P_x^m/E) - 1)]Ex^m - [(P_q^m/E) - 1]Eq^m \\ &\quad - P_n(G_n^s + Y_n^s) - Ey_x^s - V_s, \end{aligned}$$

where P_x^m and P_q^m are the domestic producer price of the export crop and the domestic price of imports marketed through the parastatal sector. Taking equations (A7.1) and (A7.2) together and adding in the operating deficit $D^b = i_g(C^c + C^s) + Ei^*r^*$ of the banking system, we obtain the following expression for the deficit of the broad government:

$$(A7.3) \quad \begin{aligned} D &= [WL^g + i_d S^p + P_n(G_n^g - Y_n^s) + P_x^m x^m - P_q^m q^m - T - E\tau] \\ &\quad + E(q^g + i^*r^* - x^m - y_x^s). \end{aligned}$$

TABLE A7.1 *Definitions of variables in fiscal calculation*

Variables appearing in the text

a^*	Foreign grants to broad government
D	Broad government budget deficit
D^d	Domestic budget balance = deficit in items denominated in local currency
E	Official exchange rate, TShs per \$
r	Net foreign assets of the banking system
b^g	Net sales of foreign exchange by (broad) government to the banking system
b^p	Net sales of foreign exchange by the private sector to the banking system
M	$M2$
m	Real money balances at the official exchange rate, $= M2/E$
m_x	Implicit tax on farmers implied by gap between producer and world price: $m_x \equiv 1 - (P_x^m/E)$.
P	Domestic price level
P_q^m	Domestic price of imports resold by import-marketing parastatals
P_x^m	Domestic producer price paid by marketing parastatals for traditional export crop
q^m	Imports of import-marketing parastatals (resold to the private sector)
q_o^p	Officially measured private sector imports (dollar value), including own-funded imports
q_{own}	Official private sector imports (dollar value) financed through the OF window
U	Unofficial (parallel) exchange rate
x^*	Net government deficit in domestic currency flows indexed to the official exchange rate
x^m	Export crop purchased from farmers by marketing parastatals
x_o^p	Private sector export proceeds remitted to the banking system
τ	Revenues from trade taxes, measured in dollars at the official rate: $\tau \equiv (t_q + s_q)q_o^p + t_x x_o^p$

Variables appearing in the Appendix and/or tables

C	Domestic credit from the banking system (Bank of Tanzania and National Bank of Commerce) to the central government and parastatals. $D = D^c + D^s + D^b$, where D^c is the deficit of central government, D^s is the deficit of non-bank parastatal sector, and D^b is the deficit of banking system
i_d	Deposit interest rate at National Bank of Commerce
i_g	Interest rate on domestic credit from the banking system to the broad government
i^*	Interest rate on foreign borrowing
G_n^c	Central government consumption of home goods
k^g	Net foreign capital inflow to broad government
L^g	Labor employed by broad government. $L^g = L^c + L^s$, where L^c is the labour employed by central government and L^s is the labor employed by parastatals.

P_n	Price of non-traded goods
q^g	Total government imports (dollar value) $= q^c + q^s + q^m$, where q^c is the central government imports (dollar value), q^m is the imports of import-marketing parastatals (resold to private sector), and q^s is the parastatal imports (dollar value)
S	Private sector time deposits
s_q	Government sales tax rate on imports
t^q	Import tariff rate
t_x	Export tax rate
T	Tax revenues (excluding trade taxes and sales tax on imports)
V_s	Central government transfers to parastatal sector
W	Nominal wage paid by government
Y_n^s	Parastatal sector production of home goods
y_x^s	Parastatal production of exports (dollar value)

The first term in square brackets in equation (A7.3) is the domestic budget balance and the second is the 'foreign budget balance' or deficit in foreign currency flows.

As noted in the text, b^*, the balance of foreign currency transactions between the private sector and the banking system, is given by

$$(A7.4) \qquad\qquad b^* = x_o^p - (q_o^p - q_{own}),$$

under the assumption that there are no private capital flows mediated through the banking system (although such flows may take place through invoicing fraud on the current account).

Using equations (A7.3) and (A7.4) to substitute for D_d and b^* in equation (3) of the text, we obtain

$$(A7.5) \quad \begin{aligned} \Delta M2 = & [WL^g + i_d S^p + P_n(G_n^g - Y_n^s) - T] \\ & + E[(P_x^m/E)\, x^m - (P_q^m/E)\, q^m - \tau] + E[x_o^p - (q_o^p - q_{own})]. \end{aligned}$$

The first term in square brackets is the portion of the domestic budget balance that is not indexed to the official exchange rate. This first term is not part of the direct monetary effect, since we treat it as fixed in real terms (that is, as indexed to the domestic price level).

The second term in square brackets in equation (A7.5) is the portion of the domestic budget balance that we will assume to be fully indexed to the official exchange rate – the counterpart to x^* in equation (7) of the text. Indexed expenditures consist of marketing board purchases of the export crop; revenues include (1) parastatal sales of imports to the private sector and (2) customs duties, export

T A B L E   A7.2   *Assumptions for simulations of direct monetary effect:*
$$DME = (U - E)x^* + (U - E)b^*$$

Baseline case (Table 7.4, column 4)
(1) Assumptions on domestic budget balance
    (a) Fully indexed to E
            (i) Customs duties. This comes from the joint assumption that
                t_x and t_q are fixed and that dollar trade volumes are
                independent of E.
            (ii) Domestic import sales tax revenues. This comes from the
                joint assumption that s^q is fixed and that dollar trade
                volumes are independent of E.
            (iii) Domestic producer prices for exports. This comes from the
                assumption that the parastatal marketing margin
                $m_x \equiv 1 - (P^m_x/E)$ is fixed.
            (iv) Domestic prices of imports sold by parastatals. We assume
                that $m_q \equiv (P^m_q/E) - 1$ is zero or equivalently that any gap
                between the domestic and world price of these imports is
                already accounted for in τ by customs duties and sales taxes.
    (b) Not indexed to E
            (i) Public sector wages
            (ii) Components of T
            (iii) Interest rate on time deposits and volume of time deposits.
(2) Assumptions on b^*
    (a) Private sector capital flows mediated through the banking sector
        (which are illegal) are zero.
These assumptions imply $DME = (U - E)[(1 - m_x)x^m - q^m - \tau] + (U - E)$
$(x^p_o - q^p + q_{own})$

Small/efficient public sector (Table 7.4, column 6)
(1) Factors decreasing indexed portion of domestic budget balance
    (a) Twenty percent rather than 15 per cent, of public sector imports are
        resold to the private sector.
    (b) Trade tax revenues are higher starting in 1991 due to a successively
        stronger tax collection effort: revenues are 5.1, 11, and 13.6 percent
        higher than the baseline in 1991, 1992, and 1993.
(2) Factors decreasing central bank losses
    (a) The public sector's share of overall imports is assumed to be 85
        percent of the baseline share.

Large/inefficient public sector (Table 7.4, column 7)
(1) Factors increasing the indexed portion of domestic budget balance
    (a) Only 10 percent, rather than 15 percent, of public sector imports are
        resold to the private sector.
    (b) A share of the marketing margin equal to 15 percent of the
        producer price paid to peasants leaks back into the private sector
        (this lowers the margin collected by the parastatals to a minimum of
        2 percent in 1985 and a maximum of 51 percent in 1989).

    (c) The trade tax collection effort is successively weaker starting in
        1991: revenues are 2.6, 6.5, and 9 percent lower than the baseline in
        1991, 1992, and 1993.
(2) Factors increasing central bank losses
    (a) The public sector's share of overall imports is assumed to be higher
        by 15 percent than the baseline share.

---

taxes, and sales taxes on imports (measured as τ in foreign currency terms). We assume no mark-up on parastatal resales of imports and a constant marketing margin m_x on export purchases from peasant producers. Thus, $P_q^m = E$, and $P_x^m / E = 1 - m_x$, so that $x^* = (1 - m_x)x^m - q^m - \tau$. In combination with equation (A7.4), this leads to equation (9) in the text.

8 The Parallel Market Premium and Exchange Rate Unification: a Macroeconomic Analysis for Zambia

Janine Aron and Ibrahim A. Elbadawi[1]

O11
O19
F31 F32
F33

INTRODUCTION

The economy of Zambia, 1964–90, provides an example of a large and thriving black market for foreign exchange. The Zambian black market has survived a long sequence of policy reforms aimed at achieving a more flexible exchange rate and price system and liberalizing trade and financial flows. Despite aggressive policies in these areas, especially with regard to the exchange rate, the black market premium (defined as the ratio of the black rate to the official rate minus one) remains high. For the 1970–88 period, the premium averaged 100 percent; it exceeded 400 percent by 1990.

The presence of sizable parallel markets with substantial premia has important macroeconomic implications. Theoretical models of dual exchange rates (Dornbusch, 1986; Lizondo, 1987a, b) and their extensions to black markets (Dornbusch et al., 1983; Pinto, 1989, 1991) derive a steady state solution for the premium that depends on the fiscal deficit ratio and the parameters of trade and exchange rate policy. Furthermore, key macroeconomic indicators such as inflation, foreign trade flows, and the real exchange rate can also be shown to be influenced by (or jointly determined with) the premium (Elbadawi, 1989). The empirical tradition on this literature, however, is still in its infancy. One of the main objectives of this chapter is to develop empirical models linking the premium to these macroeconomic indicators and to use Zambian data to assess the extent and dynamics of these linkages. Evidence from these models can shed light on the recent experience in Zambia of aborted reforms, macroeconomic instability, and recurrent policy reversals.[2]

The structure of multiple markets for foreign exchange considered in this study consists of an official market with an officially managed or auction-determined rate and an illegal unofficial market with a freely floating rate. Within this basic structure, the Zambian experience of 1964–91 includes six distinct policy episodes (Table 8.1). Figure 8.1 shows the quarterly black market premium for Zambia, with the considerable regime shifts of the last two decades clearly reflected in the evolution of the premium. The average premium declined sharply from around 100 percent in the first two episodes to approximately 50 percent in the third and fourth episodes and it rose by a factor of ten in the fifth episode. The average black market rate has continuously depreciated across the five episodes. However, as indicated by the summary statistics in Table 8.2, both the premium and the black market rate exhibit decreasing stability across exchange rate episodes (measured by the coefficient of variation of monthly data). This volatility probably reflects bubbles and crashes generated in the short term by a combination of a thin market and the responses of forward-looking, risk-averse agents to cumulative government policy errors.

This chapter examines three key aspects of the parallel market in Zambia. We begin with the origin of the parallel market and the statistical properties of the premium. We focus on the macroeconomic and political factors that account for the broad changes in the premium across episodes and for its increased volatility in the short term, and we estimate an empirical model of the premium using annual data.

TABLE 8.1   *Exchange rate policy episodes in Zambia, 1964–90*

Episode	Period	Exchange rate policy
1	1964Q4–1971Q3	Fixed to the pound sterling
	1971Q4–1976Q2	Fixed to the dollar
2	1976Q3–1983Q2	Pegged to the SDR with occasional devaluations
3	1983Q3–1985Q3	Crawling peg based on a basket of currencies of trade partners
4	1985Q4–1987Q2	Foreign exchange auction
5	1987Q3–1989Q4	Fixed rate to the dollar with occasional devaluations
6	1990Q1–1991Q1	Official dual exchange rate system

TABLE 8.2 *Basic statistics for the black market premium and black rate (monthly data)*

Period	N	Mean	Standard deviation	Minimum value	Maximum value	Coefficient of variation (%)
Black market premium						
1. October 1970–June 1976	69	89.69	38.56	29.63	177.52	43.02
2. July 1976–March 1983	84	102.27	59.50	19.32	260.10	58.18
3. July 1983–September 1985	27	49.26	32.27	9.67	102.80	65.50
4. October 1985–June 1987	21	40.26	31.69	−46.12	93.07	78.70
(excluding April 1987)	20	44.58	25.39	15.67	93.07	59.95
5. July 1987–December 1989	30	481.32	367.69	25.00	1221.48	76.39
Black rate						
1. October 1970–June 1976	69	0.82	0.15	0.55	1.08	18.73
2. July 1976–March 1983	84	0.63	0.14	0.35	0.85	21.88
3. July 1983–September 1985	27	0.40	0.14	0.21	0.59	35.60
4. October 1985–June 1987	21	0.10	0.03	0.04	0.14	29.67
5. July 1987–December 1989	30	0.03	0.03	0.01	0.10	92.26

For episode 4, statistics for the premium are calculated with and without the premium of −46 percent for April 1987, which was due to rapid devaluation of the official rate (the black rate was unaffected).

Black market data are collected monthly, apparently by the same source and in the same place, so that sampling bias is at least constant.

SOURCES: *World Currency Yearbook* and IMF, *International Finance Statistics* (various years).

Percent

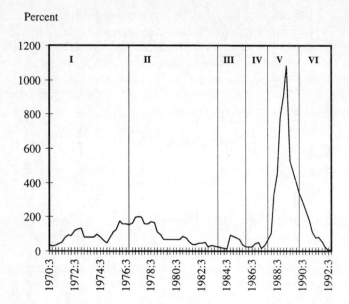

FIGURE 8.1   *Quarterly black market premium, official exchange rate episodes*
I–VI

SOURCE: International Currency Analysis, Inc., *World Currency Yearbook.*

We then investigate the effects of the premium on inflation and on
recorded and unrecorded trade flows. There is a paucity of empirical
research on the misinvoicing of trade in response to the premium and
trade policy and an attempt is made here to quantify these linkages.
Finally, we consider the implications of unifying the dual exchange
markets by trade liberalization and floating the exchange rate. Our six
episodes include two attempts to unify the foreign exchange markets,
first through a crawling peg (1983–5) and then through a foreign
exchange auction (1985–7). These episodes may usefully be contrasted
and lessons drawn from the failure to achieve unification.

The chapter is organized as follows. The next section provides an
overview of the development, structure, and operation of multiple
foreign exchange markets in Zambia. In the third section, some distributional characteristics of the premium are given and its evolution
in terms of macroeconomic policy and exogenous factors is explained.
Drawing on this discussion and the theory, an annual model for the
premium is specified and estimated. The fourth section analyzes the

effects of the premium on recorded and unrecorded trade flows using econometric models for key foreign trade aggregates and in the case of unrecorded imports, data are constructed from estimates of misinvoicing ratios computed in this section. A simple model of domestic inflation is estimated which tests for the inflationary effects of official devaluation. The final section concludes, with policy lessons concerning unification from the Zambian experience.

THE DEVELOPMENT OF MULTIPLE EXCHANGE MARKETS IN ZAMBIA

A crucial factor underlying the development of multiple foreign exchange markets in Zambia is the country's extreme dependence on copper. Between 1964 and 1991, export earnings from copper and its metal coproducts accounted for over 95 percent (on average) of total recorded foreign exchange earnings. This dependence has made Zambia highly susceptible to external shocks and indeed the size of the official market for foreign exchange has varied significantly with world mineral prices (see Table 8.6). Adverse terms of trade shocks in the early and mid-1970s drained foreign exchange reserves, bringing the pre-1976 fixed exchange rate regime under pressure. The government's response was to defend the overvalued exchange rate by imposing a more stringent rationing regime for foreign exchange. The existing capital and import controls were tightened and new restrictions were introduced. One consequences was the burgeoning of the parallel market, which had its origins in these controls.

In this section we discuss the evolution of official exchange rate policy in some detail, organizing the discussion around the six policy episodes. We then make an attempt to identify the diverse sources of supply to the parallel market and to give a lower bound on its size.

Exchange Rate Policy in Zambia

Table 8.1 identifies the six distinct exchange rate episodes and Table 8.3 the sequence of detailed parity changes. The nominal and real effective exchange rates (NEER and REER) are contrasted in Figure 8.2.[3]

TABLE 8.3   *Major parity changes since 1964*

Period	Parity change
October 1964	Zambian pound pegged to the pound sterling
January 1968	Kwacha (K) replaces Zambian pound, halving official rate (K0.714 per $), and decimalizing
December 1971	Pound sterling link substituted by US$ (K0.714 per $): a *de facto* devaluation. Gold content reduced by 7.89 percent on 18 December
February 1973	Following US devaluation, realigned to K0.643 per $
July 1976	Dollar link substituted by SDR (K1=SDR1.08479): a *de facto* devaluation of 20 percent
March 1978	Devalued by 10 percent: K1=SDR0.97631
January 1983	Devalued by 20 percent: K1=SDR0.78105
July 1983	SDR link substituted by trade weighted basket: a *de facto* devaluation of 11 percent; crawl rate of 1 percent per month
1984	Rate of crawl increased to 2.5 percent per month
October 1985	Rate determined by marginal market-clearing bid in a weekly auction administered by the Central Bank
August 1986	Dutch auction introduced: successful bidders exchange at their bid, not the marginal rate: excess accrues as tax revenue
January 1987	Auction temporarily suspended
February 1987	Official parity rate created pegged to a basket of currencies, with range K9.0–12.5 per $, for government, parastatal and Central Bank transactions
March 1987	Weekly auction reinstated for all other transactions, starting at K15 per $ (two-tier auction)
May 1987	Auction suspended: rates unified at K8 per $ for all transactions
December 1988	Devalued to K10 per $
June 1989	Devalued to K16 per $
December 1989	Devalued to K24 per $
February 1990	Two-tier system: official rate at K28 per $ and managed float initially at K40 per $. Unified in April 1991

SOURCES: *World Currency Yearbook* and Central Bank of Zambia publications.

During *episode 1* (1964–76Q2), exchange rate policy was inactive under a fixed regime. At Independence, the currency had been pegged to the pound and this fixed exchange rate was maintained until the early 1970s. Exchange controls imposed in 1961 were mildly liberalized at Independence. However, after the 1971 copper price shock, stringent controls were reimposed to protect the foreign exchange

Percent

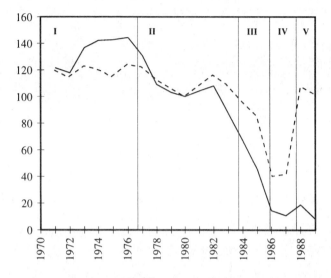

——— Nominal effective exchange rate   – – – – Real effective exchange rate

FIGURE 8.2 *Nominal and real effective exchange rates 1980=100, episodes I–V*
NOTES: An increase in the index denotes appreciation
SOURCE: Calculations using IMF, *International Financial Statistics,* and
IMF, *Direction of Trade Statistics.*

reserves. Moreover, import licensing, originally devised to reduce
congestion after the closure of transport routes in the 1960s, increasingly served to control import levels. More restrictive import controls
were introduced in 1972, when some imports were banned; however
capital and intermediate goods imports continued to be liberally
licensed.

In December 1971, the kwacha's ties to the pound were severed and
it was linked to the US$ at the rate of K0.714 per $ (a *de facto*
devaluation). Beginning in 1973 the floating dollar appreciated sharply, while the currencies of Zambia's major trading partners were
devalued. The result was that the kwacha appreciated against the
currencies of most trading partners and by mid-1976 the trade-
weighted NEER had risen by over 25 percent. Real appreciation
occurred too, though Zambian inflation (under price controls)
remained below world inflation, somewhat dampening the rise in the
REER. This appreciation contributed to the deterioration in the trade

and current account balances following the copper price shock in 1974 and the rise in oil prices from 1973. Exchange and import controls were further tightened in 1975 and strictly enforced until the liberalizing reforms of the early 1980s.

The more active exchange rate policy adopted, beginning in 1976, had its origin in conditionality associated with the various International Monetary Fund (IMF) credit agreements of 1976, 1978, 1981, 1983 and 1984. A central aim of these agreements was to redress the external imbalance by enhancing competitiveness and profitability in the export sector and by encouraging new exports and import substitutes. During *episode 2* (1976Q3–1983Q3) the link to the dollar was replaced by a peg to the SDR. Initiated in July 1976, this represented a *de facto* devaluation of 20 percent. The kwacha was devalued twice more in this episode: by 10 percent on 17 March 1978 and by a further 20 percent on 7 January 1983. The NEER thus fell sharply from 1976 and at first real depreciation was achieved. But in the aftermath of the 1979–80 copper mini-boom, higher domestic inflation (13 percent on average, 1980–3) saw the REER and NEER increasingly misaligned.

The devaluation of January 1983 initiated *episode 3* (1983Q4–1985Q3), in which the link to the SDR was broken and replaced by a crawling peg based on a basket of currencies of Zambia's major trading partners. A controlled devaluation of 1 percent per month was to be achieved, a rate that was increased to 2.5 percent in 1984. Real depreciation was achieved in this period, but continued high domestic inflation (averaging 26 percent annually, 1983–5) meant that the REER continued to be overvalued.

During 1984 and 1985 more emphasis was placed on the importance of the exchange rate as an instrument to induce the required structural adjustment. Dissatisfaction with the rate of real depreciation achieved under the crawling peg culminated in the adoption of a weekly foreign exchange auction (*episode 4*, 1985Q4–1987Q2). The principal feature of the weekly auction was that the auction rate applied to all foreign exchange transactions. Predetermined amounts of foreign exchange for essential imports were allocated outside the system, but at the auction rate.[4] The requirements for all other imports and service payments, including the remittance of profits, dividends, and transfers, were obtained through the auction. This served partially to eliminate the subjectivity of the previous manual system of foreign exchange allocation. The trade account was liberalized at the same time as the floating of the exchange rate and the black market was quasi-legalized prior to the auction, with payment for imports of goods and services out of funds held abroad allowed without restriction or declaration as to the source of the funds. External capital controls remained in place throughout the 19 month auction period. The supply of foreign exchange to the auction came from the obligatory surrender under exchange controls of exports proceeds, less the retention privilege accorded to non-traditional exporters and from external loans and grants from the World Bank, the IMF, and bilateral donors.

Substantial devaluation was achieved in the first of the weekly auctions (from K2.2 to K5.01 per $) and thereafter the rate displayed relative stability for 10 months. There was increased intervention in the auction from July 1987 (this is discussed later). Moreover, in early August, with the nominal rate at K5.01 per $, the central bank trebled foreign exchange supply to the auction. This policy was unsustainable, resulting in a foreign exchange pipeline with lags of up to 6 weeks for the disbursement of dollars and ultimately proved very costly for the central bank. From September onwards the auction entered an unstable phase, characterized by excessive speculation on the part of bidding firms and the rate depreciated sharply. The REER fell with the NEER between 1985 and 1986. While overvaluation decreased during the stable phase of the auction, high inflation in the unstable phase promoted overvaluation in 1987.

Following decontrol of the politically sensitive maize price in early December, there were food riots on the Copperbelt and in Lusaka. In January 1987, after 68 auctions, the auction was temporarily suspended with the rate at K14.92 per $ (a depreciation of 578 percent from the inception of the system). The rate was set at K9.00 per $. Beginning on 28 March 1987, six auctions were held under a two-tier auction system. In the fifth of these auctions on 24 April, the kwacha rate fell to its lowest value, K21.02 per $ and President Kaunda abolished the system on 1 May, after a final auction which served only to allocate foreign exchange at the rate of K15.00 per $.

The reversion to a fixed exchange rate of K8.00 per $ on 5 May and the reimposition of import controls, constitutes *episode 5* (1987Q3–1989Q4). The allocation of foreign exchange and issue of import licenses were decided simultaneously by a Foreign Exchange Management Committee (FEMAC). Non-traditional exporters were allowed to retain 50 percent of their export earnings and free trade of title to the retentions occurred at a premium on the official rate. Exchange rate policy was passive during the episode, save for two devaluations, to K16.00 and K24.00 per $ in June and December of 1989. Persistently high inflation saw the REER progressively more overvalued from 1987 and the real depreciation gains of the auction were eroded.

In consequence, a two-tier currency was introduced as of February 1990. An official rate of exchange was initiated at K27.80 per $ (the first window), with the 'market exchange rate' (the second window) at K40.00 per $ (*episode 6*, 1990Q1–1991Q2). The central bank sold foreign exchange through the first window under existing FEMAC procedures for imports and purchased all mineral export earnings. The second window was used for those goods eligible for foreign exchange allocation under the open general license (OGL) system. The sources to fund this window were non-traditional exports earnings and remittances received from donors (donor funding accounted for 54 percent of funding in 1990 and all of it in 1991). Only 10 percent of imports by volume were eligible for OGL allocation at the inception of the system. By 31 March 1991, most imports had been transferred from the first to the second window. In April 1991, the rates were unified at K58 per $. However, the 'market rate' was in fact a highly managed rate and with high inflation, this maintained an overvaluation in the second window. Thus, although a nominal devaluation of over 100 percent was achieved in the course of this episode, the parallel market continued unabated.

Sources of Supply to the Parallel Market

The origins of Zambia's unofficial market lie in the stringent exchange and import controls imposed to ration foreign exchange and defend the overvalued exchange rate. These controls were reinforced during periods of low world copper prices, so that the size of the unofficial market too is sensitively related to the terms of trade. It is not possible to give a measure of the number of transactions in this market, nor traded volumes over time. The only published data on the parallel market are monthly black market exchange rate figures from the *World Currency Yearbook*, which allow the calculation of monthly premia. Given official rationing, it is plausible to assume the existence of excess demand for foreign exchange in the official market, particularly when the terms of trade deteriorate. Nevertheless, a fall in the premium will not be a reliable indicator of increased supply to the

TABLE 8.4   *Potential sources of foreign exchange outside the official system,*
1987–90

---

(1) Cross-border bank deposits (IMF, International Financial Statistics)
Stocks of non-banks deposits by residence of depositor: 1988 $400
million, 1989 $420 million, and 1990 $420 million. The annual flow
from interest is approximated assuming a rate of 10 percent on
overseas dollar deposits (this is an upper bound on the London Eurodollar rate): $42 million

(2) Net short-term capital outflows (IMF, Balance of Payments Statistics)
Using the Cuddington (1986) measure of reported 'errors and
omissions': 1987 $116 million, 1988 $17 million, and 1989 $41 million

(3) Unreported capital flight: overinvoicing of imports (Table 8.9)
Partner country data comparisons up to 1986 show significant
overinvoicing of imports in years when the premium is high: however,
the trade figures from 1987 are not available

(4) No-funds import licenses (Bank of Zambia data)
These represent a quasi-legalization of the black market and thus
repatriation of flown capital: 1989 $286 million and 1990 $341 million

(5) Emerald smuggling (Gemstones Corporation, Zambia)
A widely-quoted figure for illegal exports is around $235 million per
annum

(6) Copper smuggling (Aron, 1992).
Copper shipments fraud and theft by company officials has probably
amounted to several millions of dollars per annum in recent years.

(7) Tourism (Government of Zambia, Monthly Digest of Statistics)
In 1990 visitors arriving in Zambia for holiday or business totaled
49 000: a foreign exchange inflow of $10 million per annum is a
plausible lower bound

(8) Migrants' remittances (no source)
Difficult to estimate and probably not a large figure

(9) Expatriate rent (no source)
An upper bound could be 20 000 expatriates and diplomats paying the
average rent for 1991 ($2000) in foreign exchange: $40 million per
annum

---

black market, since the premium is determined by a variety of short-
and long-term influences, including the risk of illegal dealings (see the
next section).

It remains possible to identify potential sources of supply to the
market and to quantify some of these (Table 8.4). While there is likely
to be some overlap amongst these figures, an order of magnitude
for supply can be derived. During 1991, an official at the Bank of
Zambia estimated an annual volume of $100 million or approximately
one-tenth of the official market supply of $1125 million in that year.[5]

The suggested size of the market from Table 8.4 is considerably larger than the Bank of Zambia's estimate; a conservative lower bound could be $500 million, around half the size of the official market in 1991.

DETERMINANTS OF THE PARALLEL PREMIUM IN ZAMBIA

The previous section has shown that a sizable parallel market existed alongside the official market during 1964–91, so that the premium is likely to have been a major signal in the economy. The theory of dual exchange markets shows that the premium is influenced by a variety of factors including macroeconomic and trade policies, agents' expectations, and exogenous determinants such as the terms of trade and foreign aid. Since the black market is integrated with forward-looking asset markets, expectations about political events and changes in economic policy may be apparent in the premium before these events occur, while unanticipated political and economic shocks have an immediate impact.[6] In the short term, the major determinants of the premium are probably asset portfolio considerations and expectations. In the long term these influences average out and the steady-state premium will depend on flow fundamentals such as the terms of trade, the budget deficit, capital flows, and the trade regime.

Trends in the average monthly premium for exchange rate episodes in Zambia are shown in Table 8.2. The increased volatility of the premium across episodes was attributed to bubbles and crashes arising from market thinness and agents' short-term expectational responses. It is possible to test statistically for the presence of foreign exchange bubbles by analyzing the stationarity and the second and third moments of the free exchange rate. These tests are presented in Table 8.5 for the most finely sampled data available for the black rate (monthly) and contrasted with the quarterly series. Also included are weekly data for the auction-determined exchange rate in episode 4. The table shows that none of these series is stationary in levels. However, for all the series both the Dickey–Fuller and augmented Dickey–Fuller tests reject the null hypothesis of a unit root in the first-differenced series. Further, the kurtosis and skewness statistics show a departure from normality for

TABLE 8.5   *Stationarity, skewness, and kurtosis tests for the free exchange rate*

Period	Quarterly 1970–89	Monthly 1970–89	Weekly 1985–87
Level log(E)			
Kurtosis	1.94	−0.41	−0.05
Skewness	1.70	1.01	1.06
DF	2.11	−0.21	−0.30
ADF (4 lags)	0.68	0.50	−0.20
$\Delta log(E)$			
Kurtosis	4.40	6.02	10.22
Skewness	1.82	−0.37	−2.38
DF	−7.29	−12.02	−9.28
ADF(4 lags)	−3.20	−5.52	−3.49

Weekly data refer to the official auction-determined exchange rate; all other series refer to the black market exchange rate.

Skewness is measured by the third moment around the mean standardized by the cube of the standard deviation. Kurtosis is measured by the fourth moment around the mean standardized by the square of the variance. A normal distribution displays values of 3 and 0, respectively for kurtosis and skewness.

The augmented Dickey–Fuller (ADF(k)) test (Dickey and Fuller 1981) for the integration of a variable consists of testing for the negativity of the parameter δ in the regression: $\Delta\beta_t = \delta\beta_{t-i} + \Sigma_{i=1,k}\delta_i\Delta\beta_{t-i} + e_t$ where the augmented test includes k lags of the dependent variable on the right-hand side of the standard Dickey–Fuller test to ensure serially uncorrelated errors. The critical values for small samples derive from Banerjee *et al.* (1993).

SOURCES: *World Currency Yearbooks* and Bank of Zambia.

the unconditional distribution of the free rate in both levels and differences.[7]

These tests suggest that bubbles may exist in the short term, especially for more finely sampled data. In the following subsection, where macroeconomic influences on the evolution of the premium are discussed, illustrative examples will also be given of short-term expectational responses and speculative behavior. In the estimated annual model for the premium, however, the premium will be shown to be cointegrated with economic fundamentals (see the subsection on the empirical model of the black market premium). Under these conditions, a bubbles solution is not possible (Kaminsky, 1988), suggesting that the effects of bubbles arising and collapsing in the short term are smoothed in the annual data.

Macroeconomic Influences on the Premium

The monthly premium is shown in Figure 8.3 and macroeconomic data for Zambia are given in Table 8.6.

During *episode 1*, Zambia was subject to large external shocks due to fluctuations in the world copper price. A large positive shock occurred in the decade 1964–74, the onset of which coincided with Independence in 1964. This was punctuated by several, small negative shocks in the 1970s. At the peak of the boom in 1969, the terms of trade had increased by 98 percent relative to their 1964 level. This was followed by a steep fall in the terms of trade from mid-1974, so that the average level for 1975–80 was 33 percent below the 1969 peak. The terms of trade did not again recover to the pre-boom level. The decline in Zambia's economic circumstances between the positive and negative shocks was drastic and the boom was not managed so as to smooth the transition into recession.

The positive shock induced a trade surplus and foreign reserves were accumulated while capital inflow was modest. Government savings were positive until 1970 and amounted to approximately one-third of national savings. While public sector capital and current expenditures rose strongly, in line with the ambitious First National Development Plan (1964–71), the budgetary position was sustainable until 1970 given the high mineral revenues. The first negative shocks of the early 1970s induced balance of payments and budget crises. The copper price recovered briefly in 1973, but after the crash in mid-1974, persistent budget and trade deficits were the norm. These were sustained by decumulation of reserves, external borrowing, and the appreciation of the currency. Zambia's link with the IMF was initiated with extended facility agreements in 1971–2, followed by a standby agreement in 1973.

Black market data are available only from mid-1970. However, trends for misinvoicing during the copper boom (see below) suggest that increased demand for foreign assets during the boom, as well as political uncertainty induced by nationalization of large sectors of the economy in the 1960s, induced substantial capital flight. Thus, it is likely that the premium was at least at its 1970 level in these years. In 1971, following the negative copper price shock, the premium rose to over 50 percent. Thereafter it responded appreciably to changes in the terms of trade, falling with the 1972–4 improvement and rising after the 1974 crash. From 1973 the official exchange rate, fixed to an appreciating dollar, became increasingly overvalued and

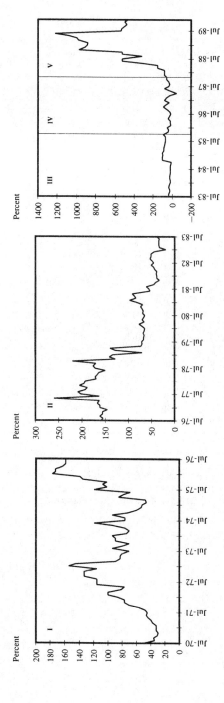

FIGURE 8.3   *Monthly black market premium, episodes I–V*

SOURCE: Country case study.

TABLE 8.6   *Macroeconomic*

Year	Premium %	Depreciation (%)		Inflation (CPI, %)	Monetary aggregates		Real GDP (K mill '90 pr)
		Offical	Black		M1 growth	M2/GDP	
1965	–	0.0	–	7.4	–	15.0	82 653
1966	–	0.0	–	10.8	38.2	17.1	79 306
1967	–	0.0	–	4.4	16.2	17.8	83 304
1968	–	0.0	–	11.0	32.0	20.6	85 454
1969	–	0.0	–	2.3	12.4	21.4	88 163
1970	36	0.0	–	3.1	2.8	29.2	91 022
1971	51	0.0	−11.0	6.0	7.0	27.0	90 955
1972	109	0.0	−38.4	5.1	1.0	25.3	99 286
1973	95	8.8	14.9	6.5	28.9	25.8	98 359
1974	80	1.2	8.8	8.1	2.7	23.4	104 985
1975	90	0.0	−5.6	10.2	24.4	31.2	102 419
1976	161	−10.9	−52.3	18.8	20.8	32.9	106 838
1977	190	−10.7	−23.0	19.8	−1.8	35.2	101 708
1978	164	−1.3	7.8	16.3	1.0	28.4	102 291
1979	85	0.8	30.5	9.7	30.2	31.3	99 178
1980	69	0.6	9.2	11.6	0.4	29.6	102 189
1981	64	−10.2	−6.9	13.0	8.7	28.1	108 492
1982	46	−6.9	4.8	13.6	22.2	36.4	105 440
1983	29	−34.7	−19.0	19.6	15.4	34.8	103 372
1984	37	−43.5	−52.4	20.0	9.4	34.6	102 993
1985	68	−51.2	−85.5	37.2	41.5	29.7	104 683
1986	31	−169.2	−109.9	51.9	87.2	31.3	105 440
1987	42	−21.7	−31.9	43.0	40.0	31.7	108 257
1988	418	7.5	−237.5	55.6	62.6	33.7	115 056
1989	749	−56.9	−157.2	127.9	51.5	30.3	113 884
1990	316	−124.6	−10.1	117.5	57.8	21.5	113 341
1991	114	−113.0	−9.6	92.6	78.3	22.0	111 334

The black market premium is defined as the black rate divided by the official exchange rate, minus 1.

The current account is valued at the official and black exchange rates.

TOT is the terms of trade or the ratio of export and import unit values.

The deflator for copper export value ($) is the US manufacturing unit value index (avoids misinvoiced indices).

SOURCES: *Government Finance Statistics* (IMF), *International Financial Statistics* (IMF), Central Bank Publications, and *World Currency Yearbook*.

indicators for Zambia

Budget			Current account		Net Foreign		Terms of trade (1963 prices)	Copper export value ($ million)
Surplus	Expend (% GDP)	Revenue	Official (% GDP)	Black	Assets (% GDP)	Reserves ($ million)		
3.4	24.6	29.4	8.7	–	21.0	196.0	195.6	468.1
3.5	20.6	25.0	6.0	–	18.6	204.8	281.1	605.0
−4.1	28.1	28.2	1.0	–	14.0	174.5	262.1	564.8
−9.9	36.9	28.0	−0.2	–	13.2	193.5	269.7	675.5
2.7	25.4	30.7	25.8	–	20.4	362.9	341.9	904.0
1.9	29.5	37.5	6.3	8.6	31.3	508.0	314.2	800.4
−16.4	40.8	26.5	−15.0	−22.6	15.4	277.1	191.8	501.2
−13.1	32.1	22.0	−11.0	−23.0	5.6	158.4	164.8	501.7
−16.7	29.5	29.5	5.3	10.4	4.2	185.5	240.5	675.1
3.4	28.1	34.4	0.5	1.0	4.0	164.4	171.7	674.2
−21.5	42.8	28.3	−29.3	−55.7	1.0	142.0	100.6	340.9
−14.2	36.1	23.9	−4.7	−12.3	−1.6	92.7	111.3	443.6
−13.1	35.5	25.1	−8.6	−25.0	−3.4	66.3	95.4	341.7
−14.4	29.7	24.7	−10.6	−28.0	−31.1	51.1	90.9	271.4
−9.1	30.5	22.3	1.1	2.0	−21.9	80.0	108.3	363.9
−18.5	37.0	25.0	−13.8	−23.4	−24.7	78.2	100.0	324.1
−12.9	36.7	23.2	−18.5	−30.3	−31.5	56.2	79.8	276.9
−18.6	39.2	23.4	−14.6	−21.3	−34.4	58.2	70.9	275.9
−7.8	32.2	24.3	−8.1	−10.5	−37.1	54.5	77.9	225.1
−8.4	29.2	22.1	−5.6	−7.6	−46.5	54.2	70.1	177.3
−15.2	35.1	22.0	−15.3	−25.7	−65.7	200.1	71.5	221.1
−21.6	41.7	23.3	−19.7	−25.8	−85.0	70.3	71.5	126.5
−12.9	34.5	21.6	−11.1	−15.8	−42.8	108.8	79.7	171.6
−11.5	28.5	17.1	−8.1	−41.9	−39.4	134.0	98.0	212.8
−5.0	21.7	11.9	−5.2	−44.1	−46.6	116.2	107.2	106.3
			−15.3	−63.5	−45.1	193.1	106.3	25.3
			−8.6	−18.5	−46.3	184.6	99.5	

the premium rose sharply to a maximum in 1977, only exceeded in the late 1980s.

Episode 2 follows in the aftermath of the 1974 copper price shock, when several conditional credit agreements were made with the IMF. The 1976–7 standby facility altered the tax base, wages were frozen, subsidies cut by 30 per cent, and development expenditure decreased by one-third. The budget deficit was reduced but three-quarters of it was funded domestically, which added to inflationary pressures. With a highly restrictive import policy and a small rise in the price of copper the current account balance showed some improvement. Thereafter the pattern of large budget and trade deficits continued, mitigated only by the rise in copper prices from 1979.

The 1978–80 standby facility reduced credit and inflationary pressures, but crowded out the private sector, most credit being absorbed by the government and mining companies. From 1975, there was little capital inflow, but payments arrears built up (amounting to $600 million by 1980) and net foreign assets declined. Foreign reserves had by this time largely been eroded. The foreign exchange constraint forced a contraction in the manufacturing sector, the decline in government demand had a similar effect on services, and agriculture continued to stagnate. Although a 1981–3 extended facility was successful in reducing the budget deficit in 1981, the facility became inoperative in 1982, when the attempt to maintain government services and employment in the face of falling revenue induced a deficit of 18 percent of GDP. The external payments deficit was financed mainly by the accumulation of arrears.

Figure 8.3 shows that during episode 2 the black market premium exhibited two phases of behavior. Until mid-1979, the level remained above 150 percent on average; it then fell by 70 percent, thereafter gradually declining with decreased volatility. The first phase saw large budget deficits and a sharp increase in inflation. Credit was rationed by foreign lenders, reserves were eroded, and the terms of trade continued to decline. Tight import and foreign exchange controls compounded these effects, keeping the premium high. The second phase began with a recovery of the copper price in 1979, which resulted in a relaxation of foreign borrowing constraints. More restrictive macroeconomic policies were pursued, which together with inflows of foreign borrowing sustained the low level of the premium despite the fall in the copper price in 1981 (when volatility briefly increased).

Exchange rate policy was passive throughout episode 2, save for two one-step devaluations. The devaluation of March 1978 had a negligible impact on the premium. However, the devaluation of 20 percent in January 1983 provides a classic instance of expectational response in the premium. Figure 8.4 shows the theoretically predicted time path for the black market premium around a fully anticipated devaluation of the official exchange rate. Speculators expect a long-term convergence to the initial steady-state level of the premium, implying a future depreciation of the black market rate. The profit opportunities this presents induce an immediate increase in the demand for foreign exchange and hence a jump in the premium from *b* to *c*. Thereafter, the premium rises over time to *d*, in combination with a growing stock of foreign currency. When the official devaluation is realized, an immediate fall in the premium from *d* to *e* occurs, due entirely to the rise in the official rate. The black market rate does not alter concomitantly with the official rate since this change was anticipated in the initial jump to *c*. The transitory accumulation of foreign currency is then gradually depleted and the premium returns to its initial steady-state level. The premium in Zambia around January 1983 follows the theoretically predicted path. The black market rate did not alter at the time of the devaluation, but depreciated subsequently.

Episode 3 coincides with the liberalizing reforms of the 1983–4 IMF standby agreement, later intensified in the auction period. A crawling peg for the official rate and a reduction in the budget deficit from 19 to 8 percent of GDP promoted a steady fall in the black market premium, from an initial 30 percent to approximately 17 percent in September, 1984. However, GDP continued to decline and inflation began to accelerate. The final purchase in the agreement was disallowed due to the postponement of paying arrears. Most measures associated with a standby facility for 1984–6 were implemented. However, GDP fell by 2.7 percent and inflation rose above 20 percent; the facility was rendered inactive from 1984 when criteria for the reduction of external payment arrears were not met. An instance of the response of the premium to news is provided by the tenfold increase in the premium when the facility was canceled in 1986. The steady decline in the premium persisted after this jump, but from the higher level and at a reduced rate despite the increased rate of crawl of the official exchange rate.

The foreign exchange auction (*episode 4*) was instituted as part of an IMF program which aimed to liberalize prices, interest rates, trade controls, and imports of black currency alongside the exchange rate reform (see earlier). A crucial aspect of expectations formulation in the context of structural adjustment is the private sector's assessment of the sustainability of liberalizing measures and the government's commitment to them. The importance of credible reform in preventing speculative attacks and policy reversals has recently been emphasized by Calvo (1987), Rodrik (1991), and others. Zambia's foreign exchange auction provides an interesting illustration of these phenomena. The path of the premium during the auction can be accurately

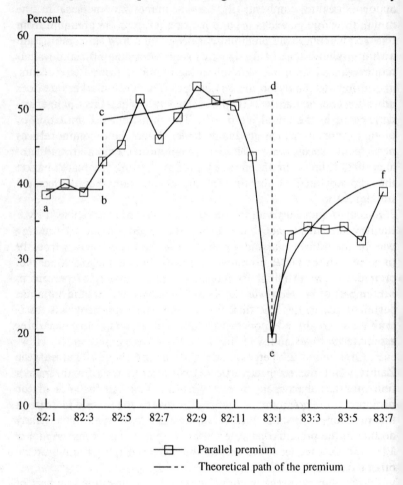

FIGURE 8.4   *Expectations of a maxi-devaluation reflected in the premium*
SOURCE: Country case study; the theoretical path *abcdef* is derived in Dornbusch, *et al.* (1983).

accounted for by short-term expectational responses to official policy changes. The premium followed a downward trend in the last quarter of 1986 and thereafter displayed considerable volatility about a fairly low mean of 40 percent, with a spectacular trough in April 1987 (Table 8.7).

Table 8.7 details the shocks and signals which dominated the behavior of the premium during the 19 month auction period. Official actions signaling commitment and sustainability decreased the premium; developments that brought sustainability into question did the reverse. Fluctuations in the amount of foreign exchange put up for auction induced uncertainty, prompting increasing excesses of dollars requested over those allocated. The degree and nature of intervention in the auction undermined credibility by suggesting a fundamental unwillingness on the part of the government to accept a market-determined exchange rate. This intervention included disqualification of bids, more stringent documentation requirements, temporary or permanent suspension of the auction, and alteration of the type of auction system. The response to political news is evident in the leap in the premium on Dr Chivuno's appointment as Governor of the Central Bank; he was well known to be opposed to the auction. Poor efficiency in implementing the system was observed at the micro-level: the large backlog in allocated dollars that built up from August 1986 was perceived as unsustainable and induced a sustained rise in the premium (disbursement delays averaged 10 weeks and were not cleared until May 1987). The implication of the speculative responses on the part of bidding firms to official signals was to impair economic sustainability of the liberalization further. Very rapid devaluation in the final stages, due to speculative overbidding, actually rendered the premium negative.

The abolition of the auction saw a termination of relations between Zambia and the multilateral organizations. In the 2-year episode following the auction (*episode 5*), Zambia followed a home-grown program. A high rate of monetary emission continued despite attempts to cut back the fiscal deficit and government expenditure and the rate of inflation rose in 1988 and then almost trebled again in 1989. The damaging effect on macropolicy credibility of the government's reversion to a fixed and appreciated rate of exchange, coupled with the opprobrium of donors, is reflected in the tenfold jump in the black market premium in 1988 (to over 400 percent) and its further near doubling in 1989. The sharp rise in inflation may in part be reflecting the feed-through of prices in the parallel market. Similarly,

TABLE 8.7 *Short-term influences on the black market premium during the auction*

Month	Auction rate	Black market rate	Black market premium (%)	Shocks and signals
September 1985	0.461	0.270	41.365	Interest rates decontrolled
October 1985	0.190	0.100	47.445	Auction instituted, import licenses abolished, no-funds import licenses
November 1985	0.171	0.120	29.825	
December 1985	0.174	0.130	25.296	
January 1986	0.168	0.110	34.468	
February 1986	0.152	0.130	14.494	Increase in dollars offered announced; IMF standby concluded; TAZARA etc. included in auction
March 1986	0.145	0.120	17.313	
April 1986	0.144	0.120	16.605	Chivuno appointed governor of BOZ
May 1986	0.141	0.100	29.200	Bids published from this date
June 1986	0.136	0.110	19.344	Stringent documentation requirements
July 1986	0.150	0.130	13.550	Dutch Auction, 'auction pipeline' begins, monetary measures to control
August 1986	0.178	0.140	21.483	money supply
September 1986	0.154	0.100	34.900	Reduction in dollars offered announced
October 1986	0.116	0.060	48.204	Bid deposit of 30 percent bank rate 30 percent
November 1986	0.081	0.050	38.511	Maize price decontrol, food riots; recontrol
December 1986	0.077	0.060	22.149	Auction suspended from 28 January for 9 weeks
January 1987	0.073	0.040	44.899	
February 1987	0.111	0.070	36.772	
March 1987	0.113	0.090	20.195	Two-tier auction from 28 March; bid deposit raised to 40 percent
April 1987	0.054	0.100	−85.586	
May 1987	0.125	0.100	20.000	Auction abolished 1 May: rate K15 per $ for allocation on 2 May, thereafter K8 per $
June 1987	0.125	0.070	44.000	

SOURCES: Economics Association of Zambia and Bank of Zambia.

the fall in government revenue despite the improved terms of trade may reflect increased use of illegal channels of trade (particularly in 1988 – for while copper tax revenue fell somewhat in 1988, it was restored to 1987 levels by 1989). The current account deficit fell in these years, but looks rather high when valued at the parallel rate.

From 1990 a dual exchange rate system was formally adopted under the aegis of a new IMF program and the premium declined dramatically in the following years, though it was not eradicated.

An Empirical Model of the Black Market Premium

Theoretical models in the dual exchange rate literature (for example, Lizondo, 1991) specify the premium as a function of asset market determinants, including the stock of money and the uncovered interest parity differential and flow determinants, which include wealth or permanent income, the real exchange rate, and the parameters of trade policy. Here we extend the standard model to endogenize the official real exchange rate as a function of its fundamentals (terms of trade and net capital flows), thus emphasizing the long-term flow determinants of the premium. The extended model is shown below:[8]

$$\log q_t - \alpha \,_t\log q_{t+1} = \beta_0 + \beta_1(i_t^* + \,_t\Delta \log E_{t+1} - i_t) + \beta_2 \log m$$

$$(1) \qquad - \beta_3 \log \left(\frac{P_X^*}{P_I^*}\right)_t - \beta_4 NKF + \beta_5(1 - t_X)_t$$

$$+ \beta_6(1 + t_I)_t + \beta_7 I_{[ENF,v,z]}.$$

Here q is the black market premium (defined as B/E, where B and E are the black market and official exchange rates), i^* and i are world and domestic interest rates, m is the real stock of broad money (measured in dollars at the official exchange rate), P_X^* and P_I^* are the world prices of exports and imports, NKF represents net capital flows, t_X and t_I are taxes on exports and imports, and $I_{[ENF,v,z]}$ is an indicator function reflecting trade policy (ENF is enforcement and v and z are the share of imports and exports passing through the official market). A subscript t preceding a variable denotes an expected value conditional on information available at time t; thus $_t\Delta \log E_{t+1}$ is the expected rate of depreciation of the official exchange rate.

The uncovered interest parity differential term requires a value for the expectations of future devaluations. One route is to use actual one-

step-ahead changes in the official exchange rate (Dornbusch *et al.*,
1983). The approach adopted here is to estimate a simple quarterly
model for expectations of future devaluations, incorporating agents'
reactions to anticipated economic policy and to political and economic
events. We begin by assuming a government reaction function in which
divergences between the official and black market exchange rates –
reflecting overvaluation of the official rate – create pressures for official devaluation. Current and past levels of the premium are therefore
useful in forecasting changes in the official exchange rate. Assuming
that the private sector also uses information contained in the previous
record of devaluations and past rates of money growth, we obtain the
following linear forecast equation for generating expectations:

$$
\Delta \log E_{t+1} = b_0 + \sum_{i=0}^{b_1} b_{1i} \log q_{t-i} + \sum_{i=0}^{b_2} b_{2i} \Delta \log E_{t-i}
$$

(2)

$$
+ \sum_{i=0}^{b_3} b_{3i} \Delta \log M2_{t-i} + \sum_{i=0}^{b_4} b_{4i} RSH_{t-i} + \epsilon_{t+1}.
$$

In equation (2) $M2$ is the nominal stock of broad money, RSH is a set
of dummy variables that account for the effects of regime shifts, and ϵ
is a stationary disturbance term. Estimation results for equation (2)
appear in the Appendix. We use the annualized fitted values from this
equation to measure expected depreciation in calculating the interest
parity differential variable.

An eclectic error-correction model for the premium based on equation (1) was then estimated by ordinary least squares (OLS) using
annual data, 1970–91 and is shown below in equation (1'). To con-
serve degrees of freedom, we imposed the condition that the real
exchange rate (RER) fundamentals (the terms of trade, taxes, and net
capital flows) influence only the long-term specification of the premium, implying that they enter equation (1') only in levels.

$$
\Delta \log q_t = 1.88 - 0.44 \log TOT_t - 0.29 \log AID_t
$$
$$
(4.81)(-2.96) \qquad (-3.86)
$$
$$
+ 0.48 \Delta \log m_t + 0.18(i_{t-1}^* + {}_{t-1}\hat{E}_t - i_{t-1})
$$

(1')

$$
(2.41) \qquad (1.46)
$$
$$
-0.37 \log q_{t-1} - 0.20 DUM(82-7) + 0.95 DUM(88-9)
$$
$$
(-3.73) \qquad (-2.00) \qquad (7.64)
$$
$$
\bar{R}^2 = 0.92, \ s.e. = 0.116, \qquad DW = 1.65.
$$

The t-statistics are in parentheses. A Chow test for splitting the sample across the subperiods 1971–80 and 1981–91 supports parameter stability ($F(6,7) = 0.54$, as compared with a critical value at the 5 percent significance level of 4.28). The explanatory power of the model is satisfactory and there is no evidence of mis-specification.[9]

Table 8.8 presents indirect diagnostic tests of the models, based on the statistical properties of the annual premium. While the unconditional distributions of the premium and its rate of change exhibit

TABLE 8.8   *The annual model of the premium: tests for normality and unit roots*

Normality tests

Variable	Skewness	Kurtosis
Unconditional distribution		
(1) $\log q_t$	1.73	3.85
	(0.005)*	(0.005)
(2) $\Delta \log q_t$	2.96	9.10
	(0.00002)	(0.14×10^{-9})
Conditional distribution		
(3) Residual of equation (1′)	−0.33	−0.96
	(0.56)	(1.09)

Dickey–Fuller and augmented Dickey–Fuller tests

Variable	DF	ADF	Differenced	DF	ADF
$\log q$	−0.213	−2.33	$\Delta \log q$	−2.81	−1.48
$\log m$	−0.98	+0.14	$\Delta \log m$	−3.54	−1.88
$\log TOT$	−3.08	−2.76	$\Delta \log TOT$	−4.71	−2.36
$\log AID$	−2.08	−1.54	$\Delta \log AID$	−4.60	−2.09
$\log E_o$	−1.69	−1.98	$\Delta \log e$	−2.92	−1.90
IPD	−2.28	−0.69	ΔIPD	−5.48	−2.57
Residual of equation (1′)	−3.62	−2.71			

q, Black market rate/official exchange rate, m, broad money/(official exchange rate* US CPI), TOT, export unit value/import unit value, AID, total net flows of ODA/US CPI, E_o, official exchange rate/CPI, IPD, $i_t^* + (\Delta \log E_{t+1}) - i_t$, where $(\Delta \log E_{t+1})$ is the fitted value from the regression in the Appendix, i_t^* is the London Eurodollar rate, and the domestic interest rate i_t is calculated as $i_t = i_t^d[M1/(M1 + M2)]$, where i_t^d is the annualized 6 month fixed Zambian deposit rate.

SOURCES: All data are from the IMF, *International Financial Statistics*, with the exception of the black market exchange rate, which is from *World Currency Yearbook* (various years), the Zambian deposit rate, which is from Bank of Zambia, and official development assistance (ODA), which is from Development Assistance Committee, OECD, *Geographical Distribution of Aid Flows*. The numbers in parenthesis are significance levels.

departures from normality,[10] such departures are not found for the conditional distribution of the rate of change of the premium (the residual of equation (1')). The economic implication of the tests is that determination of the premium, at least in the long term, is solely accounted for by economic fundamentals.

While the statistical significance of the variables is in some cases limited, the signs of the coefficients are consistent with the predictions of the theoretical model. The change in the stock of real domestic money (asset market determinants) has a significant and positive influence on the premium. The level of the stock of real domestic money (reflecting the real wealth effect) was not found to be significant. This may be because the TOT (terms of trade) and AID (a proxy for net capital flows NKF) terms are better indicators of the flow effect of permanent wealth, given the economy's substantial dependence on a single export and on foreign aid. The interest parity differential has the correct sign and is significant at the 10 percent level. This limited significance is not surprising given that interest rate controls were present in Zambia for much of the period, interspersed with interest rate liberalization episodes (for example, post-1990). Cross-dummies (not reported) for these episodes with the interest parity differential, show the differential to be strongly significant during these episodes.

The effects of the terms of trade and aid on the premium are both significant and negative. The effect due to the TOT operates through at least three channels. Two are indirect: a terms of trade improvement increases real wealth, which pushes up the premium and it also affects the real exchange rate, which raises the premium if the RER appreciates and lowers it otherwise. The third and apparently dominant channel is the direct effect of a TOT improvement on the supply of foreign exchange, which has the effect of reducing the level of the premium.

The effect of foreign aid operates through two channels. A reduction in aid (directly) worsens the official current account, as well as the unofficial current account balance, through a reduction in v (the ratio of official foreign exchange sales to imports). The reduction in foreign aid also produces a real depreciation, however and, hence, a reduction in the premium. The results show that this last channel is dominated by the direct effect on the flow balance. The evidence on the terms of trade and aid indicates that the recent sharp declines in the copper prices and increasing difficulties of external finance may have compromised economic reforms aimed at reducing the premium and achieving exchange rate unification.

The negative and significant effect of the lagged premium shows that a high premium in the previous period is likely to lead to a lower rate of growth of the premium in the following period. The negative coefficient of $\log q_{t-1}$ also implies that in the long term the premium depends negatively on *TOT* and *AID*. Finally, *DUM* (82–7) captures the reduction in the premium associated with a period of trade and exchange rate liberalization.[11] A dummy for 1988–9 captures a strong surge in the premium to over 400 percent, due to a breakdown in the government's reputation and the credibility of reform following the abolition of the auction in 1987 and the suspension of relations with the IMF during 1988–9.

LINKAGES OF THE PREMIUM WITH THE MACROECONOMY

The theoretical models of dual exchange rates develop linkages between the premium and key macroeconomic aggregates such as reported trade, illegal trade, and domestic inflation. In this section an econometric model is estimated for reported copper export supply. We also quantify capital flight and the misinvoicing of imports by various techniques and relate them to the premium in simple models. Finally, we estimate a model of inflation in which the premium operates directly through traded goods prices and indirectly through disequilibrium in the money market.

Reported Copper Export Supply[12]

Four major considerations influence the model of copper export supply developed in this section. The first issue is identifying a relevant price variable. We can treat world copper prices as exogenous given the slowing international demand for copper and the declining share of Zambian copper exports.[13] To capture the relative domestic structure of incentives for copper production, we construct a relative price, RER_X, that is the ratio of the domestic price of copper to the domestic building price index, the latter being a proxy for the domestic price of non-traded goods.[14] The domestic copper price in the numerator RER_X is generated by correcting the current

London Metal Exchange copper price for royalties and copper export taxes.

Secondly, the technology of copper export supply renders large-scale smuggling unlikely, while trading at known world prices effectively precludes the misinvoicing of copper exports. The parallel premium is therefore not likely to have a direct disincentive impact on copper export supply. The level of the premium, q, however, is a good proxy for foreign exchange rationing, which during 1975/6–1989 became the most important constraint on supply.

Thirdly, given the capital-intensive nature of deep-level copper mining, increasing production in the short term can be very costly; hence considerable inertia may be present in the production and export of copper.

The final consideration is the issue of regime shifts. There is clear evidence of a regime shift in the production and export of copper midway through the 1960–90 period (Aron, 1992). In particular, while production was not subject to notable capacity constraints during the copper boom period of 1960–74/5, shortages of foreign exchange and skilled manpower became major constraints on supply in the 1976–90 period. We handle this by estimating copper supply equations separately for the two subperiods, allowing the data to determine whether variables common to the subperiods enter identically or with impacts that depend on the regime. We use the black market premium to proxy foreign exchange shortages and the ratio of skilled expatriates to (mainly unskilled) Zambian employees (denoted *SKILLS*) to capture the evolution of the skills constraint.

A common theme across both periods is the importance of transport shocks. From 1965 onwards, landlocked Zambia incurred considerable transport costs through the disruption of export routes. We model transport constraints in both regimes by including the lagged ratio of copper export supply to the contemporaneous level of copper inventory stocks (denoted *EXP/INV*);[15] the ratio acts as a proportional control mechanism on supply.

Copper supply was also affected by idiosyncratic developments in each subperiod. For the earlier period, we use impulse dummy variables to capture the effects of the partial nationalization and introduction of a more favorable tax regime in 1969 and of the surge in exports in 1972 after recovery from the Mufulira mine disaster of late 1969. For the later period, a dummy variable for 1985–8 captures the enormous diversion of copper company resources into non-mining expenditures that was associated with increased government control (Aron, 1992).

These considerations lead to a specification for copper export supply (in thousands of metric tons) as a linear logarithmic function of the following variables: the real exchange rate for copper as defined above, expected to have a positive effect since real depreciation should improve the external competitiveness and the domestic incentive structure for copper; the level of the parallel rate premium as a proxy for foreign exchange shortages, which should have a direct negative impact and also possibly, though of lesser importance, an indirect negative effect through its influence on the domestic price of non-traded goods; the declining ratio of skilled expatriate to unskilled Zambian employees, expected to decrease productivity and thus exports; the lagged ratio of export supply to stocks of copper, which for an increased level of stocks relative to supply in the period, is expected to increase exports in the next period; and, finally, a host of dummies reflecting the various regime shifts we discussed above. The regression is shown in equation (3) and uses annual data from 1960 to 1989.

$$
\begin{aligned}
\log EXP_t = \alpha(5.0 \quad &+ \quad 0.25 \log REX_{Xt} - 0.05 \log(EXP/INV)_{t-1} \\
(14.08) \quad &(4.40) \quad\quad\quad (-3.75) \\
&+ 0.10\, D69 + 0.12\, D72 \\
&(1.77) \quad\quad (2.25) \\
+ (1-\alpha)(6.11 \quad &- \quad 0.18 \log q_t + 0.36 \log SKILLS_t \\
(67.82) \quad &(-5.83) \quad\quad (7.09) \\
&- 0.05 \log(EXP/INV)_{t-1} - 0.17D8588) \\
&(-3.75) \quad\quad\quad\quad (-4.49)
\end{aligned}
$$

(3)

$$\bar{R}^2 = 0.91,\ s.e. = 0.052,\ DW = 1.92.$$

The parameter α takes the values 1 for 1960–75 and 0 for 1976–89.[16] Individual effects in equation (3) are statistically significant and consistent with prior expectations. The model explains over 90 percent of the variation in the dependent variable. During the first regime (1960–75), export supply was strongly influenced by the relative structure of incentives in the domestic economy, as reflected by a short-term elasticity of 0.25 for the real exchange rate for copper, RER_X. Thus, copper export, despite the technology of production and international export arrangement, is strongly linked to the rest of the economy. For the period after 1974–5, the real exchange rate for copper proves insignificant for the evolution of copper exports. The relevant determinants were foreign exchange shortages, the increasing skills deficit, transport shocks, and the diversion of mining resources. Skills shortages are very important: a 100 percent rise in the skills ratio reduces copper exports by approximately one-third. The lagged supply : stocks ratio, which indirectly captures transport shocks and the inertia of supply in the industry, displays the expected negative partial elasticity of supply in both regimes. The estimated effects of the dummies are consistent with the likely influences of the episodes they represent.

Finally, the premium, q, has a pronounced negative effect on copper supply in the second regime, reflecting foreign exchange constraints.[17] A 100 percent rise in the premium will lead to an approximately 18 percent decline in the export of copper in the short term. As suggested earlier, the premium is probably capturing the direct effect of foreign exchange shortages. The estimated effects for the real exchange rate and the premium on Zambia's copper exports thus provide a strong argument for unification based on its macro-level resource allocation effects (Pinto (1989) makes a similar argument for Ghana).

Illegal Trade Flows and Capital Flight

Capital flight is usually defined as net private short-term capital outflow, occurring in response to such factors as political or financial crises, high levels of inflation, increased taxation, expectations of devaluation, or the tightening of exchange controls. While there are clearly problems of measurement and definition, an estimate of net capital flight is possible. Part (2) of Table 8.4 shows the narrow Cuddington (1986) measure of capital flight, which refers to short-term speculative capital outflows by the private non-bank sector, net of unrecorded capital inflows. For countries like Zambia that enforce capital controls, the outflows have to be concealed and the Cuddington (1986) measure reduces to the 'errors and omissions' entry in the balance of payments. Capital flows thus measured will still under estimate additions to the stock of flown capital, since interest is earned on assets held abroad. The definition needs further to be appended by a measure of the private sector's unrecorded current account (for example, misinvoiced trade, migrants' remittances, and tourism).

Trade may be misinvoiced in order to avoid trade taxes or inflate the value of subsidies, to gain rents from supplying a quota constrained market for imports, or to divert foreign exchange from official channels to the black market. A large premium, for example, gives importers an incentive to overinvoice imports (and exporters an incentive to underinvoice exports) and to sell the additional foreign exchange on the black market. Import restrictions work in the opposite direction: larger tariffs or greater quota rents encourage the underinvoicing of imports. The strength and direction of the incentive for misinvoicing may be expected to vary both across traded commodities and over time, responding not only to trade interventions and the premium but also to variations in penalties and degrees of enforcement. A mix of channels for capital flight may therefore be operative at any one time.

In what follows, we use partner trade data to estimate the extent of import misinvoicing in Zambia. Zambia has a high import dependence, with imports averaging over 30 percent of GDP between 1964 and 1990. Misinvoicing of exports is unlikely to be a significant component of capital flight in Zambia, given the predominance of metals that trade at known world prices in the export basket.[18] On the import side, however, product differentiation probably facilitates misinvoicing by making the confirmation of prices more difficult. Disaggregating to the level of manufactured imports (SITC categories 5–8[19]) would be likely to amplify disparities (Bhagwati *et al.*, 1974), but since the majority of Zambian imports (70 percent in 1970 and 77 percent in the early 1980s) already fall in this category we confine the analysis to aggregate imports.

Table 8.9 compares the recorded exports of Zambia's trading partners with Zambia's recorded imports from 1965 to 1985. Discrepancies are given by non-zero values of the ratios $R = (M_Z - X_F)/X_F$, where M_Z and X_F are Zambian-recorded f.o.b. imports and partner country-recorded f.o.b. exports; a positive ratio indicates overinvoicing and a negative ratio underinvoicing. The table shows results for trade with the UK and the USA (which comprise on average 22 and 10 percent of Zambian imports, respectively), for the six main trading partners (excluding South Africa and Saudi Arabia[20]) and for the Organization for Economic Cooperation and Development (OECD) as a whole (comprising 60 percent of imports). Outside of these countries, trade is erratic and the data patchy, suggesting that further comparisons were unlikely to be useful.

The misinvoicing series in Table 8.9 shows a correspondence with changes in the premium and the trade regime. All four series suggest that capital flight through overinvoicing was rife during the copper

TABLE 8.9 *Partner country data trade comparisons: percentage misinvoicing*

Year	UK	USA	Six major partners	OECD
1965	38.3	.	40.8	65.1
1966	13.1	12.7	8.0	8.2
1967	21.1	22.3	8.1	5.6
1968	36.86	73.76	35.98	36.34
1969	30.61	76.16	34.15	31.89
1970	36.48	64.51	29.80	29.31
1971	13.25	58.49	20.02	20.77
1972	15.86	44.41	13.22	16.91
1973	13.17	22.56	−1.10	2.20
1974	3.69	−9.41	−12.59	−15.85
1975	3.32	34.54	14.05	9.41
1976	32.77	47.71	9.69	2.97
1977	2.67	48.98	12.91	8.59
1978	12.54	8.18	7.05	6.41
1979	6.10	2.65	0.03	−4.10
1980	2.23	−21.63	−8.76	3.76
1981	17.52	32.94	15.50	2.37
1982	20.00	37.83	10.78	10.61
1983	–	–	–	–
1984	−14.27	−56.44	−30.71	−29.27
1985	−8.09	2.67	−14.79	−14.55

The trade ratios are $R = 100.(M_Z - X_F)/X_F$, where M_Z are Zambian-recorded f.o.b. imports and X_f partner country-recorded f.o.b. exports (there is thus no need to correct for transport costs).

The six main trading partners, excluding South Africa and Saudi Arabia, are the USA, the UK, France, Italy, Japan, and Germany.

No data were available before 1965; the 1965 figure for the six main trading partners is an average of five countries, excluding the USA for which figures were unavailable. Further, OECD figures for 1965–7 were available as monthly averages only.

For all imports in 1983 and 1986–91, only partner country data were available.

SOURCES: IMF, *Direction of Trade Statistics*; OECD, *Foreign Trade Statistics*.

boom, 1966–74.[21] The imposition of more restrictive exchange and import controls in 1971 saw the premium double and overinvoicing was sustained. With the terms of trade recovery in 1973 and the first two quarters of 1974, the premium and overinvoicing fell. The negative copper price shock in 1974 induced a further tightening of trade and exchange controls. The premium more than doubled from 1975–7, influenced by an increasingly overvalued exchange rate and the persistence of poor terms of trade: the UK and USA data suggest a rise in overinvoicing. From a peak of 190 percent in 1977, the premium fell steadily during the second and third exchange rate policy episodes until the auction. Between 1978 and 1979 alone, the fall amounted to almost 40 percentage points, induced primarily by favorable copper prices. Overinvoicing was negligible in these years, but revived in 1981 with a sharp deterioration in the terms of trade. During the crawling peg episode preceding the auction of October 1985, the premium averaged 30 percent (a low level compatible with the maintenance of exchange controls) and underinvoicing predominated.

The correspondence between misinvoicing and changes in the premium and trade policy can in principle be shown more formally by regressing the R-values on a constructed series for the smuggling incentive. Following McDonald's (1985) study of export misinvoicing, for example, the import invoicing incentive can be defined as $I = [(1 + q)/(1 + t_I)] - 1$, where q is the parallel premium and t_I is the implicit import tax rate (implicit because import controls mainly take the form of quotas rather than tariffs). In the extended version of this chapter, we construct a proxy for t_I and find limited empirical support for a positive link between I and misinvoicing (Aron and Elbadawi, 1992). Perhaps unsurprisingly given the quality of the data and the prevalence of institutional and regime changes, the results are sensitive both to the period examined and to the dummy variables used to capture regime changes.

Domestic Inflation

A final topic we examine is the role of the parallel rate (or premium) in the domestic inflationary process. Inflation in the consumer price index (CPI) was relatively low and stable until the late 1980s and gives little evidence of influence by black market depreciation. The main components of the CPI were price controlled, however, making this variable a poor measure of underlying inflation pressures. We therefore focus on the manufacturing sector, which is the only sector for which it is possible to separate out controlled and uncontrolled prices. We extracted the manufacturing components from the wholesale price index (WPI) and then excluded the parastatal-dominated food, beverage, and tobacco subsectors where price controls were most likely to dominate. The resulting disaggregated wholesale price for manufacturing (WMI) shows similar volatility to the black market exchange rate and its inflation rates move as the mirror image of black market depreciation. To assess the role of parallel market depreciation in the inflationary process, we specify the price level as a geometric average of traded and non-traded components and derive the following simple model of inflation π_t:[22]

$$(4) \qquad \pi_t = \delta_0 + \delta_1[\hat{P}_t^* + \hat{E}_t] + \delta_2\hat{q}_t + \delta_3 \log p_{ct} + \delta_4\hat{B}_t$$

In equation (4), the coefficient of δ_1 on foreign inflation $\hat{P}^*$ reflects the direct pass-through of foreign prices into the prices of traded final goods and an additional possible cost-push effect through imported intermediates in the production of non-traded goods. The change in the official exchange rate, which is a component of $\hat{q}$, enters with a net effect of $\delta_1 - \delta_2$, which is lower than δ_1 because a portion of traded goods enters the economy at the black market rate. Goods entering at the latter rate provide a direct channel for the depreciation in the black market rate. The real price of copper, p_c, is in the equation as a determinant of excess demand for non-traded goods, along standard Dutch disease lines. The rate of depreciation of the parallel rate also enters separately, as a sensitive indicator of the excess supply of money and thus of the excess demand for non-traded goods.

We estimated equation (4) using annual data from 1970 to 1986, but with unsatisfactory results. Estimation in terms of acceleration of inflation (that is, using $\Delta\pi_{t+1}$ as the dependent variable) was successful, however, as indicated below:

$$\Delta\pi_{t+1} = 1.40 + 0.50[\hat{P}_t^* + \hat{E}_t] + 0.60\hat{q} + 0.30 \log p_{ct} + 0.12\Delta\hat{B}_t$$
$$(4') \qquad\quad (4.87)\ (2.29) \qquad\quad (3.20) \qquad (4.67) \qquad\quad (1.12)$$
$$\bar{R}^2 = 0.75, \quad DW = 2.38.$$

$$\Delta\pi_{t+1} = 1.45 + 0.57[\hat{P}_t^* + \hat{E}_t] + 0.31 \log p_{ct} + 0.11\Delta\hat{B}_t$$
$$(4'') \qquad\qquad (5.70)\ (3.32) \qquad\quad (5.68) \qquad\quad (1.09)$$
$$\bar{R}^2 = 0.77, \quad DW = 2.38.$$

Equation (4') is the unrestricted version of equation (4), while equation (4'') imposes the restriction $\delta_1 = \delta_2$. This restriction could not be rejected at any reasonable significance level ($t = -0.56$). The acceptability of this restriction by the data is also reflected in the similarities of the two empirical results in equations (4') and (4").

With the above restriction taken as a maintained hypothesis, the result in equation (4") indicates that foreign inflation and depreciation of the parallel rate are important cost-push factors causing acceleration in uncontrolled manufacturing prices. Furthermore, previous-period devaluations of the official exchange rate were shown not to influence the current-period change in inflation. The income effect channeled through the balance of payments is also found to lead to an increase in the inflation. The other channel of excess demand for non-traded goods – working through the money market and reflected by the change in the rate of depreciation of the parallel rate – has a smaller and only slightly significant effect on inflation in uncontrolled manufacturing prices in Zambia.

CONCLUSIONS

In Zambia, where the foreign exchange black market is pervasive and strongly linked to macroeconomic performance, the traditional macroeconomic objectives of stabilization and real depreciation are closely related to those of stabilizing the free-market rate and achieving a sustainable reduction in the premium. Exchange rate unification, at least for current account purposes, was therefore a theme of policy during the 1980s. In this concluding section we discuss Zambia's largely unsuccessful experience with exchange rate unification. Drawing on our analysis of earlier sections, we ask three questions. First, what problems for macroeconomic management or economic reform did the existence of a large parallel market cause? Second, what was the actual experience with attempted unification? Finally, what lessons does the Zambian experience suggest?

Our econometric analysis shows that a large premium can have a deleterious effect on copper exports, directly as an indicator of foreign exchange shortages and indirectly through its negative influence on the domestic structure of incentives for the officially sanctioned copper economy. A high premium also encourages overimporting (and probably overinvoicing) of officially traded imports. The black market rate was found to have a significant effect on domestic inflation through at least two channels: directly through the cost-push channel and indirectly through money market disequilibrium.

Analysis with monthly data revealed that the short-term evolution of the premium reflects the impact of anticipated political events and changes in economic policy. Thus, the premium not only affects inflation and the real exchange rate, but also serves as a signal for the credibility of economic reform and the sustainability of macro-economic policy.

These empirical results point to the importance of liberalizing major trade and financial markets in a way that will compress the parallel market and prevent the premium from serving as a major signal to the economy.[23] As such, some form of exchange rate unification must have been either an explicit or an implied objective of recent economic reform. Considerable official depreciation was achieved during the crawling peg period (July 1983 to October 1985) with the rate of annual nominal devaluation averaging 27 percent compared with less than 8 percent during the preceding 2 years; however, the premium remained high and rose in the final year to match the pre-crawl historical average. The premium declined sharply when the auction system was introduced, as part of the IMF-supported economic reform in the fourth quarter of 1985, but this decline was reversed in the second year of the auction and in 1988 it soared to 418 percent.

The empirical analysis of this chapter gives a potential role to both policy fundamentals and exogenous shocks in explaining the failure of exchange rate unification in Zambia. With regard to economic policy, we find that expansive fiscal and monetary policies raise the premium both directly through their effects on wealth and spending and indirectly through expectations of depreciation of the official exchange rate. Reductions in the terms of trade or in foreign aid also increase the premium, implying that the direct effects of these variables on the flow supply of foreign exchange dominate their indirect effects through wealth and the real exchange rate.

The relative importance of policy and external fundamentals shifted over the 1980s, with adverse terms of trade shocks preventing a meaningful reduction in the premium during most of the crawling peg period and loss of control over macroeconomic policy becoming the driving force starting in 1985. During the first 2 years of the crawling peg regime (1983 and 1984), the fiscal deficit was reduced to a level of only 7.5 percent of GDP, from 18 percent a year earlier. The rate of growth in the supply of (narrow) money declined from 22 percent in 1982 to 15 and 9 percent for the following 2 years. The terms of trade, in contract, declined dramatically throughout the 1980s. Compared with their 1980 level, the terms of trade declined by 43 percent in 1981 and by 80 percent for the first 2 years of the crawling peg regime. The result was that a policy of considerable macroeconomic restraint (at least compared with the history of macroeconomic policy in the country) and substantial nominal devaluation (effected by the crawl policy) was clearly undermined by adverse external developments. For the last year of the peg regime and the 2 years of the auction (1985–7), the terms of trade continued to be low and stable at around 30 percent of the 1980 index. The driving force behind the persistence of the premium during this period, however, was outright laxity in fiscal and monetary policy. The fiscal deficit ratio doubled to an average of 15 percent for the period and money growth increased from 12 percent for the previous period to 41 percent in 1985 and more than 60 percent for 1986–7.

While the Zambian experience indicates that exchange rate reform without fiscal reform may be futile, it also suggests that considerations of the political economy may significantly influence the sustainability of fiscal retrenchment. Zambia is one of the most urbanized countries in Africa with an estimated 45 percent of its population in urban areas. Until October 1991 the urban classes constituted the main support base for the ruling single party (UNIP) and a desire to maintain this support helps explain the pervasive ensemble of price control and subsidy schemes that survived the reform attempts of the last decade. On the other hand, government revenue as a ratio to GDP has never been less than 20 percent despite sharp declines in the terms of trade, this rate being one of the highest in Africa. These observations suggest that more emphasis be given to political–economic and distributional consequences, and especially to the rural–urban nexus, in the early stages of economic reform.

Finally, it is evident that the economy of Zambia, being heavily dependent on copper, is particularly susceptible to external shocks. Increased foreign aid could be very effective in mitigating the destabilizing effects of terms of trade shocks during unification. This is likely to be most helpful in the early stages of reform in stabilizing the free rate and fostering credibility in the face of a potentially tentative and inevitably gradual private sector supply response to real depreciation. With program credibility underpinned by sufficiently supportive aid flows early on, the stronger supply response would imply less need for aid to continue at initial levels.

NOTES

1. The authors are grateful to David Bevan, Charles Harvey, Miguel Kiguel, Saul Lizondo, John Muellbauer, and Stephen O'Connell for comments. Janine Aron gratefully acknowledges funding through an Economic and Social Research Council Fellowship at the Centre for Study of African Economies, University of Oxford. The views expressed in this chapter are not necessarily those of the World Bank or affiliated organizations. The authors would like to acknowledge able research assistance from Nita Ghei.

2. Pinto and van Wijnbergen (1987) argued that the failure to adjust policy for the existence of parallel markets may be the main cause behind recent macroeconomic instability in sub-Saharan Africa.

3. The real effective exchange rate (*REER*) is the geometric average of trade-weighted real exchange rates (RER_i) for the six major trading partners, excluding South Africa, where $RER = NER \cdot CPI(Zambia)/CPI$ and *NER* is the nominal bilateral exchange rate in foreign currency per kwacha. The weights are import weights, based on partner country-recorded exports to avoid the misinvoicing bias (South Africa does not record exports to Zambia). Weights were redefined for 1968–72, 1973–7, 1978–82, and 1983–8. The CPI rather than WPI was used as there are less likely to be definitional discrepancies across countries (as noted in the IMF's monthly *International Financial Statistics*).

4. This applied to the government's imports, the copper company, and non-traditional exporters' export earnings retention quotas, crude oil imports and related port charges, and IATA payments by Zambia Airways. Petroleum and IATA payments were included in the auction from February 1986.

5. Interview at the Bank of Zambia (April 1991).

6. Dornbusch *et al.* (1983) found that in addition to variables capturing changes in asset stocks and the flow of foreign exchange, expectations of major devaluations are significant in explaining the Brazilian black market premium. Politics and interest rates play a major role in determining the Argentinean premium (Dornbusch and Moura Silva, 1987).

7. Similar empirical distributional characteristics have been found for black market exchange rate changes in 12 Latin American countries (Akgiray *et al.*, 1988).

8. The model is formally derived in Aron and Elbadawi (1992).

9. Along with the Chow test for parameter stability, we conducted an out of sample forecast for 1990 and 1991 (that is, using data only up to 1989). The *F*-value for the forecast test was $F(2, 11) = 2.27$, which is well below the critical value (again at the 5 percent level) of 3.98. Also, a Lagrange multiplier test for first-order serial correlation generated a parameter of $\rho = 0.21$, which was insignificantly different from zero (*t*-ratio $= 0.54$).

10. As shown earlier, in the very short term, a combination of market thinness and agents' reactions to frequently changing policies might have caused the premium to follow a skewed or non-stationary process.

11. No satisfactory measure was available for the relative tax variable and it was dropped from the regression. A term given by import tax revenue to GDP was included, but the results worsened substantially.
12. In the extended version of this paper (Aron and Elbadawi, 1992), we estimate a model for reported import demand and find that a high premium encourages overimporting of officially traded imports.
13. The Zambian share of world copper production fell from 13 percent in 1961 to 6.7 percent in 1982–4.
14. Further, the building price aggregate is the only domestic price series extending back to 1960 that reflects the structure of domestic costs (including transport costs) to the copper sector.
15. In the absence of suitable data, these stocks were proxied by the cumulative difference between production and exports in each year, assuming quite reasonably that domestic consumption is negligible.
16. Coefficients on *EXP/INV* were the same in both regimes, so this restriction was imposed in the final estimation. To verify the presence of a regime shift in 1976, we re-estimated the equation in the form $\log EXP_t = aD_t(\beta_1' X_{1t}) + (1 - aD_t)(\beta_2' X_{2t})$, where D_t is a dummy variable taking the value 1 in 1960–75 and 0 in 1976–89 and X_{1t} and X_{2t} are the vectors of variables relevant to each regime after the general to specific estimation process. The value of a estimated by non-linear least squares was 1.19, with a t-statistic of 10.0. The null hypothesis of $a = 0$ is thus clearly rejected against the alternative of $a = 1$ and a null of $a = 1$ cannot be rejected at the 10 percent level of significance (t-ratio = 1.6) against the general alternative $a \neq 1$.
17. Since the parallel exchange rate is not available before 1970, we used the 1970 value of the premium (1.36) for the earlier years 1960–9, judging that this was a reasonable ceiling in the presence of exchange controls but with a booming copper sector. While this gives a static premium for much of the first period, the premium moves considerably during 1970–5. The premium was not statistically significant for the first regime and was therefore excluded for this regime in the general to specific estimation.
18. This has been confirmed by Yeats (1990) who found that discrepancies in the data for Zambia's exports to industrial countries in 1982–3 were in the range of transport correction factors.
19. SITC categories 1–4 comprise food, beverages and tobacco, crude materials, animal fats, and mineral fuels.
20. South Africa reports only its total exports to sub-Saharan Africa, not its exports to Zambia; in the Zambian data, South Africa accounts for some 20 percent of imports. Saudi Arabian trade is predominantly in oil, which by analogy with copper seems unlikely to be misinvoiced; however, other studies have shown significant discrepancies in oil trade data due to confusion over the ownership of refineries and petroleum (Bhagwati *et al.*, 1974).
21. *R*-values are larger for the individual countries, in part because cancellation effects are diminished.
22. See Aron and Elbadawi (1992) for a more detailed derivation.

23.   The concept of unification we have in mind does not call for a zero level
      of the premium, however. At least for the case of capital controls,
      liberalization may not be possible nor desirable for some time to come
      in Zambia.

REFERENCES

Akgiray, V., G. Booth, and B. Seifert (1988) 'Distribution Properties of Latin
   American Black Market Rates', *Journal of International Money and
   Finance*, vol. 7, pp. 37–48.
Aron, Janine (1992) 'Regulatory Capture in a Mining Parastatal: Zambia
   Consolidated Copper Mines Limited, 1981–91', Working Paper (Durham,
   NC: Center for International Development Research, Duke University).
Aron, Janine, and Ibrahim Elbadawi (1992) 'Parallel Markets, the Foreign
   Exchange Auction and Exchange Rate Unification in Zambia', *World Bank
   Policy Research Working Papers* No. 909 (Washington, DC: World Bank).
Banerjee, Anindya, Juan Dolado, John W. Galbraith, and David F. Hendry
   (1993) *Co-integration, Error Correction and Econometric Analysis of Non-
   stationary Data* (Oxford: Oxford University Press).
Bhagwati, Jagdish, N., Anne Krueger, and C. Wibulswasdi (1974) 'Capital
   Flight from LDCs: a Statistical Analysis', in J. Bhagwati (ed.), *Illegal
   Transactions in International Trade* (Amsterdam: North-Holland), pp.
   148–54.
Calvo, Guillermo A. (1987) 'On the Costs of Temporary Policy', *Journal of
   Development Economics*, vol. 27, pp. 245–61.
Cuddington, John T. (1986) 'Capital Flight: Estimates, Issues, and Explana-
   tions', *Princeton Studies in International Finance* no. 58 (Princeton, NJ:
   International Finance Section, Department of Economics, Princeton Uni-
   versity).
Development Assistance Committee (various years) *Geographical Distribution
   of Aid Flows* (Paris: Organization for Economic Cooperation and Develop-
   ment).
Dickey, D. and Fuller, W. (1981) 'Likelihood Ratio Statistics for Autoregres-
   sive Time Series with a Unit Root', *Econometrica*, vol. 49, pp. 1057–72.
Dornbusch, Rudiger (1986) 'Special Exchange Rates for Capital Account
   Transactions', *World Bank Economic Review*, vol. 1, no. 1, pp. 1–33.
Dornbusch, Rudiger and A. Moura Silva (1987) 'Dollar Debts and Interest
   Rates in Brazil', *Revista Brasileira de Economica*.
Dornbusch, Rudiger, Daniel V. Dantas, Clarice Pechman, Roberto Rocha,
   and Demetri Simoes (1983) 'The Black Market for Dollars in Brazil',
   Quarterly Journal of Economics, vol. 98, pp. 25–40.
Elbadawi, Ibrahim (1989) 'Terms of Trade, Commercial Policy and the Black
   Market for Foreign Exchange: an Empirical Model of Real Exchange Rate
   Determination', *Economic Growth Center Discussion Paper* No. 570 (New
   Haven: Yale University).

Government of Zambia (various issues) *Monthly Digest of Statistics* (Lusaka: Government Printer).

International Currency Analysis, Inc. (various years) *World Currency Yearbook* (Brooklyn, NY: International Currency Analysis, Inc.). (Formerly *Pick's Currency Yearbook*; continued as monthly *Currency Alert*).

International Monetary Fund (various years) *Balance of Payments Statistics* (Washington, DC: International Monetary Fund).

International Monetary Fund (various years) *Direction of Trade Statistics* (Washington, DC: International Monetary Fund).

International Monetary Fund (various years) *Government Finance Statistics* (Washington, DC: International Monetary Fund).

International Monetary Fund (various years) *International Financial Statistics* (Washington, DC: International Monetary Fund).

Kaminsky, Graciela (1988) 'The Real Exchange Rate Since Floating: Market Fundamentals or Bubbles?', mimeo (San Diego: University of California at San Diego).

Lizondo, J. Saul (1987a) 'Exchange Rate Differential and Balance of Payments Under Dual Exchange Markets', *Journal of Development Economics*, vol. 26, no. 1, pp. 37–53.

Lizondo, J. Saul (1987b) 'Unification of Dual Exchange Rate Markets', *Journal of International Economics*, vol. 22, nos 1/2, pp. 57–77.

Lizondo, J. Saul (1991) 'Alternative Dual Exchange Rate Regimes: Some Steady-state Comparisons', *IMF Staff Papers*, vol. 38, no. 3, pp. 560–81.

McDonald, Donough (1985) 'Trade Data Discrepancies and the Incentive to Smuggle', *IMF Staff Papers*, vol. 32, no. 3, pp. 668–92.

Organization of Economic Cooperation and Development (various years) *Foreign Trade Statistics* (Paris: Organization for Economic Cooperation and Development).

Pinto, Brian (1989) 'Black Market Premia, Exchange Rate Unification, and Inflation in Sub-Saharan Africa', *World Bank Economic Review*, vol. 3, no. 3, pp. 321–38.

Pinto, Brian (1991) 'Black Markets for Foreign Exchange, Real Exchange Rates and Inflation', *Journal of International Economics*, vol. 30, pp. 121–36.

Pinto, Brian and Sweder van Wijnbergen (1987) 'Exchange Rate Regimes in Africa', mimeo (Washington, DC: World Bank).

Rodrik, Dani (1991) 'Promises, Promises: Credible Policy Reform via Signalling', *Economic Journal*, vol. 99, pp. 756–72.

Yeats, Alexander (1990) 'On the Accuracy of Economic Observations: Do Sub-Saharan Trade Statistics Mean Anything?', *World Bank Economic Review* vol. 4, no. 2, pp. 135–56.

APPENDIX: THE ESTIMATED QUARTERLY MODEL OF EXPECTED DEVALUATION

$$\Delta \log E_{t+1} = -1.53 + 0.05\Delta \log q_{t-1} - 0.16\log E_{t-2} + 0.44\Delta \log E_{t-3}$$
$$(-5.92) \quad (0.99) \quad\quad (-5.06) \quad\quad (6.89)$$
$$+ 0.22\log M2_t + 0.86DUM85:3$$
$$(5.99) \quad\quad (11.86)$$

Sample period 1971:3–1992:2.

$\bar{R}^2 = 0.76$, *s.e.* $= 0.072$, $DW = 2.36$.

$D85$:3 is a dummy variable for the third quarter of 1985, just prior to the start of the auction. $M2$ is money plus quasi-money, measured in dollars at the official exchange rate and deflated by the US import unit value index, 1985 = 100. The premium q is defined as the ratio of the black market exchange rate to the official exchange rate E.

9 Black Market Exchange Rates in Turkey

Sule Özler[1]

619
F31 F32
017 F33

INTRODUCTION

Black markets for foreign exchange have had an uninterrupted existence in Turkey's history. The nature of the black market, however,
showed a dramatic change with the onset of path-breaking, market-
oriented economic reforms in the 1980s. From a position of very
significant activity before 1980, both the level of activity and the
premium on foreign exchange in the black market declined throughout the 1980s, becoming negligible as the Turkish lira gained convertibility in 1989. The importance of the Turkish experience is that a
successful unification was achieved without an immediate threat of
reversal.

In this study we focus on economic factors that had an impact on
the black market during two contrasting decades: the 1970s, which
culminated in a balance of payments crisis and the 1980s, which saw
major reforms and unification. The 1970s were characterized by pervasive controls, including significant restrictions on foreign trade
and the financial system and a fixed exchange rate regime with a
non-convertible lira. The black market for foreign exchange was an
integral part of the economy. The premium and the volume of transactions in the black market reached unprecedented levels at the end of
the decade, a time of major balance of payments crisis.

The reforms of the 1980s contained a mix of stabilization and
liberalization programs. Liberalization policies were addressed first
towards foreign trade and financial markets and later towards capital
movements. Management of the foreign exchange regime was a very
important policy tool throughout. Exchange rate unification was
achieved gradually over the decade, with the black market becoming
less prominent over time. The black market premium – defined as the
percentage excess of the black market price of foreign exchange over
the official exchange rate – initially disappeared in response to the
major devaluations that were undertaken as a part of the economic

reform program of the 1980s. The premium then re-emerged over the next few years, but at lower and more stable levels. This was a period of managed float with ongoing real depreciation of the Turkish lira (TL), continued capital account and import restrictions, but high export subsidies. The prominence of the black market diminished further with the opening of foreign exchange deposit accounts at the end of 1983. After this date, until the currency became convertible in 1989, policy experiments concerning the regulation of foreign exchange activities of commercial banks were the major sources of activity in the black market. By the end of the decade, the premium had become negligible and the black market no longer played a significant economic role.

The remainder of the chapter is organized as follows. In the following section, we focus on the main macroeconomic events of 1970s and their connections with the black market for foreign exchange. In the third section we focus on the 1980s, describing and evaluating the policy measures that were implemented to achieve exchange rate unification. In the fourth section, we undertake a statistical investigation of the determinants of black market premium, with particular attention to the presence of sample breaks. The final section concludes the chapter and discusses policy lessons.

THE BLACK MARKET IN THE 1970s

Through the 1970s, Turkish economic policy reflected the official ideological position of statism, which had strongly influenced Turkish policy since a decade after the formation of the Turkish Republic in 1923. The key component of statism was an active role for the state in the industrial development strategy. As a consequence, the Turkish economy evolved as a mixed economy that embedded features of a planned economy and a market system.

Trade and exchange rate policy were largely used as instruments of import-substituting industrialization, with the aim of achieving an independent national industrial base. Import restrictions were severe.[2] The lira was an inconvertible currency pegged to the dollar and was often kept overvalued. The available foreign exchange and import licenses were allocated to importers administratively.

As a consequence of controls in the foreign exchange regime, a foreign exchange black market developed. As *Pick's Currency Year-*

book characterized the situation in 1979, 'Black markets in Turkey, with an uninterrupted existence for over 30 years, have become an integral part of the country's economic organization' (p.639). Though these markets were mostly tolerated, they were occasionally the subject of strong restrictive measures.[3]

As in all economies with exchange controls, black markets served to satisfy foreign exchange demands that were not met through official channels. In general one can distinguish between demands arising from current account transactions and demands arising from portfolio transactions. Systematic evidence on the nature of demand in Turkey is limited. However, existing studies suggest that a large component of the demand for black market currencies in the Turkish economy was a consequence of current account transactions and in particular the unmet demands of industrialists and licensed importers (see Olgun, 1984). Limitations on the acquisition of foreign exchange by citizens traveling abroad are also known to have spilled over to the black market.

Since capital account transactions were illegal during the period (Turkish citizens were not permitted to hold foreign securities or bank balances abroad), the demand for black market currency to purchase foreign securities is argued to have played a more minor role (Olgun, 1984). There was undoubtedly a portfolio demand for foreign currency itself, however, both for speculative purposes and as a hedge against inflation. The domestic financial system was highly repressed, with negative real interest rates prevailing in an inflationary environment through the period. Gold and black market foreign exchange therefore became important alternatives to domestic monetary assets (the import or export of gold was also prohibited during the period).

The supply of foreign exchange to the black market can also be from a variety of sources. The remittances of Turkish workers abroad have been suggested as the main source. In addition, both tourism from abroad and underinvoicing of exports were potential sources of supply.

The Premium and Macroeconomic Developments in the 1970s

Figure 9.1 shows the monthly black market premium from 1973 to 1989. There are two distinct phases in the 1970s. In the first phase, lasting to mid-1977, the premium varied between 3 and 20.4 percent. In the second phase the premium reached higher levels, hitting the

Percent

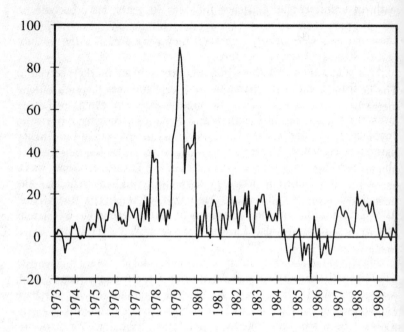

FIGURE 9.1   *Monthly black market premium*
SOURCES: International Curency Analysis, Inc., *World Currency Yearbook*
and IMF, *International Financial Statistics.*

historic high of 91.4 percent in 1979. Corresponding to the two phases
of the premium in the 1970s are two distinct phases in the macroeconomic environment. The 1973–7 phase followed the first oil shock
and was a period of rapid debt accumulation. The debt build-up of the
early 1970s took place under the new rules of the international financial system, with reliance on commercial bank credits. The incentives
for external borrowing provided by the Turkish government (see
below) and the eagerness of foreign banks to lend led to a rapid
build-up of short-term debt. Continual access to commercial bank
loans, however, required regular servicing of the debt. This in turn
required sufficient export earnings, which the Turkish economy was
not generating. When it became apparent that the government could
not service the debt, lending came to a halt and Turkey entered the
balance of payments crisis phase of 1978–9, with severe internal and
external imbalances.

In the rest of this section these two phases of the economy[4] and the evolutions of the black market will be discussed.

Phase 1: the Debt Build-up, 1973–7

The debt build-up of the 1973–7 period was largely a consequence of increases in the public sector's savings–investment gap. The public sector in Turkey accounted for 50 to 55 percent of GNP during the 1970s. Large public expenditures were undertaken so as to provide basic infrastructure and basic heavy industries. Public investment increased from 7 to 13 percent of GNP between 1973 and 1977, accounting for nearly the entire increase in total domestic investment during the period. Domestic saving changed very little, showing a decline of close to 2 percent of GNP over the period. Increased public sector investment therefore accounted for approximately the entire increase in the investment–savings gap.

The current account balance reflected the public savings–investment gap, with a surplus of 2.4 percent of GNP in 1973 and a deficit of 7.1 percent by 1977.[5] The public sector investment program, despite its contribution to GNP growth and to basic industrial infrastructure, had a negative impact on the current account balance even from a longer run perspective: public investment was not directed towards exportables, nor did it promote exports. Turkey's total export to GNP ratio during the 1974–7 period was 6.2 percent, compared with an import to GNP ratio of 13.7 percent.

The expanding public sector deficit meant that the borrowing requirement of the public sector increased from 2 percent of GNP in 1973 to nearly 10.6 percent of GNP in 1977. Direct foreign borrowing of the public sector constituted only 0.05 percent of GNP in 1977. The Central Bank provided the most important component of deficit financing, amounting to 6.6 percent of GNP in 1977. The financing of the current account, on the other hand, indicates a substantial reliance on short-term external borrowing, which constituted approximately 54 percent of current account financing in 1977, a dramatic increase from a share of 6.4 percent in 1973. Furthermore, with a share of 37 percent of all short-term liabilities, the most important source of short-term financing was in the form of convertible Turkish lira deposit accounts (CTLDs).

CTLDs were deposit accounts at Turkish commercial banks that could be opened by non-residents. The recipient bank would turn over the foreign currency to the Central Bank and its account with the Central Bank would be credited with the TL equivalent of the deposit. This amount could then be extended as loans to domestic firms. Typically, foreign lenders willing to make CTLDs were located by a Turkish firm, who would then be the beneficiary of the credit extended.

The Central Bank guaranteed the repayments on these accounts (both interest and principal) against foreign exchange risk. The exchange rate guarantees of the Central Bank generated an element of subsidy equal to the expected rate of depreciation of the local currency. If expected depreciation of the local currency is captured by the spread between the official and black market rate, one finds a significant amount of subsidy for borrowing through CTLDs: the lira was overvalued by at least 20 percent in 1977 as reflected in the black market premium.[6] The combination of Central Bank guarantees against foreign exchange risk and the interest spreads and fees offered on CTLDs easily attracted foreign lenders, leading to a rapid debt build-up.[7]

Phase 2: the 1978–9 Crisis

Debt servicing difficulties became apparent in mid-1977, bringing foreign capital inflows to a halt and ushering in a period of severe economic and political crisis. Foreign exchange constraints, shortages in the economy, unprecedented levels of inflation, real appreciation of the domestic currency, a collapse of the investment boom, excess industrial capacity, and declining economic growth characterized the economy. Politically, the period from 1977 to 1979 saw a succession of three unstable and weak governments, two of which were coalition governments and a third a minority government. Social and political unrest increased dramatically according to any conventional measure, such as protests, armed attacks, deaths, and increased repression.

The black market premium reached historically high rates during the crisis period, moving to some 40 percent during mid-1977 and to nearly 92 percent at beginning of 1979. The Central Bank of Turkey was not able to satisfy the demand for foreign exchange at the official rate. The reserve position of the Central Bank steadily declined from a peak of nearly 10 percent of GDP in 1974 to approximately 1 percent of GNP by 1978. A major contributing factor to the declining reserve position was a drop in the remittances of workers through official channels. Remittances sent by Turkish workers abroad had consti-tuted a large source of foreign exchange until the mid-1970s, covering 51 percent of imports in 1973. Increasing overvaluation of the official exchange rate following the first oil shock, however, led to a diversion of these remittances to the black market, with the result that remit-tances through official channels declined to only 15 percent of imports in 1977.

Another factor contributing to the scarcity of official reserves was underinvoicing of exports. Though the impact of this is much smaller than that of remittances, the average rate of underinvoicing of trade with the Organization for Economic Cooperation and Develop-ment (OECD) was in the order of 4 percent (Celasun and Rodrik, 1989).

As the foreign exchange reserves of the Central Bank were depleted, the available foreign exchange was rationed administratively and 'commercial enterprises turned to the black market for hard currencies to pay for necessary imports, legal and smuggled, to stay in business' (*Pick's Currency Yearbook*, 1979, p. 639). The black market premium was at a historic high of 91.4 percent at the beginning of 1979 and widespread shortages of imported commodities emerged.

The foreign exchange bottleneck resulted in a drop of the capacity utilization rate to approximately 40–45 percent. Furthermore, the inflation rate reached historically high levels, with wholesale prices registering an increase of 64 percent in 1979, in contrast to an average of 20 percent in 1974–7. In the inflationary environment of the period, foreign exchange and gold became more attractive as hedges against inflation. This is not surprising considering that interest rates on government bonds and 6–12 month bank deposits were 18 and 20 percent in 1979, respectively, while the inflation rate was 64 percent. In contrast to the negative real returns on these financial assets, the black market exchange rate increased threefold between 1976 and 1979, keeping up fully with the increase in the consumer price index (the price of gold increased a phenomenal sevenfold).

Several attempts were made to address the balance of payments problems through stabilization programs with the International Monetary Fund (IMF). Devaluations of close to 30 percent were implemented in March 1978 and June 1979, in connection with an IMF agreement and the signing of a letter of intent for a new agree-ment, respectively. While these devaluations produced significant drops in the black market premium, the reductions proved short-lived in the absence of consistent macroeconomic adjustment.

In an attempt to address the severe balance of payments problems, further foreign exchange restrictions were introduced. In February 1978, for example, Turkish tourists were restricted to travel abroad only once every 2 years, with a foreign exchange advance of only $300–$500 per trip. The number of trips allowed was reduced further in January 1979, to one every 3 years. Needless to say, the associated excess demand for foreign exchange spilled over to the black market.

The authorities also experimented with various incentive schemes to increase official reserves. More favorable exchange rate and interest rate incentives were offered to increase remittances of workers through official channels. Exporters were subsidized by expanded tax rebates and permission to retain a portion of foreign exchange earnings. Though these incentives generated a positive response, the foreign exchange bottleneck was far from being resolved due to the *ad hoc* and uncertain nature of these policies. The burden of adjustment therefore fell primarily on imports.

THE BLACK MARKET AND EXCHANGE RATE UNIFICATION IN THE 1980s

In response to the deep economic crisis, the minority government, which took office in October 1979, introduced an economic package known as the January 1980 measures. This package was the first step on a new economic path. It consisted of a mix of stabilization and liberalization policies, including export subsidies, devaluation of the TL, substantial price increases for the products of state enterprises, and an increase in interest rates. These measures were aimed at export-led recovery, liberalization, and institutional change. *Ex post*, it is clear that the Turkish economy made a major break with its past in 1980.[8]

In this section we focus on the linkages between the economic reforms of the 1980s and developments in the black market. We focus particularly on the roles played by exchange rate policies, trade policies, capital account policies, and financial policies in achieving a gradual unification of the black market and official exchange rates.[9] It will be the conclusion of this overview that unification, defined as the elimination of the black market without an immediate threat of reversal, was successful. However, high domestic inflation has remained a problem for the Turkish economy. The section will end with a discussion of how policies that helped a successful unification may have accentuated the inflation problem.

Exchange Rate Practices

Figure 9.2 shows the monthly devaluation of the official exchange rate from 1973 to 1988. On 25 January 1980 the lira was devalued by nearly 33 percent, from 47.1 to 70 TL per US$. Multiple exchange rate practices were simultaneously abolished, with the exception of a special (55TL per $) exchange rate for imports of fertilizers and agricultural pesticides and a proviso that students who left Turkey prior to 25 January 1980 would continue to be provided with foreign exchange at the rate in effect at the time of their departure.[10] Between the January 1980 devaluation and 1 May 1981, there were 12 small devaluations in the order of 1.5–5.5 percent.[11] On 1 May 1981 the

Percent

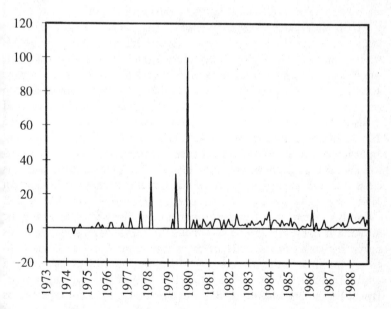

FIGURE 9.2 *Percent change in official rate monthly*
SOURCES: IMF, International Financial Statistics.

Central Bank of Turkey was authorized to publish daily exchange rates for foreign currencies, adopting a crawling peg. The exchange rate was determined taking into account both the inflation differential between Turkey and its main trade partners and developments in foreign exchange markets.

During 1981 multiple exchange rate practices continued to be phased out by abolishing the special rates for students and fertilizer importers. The phasing out was completed in 1982 by the modification of an arrangement that had allowed exporters of selected products to retain and transfer a portion of foreign exchange earnings.

The next major policy change, the authorization of commercial banks to determine their buying and selling rates for foreign exchange transactions, was implemented on 1 July 1985.[12] Initially, the banks continued to set rates close to those of the Central Bank. In early 1986, however, banks started speculating and accumulating foreign deposits. As a consequence, in March 1986 the government stopped allowing deposit money banks to set their own buying and selling rates. The Central Bank reverted to fixing the rates daily and the rates applied by banks could not differ by more than 1 percent from the buying and selling rates used by the Central Bank.

Starting in August 1988, commercial banks, special finance institutions, and authorized institutions participated in the daily fixing of rates under the leadership of the Central Bank. The Central Bank's role was to act as a blind broker and charge a commission of 0.005 percent of the TL value of the transaction. Participants were subject to collateral requirements of 100 percent on realized bids and 5 percent on realized offers. The exchange rates determined in these sessions became the official rate for the following day. The official rate was applicable to small transactions between commercial banks and private customers and to transactions between the Central Bank and the public sector or commercial banks. Given these rates, banks were free to set their exchange rates. For transactions that exceeded 50 000 US$, however, the lowest and highest rates applied were to be reported to the Central Bank.[13] The exchange rates for non-dollar currencies were set on the basis of cross rates in international markets.

Export Promotion and Import Liberalization

Export promotion was one of the key features of the January 1980 economic program. A set of export incentives was introduced that included tax rebates, foreign exchange allocations that allowed for the duty-free import of intermediate goods and raw materials, and credit subsidies. The value of these direct subsidies averaged approximately 20 percent of the value of manufactured exports during the 1980–6 period, though the subsidy value varied considerably across different commodity categories.[14] The relative importance of alternative forms of export subsidy also changed over time, with a declining importance of export credits and an increasing importance of tax rebates and preferential foreign exchange allocations. Later, a more active exchange rate policy, import liberalization, and direct cash incentives were introduced.

Import liberalization was more gradual. Initial measures, introduced between 1980 and 1983, included a reduction of the stamp duty, abolishment of the explicit import quota list, simplification of import procedures, and a gradual shift of goods from more restrictive to more liberalized lists. However, the most dramatic changes in import liberalization were delayed until the end of 1983, when commodities which had their importation banned or subject to license were explicitly listed, in sharp contrast to the previous system under which all commodities not specifically mentioned were effectively prohibited. With this transition from the positive to negative list it became possible to import all products not specifically listed. The associated elimination of quantity restrictions affected close to half of imports. The resulting regime was less protective overall and was one in which price measures played a much greater role than quotas.

Capital Account Liberalization

The first step in capital account liberalization, taken in December 1983, represented a major break with the 1930 law on the protection of the value of the Turkish currency. Residents and non-residents were allowed to possess foreign currency and to open foreign exchange deposit accounts in banks, with no restrictions on the use of these funds.[15] Restrictions on the importation of currencies, notes, securities, bills, and other commercial payments were abolished. While restrictions on capital exports remained for another 6 months, the December 1983 decree was replaced in July 1984 by a decree that integrated all regulations concerning foreign exchange transactions, including those relating to exports and foreign investment.[16]

The final major steps in liberalizing capital account transactions were taken in August 1989 and resulted in the TL becoming a convertible currency. Turkish nationals were permitted to purchase foreign securities abroad and foreigners to buy Turkish securities quoted on the Istanbul stock exchange, Turkish and foreign nationals were allowed to open TL deposit accounts convertible into foreign exchange, and Turkish residents were no longer obliged to secure government permission to obtain foreign credits. Curbs on the import and export of gold and other precious stones were also lifted in August 1989. This followed the opening of an official gold market in April 1989, at which banks participating in the Central Bank foreign exchange market were able to purchase gold with foreign currencies, provided that they opened special foreign currency accounts at the Central Bank.

Financial Policies

The 1980s also saw a major evolution in government policies towards the financial sector. The first step towards financial deregulation was taken in July 1980 when the authorities lifted ceilings on personal time deposit rates.[17] Initially the interest rates did not increase much, due to a gentleman's agreement among the large banks, but as competition from the smaller banks increased, interest rates started to rise rapidly. A financial crisis that emerged with a loss of confidence in mid-1982 led to more direct government involvement and in December 1983 the Central Bank was authorized to determine deposit rates. Deposit rates were raised sharply starting in early 1984 and have in general been kept above the rate of inflation. In mid-1987, interest rates on 1 year deposits were allowed to be determined freely by the banks. However, as large banks were again reluctant to raise such rates the Central Bank control increased substantially.[18]

Commercial banks became more directly involved with foreign exchange transactions during the 1980s, due to the opening of foreign currency deposit accounts and the transfer of exchange transactions on trade from the Central Bank to commercial banks. Commercial banks remained subject, however, to special reserve, liquidity, and loan restrictions that depended on their foreign exchange deposits. These restrictions were changed several times through the period to relieve pressure on the lira. Thus in October 1984, the reserve requirement ratio was raised to 20 percent from its previous level of 10 percent; it was then reduced to 15 percent in March 1986, only to be increased back to 20 percent in July 1987 and raised further to 25 percent in October 1988.

The Black Market Through Unification

The black market spread disappeared briefly in response to the 33 percent devaluation of January 1980 (Figure 9.1). However, since the underlying macroeconomic imbalances were not yet eliminated, this effect was short-lived. The spread soon moved into the 15–20 percent range and stayed there for most of the 1980–3 period.

With the onset of capital account liberalization in December 1983, which included the introduction of foreign exchange deposit accounts, the spread dropped markedly. Spreads were in fact negative for most of 1984 and 1985, perhaps reflecting the disposal of illegal export revenues through the black markets.

The spikes of the premium in early 1986 and late 1987 were primarily a consequence of financial policy measures. In 1986 the government imposed a set of restrictions on the banking sector in response to pressures in the foreign exchange market and an emerging excess of banks' foreign exchange liabilities over their foreign exchange assets. These included tighter liquidity and reserve requirements, restrictions on foreign currency deposits, and limits on the ratio of foreign exchange liabilities to assets. Banks turned to the black market to meet these requirements, causing the premium to jump by nearly 25 percentage points, from its negative levels to a positive range.

During the latter half of 1987 the premium again jumped from negligible levels to above 20 percent. This was primarily a consequence of the response of commercial banks to accelerating inflation. Specifically, banks started making large purchases in the black market to cover themselves because they expected a large devaluation. These expectations were evident in the fact that banks were charging a commission on sales to importers at a rate of 20–30 percent over the maximum selling rate set by the Central Bank.[19] In February 1988 a set of measures was introduced in response to the deepened instability. The implementation of these measures, which included incentives for the speedy surrender of foreign exchange, penalties for delay, increased deposit rates, and increased reserve and liquidity ratios, resulted in a fall in the black market premium to negligible levels.

In addition, the August 1989 measures of capital account liberalization and the opening of the official gold market are among the factors that helped a sustained disappearance of the premium in the black market.

As for the 1970s, we lack systematic data on the sources of supply and demand in the black market for the 1980s. However, the policy measures undertaken suggest some insights. In the first couple of years of the 1980s a series of incentives were created to attract the workers' remittances through official channels. It appears that remittances responded to these incentives, reducing the available supply to the black market. Exporters overinvoiced their exports during this period or simply declared 'fictitious' exports, as the subsidies to exporters were particularly attractive. This overinvoicing led to purchases in the black market as the exporters tried to make up the fictitious component of exports. This may be the major reason for the sustained premium in the black market through 1983, after its initial disappearance in early 1980s.[20]

On the demand side, financial deregulation and the introduction of foreign currency deposit accounts played important roles in reducing the demand for black market currency as an asset. Deregulation in financial markets and particularly the high real interest rates of 1981 and 1982 that followed the abolition of interest rate ceilings, suggests the possibility of a substitution of bank deposits for black market currency. The financial crises of mid-1982 reversed this trend somewhat, increasing the demand for foreign currency through the black market. The introduction of foreign exchange deposit accounts at the end of December 1983 is likely to have diminished the demand for foreign exchange through unofficial channels. While the magnitude of this substitution year to year is not known, black market activity became negligible in the later part of the 1980s (the exceptions being the periods of speculation against the lira by the commercial banks).

Unification and Some Policy Dilemmas

If a successful unification is narrowly defined as the elimination of the black market without an immediate threat of its re-emergence, the Turkish experience was a success story. If, on the other hand, one is concerned with policy inconsistencies and macroeconomic performance more broadly, then points of caution emerge and evaluation of the experience as a success story becomes more dubious.

The single most persistent macroeconomic problem of the 1980s was the high rate of inflation. The inflation rate (using the GDP deflator) was initially brought down from 107 percent in 1980 to 25 percent in 1982 with the introduction of the stabilization program of 1980. Inflation then rebounded to 51 and 41 percent in 1984 and 1985, before being brought back down during 1986 and 1987. However, inflation rose again starting in 1988, reaching approximately 65 percent in 1989.[21]

The continual depreciation of the real exchange rate, which was an essential component of the unification program and the shift to an outward-oriented macroeconomic framework is likely to have accentuated the inflation problem. From January 1980 to May 1981, real exchange rate depreciation was achieved through discrete devaluations. The lira depreciated by 23 percent in real effective terms in 1980 and by another 13 percent in 1981. The lira then continued its real depreciation after the adoption of daily exchange rate fixing, Depreciation was approximately 8 percent in 1982. From 1982 to 1985 real depreciation was at a lower rate of approximately 3 percent. The rate of real depreciation then accelerated markedly in 1986–7, in response to policy concerns over worsening export performance.

Despite its favorable contribution to strong export growth, restriction of import demand, a strengthened reserve position of the central bank, and a unified exchange rate, the exchange rate policy is believed to have put pressure on the fiscal balances. First, real devaluation increased the real burden of external debt. This is a straightforward implication of the public sector budget constraint, which states that holding the real value of the external debt constant, a depreciation of the real exchange rate requires a corresponding increase in the real primary surplus. Since the debt : output ratio was 60 percent, a 10 percent permanent real depreciation had to be accompanied by an increase in the public sector's primary surplus by no less than 6 percentage points of GNP in order to neutralize the capital loss (see Rodrik, 1990a).

The second channel through which real depreciation put pressure on the fiscal balance was through its impact on domestic interest rates. Uncovered interest arbitrage suggests that the interest rates on Turkish lira assets should incorporate the expected rate of depreciation of the lira. Since the real exchange rate depreciated through most of the 1980s, it is not implausible to suppose that investors came to fully anticipate the real depreciation. In fact, the gap between Turkish interest rates and dollar interest rates steadily increased in the 1980s. This, of course, increased the domestic cost of borrowing for the government, which had become an important source of financing in Turkey in the later part of the 1980s.

Another caveat concerning the inflationary impact of unification policies is the timing of capital account liberalization. The relaxation of capital account restrictions that started in December 1983 facilitated an ongoing process of currency substitution and may well have reduced the demand for the monetary base. A cursory inspection of the composition of the stock of financial assets indicates that foreign exchange deposits rose from negligible levels before 1983 to 16 percent of all financial assets in 1986.[22] Over the same period, the ratio of the monetary base to GNP declined steadily, from 11.2 percent of GNP in 1983 to 6.6 percent by 1988. This erosion of the base for the inflation tax would have increased the inflation rate consistent with any combination of fiscal deficit and non-monetary financing.[23]

AN EMPIRICAL MODEL OF THE BLACK MARKET PREMIUM

The discussion in the previous sections suggests that current account transactions and financial transactions both played important roles in determining the black market premium during the 1970s and 1980s. At the same time the significance of various types of transactions in influencing the premium has changed over time. In this section we use data for 1973–88 to estimate a model of the premium as a function of variables affecting illegal current account transactions as well as portfolio transactions. It goes without saying that this undertaking is limited by the availability of systematic data sources. A main objective of our undertaking is to identify whether the motives for trading black market currency have had a differential impact on the spread over the distinct policy episodes.[24]

Specification

In order to investigate the factors that determine the black market premium, we implement a version of the forward-looking dynamic model of the premium developed in Dornbusch *et al.* (1983). Since this model has been used in a number of recent studies (for example, Kaufmann and O'Connell (1991); see also Chapter 1), we give only a brief heuristic description here. In this model, the portfolio preferences of investors determine the premium in the short term, given the existing stocks of domestic and illegal foreign assets (illegal foreign exchange holdings). The premium then feeds into the illegal current account balance by altering the costs and benefits of illegal trade. Since the illegal current account balance equals the change in the net stock of illegal foreign exchange holdings, this creates a new (momentary) portfolio disequilibrium that is cleared by a further change in the premium and the dynamic process continues.

Since the stock of illegal foreign exchange holdings is not directly observable, neither the portfolio equilibrium condition nor the illegal current account balance can be estimated directly. Instead, an equation for the black market premium can be derived by using the portfolio equilibrium condition to eliminate the stock of foreign exchange from the illegal current account equation. Assuming rational expectations, this yields an equation for the black market premium as a function of its own lagged value and expected future values of the other variables that determine portfolio equilibrium and the illegal current account balance.

The model suggests that the premium is an increasing function of both the real stock of domestic financial assets and the interest parity differential in favor of foreign assets, since an increase in either of these variables produces a desired portfolio shift towards illegal foreign currency holdings. A real appreciation of the exchange rate is expected to shift incentives towards import smuggling, increasing the premium. The model suggests that the portfolio determinants have no long-term influence on the premium if foreign assets do not bear interest. The following equation, which can be interpreted as the reduced-form solution of the model, is a typical estimated equation:

$$\text{PREM}_t = a_0 + a_1 \text{PREM}_{t-1} + a_2 d(M2)_t + a_3 d(IPD)_t + a_4 M2_{t-1}$$
$$+ a_5 IPD_{t-1} + a_6 RER_{t-1} + a_7 d(RER)_t$$

where PREM is the black market premium, $M2$ is the dollar value of domestic assets at the official rate, IPD is the uncovered interest parity differential using the official exchange rate (the foreign interest rate plus the expected rate of change of the official rate, minus the domestic interest rate), *RER* is the official real exchange rate (a domestic price index scaled by a trade weighted average of foreign price indices converted at the official exchange rate; an increase is an appreciation), and where the notation '*d*' indicates a first difference (for example, $dM2 = M2_t - M2_{t-1}$).

In applying this specification to the Turkish case, an adjustment must be made for the presence of foreign exchange deposit accounts as a third asset in the relevant periods. Accordingly, we include the stock of foreign exchange deposit accounts *(FX)* and the difference between the foreign deposit rate and the domestic foreign exchange deposit account rate *(DIFF)* in the equation in order to see if the opening of deposit accounts had a significant impact on activity in the black market. We also include the short-term deviations of these two variables, *dFX* and *dDIFF*.

An important consideration for the estimation is the possible correlation between the theoretical disturbance terms and some of the right-hand side variables, notably the real exchange rate and the interest parity deviation (the interest parity deviation uses the actual future depreciation of the official rate, introducing an errors in variables-type correlation between this proxy and the disturbance term, which by construction includes the *ex post* forecast error). We handle these issues using an instrumental variables estimation method. Instruments used include lagged values of the endogenous variables and of the terms of trade index, the reserves to GNP ratio, indicators of the political climate, and the official exchange rate. The terms of trade enter through several channels of influence, including resource movements between the export- and import-competing sectors and effects on aggregate demand. The reserve position of the Central Bank is incorporated because the importers who are licensed by the government but unable to buy the foreign currency from the Central Bank are likely to shift their demand to the black markets. The terms of trade index and the reserves to GNP ratio are therefore potential instruments for the current account transactions. Several political indicators, such as armed attacks against the government and demonstrations against the government are also incorporated. These are included to capture expectations concerning the possibility of a change in government and, hence, in government policy that might be relevant for exchange rates.

The Data

The data employed are monthly and cover the period from 1973 to 1988. The real exchange rate is defined as the Turkish consumer price index scaled by a trade-weighted wholesale price for the US and Germany, converted to TL using the official exchange rate. This measure appreciated at a trend rate of approximately 3 percent a year over the 1970s, with more explosive appreciation late in the decade barely offset by the maxi-devaluations of 1978 and 1979. The January 1980 devaluation erased the real appreciation of the 1970s on impact and the accompanying reform package initiated a period of real depreciation that lasted until the mid-1980s. A mild real appreciation occurred between 1985 and 1988. To measure the dollar value of domestic assets, we use the $M2$ measure of money (currency in circulation plus the sight deposits plus the time deposits of lira accounts only), converted to US dollars at the official exchange rate. In constructing the interest parity deviation (at the official rate), *IPD*, we use the 3 month London interbank (libor) rate on US dollars and the 3 month rate on TL deposits and as a proxy for expected depreciation of the official rate, we use the actual depreciation of the official exchange rate (Figure 9.2).

Variables capturing the political climate have been coded from the *New York Times*. These are dummy variables indicating the presence of armed attacks against the government and reports of deaths in demonstrations against the government.

Results

The results of our estimation for the entire period are presented in Table 9.1, column 1. These results basically confirm the earlier discussion that both current account and portfolio transactions have been important in determining the extent of premium. The level of the real exchange rate *(RER)* and its short-term deviation are both estimated statistically significantly and with the expected positive sign. The level of domestic assets ($M2$) is estimated statistically significantly, but the short-term effect is not. In contrast, the interest parity deviation has a statistically significant short-term effect, but not a significant long-term effect.

TABLE 9.1   *The black market premium*

	(1)	(2)	(3)
PREM (-1)	0.70	0.72	0.68
	(12.04)	(12.23)	(11.65)
dRER	0.57	0.45	0.48
	(2.58)	(2.36)	(2.25)
RER	0.009	0.005	0.007
	(3.32)	(2.30)	(2.20)
dM2	−0.30	−0.50	−0.40
	(−0.30)	(−0.28)	(−0.28)
dM2 × pre-1980		3.22	
		(2.34)	
dM2 × post-1983		−3.20	
		(−1.42)	
M2	1.52	1.25	1.13
	(2.63)	(2.56)	(2.38)
dIPD	0.51	0.49	0.42
	(3.25)	(3.19)	(2.64)
dIPD × pre-1980			0.35
			(2.22)
dIPD × post-1983			−0.16
			(−1.23)
IPD	−0.09	−0.11	−0.14
	(−0.90)	(−1.00)	(−1.10)
dFX	−3.45	−2.45	−2.65
	(−0.60)	(−0.45)	(−0.48)
FX	−1.82	−1.75	−1.63
	(−2.62)	(−1.98)	(−1.97)
dIDIF	0.15	0.53	0.41
	(0.05)	(0.47)	(0.10)
IDIF	0.24	0.12	0.14
	(0.23)	(0.45)	(0.10)
Constant	−5.03	−3.74	−4.63
	(−5.04)	(−2.68)	(−3.12)
Adjusted R^2	0.83	0.85	0.85

The dependent variable is the black market premium. All regressions are estimated by two-stage least squares. The number of observations is 175. The numbers in parentheses are *t*-values.

An interesting finding here concerns the impact of foreign exchange deposit accounts. The stock of foreign exchange deposits, *FX*, has a statistically significant negative effect on the premium. This finding might suggest that a significant substitution towards foreign exchange deposits has come from black markets. Other variables concerning the short-term effects of foreign exchange deposit accounts and the return differentials associated with these accounts, are not estimated statistically significantly.

We next investigate whether there is evidence of sample breaks in the impact of portfolio variables on the premium. In particular, we consider three subperiods: the pre-1980 period of a fixed exchange rate regime with capital controls, the 1980–3 period of a managed exchange rate regime with capital controls, and the post-1983 period with a managed exchange rate regime and less restrictive capital controls.

In column 2 results concerning the d$M2$ variable are presented. The effect of an increase in $M2$ on the premium is significantly stronger in the pre-1980 period than in the 1981–3 period. The impact in 1981–3, in turn, is stronger than in the post-1983 period, though the difference is not statistically significant. These results are interesting in suggesting that trading in the black market for portfolio purposes became less important during the period of financial deregulation, and even less so once capital market liberalization was under way.

In column 3 we allow for a sample break in the effect of the dIPD variable. The parameter estimates again suggest an interesting pattern over the three subperiods. The impact of this variable during the period up to 1980 is measured as 0.79 (the sum of the coefficients on dIPD (0.44) and dIPD interacted with the pre-1980 dummy variable (0.35)). The parameter estimate for the period of 1980–3 is 0.44 and the impact for the post-1983 period is 0.25. The impact appears to decline in two stages, first with the move in 1980 towards realistic official exchange rates and unification and then further with the creation of foreign exchange deposit accounts.

We considered several other specifications. There is no evidence of a sample break in the impact of the real exchange rate. We also considered sample breaks in the other long-term variables such as $M2$ and IPD, again finding no evidence of sample breaks. Finally, the lag structure of the variables does not appear to be driving the results, as adding an additional lag of the explanatory variables did not change the results.

Overall, our investigation of the black market spread suggests that both current account transactions and portfolio considerations have been important determinants of the spread through the entire period considered here. The short-term impact of the portfolio variables appears to be strongest in the pre-1980 period. The impact of these variables declines with the onset of unification and again with the opening of foreign exchange deposit accounts.

CONCLUDING REMARKS

This chapter has described the Turkish experience with black market exchange rates, from the significant policy distortions and high premia of the 1970s through the decade of liberalization and exchange rate unification in the 1980s. The unification of the 1980s was successful from the point of view of eliminating the black market for foreign currency. The black market has become a negligible part of the economy and the premium has disappeared. This was achieved by implementing a comprehensive mix of stabilization and liberalization policies: a major devaluation accompanied with elimination of official multiple rates, adoption of an active crawl that followed a path of steady real depreciation, export promotion, elimination of import restrictions, financial deregulation, and capital account liberalization.

A major devaluation and adoption of a crawling peg were undoubtedly keys to successful unification. In particular, since fiscal deficits and inflation continue to be problems for the Turkish economy, unifying to a fixed exchange rate could eventually have produced a failure of the system. In fact, our statistical investigation of the determinants of the black market premium identifies the official real exchange rate as an important determinant of premium over the entire period. Moreover, the importance of this variable during the periods prior to or post-1980 is approximately the same.

The evidence also suggests the significance of capital account liberalization in unification. It is after the onset of capital account liberalization by the creation of foreign exchange deposit accounts that the level of black market activity and the premium became more or less negligible. Our empirical results suggest that the demand for black market currency as an asset became less important in explaining the premium over time. In particular, portfolio factors were most important in the period prior to 1980. In contrast, portfolio factors became less important in influencing the premium during the 1980–3 period of financial deregulation and finally declined further in the aftermath of capital account liberalization.

The periods of relatively high premium through the decade of unification raise several caveats. The first concerns the trade regime. During 1980–3, the trade regime included both import restrictions and substantial export subsidies. There was significant overinvoicing of exports and smuggling of imports through the period, both of which resulted in continued activity in the black market, slowing down unification.

The second qualification concerns domestic financial policies. The Turkish deregulation of the early 1980s contributed to a declining demand for foreign currency in the black market, but the financial crisis in 1982 led to increased activity in the black market. Later in the decade, uncertain and *ad hoc* policy experiments in regulating the foreign exchange holdings of commercial banks resulted in major purchasing activity in the black market by commercial banks attempting to meet Central Bank demands or to speculate against the TL.

The broader macroeconomic implications of the exchange rate regime and capital account policies pursued in the 1980s are less clear. Economic performance was good on many fronts in the 1980s and particularly so as measured by increased export volumes and higher growth. High fiscal deficits and high inflation, however, remained as problems through most of the period. Cursory evidence suggests that continual real depreciation may have contributed to higher inflation by worsening the fiscal balances. Furthermore, it has been suggested that capital account liberalization may have contributed to ongoing currency substitution, decreasing the demand for the domestic monetary base. Our empirical results suggest that the onset of capital account liberalization with the opening of foreign account deposits led to a decrease in the black market premium, indicating the presence of substitution from black market holdings into foreign exchange deposit accounts. But this is not inconsistent with substitution away from domestic money as well, an issue that invites more thorough investigation.

NOTES

1. I am grateful to Stephen O'Connell for many helpful comments and to Hasan Ersel for his invaluable help in enabling me to have access to data from the Central Bank of the Republic of Turkey.
2. Import licensing policies and other quantitative restrictions on imports were in place and implied high rates of effective protection. Protection was biased against consumer durables, with a wide variation of effective rates of protection across sectors.
3. *Pick's Currency Yearbook* (1957) notes that during a period of martial law in Istanbul, black market transactions carried penalties of death or jail.
4. The data concerning these phases of the economy are largely from Celasun and Rodrik (1989) and Özler (1989).

5. The oil shock of 1973–4 had severe consequences for the Turkish economy. Initially the current account deficit deteriorated more severely than the average for developing countries. Moreover, after 1975, as oil-importing countries managed to reduce their deficits on average, the Turkish current account deficit continued to grow.

6. If alternatively expected depreciation of the lira is assumed to be equal to the actual rate of depreciation during the following year, implicit subsidy payments amounted to 0.5, 1.1, and 1.7 percent of GNP during the years 1975–7, respectively (Celasun and Rodrik, 1989).

7. The cost of funds to the borrowers included a spread over the relevant base Euromarket interest rate, a front-end fee to the lender, and a margin to the local intermediary. Interest spreads offered on these deposits were set by the Turkish government, at a maximum of 1.5 percent for deposits with maturity of up to a year and 2.25 percent for maturities of more than 5 years. Front-end fees paid were approximately 4 percent.

8. Several factors contributed to the realization of this break. First, the military rule of September 1980–November 1983 retained the primary technocrat, Korkut Ozal, behind the January economic package. Second, major debt relief, balance of payments assistance, and policy support were made available by the major bilateral creditors and multilateral lending institutions. Finally, the Iran–Iraq war in the Middle East generated special trading opportunities.

9. See Krueger and Aktan (1992) for an overview of reforms in the trade and payments regime.

10. More depreciated rates resulted from the arrangement for retention and transfer of specified portions of the foreign exchange obtained from exports of mining products and manufacturers, fresh vegetables, fruits, and Turkish contractors working abroad.

11. The lira (TL) dollar rate and the devaluation dates are as follows: 25 January 1980 70 TL per $, 2 April 1980 73.7, 9 June 1980 78, 4 August 1980 80, 12 October 1980 82, 25 October 1980 82.7, 8 November 1980 84.8, 10 December 1980 89.25, 27 January 1981 91.9, 5 February 1981 95.95, 22 March 1981 95.65, and 15 April 1981 98.2.

12. As of January 1984 the commercial banks were free to establish their exchange rate within a band of ±6 percent around the central rate established by the Central Bank. The spread between the buying and selling rates of a commercial bank could not exceed 2 percent. For its own transactions with commercial banks and with the non-bank sector, the Central Bank set up daily buying and selling rates which fell within the spread established by the leading banks.

13. In August 1989 the 50 000 US$ limit was changed to a 10 000 US$ limit.

14. See Baysan and Blitzer (1990).

15. There are two types of foreign exchange account in Turkey: Dresdner accounts (introduced in 1978) and foreign exchange accounts at Turkish commercial banks (introduced in 1983). Dresdner accounts can only be held by non-resident nationals and operate under the coordination of the Turkish Central Bank and Dresdner Bank. Foreign exchange accounts held with commercial banks can be opened by both residents and non-residents.

16.	During the 6 month transition period, Turkish residents were allowed to export capital in amounts up to $2 million with the permission of the office of the Under-secretary for the Treasury and Foreign Trade. For investment exceeding this amount, the approval of the Council of Ministers was required.

17.	See Atiyas (1990) for a study of the private sector response to financial liberalization in Turkey.

18.	In addition, the major policy reforms for the financial sector included the establishment of the Capital Market Board in 1981, the introduction of a new framework for the stock exchange in 1983, legislation of a new banking law and regulatory system in 1983–5, and the creation of an interbank money market in 1986.

19.	See Akyuz (1990).

20.	On average, the actual level of Turkish exports to the OECD was overstated by approximately 13 percent between 1981 and 1985. However, overinvoicing of exports appears to have diminished over time as the export subsidies declined (Celasun and Rodrik, 1989).

21.	The jumps in the inflation rate during 1984 and 1987 correspond to increases in the fiscal deficit. The fiscal deficit to GDP ratios for 1980 through to 1989 are 4, 1.7, 2.3, 3, 5.3, 2.8, 3.6, 4.5, 3.4, and 2.6.

22.	See Akyuz (1990).

23.	See Rodrik (1990b). He suggested that the entire increase in the inflation rate by approximately 32 percentage points between 1983 and 1988 can be explained by the erosion of the money base, as the fiscal deficit in 1988 was nearly the same as that of 1983.

24.	In a related study, Olgun (1984) estimated a system of equations in which the explained variables are the domestic price level, the black market exchange rate, real income, and the real money stock. Explanatory variables are foreign prices, the official exchange rate, capacity output, and expected inflation. Using data for the 1963–81 period, Olgun (1984) found that the official exchange rate affects the black market rate positively and significantly, but that the ratio of domestic prices to foreign prices and the expected rate of inflation do not affect the black market rate significantly.

REFERENCES

Akyuz, Yilmaz (1990) 'Financial Systems and Policies in Turkey in the 1980s', in T. Aricanli and D. Rodrik (eds), *The Political Economy of Turkey* (New York: St Martin's Press), pp. 98–131.

Atiyas, Izak (1990) 'The Private Sector's Response to Financial Liberalization in Turkey: 1980–82', in T. Aricanli and D. Rodrik (eds), *The Political Economy of Turkey* (New York: St Martin's Press), pp. 132–56.

Baysan, Tercan and Charles Blitzer (1990) 'Turkey's Trade Liberalization in the 1980s and Prospects for Sustainability', in T. Aricanli and D. Rodrik (eds), *The Political Economy of Turkey* (New York: St Martin's Press), pp. 9–36.

Celasun, Merih and Dani Rodrik (1989) 'Debt, Adjustment and Growth', in Jeffrey D. Sachs and Susan M. Collins, (eds), *Developing Country Debt and Economic Performance*, Volume 3 (Chicago: University of Chicago Press for the NBER), pp. 615–808.

Dornbusch, Rudiger, Daniel V. Dantas, Clarice Pechman, Roberto Rocha, and Demetri Simoes (1983) 'The Black Market for Dollars in Brazil', *Quarterly Journal of Economics*, vol. 98, pp. 25–40.

International Currency Analysis, Inc. (various years) *World Currency Year-book* (Brooklyn, NY: International Currency Analysis, Inc.). (Formerly *Pick's Currency Yearbook*; continued as monthly *Currency Alert*.)

Kaufmann, Daniel and Stephen A. O'Connell (1991) 'The Macroeconomics of the Unofficial Foreign Exchange Market in Tanzania', in Ajay Chhibber and Stanley Fischer (eds), *Economic Reform in Sub-Saharan Africa* (Washington, DC: World Bank), pp. 50–65.

Krueger, Anne O. and Okan H. Aktan (1992) *Swimming Against the Tide* (San Francisco: International Center for Economic Growth).

Olgun, Hasan (1984) 'An Analysis of the Black Market Exchange Rate in a Developing Economy: the Case of Turkey', *Weltwirtschaftliches Archiv* vol. 120, pp. 324–47.

Özler, Sule (1989) 'Sources of Debt Rescheduling: Turkey in the 1970s', *UCLA Journal of Middle Eastern Studies*, pp. 45–55.

Rodrik, Dani (1990a) 'Some Policy Dilemmas in Turkish Macroeconomic Management', in T. Aricanli and D. Rodrik (eds), *The Political Economy of Turkey* (New York: St Martin's Press), pp. 183–98.

Rodrik, Dani (1990b) 'Premature Liberalization, Incomplete Stabilization: the Ozal Decade in Turkey', *Discussion Paper Series* No. 402 (London: Centre for Economic Policy Research).

10 European Dual Exchange Rates

Nancy P. Marion[1]

INTRODUCTION

In the early 1970s, many European countries faced a difficult predicament. Uniform fixed exchange rates allowed speculative capital movements to deliver large international reserve fluctuations, yet abandoning fixed exchange rates in favor of flexible rates could possibly deliver large exchange rate fluctuations that would disrupt trade. Between 1971 and 1974, several European countries, such as Belgium, France, and Italy, used a dual exchange market as a temporary middle-ground between the fixed and flexible rate extremes. Such an arrangement involved the formal establishment of separate exchange markets, with separate exchange rates, for current and capital account transactions.

The European experience has inspired a large theoretical literature.[2] Nevertheless, there has been no attempt to assemble a set of empirical regularities from the European data. The purpose of this paper is to uncover some important empirical features of the European dual exchange markets. This task is of more than historical interest. An understanding of the European experience may contribute to our understanding of the more recent experiences with dual exchange markets in many developing countries.

The paper is divided into five sections. The following section sets out a theoretical framework that describes the distortion created by dual exchange rates and examines the magnitude of this distortion in several European countries. The third section identifies some of the economic factors that influence the distortion and looks at the empirical evidence. The fourth section examines whether the dual exchange market provides insulation of domestic interest rates from foreign interest rate disturbances and insulation of international reserves from speculative activity. The last section contains some final thoughts.

359

A THEORETICAL FRAMEWORK

The defining feature of a dual exchange market is that current and capital account transactions are channeled into separate exchange markets – a commercial exchange market for current account transactions and a financial exchange market for capital account transactions. Foreign exchange may stand at a premium or a discount in the financial exchange market as compared with its price in the commercial exchange market (Fleming, 1971; Lanyi, 1975). The exchange rate for current account transactions is generally pegged by the authorities, while the rate for capital account transactions is free to fluctuate.

The Distortion Created by Dual Rates

The classic dual rate system introduces a distortion into asset portfolios. The distortion is created by the spread between the two exchange rates and its evolution over time.

To illustrate, consider the case where a resident of a country that operates a dual exchange market wishes to hold a foreign currency-denominated asset for one period. The resident must purchase capital account-eligible foreign exchange at the financial exchange rate, the applicable rate for financial transactions. In the next period, the resident repatriates the principal at next period's financial exchange rate and repatriates the interest income at next period's commercial exchange rate, the rate applicable for current account transactions. Letting S and X be the home country prices of foreign currency in the commercial and financial markets, respectively, this period's expected nominal return from holding the foreign currency-denominated security for one period, N, is therefore

$$(1) \qquad N = (\frac{i_t^*}{z_t})(1 + \delta_t) + (1 + f_t),$$

where i_t^* is the interest rate on the foreign currency-denominated asset, z_t is the spread between the two exchange rates ($z_t = X_t/S_t$), δ_t is the expected rate of depreciation of the commercial rate, and f_t is the expected rate of depreciation of the financial rate.

The expected nominal return to a foreign agent from holding a foreign currency-denominated asset for one period is merely $N^* = (1 + i_t^*)$. Consequently (one plus) the wedge created by dual exchange rates is equal to the return received by the home resident relative to the return received by the foreign agent or

$$(2) \qquad \frac{N}{N^*} = 1 + \text{wedge} = [1 + (\frac{i_t^*}{z_t})]\frac{1 + \delta_t}{1 + i_t^*} + \frac{f_t - \delta_t}{1 + i_t^*}.$$

Equation (2) shows that the dual exchange market distorts the effective rate of return and thereby influences international capital flows by means of the spread and the expected rates of change of the financial and current account exchange rates. The first term on the right-hand side of equation (2) represents the distortion that arises when there is a difference between the financial and commercial rates at a point in time. It is the static effect of the dual exchange market. The second term represents the distortion that arises when there is a difference between the rates of depreciation of the financial and commercial rates. It is the dynamic effect. The dual exchange market may provide insulation from foreign interest rate shocks if such shocks generate offsetting movements in the spread or offsetting movements in the expected rates of exchange rate change.

While theoretical work on dual exchange markets often assumes a complete segmentation of the two exchange markets, in practice this is not possible (Bhandari and Decaluwe, 1987; Gros, 1988). When the spread widens, agents have an increased incentive to channel transactions through the market with the more attractive rate. The authorities have sometimes tried to discourage fraudulent leakages across markets by reclassifying transactions in such a way as to narrow the spread. Moreover, current account transactions that are difficult to monitor, such as tourist expenditures and remittances, are often assigned to the financial exchange market from the start. These cross-market leakages change the nature of the distortion facing asset holders because only a fraction of foreign assets is purchased or repatriated at the financial rate and only a fraction of interest income is repatriated at the commercial rate. The distortion in asset portfolios still depends on the spread and rates of exchange rate change, but in a much more complicated way. Cross-market leakages also distort relative prices of goods and services.

The nature of the distortion is also altered by the perceived temporariness of the dual exchange market. The domestic rate of return described in equation (1) was derived assuming that the dual exchange market would be in place when repatriation occurs. If, instead, the investor believes the dual market is temporary, then the calculation of the return must take into account not only the possible exchange rate regimes to follow, but the probability of each being in effect at the time of repatriation. Clearly, the perceived temporariness of the dual exchange market combined with uncertainty about the regime to follow can alter the nature of the distortion, particularly as the date of reunification approaches and probability estimates are revised (Flood and Marion, 1982a).

A Look at the Data on Spreads

Among the European countries, Belgium (actually the Belgium–Luxembourg Economic Union, or BLEU), France, and Italy were the major European countries that used dual exchange markets in the early 1970s, although Belgium adopted its system in 1957 and kept it in place until 1990. The UK and the Netherlands used a second exchange rate for a small group of capital account transactions, as

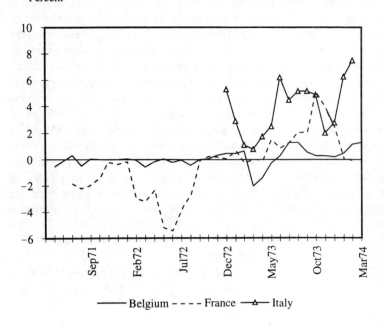

FIGURE 10.1 *European spreads percentage*
SOURCE: Country case study.

did France both before adopting its fully-fledged dual rate system and again in the 1980s. Due to limited availability of financial exchange rate data for some countries or time periods, we limit our investigation to the dual exchange market in Belgium between 1963 and 1988, in France between 1971 and 1974, and in Italy between 1973 and 1974.[3]

The spread between the commercial and financial exchange rates represents the observable part of the distortion created by the dual exchange market. Some sense of the magnitude of the distortion is revealed by the data on spreads for these three countries. Figure 10.1 illustrates monthly movements in the spreads in Belgium, France, and Italy during the early 1970s. Table 10.1 summarizes key statistics on the spreads.

Figure 10.1 reveals that the spreads between the commercial and financial exchange rates were quite small for the three European countries, generally under 4 percent. This is in sharp contrast to the experience of many developing countries where black market premiums are often over 100 percent. The Belgian spread was generally 1 percent or less. In March 1973, a spread of −2.05 percent emerged but lasted less than 1 month. Over the period May 1971 to March 1974, the mean spread was 0.04 percent, with a standard deviation of 0.67 percent. In France, the mean spread over the duration of the dual exchange market was −0.46 percent, with a standard deviation of 2.35 percent. Italy experienced somewhat larger spreads, on average, than its two European neighbors; spreads between 4 and 7 percent

TABLE 10.1   *Spreads (%)**

	Belgium[†]	*France*[‡]	*Italy*[§]
Mean	0.04	−0.46	3.90
Maximum	1.27	5.03	7.48
Minimum	−2.05	−5.54	0.76
Standard deviation	0.67	2.35	2.08

*   The spread is defined as $[(X - S)/S] \times 100$, where X is the financial exchange rate and S is the commercial exchange rate. Rates are expressed as domestic currency per US\$. Calculations are based on monthly data and are period averages for Belgium and Italy and end of period observations for France.

†   For the period May 1971–March 1974. Source: IMF *International Financial Statistics*.

‡   For the period August 1971–March 1974. Source: Central Bank of France.

§   For the period January 1973–March 1974. Source: Central Bank of Italy.

Percent

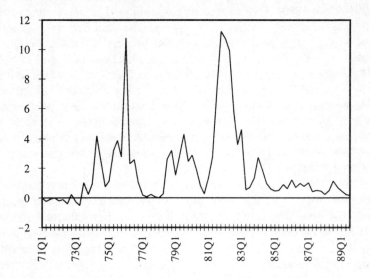

FIGURE 10.2   *Quarterly spread of the period average data (Belgium)*
SOURCE: Country case study.

prevailed during 8 of the 15 months in which the Italian system operated. The mean spread was consequently a bit higher, at 3.9 percent, with a standard deviation of 2.08 percent. In all three countries, spreads in excess of 5 percent never persisted for more than 2 consecutive months in the early 1970s.

Figure 10.2, which shows the Belgian spread during a 20 year period, reveals that the early period was not an aberration. Over the last two decades of Belgium's dual exchange market, the mean spread was 1.8 percent, with a standard deviation of 2.6 percent. The only big jumps in the spread occurred in the first quarter of 1976, when the spread exceeded 10 percent and between the third quarter of 1981 and the second quarter of 1982, when spreads of 6–11 percent emerged.

DETERMINANTS OF THE SPREAD

A model is used to identify key determinants of the spread and to derive a reduced-form equation for the spread. The equation is estimated using European data to see whether the predictions of the model are sensible.

The Theory

The simplest model for highlighting determinants of the spread between dual exchange rates is a stock-flow model that assumes a fixed or crawling commercial rate, a flexible financial exchange rate, domestic money and foreign bonds, purchasing power parity, and perfect foresight.[4] All commercial transactions are conducted at the commercial exchange rate and all financial transactions at the financial exchange rate. Complications arising from leakages are discussed later.

In the asset markets, the desired ratio of domestic money to foreign interest-bearing assets, M/XF, depends on the rate of return on foreign assets:

$$(3) \qquad \frac{M}{XF} = L\left[\left(\frac{i^*}{z}\right)(1 + \delta) + f\right], \quad L' < 0.$$

Domestic money earns no return. The return on foreign assets is calculated under the assumption that interest income, a current account transaction, is repatriated at the commercial exchange rate. The stock of foreign assets is denoted by F and the value of foreign assets in domestic currency by XF.

The rate of change of the spread, $\dot{z}/z$, is equal to the difference between the rate of depreciation of the financial exchange rate and the rate of crawl (managed depreciation) of the commercial exchange rate:

$$(4) \qquad \frac{\dot{z}}{z} = f - \delta.$$

Substituting equation (4) into equation (3) and inverting gives the evolution of the spread over time:

$$(5) \qquad \frac{\dot{z}}{z} = h\left(\frac{m}{zF}\right) - \left(\frac{i^*}{z}\right)(1 + \delta) - \delta, \quad h = L^{-1}, \quad h' < 0,$$

where $m = M/S$ and $z = X/S$. Equation (5) is the first dynamic equation of the model.

The other dynamic equation comes from equating expected real asset accumulation to planned real saving:

(6) $\dot{m} + \left[h\left(\dfrac{m}{zF}\right) - \left(\dfrac{i^*}{z}\right)(1 + \delta) - \delta \right] zF = s(y, m + zF), \quad s_1 > 0, s_2 < 0.$

Households may increase their domestic currency wealth in several ways. They can add to their money holdings as the economy acquires reserves through current account surpluses or as the government undertakes domestic credit creation to finance budget deficits. They can also experience capital gains on their foreign asset holdings as a result of a depreciation of the financial exchange rate. They cannot increase their holdings of foreign assets, however. The flexible financial exchange rate prevents net capital flows through the capital account exchange market. Households cannot acquire foreign assets through the current account exchange market either since proceeds from commercial transactions must be exchanged at the commercial exchange rate for domestic assets.

Assuming purchasing power parity and a fixed foreign price level normalized to one, the domestic price deflator is $P = S$. Then using equations (4) and (5) and setting $\dot{F}/F = 0$ and $\dot{m} = \mathrm{d}(M/S)/\mathrm{d}t$, expected real asset accumulation is

$$\frac{\mathrm{d}[(M + XF)/P]}{\mathrm{d}t} = \dot{m} + (f - \delta)zF = \dot{m} + \left[h\left(\frac{m}{zF}\right) - \left(\frac{i^*}{z}\right)(1 + \delta) - \delta \right] zF,$$

which is the left-hand side of equation (6).

The right-hand side of equation (6) specifies saving behavior. Planned real saving is assumed to depend positively on real income, y and negatively on real wealth, $m + zF$. Using the national income identity and ignoring investment spending, saving represents the sum of the current account surplus and the government budget deficit, all in real terms. Equation (6) describes the evolution of real wealth over time.

The steady state is attained when $\dot{z} = \dot{m} = 0$. In the steady state, the spread is constant. The financial and commercial exchange rates depreciate at the same rate. The real money stock is also constant. The growth of the nominal money stock is offset by the depreciation of the commercial exchange rate. The current account is balanced and the government deficit is financed by credit creation, with the depreciation of the commercial exchange rate generating an inflation tax on money balances.

Combining equations (5) and (6) and assuming convergence to the steady state, a reduced-form equation for the spread, z, depends on the foreign interest rate, the rate of depreciation of the commercial exchange rate, real income, and the initial stock of foreign assets at the onset of the dual exchange market:

(7)
$$z = z(i^*, \delta, y, F).$$
$$+ + +$$

An increase in the foreign interest rate or the rate of depreciation of the commercial exchange rate shifts asset holders from money to foreign assets. Given the fixed supply of foreign assets, the spread must widen to restore portfolio balance. An increase in income will stimulate saving, generating current account surpluses that cause the real money stock to rise as the central bank intervenes in the commercial exchange market. The spread will rise as asset holders attempt to shift some of their new wealth into foreign assets.

An increase in the government budget deficit also widens the spread. With money demand inelastic with respect to inflation, an increase in the deficit financed by credit creation requires an increase in the rate of depreciation of the commercial rate to raise the needed inflation tax revenue. A faster depreciation of the commercial rate in turn widens the spread.

A shift in expectations also has an impact on the spread. For example, if agents believe that the government will increase the budget deficit and the rate of depreciation of the commercial exchange rate at some time in the future, they will now attempt a portfolio shift from money to foreign assets, which will lead to a jump in the spread. Thus, as described by Dornbusch (1986), changing expectations about the future course of fiscal policy can generate large fluctuations in the spread. In addition, a shift in expectations about future income affects the spread since saving depends on some notion of expected permanent income.

Empirical Estimation of the Spread

Equation (7) guides the choice of economic variables in the regression analysis of the determinants of the spread in the European dual exchange markets. The European spreads are estimated with quarterly data using the following initial specification:

(8)
$$\log z_t = \beta_0 + \beta_1 \log z_{t-1} + \beta_2(i_t^*) + \beta_3(L)(\log y_t - \log y_{t-1})$$
$$+ \beta_4(L)(\log S_{t+1} - \log S_t) + \varepsilon_t,$$

where $\beta(L)$ is a polynomial in the lead/lag operator L, $\log z_t$ is the log of the spread in time t, i^* is the nominal foreign interest rate in percentage terms, $(\log y_t - \log y_{t-1})$ is the growth of real income, and $(\log S_{t+1} - \log S_t)$ is the actual rate of depreciation of the commercial exchange rate, which is equal to the expected rate of depreciation plus a random component under rational expectations.

Although the spread is a real variable, its variance is dominated by the variance of the financial exchange rate because the commercial rate is generally fixed. Economists have had no success in explaining the variance of a flexible exchange rate solely in terms of fundamentals, so there is no reason to expect considerably more success in explaining the variance of the spread on the basis of fundamentals alone. Hence the lagged spread is included on the right-hand side as well. Dickey–Fuller tests confirm that the European spreads are stationary, so the regression is run using the log-level spread rather than its rate of change. The right-hand side variables are also constructed to be stationary processes.[5]

Recognizing that the expected rate of depreciation of the commercial exchange rate may in fact deviate from its actual rate of depreciation, some other specifications for expectations are also considered. Expectations may be influenced by factors such as movements in international reserves, the evolution of the real commercial exchange rate, and the size of the real budget deficit. A faster rate of reserve depletion brought about by increasing current account deficits may signal that the authorities are under pressure to increase the rate of depreciation of the commercial exchange rate. An increasing appreciation of the real commercial exchange rate that worsens the current account balance may also indicate the need to increase the rate of depreciation of the nominal commercial exchange rate. Finally, an increase in the real budget deficit may signal an eventual increase in the rate of depreciation of the commercial exchange rate to raise seigniorage revenue. Thus a modified version of equation (8) substitutes the terms $(\log R_t - \log R_{t-1})$, $(\log r_t - \log r_{t-1})$ and def_t for the term $(\log S_{t+1} - \log S_t)$, where R is the foreign currency value of international reserves, r is the real commercial exchange rate, and def is the real budget deficit.[6]

In the regressions, the spread is calculated using end of quarter observations for the financial and commercial exchange rates. Foreign variables are proxied by US data. The 3 month US Treasury Bill rate is used for the foreign interest rate. Quarterly data on the gross national product (GNP) are unavailable, so an index of industrial production is used for the income measure. Data on the net stock of foreign assets are also unavailable, but since the net stock does not change during the operation of dual exchange markets, F can be subsumed in the constant term. The stock of non-gold international reserves is chosen as the reserves variable. The real commercial exchange rate is measured by the consumer price-adjusted bilateral exchange rate with the US. The real budget deficit is calculated by deflating the nominal budget deficit (in billions of national currency units) by the domestic consumer price index.

The set of regressions based on equation (8) is reported in Table 10.2. Because the French and Italian dual exchange market episodes are too short for estimation procedures, their data are pooled with the Belgian data. Belgium had a long continuous experience with dual

TABLE 10.2 *Dependent variable: (log) spread; quarterly data*

Sample size	(1) Europe 103	(2) Belgium 94	(3) Belgium 94
Constant	−0.008*	−0.008	−0.003
	(−1.65)	(−1.56)	(−0.72)
$logz_{t-1}$	0.512**	0.55**	0.58**
	(6.26)	(6.88)	(8.02)
i^*	0.009**	0.008**	0.005*
	(3.20)	(2.83)	(1.82)
$\log y_t - \log y_{t-1}$	0.12	0.13*	0.006
	(1.64)	(1.78)	(0.09)
$\log y_{t+1} - \log y_t$	0.14**	0.16**	0.11*
	(1.99)	(2.28)	(1.67)
$logS_{t+1} - logS_t$	0.03	0.04	−
	(0.96)	(1.12)	
$logS_{t+2} - logS_{t+1}$	0.05	0.07**	−
	(1.51)	(2.05)	
$logR_t - logR_{t-1}$	−	−	−0.06**
			(−5.03)
$logr_t - logr_{t-1}$	−	−	−0.02
			(−0.79)
Real budget deficit	−	−	0.0036*
			(1.71)
Adjusted R^2	0.57	0.56	0.63

t-statistics are in parentheses.
** indicates significance at the 95 percent significance level,* indicates significance at the 90 percent significance level. Regression (1) uses pooled data for Belgium, France, and Italy and regressions (2) and (3) use data for Belgium.

exchange markets, so separate regressions of the Belgium spread are
also reported.

The first regression reported in Table 10.2 uses pooled Belgian,
French, and Italian data. The results show that all the explanatory
variables affect the spread in ways consistent with the stock-flow
model and that some are significant at the 95 percent confidence
interval. An increase in the foreign interest rate has a positive and
highly significant effect on the spread, as does an expected increase in
income growth. An expected increase in the rate of depreciation of the
commercial exchange rate also widens the spread, but the effect is not
significant. Together with the lagged spread, these variables explain 57
percent of the variation in the European spreads.[7]

The results are quite similar for the same regression run on Belgian
data alone, although the expected rate of depreciation of the commercial exchange rate is now highly significant as well. The strong correlation between the expected increase in the rate of depreciation and
the spread helps explain the behavior of the Belgian spread in the first
quarter of 1976 and from the third quarter of 1981 to the second
quarter of 1982 (Figure 10.2). The dramatic widening of the Belgian
spread in the first quarter of 1976 corresponded to speculative pressures against the French franc that spilled over to the Belgian commercial franc when the French franc departed from the snake and the
Belgian current account shifted into deficit that quarter.[8] The wider
spread during the period from the third quarter of 1981 to the second
quarter of 1982 (7–11 percent range) reflected speculative activity
surrounding three devaluations of the Belgian commercial franc
against the Deutschmark that occurred within the European Monetary System in the fourth quarter of 1981 and the first and second
quarters of 1982.

The third regression in Table 10.2 uses the real budget deficit and
the rates of change in both international reserves and the real commercial exchange rate to capture expectations about future movements in the nominal commercial exchange rate. Because the
European and Belgian regression results are nearly identical, only the
Belgian regression is reported.

The regression for Belgium shows that the variables proxying for
expectations have sensible and important effects on the Belgian
spread. An increase in the real budget deficit widens the spread as
does a more rapid rate of reserve depletion. The coefficient is significant at the 90 percent confidence level on the deficit variable and at
the 95 percent level on the reserve variable. A faster real appreciation

of the commercial exchange rate has no significant effect on the spread, however. Using a different real exchange rate specification, such as the bilateral rate with Germany, did not change the insignificance of the real commercial exchange rate variable. Expected future income growth and current increases in the foreign interest rate have positive and significant effects on the Belgian spread, as in the earlier regressions.

Although the coefficient on the real deficit variable is positive, it is significant at the 90 rather than the 95 percent level. One possible reason may be that, in practice, an increase in the budget deficit has opposing effects on the spread. As described by the theoretical model, a budget deficit financed by credit creation ultimately requires a more rapid depreciation of the commercial exchange rate, which raises the return on foreign assets, triggers an attempted portfolio shift, and widens the spread. However, an increase in the deficit may also be financed by domestic bond sales. In that case, although the accumulation of domestic bonds tends to widen the spread as agents try to diversify their new wealth, higher domestic interest rates tend to narrow the spread as agents try to shift into the higher-yielding domestic assets. The positive coefficient on the deficit term suggests that the wealth effects may dominate the interest rate effect, but not by much. Additional regressions were run using both the foreign and domestic interest rates or the interest differential as right-hand side variables. The results must be treated cautiously because the domestic interest rate is not really an exogenous variable. Nevertheless, it is interesting to note that, controlling for domestic interest rates, an increase in the real budget deficit has a highly significant positive effect on the spread.[9]

Drawbacks in Empirical Estimation

Some important caveats about the empirical tests are in order. The spread has been analyzed on the assumption that there is a structural relationship between the spread and its determinants. However, because the dual exchange market is generally a temporary arrangement and because institutional practices vary during its operation, this assumption may not be appropriate.

Consider first the issue of temporariness. While Belgium operated a dual exchange market for more than 30 years, France used the arrangement for only 31 months and Italy for 15 months. When private agents believe the dual exchange market is temporary, the spread will be influenced by probability-weighted beliefs of the possible regimes to follow. These beliefs build into the data elements that are difficult to model in empirical work and contaminate the link between the spread and its determinants, particularly around the time of reunification.

Changes in institutional practices during the operation of a dual exchange market also affect the structural stability of the regression equation. Determinants of the spread can differ in their importance across time as institutional practices change. There are numerous examples of these institutional changes. For purposes of illustration, consider three categories of institutional practices: market access, market segmentation, and intervention to support the commercial exchange rate.

In all three European countries, transactors were allowed free access to the appropriate exchange market. This was particularly true in Belgium, where current and capital account transactions were substantially free from restrictions. In France and Italy, the introduction of a dual exchange market was not accompanied by the lifting of certain capital account restrictions, so access was not completely free. For instance, the French authorities continued to place restrictions on banking operations, borrowing abroad, and direct and portfolio investment.[10] In the Italian case, certain controls such as the 50 percent deposit on capital exports (established in July 1973) pushed some transactions to a black market for bank notes, where the black rate for dollars was even higher than the financial rate.

Regarding market segmentation, current account transactions were broadly channeled through the commercial exchange market and capital account transactions through the financial exchange market in all three European countries. Nevertheless, the separation of the two markets was not complete, because of both officially sanctioned and illegal leakages across markets.[11]

For example, in some cases the authorities allowed a few transactions to go through either market at the agent's discretion. If speculative capital outflows led to a premium in foreign financial exchange, then some transactors wanting to sell foreign exchange for home currency could switch to the financial exchange market while other transactors who wanted to buy foreign exchange could switch to the commercial exchange market. The discretion to switch markets moderated the spread. Incomplete separation of current account and capital account transactions was also permitted because, in practice, it proved difficult to monitor certain transactions, particularly those related to tourism, remittances, and profits from foreign investments. Thus the authorities sometimes required specific current account transactions to be carried out in the financial market or capital transactions in the commercial market. In addition, the authorities sometimes reclassified certain transactions with the intent of dampening a growing spread. For example, if financial foreign exchange began to sell at a larger premium, the authorities occasionally shifted some commercial transactions in surplus at the commercial rate to the financial market. It was hoped that the net sales of foreign exchange induced by the reclassification would moderate the premium and lessen speculative activities against the commercial exchange rate.[12]

In addition to officially sanctioned arbitrage between the two exchange markets, it was widely conjectured by central bank authorities that illegal private arbitrage activities occurred, becoming more prevalent the bigger the spread and the longer that spread persisted. Lanyi (1975) provides a detailed description of how such illegal transactions can take place. As an illustration, consider the case where financial foreign exchange goes to a premium. Individuals have a bigger incentive to try to obtain foreign exchange for asset trades by going through the commercial exchange market. They can do this by falsely invoicing exports and imports. The demand for foreign exchange to finance asset purchases can be disguised by overinvoicing imports or by underinvoicing exports. In fact, Gros (1988), Bhandari and Decaluwe (1987), and others have appealed to fraudulent leakages as a rationale for the subsequent reduction of a large spread created by a one-time shock to the economy. A careful look at cross-country trade data along the lines of Bhagwati (1964) is still needed to reveal the extent of false invoicing under the European dual exchange market.

During periods of heightened speculative activity, not only did officially sanctioned and fraudulent leakages occur, but the authorities sometimes relieved pressure on official reserves by allowing the commercial exchange rate to float in its separate market. For instance, before August, 1971, the Belgian commercial franc was pegged to the dollar within a narrow band, but between August and December of 1971, the Belgian commercial franc floated against all currencies except the Dutch guilder. With the Smithsonian Agreement at the end of 1971, the commercial franc rate was again confined to specific margins for the dollar. During the rest of the 1970s and the 1980s, the authorities maintained a peg for the commercial franc, but not always to the dollar.[13] Under the French dual exchange market, the authorities initially pegged the commercial rate to the dollar and then to a group of European currencies (the snake). The commercial franc dropped out of the European snake in January 1974 and the commercial franc floated from that point until March 1974, when the dual exchange market was abolished. Under the Italian system, the authorities initially pegged the commercial lira to the snake currencies, but abandoned the peg on 13 February 1973, just weeks after the dual exchange market was established. The commercial and financial lira then floated in separate markets until the regime was abolished in March 1974.[14]

MOTIVES FOR ADOPTING DUAL EXCHANGE MARKETS IN EUROPE

Insulation of Domestic Interest Rates

Because the dual exchange market drives a wedge between the domestic and foreign interest rates, it is thought that it preserves a measure of monetary autonomy without resorting to discretionary restrictions on capital transactions. An increase in the foreign interest rate that induces a reallocation of portfolios towards foreign securities may alter the level and evolution of the spread so as to limit the response of domestic interest rates.

Actually, no empirical work has been conducted on how well the dual exchange market insulated European interest rates from foreign interest rate disturbances. One simple test would be to regress an onshore interest rate on an exogenous foreign interest rate and lags of the onshore and foreign interest rates. The problem with such a test is that nominal interest rates often follow non-stationary processes, so a regression of one interest rate against another leads to spurious results. In such cases, differencing can result in stationary series. The empirical evaluation of interest rate insulation thus proceeds in two steps. First, the time series properties of relevant interest rate series are examined. Second, a regression is run to test whether the dual exchange market altered the transmission of foreign interest rate disturbances to domestic interest rates in the early 1970s.

The properties of two onshore rates are examined: the 3 month treasury bill rate and 3 month money market rate. The 3 month US Treasury Bill rate is selected as the foreign interest rate and its properties are also examined. End of the week observations are obtained from the Harris Bank *Foreign Exchange Weekly Review*. The data start in 1967 for Belgium and the US and mid-1970 for France and Italy. Quarterly observations are obtained from the International Monetary Fund's (IMF) *International Financial Statistics*. The data start in 1967 for Belgium and France and in 1971 for Italy.

Augmented Dickey–Fuller tests on the weekly and quarterly series for Belgium, France, Italy, and the US confirm the random walk property of nominal interest rates documented in previous studies (for example, Wasserfallen, 1986). First differencing yields stationary series, however. Consequently, interest rate insulation tests are carried out by regressing the change in each European country's onshore interest rate (i) on changes in the US interest rate (i^*) and lagged changes in onshore and US interest rates. To the extent that the dual exchange market is an effective device for insulating domestic interest rates, changes in the foreign interest rate will have a different impact on onshore rates during the period when the dual exchange market operates. Absent a model, we can test for this differential impact by adding constant and slope dummies for the time period when dual markets were in effect. The variable '*drs*' equals one when the dual rate system operates and zero otherwise. The basic regression equation to be estimated is thus of the form

$$(9) \quad \Delta i_t = \alpha_0 + \sum_{k=1}^{4} \alpha_k \Delta i_{t-k} + \sum_{k=0}^{3} \gamma_k \Delta i_{t-k}^* + \mu drs + \sum_{k=0}^{3} \lambda_k \, drs \Delta i_{t-k}^* + \varepsilon_t$$

where $\Delta i_t = (i_t - i_{t-1})$. The weekly Italian and US interest rates are cointegrated, so we add the estimated linear combination of those two variables to the right-hand side of the Italian regression equation in order to utilize information about the long-term relationship between domestic and foreign interest rates. (Neither Belgian–US rates nor French–US rates are cointegrated.)

If any of the coefficients γ_0–γ_3 is positive and significant, then an increase in foreign interest rates is positively transmitted to onshore rates, just as one would expect in a world of fixed exchange rates and high capital mobility. In that case, if any of the coefficients on the slope dummies λ_0–λ_3 is negative and significant, we can infer that the dual exchange market dampened the transmission and hence provided some insulating effect. Alternatively, if γ_0–γ_3 are insignificant, then a finding that λ_0–λ_3 are also insignificant would be consistent with the view that the dual exchange market preserved interest rate insulation. Alternatively, it could reflect the fact that other measures provided interest rate insulation and the dual exchange market was redundant. Thus, a finding that all coefficients on the foreign interest rate terms are insignificant provides weaker evidence of insulation.

Regressions are run for each European country separately. The results are reported in Tables 10.3 and 10.4. They provide some evidence in support of the view that the dual exchange market insulated domestic interest rates from foreign interest rate disturbances during the turbulent early 1970s.

Table 10.3 examines whether domestic *treasury bill* rates were insulated from changes in US Treasury Bill rates using weekly data. For Belgium, the dual exchange market was in effect over the entire sample period. Between 14 May 1971 and 15 March 1974, regulations aimed at achieving a complete separation of the two exchange markets were put into effect. We capture any difference in the two periods with the help of the dummy variable. Table 10.3 indicates that the dual exchange rate insulated domestic rates from changes in foreign rates. The coefficients γ_0–γ_3 are not significantly different from zero at the 95 percent confidence level. The dual exchange market also prevented positive changes in US rates from generating positive changes in domestic rates during the 1971–4 period. In fact, during this more turbulent period, the coefficient on the prior week's change in US rates is negative and significant at the 95 percent level, suggesting that Belgian onshore rates even moved in the opposite direction from the earlier change in foreign rates. Overall, then, there is evidence in the weekly data that the Belgian dual exchange market prevented the positive transmission of foreign interest rate changes to domestic treasury bill rates in the early 1970s. For France, the regression is run for the period 5 June 1970 to 15 March 1974 since onshore rates are not available before mid-1970. Over this period, France either operated the *devise titre*, where a second exchange rate applied to resident transactions in foreign securities or it operated a fully-fledged dual exchange market. We capture any difference in the two regime periods with the dummy variable. The results are similar to those of Belgium. The French dual exchange market prevented changes in foreign interest rate changes from being positively transmitted to domestic treasury bill rates.

Unlike the other two European countries, Italy did not have some form of the dual exchange market in effect over the entire sample period. The dummy variable distinguishes between the period when

TABLE 10.3   *Interest insulation of onshore treasury bill rates*

Country Number of observations Frequency Dependent variable	(1) Belgium 349 weekly Δi	(2) France 178 weekly Δi	(3) Italy 193 weekly Δi
Constant	−0.0083	−0.0281	−0.0229
	(−0.73)	(−1.04)	(−0.11)
$\Delta i(-1)$	−0.0927	−0.0392	−0.5011
	(−1.73)	(−0.50)	(−3.92)
$\Delta i(-2)$	0.0478	0.0901	−0.5256
	(0.89)	(1.19)	(−4.37)
$\Delta i(-3)$	0.1684	−0.0540	−0.2973
	(2.92)	(−0.71)	(−2.93)
$\Delta i(-4)$	0.2231	−0.0498	−0.0112
	(3.86)	(−0.65)	(−0.15)
Δi^*	−0.0418	0.2160	−0.0385
	(−0.60)	(1.61)	(−0.03)
$\Delta i^*(-1)$	0.1088	0.1316	−0.1578
	(1.57)	(0.92)	(−0.13)
$\Delta i^*(-2)$	0.0198	−0.0449	−0.1476
	(0.29)	(−0.32)	(−0.13)
$\Delta i^*(-3)$	0.0413	0.1595	−0.1690
	(0.59)	(1.13)	(−0.15)
drs	0.0323	0.0545	0.1237
	(1.79)	(1.63)	(0.34)
$drs\Delta i^*$	0.0014	−0.1885	−0.2044
	(0.01)	(−1.18)	(−0.13)
$drs\Delta i^*(-1)$	−0.1882	−0.0851	−0.7859
	(−2.03)	(−0.51)	(−0.49)
$drs\Delta i^*(-2)$	0.0260	0.0850	2.3218
	(0.28)	(0.52)	(1.47)
$drs\Delta i^*(-3)$	0.0216	−0.3357	−1.4796
	(0.23)	(−2.04)	(−0.95)
res (−1)	–	–	−0.4739
			(−3.74)
Adjusted R^2	0.06	0.02	0.051

The variable i is the onshore 3 month treasury bill rate, where $\Delta i_t = i_t - i_{t-1}$. The variable i^* is the US 3 month Treasury Bill rate. The variable *drs* is a dummy variable that takes on the value of 1 when the dual market is in operation and a value of 0 otherwise. The variable *res* is the residual from the cointegrating vector.

dual exchange rates were in effect and when they were not. The results indicate that Italian treasury bill rates were insulated from foreign interest rate disturbances over the entire sample, regardless of whether

TABLE 10.4   *Interest insulation of onshore money market rates*

Country Number of observations Frequency Dependent variable	(1) Belgium 43 quarterly Δi	(2) France 43 quarterly Δi	(3) Italy 11 quarterly Δi
Constant	0.0198	0.0065	−0.3010
	(0.14)	(0.05)	(−1.12)
$\Delta i(-1)$	0.1122	0.2574	−1.0856
	(0.63)	(1.73)	(−1.49)
Δi^*	0.7013	0.4573	−0.3194
	(2.26)	(1.79)	(−0.84)
$\Delta i^*(-1)$	0.0488	0.2776	0.0480
	(0.13)	(1.03)	(0.13)
drs	0.0544	0.2771	1.8851
	(0.19)	(1.04)	(2.63)
$drs\Delta i^*$	−0.0169	−0.2678	0.1205
	(−0.03)	(−0.74)	(0.28)
$drs\Delta i^*(-1)$	0.4514	0.1889	−0.0873
	(1.00)	(0.52)	(−0.15)
Adjusted R^2	0.27	0.30	0.43

i is the onshore 3 month money market rate, i^* is the 3 month US Treasury Bill rate, and *drs* is a dummy variable that takes on the value of 1 during the dual exchange market period. The observation period is 1967:1–1974:1 for Belgium and France and 1971:1–1974:1 for Italy.

the dual exchange market was in operation. Since Italy had extensive capital controls, they may have insulated domestic interest rates prior to the adoption of the dual exchange market. Whether the dual rate regime provided additional insulation from foreign interest rate disturbances or was merely a redundant device cannot be determined.

Table 10.4 provides some evidence on whether the dual exchange market insulated domestic *money market* rates from changes in US Treasury Bill rates using quarterly data. In Belgium, the evidence is mixed. A positive change in US Treasury Bill rates is positively correlated with a change in the Belgian money market rates. The transmission process is not complete, however, since the change in Belgian rates is approximately 70 percent of the change in US rates. In France and Italy, changes in domestic money market rates are not significantly correlated with changes in US Treasury Bill rates. The evidence here is thus consistent with the view that the dual exchange market provided some insulation from foreign interest rate disturbances.

Insulation of International Reserves

Another motive for adopting a dual exchange market is the desire to insulate official reserves from speculative capital flows. A fluctuating exchange rate for capital account transactions can remove pressure from official reserves caused by large speculative shifts in capital flows. Nevertheless, this does not mean that official reserves are fully protected against speculative forces. Trade financing (a capital account item included in the commercial exchange market) may potentially be an important vehicle for speculating against the commercial rate. Lanyi (1975, p. 719) wrote

> 'Leads and lags' in the settlement of commercial claims, or variations in the initial terms of commercial financing, are believed to have been responsible for a large proportion of the short-term capital movements occurring during the foreign exchange crises of recent years. Thus, so long as trade financing remains in the official market, the dual exchange market cannot effectively act as a buffer for official reserves against speculative forces. However, a separation of trade financing from the exchange market for current transactions would not only be extremely difficult to administer but would also eliminate an important advantage of separate exchange markets – namely, that they shield current account transactions from the exchange rate fluctuations caused by capital movements.

In order to see if there is any evidence that trade financing was a source of speculative pressure on international reserves under dual exchange rates, we examine the value of short-term trade credits as a percent of total short-term capital transactions by the private non-bank sector. According to Giavazzi and Giovannini (1989), during periods of heightened speculative activity, the bulk of short-term capital will flow in and out through the financial market when there are no capital controls but may occur through trade credits when capital controls are in place. In Table 10.5, we report some evidence on the importance of trade credits as a vehicle for moving capital in and out of a country during the 1970–5 period. Since only France and Italy provide disaggregated trade credit figures in their balance of payments accounts, Table 10.5 displays the data for just those two countries.

The data are somewhat difficult to interpret. For France, when pressures mounted in 1971 in favor of the franc, short-term capital

TABLE 10.5   *Trade credits as speculative capital movements*

	1970	1971	1972	1973	1974	1975
France						
Credits/inflows*	41.6	18.2	41.6	42.6	47.6	–
Credits/outflows	77.5	28.9	73.7	92.4	72.0	–
Inflows/trade[†]	3.8	5.4	2.8	4.1	5.0	–
Outflows/trade	2.0	2.7	1.9	1.3	2.7	–
Italy[‡]						
Credits/inflows	20.1	24.8	17.3	6.9	51.0	76.4
Credits/outflows	33.1	28.6	34.0	7.7	53.8	74.4
Inflows/trade	17.0	18.6	16.6	46.4	37.3	28.7
Outflows/trade	17.9	20.6	22.9	40.2	33.8	30.0

The French dual exchange market operated between August 1971 and March 1974. The Italian dual exchange market operated between January 1973 and March 1974.
* Short-term trade credits (liabilities to foreigners) as a percent of total short-term capital inflows by the private non-bank sector and short-term trade credits (claims on foreigners) as a percent of total short-term capital outflows by the private non-bank sector.
† Short-term private capital inflows as a share of imports plus exports.
‡ Separate data for short-term capital flows not available. Shares based on all capital transactions, both short and long term. Share of trade credits is underestimated.
SOURCES: *Balance des Paiements entre La France et L'Exterieur*, Direction du Tresor; *Bolletino Statistics*, Banca d'Italia.

seemed to move mostly through the financial market rather than through changes in trade credits. Short-term capital inflows as a share of trade rose from 3.8 percent in 1970 to 5.4 percent during 1971, while trade credits as a share of short-term capital inflows fell from 41.6 percent to 18.2 percent. Of course, the dual exchange market was not adopted until August 1971, so trade credits may have become a more important channel for speculative activity in the latter part of the year. When pressures mounted again in 1973, this time *against* the franc, trade credits were a more important channel. Trade credits as a share of short-term capital outflows rose from 73.7 percent in 1972 to 92.4 percent during 1973 while capital outflows as a share of trade fell from 1.9 to 1.3 percent.

The Italian data provide some additional insights into the vehicles for speculative activity under dual exchange rates. Rising pressure against the lira brought about the adoption of dual exchange rates in January 1973, yet for the year 1973 the bulk of short-term capital seemed to move through the financial market rather than through changes in trade credits. Trade credits as a share of capital outflows fell from 34 percent in 1972 to only 7.7 percent during 1973, while capital outflows as a fraction of total trade rose from 22.9 to 40.2 percent. The drop in the share of trade credits may have been due in part to regulations imposed by the authorities on leads and lags. Worried about capital outflows via trade financing, the Italian central bank shortened the maturity of export credits and limited the possibility of pre-paying imports.

Based on the French and Italian balance of payments data, we tentatively conclude that the dual exchange market cannot fully insulate official reserves from speculative activity. Trade financing becomes a vehicle for moving capital in and out of the country unless additional regulations on leads and lags are imposed.

CONCLUSION

While the European experience with dual exchange markets has been commented on by numerous authors, there has been no attempt to put together a set of correlations in the data for that period. This paper is an attempt to fill part of that gap by uncovering some of the empirical regularities in the Belgian, French, and Italian dual exchange markets.

In the second section we examined the nature of the distortion created by the dual exchange market and examined the observable part of the distortion in the European data. In the third section we laid out a standard stock-flow portfolio model to isolate the economic determinants of the spread between the two official exchange rates. We then presented a reduced-form equation for the spread based on the stock-flow model and fitted it to quarterly Belgian, French, and Italian data. The spread regressions showed that portfolio variables were important determinants of the spread. In Belgium, the foreign interest rate, the rate of change of international reserves, and the real budget deficit, along with the lagged spread, explained almost two-thirds of the variation in the spread. The chapter were similar for the panel data on Belgium, France, and Italy. The chapter also provided some evidence suggesting that the dual exchange market insulated domestic interest rates from foreign interest rate disturbances but could not fully insulate official reserves from speculative activity.

One reason for the absence of empirical work on official dual exchange markets is the transitional nature of most of these regimes. Except for Belgium, official dual exchange market episodes are either too short for estimation procedures or agents' beliefs about the temporariness of the regime build into the data elements that are difficult to capture. The regression results presented in this paper should be treated with caution since the inherent temporariness of these regimes casts doubt about the stability of the structural relationship between the spread and portfolio variables. Frequent rule changes during the operation of a dual exchange market further weaken the claim that a dual exchange market episode can be treated as a single event.

NOTES

1. I am indebted to Robert Flood, Andrew Oswald, and Alex Zanello for helpful discussions. I also wish to thank project organizers Miguel Kiguel, Saul Lizondo, and Steve O'Connell, my discussant, Pablo Guidotti, as well as Joshua Aizenman, Mike Knetter, and Carsten Kowalczyk for comments on an earlier draft. I thank Robert Cumby, Kellett Hannah, and Saul Lizondo for assistance in acquiring some of the data. John Dean and Murtaza Moochhala provided helpful research assistance.
2. For early examples, see Fleming (1971), Lanyi (1975), Flood (1978), Marion (1981), and Flood and Marion (1982b).
3. Belgium operated a dual exchange market from 1957 to 1990. Between May 1971 and May 1983 both capital inflows and capital outflows were assigned to the market for capital account transactions, whereas before May 1971 and after May 1983 capital inflows could go through either exchange market. France used a dual exchange market from 23 August 1971 to 21 March 1974. It operated a *devise titre*, a second exchange rate applicable to resident purchases and sales of foreign securities, during the period 11 August 1969 to 20 October 1971 and again during the period 21 May 1981 to 22 May 1986. Italy operated a dual exchange market from 22 January 1973 to 22 March 1974. The Netherlands established an O-guilder market for non-residents investing in Dutch guilder bonds between 6 September 1971 and 1 February 1974. The UK operated a separate investment currency exchange rate for certain capital account transactions conducted by UK residents from 1947 until 23 October 1979. In the 1970s and 1980s, a number of developing countries, including Argentina and Mexico, used two-tier exchange rates as an interim measure prior to devaluing their currency.
4. For examples of models with most or all of these features, see Flood (1978), Marion (1981), Flood and Marion (1982b), Dornbusch *et al.* (1983), Dornbusch (1986), Lizondo (1987), Pinto (1991), and Ghei and Kiguel (1992). Optimizing models can also be used to isolate economic

determinants of the spread. See Adams and Greenwood (1985), Frenkel and Razin (1986), Flood and Marion (1989), and Guidotti and Vegh (1992).

5. Dickey–Fuller tests fail to reject the hypothesis of a unit root for the foreign interest rate, but on *a priori* grounds we would expect the interest rate to be bounded by reasonable limits.

6. The deficit variable is not logged because some observations (surpluses) have negative values. Various lag/lead structures for these variables are also considered. Note that the empirical work departs from the theoretical model by allowing for variation in the real commercial exchange rate.

7. Since country and time dummies were all insignificant, they are not reported. Additional lags on the spread or leads on the rate of depreciation and on income growth were also insignificant.

8. The snake refers to the close margins for the bilateral exchange rates of European currencies that were negotiated near the end of the Bretton Woods system.

9. The regression using Belgian data is

$$\log z_t = 0.001 + 0.76 \log z_{t-1} + 0.01(i_t^* - i_t) - 0.06(\log y_t - \log y_{t-1})$$
$$\quad (0.56) \quad (13.51) \qquad (4.08) \qquad (-1.06)$$
$$\quad + 0.017(\log y_{t+1} - \log y_t) + 0.44E - 05def_t$$
$$\quad (0.26) \qquad\qquad (2.55)$$
$$\quad - 0.059(\log R_t - \log R_{t-1}) - 0.064(\log r_t - \log r_{t-1})$$
$$\quad (-4.94) \qquad\qquad (-1.95)$$
$$R^2 = 0.75, \quad n = 94.$$

t-statistics are in parentheses. A correction has been made for serial correlation. Regressions of the *black* spread commonly include the interest differential on the right-hand side in the belief that activities in the black market do not affect domestic variables such as the interest rate. For the European dual market episodes, however, the financial exchange rate and domestic interest rate are jointly determined endogenous variables.

When regression equation (1) was rerun using current and future values of the real budget deficit, the coefficient on the one-quarter ahead deficit was negative and highly significant. One explanation consistent with this result is that an increase in next period's budget deficit puts upward pressure on current domestic interest rates, causing a portfolio shift into domestic assets that narrows the current spread.

10. See the IMF's *Exchange Arrangements and Exchange Restrictions* (various issues), for details.

11. The exact classification of transactions by exchange market for each of the European countries can be found in the IMF's *Exchange Arrangements and Exchange Restrictions*.

12. During May 1971, a period of heightened speculation against the dollar, Belgium made important changes in the classification of trans-

actions which resulted in almost complete separation of the commercial and financial exchange markets. Nevertheless, a small number of current transactions could be undertaken in either exchange market and individual licenses could be granted to allow certain capital account transactions through the commercial market. In addition, domestic and foreign bank notes, representing private travel expenses and so forth, could be bought and sold on the financial market. In January 1974, outward payments of investment earnings were again permitted to be channeled through either market, thereby establishing a major link between the markets. Under the French scheme, there was also a broad separation of commercial and financial transactions, but it was by no means complete. Some current account items, such as travel, tourism, investment income, workers' remittances, and bank note transactions, were channeled through the financial market. A few financial transactions, such as those related to commercial credits, were channeled through the commercial exchange market.

13. Belgium became a member of the European 'snake' in April 1972, thereby limiting the fluctuations in the commercial franc relative to other European members. In March 1973, Belgium abandoned the peg against the dollar but kept the commercial franc in a narrow band with the other snake countries. In March 1979, it joined the European Monetary System (EMS). The arrangement called for the commercial franc to move within narrow margins for EMS currencies, but allowed it to float against the dollar. The commercial franc has been adjusted periodically as part of EMS realignments, while throughout the period the financial franc has floated freely.

14. The lack of data makes it impossible to measure the extent of foreign exchange intervention in the financial market. In the Belgian case, it appears that neither systematic intervention over the long term nor large-scale short-term intervention occurred in the financial exchange market (see Bindert-Bogdanowicz, 1979). The main reason given by the Belgian authorities for not intervening in the financial market was that such intervention could have a destabilizing effect on expectations. The lack of data also makes it impossible to assess the extent of intervention by the French and Italian authorities in their financial exchange markets. The general view is that there was little or no management of the financial exchange rate, at least via direct foreign exchange intervention. More indirect ways of influencing the rate, such as changing the mix of transactions going through the financial market, altering quantitative controls, or encouraging public sector borrowing/lending through the financial market, were attempted.

REFERENCES

Adams, Charles and Jeremy Greenwood (1985) 'Dual Exchange Rate Systems and Capital Controls: an Investigation', *Journal of International Economics*, vol. 18, pp. 43–63.

Bhagwati, Jagdish N. (1964) 'On the Underinvoicing of Imports', *Bulletin of the Oxford University Institute of Statistics*, vol. 26, no. 4, pp. 389–97. (Also in Bhagwati, J. (ed.) (1974) *Illegal Transactions in International Trade* (Amsterdam: North-Holland).)

Bhandari, Jagdeep, S. and Bernard Decaluwe (1987) 'A Stochastic Model of Incomplete Separation Between Commercial and Financial Exchange Markets', *Journal of International Economics*, vol. 22(1/2), pp. 25–55.

Bindert-Bogdanowicz, C. (1979) 'The Dual Exchange Rate System', *Revue de la Banque Bruxelles*, June.

Dornbusch, Rudiger (1986) 'Special Exchange Rates for Capital Account Transactions', *World Bank Economic Review*, vol. 1, no. 1, pp. 1–33.

Dornbusch, Rudiger, Daniel V. Dantas, Clarice Pechman, Roberto Rocha, and Demetri Simoes (1983) 'The Black Market for Dollars in Brazil', *Quarterly Journal of Economics*, vol. 98, pp. 25–40.

Fleming, J. Marcus (1971) 'Dual Exchange Rates for Current and Capital Transactions: a Theoretical Examination', in J. Marcus Fleming (ed.), *Essays in International Economics* (Cambridge, Mass: Harvard University Press), pp. 296–325.

Flood, Robert P. (1978) 'Exchange Rate Expectations in Dual Exchange Markets', *Journal of International Economics*, vol. 8, pp. 65–77.

Flood, Robert P. and Nancy P. Marion (1982a) 'Exchange-rate Regimes in Transition: Italy 1974', *Journal of International Money and Finance*, vol. 2, pp. 279–94.

Flood, Robert P. and Nancy P. Marion (1982b) 'The Transmission of Disturbances Under Alternative Exchange-rate Regimes with Optimal Indexing', *Quarterly Journal of Economics*, vol. 97, pp. 43–66.

Flood, Robert, P. and Nancy P. Marion (1989) 'Risk Neutrality and the Two-tier Foreign Exchange Market: Evidence from Belgium', *Working Paper No. 89/83* (Washington, DC: IMF).

Frenkel, Jacob and Assaf Razin (1986) 'The Limited Viability of Dual Exchange-rate Regimes', *Working Paper No. 1902* (Cambridge, Mass.: National Bureau of Economic Research).

Ghei, Nita and Miguel A. Kiguel (1992) 'Dual and Multiple Exchange Rate Systems in Developing Countries: Some Empirical Evidence', *Policy Research Working Paper Series* No. 881 (Washington, DC: World Bank).

Giavazzi, Francisco and Alberto Giovannini (1989) *Limiting Exchange Rate Flexibility: the European Monetary System* (Cambridge, Mass: The MIT Press).

Gros, Daniel (1988) 'Dual Exchange Rates in the Presence of Incomplete Market Separation', *IMF Staff Papers*, vol. 35, pp. 437–60.

Guidotti, Pablo and Carlos Vegh (1992) 'Macroeconomic Interdependence under Capital Controls: a Two-country Model of Dual Exchange Rates', *Journal of International Economics*, vol. 32, no. 34, pp. 353–67.

International Monetary Fund (various years) *Exchange Arrangements and Exchange Restrictions* (Washington, DC: International Monetary Fund).

International Monetary Fund (various years) *International Financial Statistics* (Washington, DC: International Monetary Fund.

Lanyi, A. (1975) 'Separate Exchange Markets for Capital and Current Transactions', *IMF Staff Papers*, vol. 22, pp. 714–49.

Lizondo, J. Saul (1987) 'Unification of Dual Exchange Rate Markets', *Journal of International Economics*, vol. 22, nos 1/2, pp. 57–77.

Marion, Nancy P. (1981) 'Insulation Properties of a Two-tier Exchange Market in a Portfolio Balance Model', *Economica*, vol. 48, pp. 61–70.

Pinto, Brian (1991) 'Black Markets for Foreign Exchange, Real Exchange Rates and Inflation', *Journal of International Economics*, vol. 30, pp. 121–36.

Wasserfallen, W. (1986) 'Non-stationarities in Macro-economic Time Series – Further Evidence and Implications', *Canadian Journal of Economics*, vol. 19, pp. 498–510.

Author Index

Subject Index

Bold page numbers refer to selected figures and tables. Footnotes are identified by page and note number (e.g., 64 n3).